Cookery Americana

AMERICAN REGIONAL COOKING

FAVORITE RECIPES FROM THE PAST

THE RICH SOIL OF TEXAS DREW MANY EUROPEAN FARMERS DURING THE 19TH CENTURY.
THIS TYPICAL PICTURE FROM 1883 SHOWS THE MOST MODERN PLOWING EQUIPMENT OF THE TIME

SOUTHWESTERN COOKERY

Indian and Spanish Influences

Introduction and Suggested Recipes

by

Louis Szathmáry

PROMONTORY PRESS

New York · 1974

COOKERY AMERICANA is a series of 27 cookbooks in 15 volumes that chronicles a fascinating aspect of American social life over the past 150 years. These volumes provide unique insight into the American experience and follow the movement of pioneer America from the original colonies to the Great Plains and westward to the Pacific. More than cookbooks, these works were manuals for daily living: household management, etiquette, home medicinal remedies, and much more. See the last pages of this volume for a complete listing of the series.

LOUIS I. SZATHMARY, Advisory Editor for this series, is an internationally known chef, food management consultant, owner of the renowned Chicago restaurant, The Bakery, and author of the best selling *The Chef's Secret Cookbook* (Quadrangle Books, 1971). As a serious student of the history of cookery, he has collected a library of several thousand cookbooks dating back to the 15th century. All of the works in *Cookery Americana* are from his private collection.

Published by Promontory Press, New York, N.Y. 10016

Introduction Copyright © 1973 by Louis Szathmáry

Reprinted from a copy in the private collection of Louis Szathmáry

Library of Congress Catalog Card No.: 73-92639
ISBN: 0-88394-018-3

Printed in the United States of America

Contents

INTRODUCTION

SUGGESTED RECIPES

FAVORITE RECIPES OF COLFAX COUNTY CLUB
WOMEN. Compiled by the Colfax County Home Demonstration
Clubs. Colfax County, New Mexico, 1946

THE GARFIELD WOMAN'S CLUB COOK BOOK.
Compiled and Published by The Garfield Woman's Club.
Garfield, Utah, 1916

CHOCTAW INDIAN DISHES. Compiled by Amanda and
Peter J. Hudson. Tuskahoma, Oklahoma, 1955

THE INDIAN COOK BOOK. By The Indian Women's Club of
Tulsa, Oklahoma. Tulsa, Oklahoma, 1933

THE JUNIOR LEAGUE OF DALLAS COOK BOOK.
Compiled and Edited by Members of the Dallas Chapter of
The Association of Junior Leagues of America. Second edition.
Dallas, Texas, n.d.

Introduction

During the 1700s, sixty million buffalo roamed freely throughout the western and southwestern parts of what later became the United States. Around the mid-1850s, when a kinetic America was constructing a railroad across the Great Plains, the buffalo became the staple food of the railroad builders. As a consequence, the buffalo was slaughtered by the thousands. Buffalo Bill (William F. Cody) is reputed to have himself killed 4,280 of these native American animals in less than eighteen months. In 1889, when the United States government finally began to count how many of the sixty million bison were still alive, the exact nose count was only 800!*

Although the population of the American Indians and that of the first European conquerors, the Spaniards, have also diminished greatly, their influence upon the culture of the Southwest is still apparent. As Americans moved westward, they brought new ideas, new dishes, and new knowledge to the Southwest, yet the Indian and Spanish heritages are still visible in the gastronomy of that area.

The five cookbooks combined in this volume span a fifty-year period and mirror the many changes and new influences which affected the ingredients used in cookery as well as its methods and equipment. These changes in methods and equipment were due to shifts from the use of wood to coal, from coal to gas, and from gas to electricity. In addition, aluminum foil replaced cheesecloth and electric mixers superseded copper bowls and hand beaters.

The forty-five menus found in the *Junior League of Dallas Cook Book* (pp. 11-24) probably have greater social significance than many in other cookbooks of that or any other period. The menus reflect the newly acquired affluence of that community; the best is not good enough—the food is "embellished," "surrounded," and "stuffed." The Valentine Dinner (p. 17) for example, begins with fresh strawberries on the stem, followed by crown of lamb filled with creamed potatoes and surrounded by baked whole

---

*Arehart-Treichel, Joan. "Saving the Last of the Free-Roaming Buffalos," *Science News,* Volume 102, Number 10, pp. 158 and 159.

tomatoes stuffed with deviled ham filling. The salad is also elaborate—cut lettuce heads across in slices, stuff a green gage plum with cheese and nuts and surround with grapefruit sections. Even the Charlotte Russe is surrounded with lady-fingers and garnished with whipped cream topped with one glacé cherry!

At a simple *Luncheon* (p. 12) where creamed sweetbreads and fresh mushrooms are served in a patty shell, examine the garnish—instead of the classic garnish of minced egg white, egg yolk, and green parsley which mixes into a dainty garnish called "mimosa," broiled ham is used.

Interestingly, the local or regional dishes are confined to the informal meals, and while the *Luncheons* sparkle with such French culinary expressions as Toast Melba (p. 11), Glacé Fruit (p. 11), and Chicken Mousse (p. 12), the *Informal Luncheons* offer Moulded Hot Tamale Loaf (p. 13), Biscuits and Preserves; the *Dinner* menus offer Caviare (p. 16), Bouillon (p. 20), and Artichokes in many forms, and the *Suppers* include such lowly "delicacies" as Barbecue Chicken, Chili, Scrambled Eggs, Little Pig Sausages, Fried Chicken, and Baked Virginia Ham (p. 23).

Many interesting and useful ideas can be found in the book. For example, to make a good chili, the meat used should be round steak and it should be cut with scissors (p. 240)—a good suggestion, we believe, for preserving flavor. Many other useful instructions are provided, including the secrets of successful sandwich making (p. 228) and how to skillfully transfer a pudding to the serving dish without breaking the mass of the pudding (p. 191).

Not too many of the recipes reveal their Spanish heritage in their names. However, people who know about Spanish cuisine know that one of the forebears of the American breakfast sausage is the Spanish Chorizo and that Tomato Stuffed with Rice (p. 70) and Caramel Custard (p. 167) are just as Spanish in origin as are Spanish Chili Con Carne (p. 237), Spanish Stew (p. 230), and Tamale Loaf (p. 77).

The Indian influence is represented by recipes which use such ingredients as corn, turkey, squash, and sweet potatoes. Equally significant are the contributions made by the combined Spanish and Indian elements which created the excellent Latin cuisine of Mexico, and its close relative, the Texan-Mexican cuisine, characterized by the different versions of chili (pp. 234, 236, 237, 239, and 243).

Favorite Recipes of Colfax County Club Women, although published in New Mexico somewhat later, is close geographically

CORNMEAL BECOMES MUFFINS IN NEW ENGLAND;
CORN BREAD IN THE CAROLINAS; HUSH PUPPIES IN LOUISIANA;
AND TORTILLAS IN NEW MEXICO, ARIZONA, AND TEXAS

to the *Junior League of Dallas Cook Book*. Chili (pp. 72-73) is still one of the leading local dishes, but recipes for Enchiladas (p. 80), Tamale Pie (p. 79), Chicken Mexicana (p. 72), and several other dishes indicate that, although the population was changing with the passage of time, the new settler, wherever he came from, adapted quickly to the local taste spectrum.

Among the *Vegetables,* Cauliflower Mexican (p. 113) and Chili Con Carne and Green Beans (p. 114) are the local dishes. The European influence is also represented in such recipes as Asparagus Au Gratin (p. 113), Italian Spaghetti (p. 116), and Stuffed Cabbage (p. 118).

Before the white settlers came to this continent the North American Indians ate only the organs of the animals they killed for food—the eyes, tongue, lungs, liver, kidneys, stomach, testicles, and other internal organs. They skinned the animal and left the muscles and the flesh for the birds and other predators. This custom is reflected throughout the books in this volume; note for example how many entries in *Favorite Recipes* are for dishes prepared from internal organs—Breaded Brains (p. 75); Calf, Lamb, or Beef

Heart (p. 75); Veal, Lamb, Pork or Beef Kidney (p. 75); Calf, Lamb, Beef, or Pork Liver (p. 75); Sweetbreads and Brains (p. 76); and Beef, Calf, and Pork Tongue (p. 76).

The recipe for Venison or Elk Roast (p. 80) could have been used for a festive Indian occasion by merely substituting a wild onion for the large onion and a native condiment for the Worcestershire Sauce.

As in most regional cookbooks, the largest and most elaborate section is on *Cakes* (pp. 15-35). On the other hand, the chapter on *Soup* has only one recipe—Peanut Butter Soup (p. 111). Among the *Meats* are seven recipes for stew and chili which, like soup, can be eaten with a spoon. Most of the recipes in this book come from all over the United States, and disclose a heritage that can be traced from New England to Louisiana, and from Boston to Seattle. Thus we see that the country had become a continent-sized neighborhood by the 1940s.

The Indian Cook Book compiled by The Indian Women's Club of Tulsa, Oklahoma, and the manuscript entitled *Choctaw Indian Dishes* transcribed by Peter J. Hudson of Tuskahoma, Oklahoma, for his wife, are more memorabilia than recipes to follow; nevertheless, both are exciting, interesting reading. This does not mean, however, that these books are mere curiosities. The recipes are not only useful and easy to follow, but they would make eating a memorable experience. Those that we have selected from *The Indian Cookbook* and adjusted to today's style of cooking, for example, can be part of a very well-balanced, up-to-date menu. We don't expect the reader to cook Ma-Ching-Wah Ming-Zah (p. 17) which is burr oak acorns in wood ashes, or to make Wah-We-No-Kone-Min-Guy (p. 11) which is a corn dish using, for lack of any other type of grater, the jaw of a deer so that the corn can be grated on its teeth, but the recipes for Wild Rice (p. 11), several of the unique soups, and the teas (p. 15) made from spice wood, raspberry vine, or sassafras are not only educational and entertaining, but pleasant alternatives to everyday meals as well.

The Garfield Woman's Club Cook Book, as stated in the preface, was a fund-raising effort, intended by its editors and compilers to be a cosmopolitan book, reflecting the best recipes from every section of this nation as well as from those nations across the seas. Whichever section of the book we thumb through, though, we find that the local color and circumstances tinted, altered, and influenced many of the dishes. In the *Meats* section, recipes for

GAME BIRDS, SUCH AS THE CALIFORNIA QUAIL
WERE ABUNDANT THROUGHOUT THE SOUTHWEST

Wild Rabbit Friscassee (p. 11) and Steamed Wild Duck (p. 13) indicate the abundance of game, while entries for Baked Lamb Hearts and Spanish Stew (p. 13), Chili Con Carne (p. 47), Spanish Rice (p. 49), Chili Stew (p. 54), Cheese and Chili (p. 55), Green Tomato Pickle (p. 71), Cold Chili Sauce (p. 71), Chili Sauce (p. 69), and Spanish Beans (p. 15) reflect the Spanish and Indian influence.

The chapters begin with charming poetical quotes. "Little Tommy had some candy, on a painted stick, Little Tommy ate that candy and it made him sick," introduces the chapter on *Candies* (p. 61). "What moistens the lips and brightens the eye? What calls back the past like a rich, juicy pie?" is a tempting opener to *Desserts* (p. 39). These statements probably won't make you eat more candy or bake more pies, but there is much domestic wisdom to be found, as for example, in the *Meats* section (p. 11): "Jack Sprat could eat no fat, his wife could eat no lean—And so between them both, they licked the platter clean."

The advertisements are interesting, and not without social significance—large grafonolas, modern ranges, pianos, and furniture are offered to the modern family. Full page ads, such as the one by the National Copper Bank, "How Much of Your Pay Check Is Yours," (p. 64) and numerous other ads by bank and money institutions which give advice point to the economic situation of the time. Pictures of kitchens (p. 18) and household gadgets (p. 22) add additional charm to the book.

Louis Szathmáry
CHICAGO, ILLINOIS

SUGGESTED RECIPES

The following recipes have been tested and adjusted to today's ingredients, measurements, and style of cooking by Chef Louis Szathmáry.

FAVORITE RECIPES OF COLFAX COUNTY CLUB WOMEN

FIVE MINUTE DEVIL'S FOOD CAKE (p. 20)

INGREDIENTS:

- 2 cups sugar
- ½ cup butter (1 stick)
- 2 eggs
- ½ cup buttermilk
- 3 heaping tablespoons cocoa
- 2 cups flour
- 1 teaspoon baking soda
- 1 teaspoon vanilla
- 1 cup boiling water

METHOD: With an electric mixer, cream together the butter and sugar. Gradually add the eggs, continuing to beat until the mixture is light and fluffy. Dissolve the soda in the buttermilk. Blend the cocoa into the flour. Beating on low speed, alternately add the buttermilk mixture and the flour mixture, beating just until the batter is smooth. Add the vanilla, and finally, add the boiling water. Pour the batter into 2 8-inch cake pans which have been greased and dusted with flour, and bake in a preheated 350° oven for about 30 minutes. Makes a moist cake.

To serve, split each layer and frost with your favorite icing. You may wish to dust the top with some powdered sugar.

IN TEXAS, FRUIT AND VEGETABLE MERCHANTS BROUGHT THEIR
GOODS TO MARKET IN WAGONS DRAWN BY MULES AND OXEN

WESTERN RANCH MEAT LOAF (p. 77)

INGREDIENTS FOR 8:

- 2 pounds ground beef, or a mixture of ground beef and lamb
- 1 medium-sized onion, finely minced
- ½ cup finely minced celery
- ¼ cup finely minced carrot
- ⅓ cup finely minced green bell pepper
- 4 tablespoons lard, bacon drippings, or butter, or a combination of two
- 2 teaspoons salt
- ½ teaspoon freshly ground black pepper
- 2 eggs
- 3 cups soft bread crumbs
- ½ cup water
- ½ cup tomato juice

METHOD: Heat the shortening in a frying pan or skillet, and add the minced onion, celery, and carrot. Brown the mixture over medium heat. Cool slightly, then add the bell pepper, salt, pepper, eggs, bread crumbs, and water. Thoroughly mix together with your hands. Divide the mixture in ½, and mix ½ with the ground meat. Pat ½ of the ground meat mixture into the bottom of a 2-quart loaf pan. Spread the remaining ½ of the dressing over the meat mixture, and then place the remaining ½ of the meat mixture on top. Brush the top with tomato juice, and bake in a pre-heated 350° oven for 1 hour and 15 minutes, basting several times with the remaining tomato juice.

QUICK CAKE

INGREDIENTS:

2	cups sifted cake flour
2	teaspoons baking powder
¾	cup milk
½	cup shortening, preferably butter
¾	teaspoon salt
1¼	cups sugar
2	eggs
1	teaspoon vanilla

METHOD: Sift flour once before measuring, then sift again, adding the baking powder and salt. Cream the butter and sugar together with an electric mixer, then add the eggs, 1 at a time, and continue to beat until the mixture is light and fluffy. On low speed, add the dry ingredients, alternately with the milk and vanilla, until both are incorporated into the batter. Pour the batter into 2 greased and floured 8-inch cake pans, and bake in a preheated 350° oven for approximately 25 minutes, or until a cooking needle inserted into each layer, comes out dry. Cool for about 10 minutes, then invert onto a rack to cool.

THE GARFIELD WOMAN'S CLUB COOK BOOK

NUT BREAD (p. 25)

INGREDIENTS:

3	cups flour
1½	cups milk
½	cup brown sugar or
	½ cup molasses
1	cup chopped walnuts or pecans
1	cup raisins
1	tablespoon baking powder
¼	teaspoon salt

METHOD: Preheat oven to 350°. Sift the flour and baking powder together. Add the salt and brown sugar (or molasses if used), then stir in the milk. Beat with a wooden spoon until the batter is smooth, but do not over beat. Fold in the nuts and raisins. Bake in a 1-pound loaf tin or a round baking pan 5-inches in diameter, approximately 3-inches deep, which has been greased, for approximately 45 minutes to 1 hour. Cool before removing from pan.

SMOTHERED CHICKEN (p. 11)

INGREDIENTS FOR 8:

4	small broilers, approximately
2½	pounds each, split in ½
1	tablespoon salt mixed with
½	teaspoon black pepper and
½	teaspoon paprika
1	cup boiling water
1	tablespoon butter
8	thin slices bacon, each slice cut in ½
1	tablespoon flour kneaded together with 1 additional tablespoon room temperature butter
½	medium-sized onion, sliced
1	small carrot, sliced
1	rib celery, sliced (optional)

METHOD: Rub the skin and flesh side of each ½ chicken with the salt mixture. Place the sliced vegetables in a large roasting pan and lay chicken on it, flesh side up. Bring the water to a vigorous boil and stir in the tablespoon butter. Pour the boiling mixture over the chicken. Cover the roasting pan and place in a preheated 350° oven. After 30 minutes, remove from the oven, turn chicken skin side up, and place 2 ½-strips of bacon over each breast, covering the breast as much as possible. Increase the oven temperature to 400°, and place the chicken back into the oven, uncovered. After 10 to 15 minutes, remove chicken. Take off the bacon slices, drain on absorbent paper, set aside. Place the chicken on a serving platter. Strain the cooking juices. Discard the vegetables, and add enough boiling water to the pan juices to have a total of 2 cups. Bring the liquid to a vigorous boil, and add the flour mixture, little by little, stirring constantly to avoid any lumps. Pour a part of the sauce over the chicken arranged on the serving platter. Decorate with the bacon slices and watercress or parsley, and serve. Offer the remaining sauce separately in a sauceboat.

Spanish Rice (p. 49)

INGREDIENTS FOR 8:

- 1 cup uncooked rice
- 1 medium-sized onion, finely minced
- 1 medium-sized green bell pepper, finely minced
- 1 No. 2 can tomatoes, chopped
- 1 bay leaf
- Salt and freshly ground black pepper to taste
- 2 tablespoons bacon drippings or lard
- ½ cup water

METHOD: Place the cold shortening in a cold frying pan, add the minced onion, and begin to heat over medium heat. Saute until the onion turns glossy and begins to brown around the edges. Add the rice and brown over medium heat, stirring constantly. Then add the bell pepper, tomatoes, with the juice from the can, bay leaf, salt and black pepper to taste, and water. Cover and simmer for approximately 30 minutes, or until rice is tender and most of the liquid is absorbed.

THE INDIAN COOK BOOK

Apple Butter (p. 16)

INGREDIENTS:

- 2 quarts unpeeled, cored, chopped apples, tightly packed
- ½ cup cider vinegar
- 3 cups light brown sugar, tightly packed
- Cinnamon to taste

METHOD: Place the chopped apples in an enamel pot, which has a lid. Pour in enough water to cover apples, place over medium heat,

THE AVOCADO PEAR, OR ALLIGATOR PEAR,
IS A NOT-TOO-DISTANT RELATIVE OF THE CINNAMON.
ALTHOUGH NATIVE TO THE WEST INDIES,
IT BECAME POPULAR IN THE AMERICAN SOUTHWEST.

bring to a boil, and then reduce heat and simmer apples until they are thoroughly cooked. Strain cooking liquid and discard it. Press the apples through a food mill or sieve. Discard skin. Add vinegar and brown sugar to apple pulp, return to the fire, and slowly boil the mixture down to ⅔ of the original amount. Flavor with some cinnamon if desired. Yield: Approximately 1 quart.

SHAWNEE RECIPE FOR DRYING CORN (p. 10)

INGREDIENTS FOR 8:

    8 ears of mature, but not hard, corn
      Enough water to steam cook thoroughly
    2 tablespoons bacon grease for each
      cup corn (after removing from cob)

METHOD: Steam the corn until tender. With a sharp, small knife, cut the kernels from each cob. Don't cut too much of the cob with it. Scrape each cob with the edge of a tablespoon, to remove all the juices left on the cob. Measure amount of corn and juice. In a frying pan or skillet, heat enough bacon drippings, add corn, and heat thoroughly. This is especially good, according to Roberta

Campbell Lawson (Delaware) who contributed this recipe, served with turkey or wild meats.

WA-LUX-SIA (p. 17)

INGREDIENTS FOR 8:

- 8 medium-sized pears, not overripe
  Water to cover
- 2 eggs
- 1 pint milk
- ½ teaspoon salt
- 2 tablespoons flour
- 1 tablespoon butter
- 1 cup sugar plus additional ½ cup
  to cook pears
  Pinch nutmeg

METHOD: Peel and core the pears, leaving them whole. Place in a pot, add the ½ cup sugar and enough water to cover, and simmer over medium heat until they are slightly done. Remove from the heat, pour off the liquid, and keep the pears covered for 10 to 15 minutes more, then cool.

Make a batter by beating the eggs until light and fluffy, then add the milk, salt, flour, butter, sugar, and nutmeg. In a heavy saucepan, bring the mixture to a boil, beating constantly with a wire whip, until it slightly thickens. Remove from the fire, and continue beating with the whip for a few minutes. Pour over the fruit and serve hot or cold.

THE JUNIOR LEAGUE OF DALLAS COOK BOOK

KENTUCKY HAM (p. 75)

INGREDIENTS FOR 8:

- 2 1-pound lean ham steaks, or
  1 2-pound cut of ham
- 1 cup milk
- 2 tablespoons prepared mustard
  (not the salad type, but the dry,
  tart prepared mustard with no
  sugar added)

METHOD: Completely dissolve the mustard into the milk. Place ham in a heavy skillet, preferably iron or enameled with a lid, or in a heavy duty aluminum skillet with a lid. Pour the milk-mustard mixture over ham. Place cold pan over medium heat, and when the liquid begins to boil, cover, adjust heat to low, and cook just below the boiling point, basting occasionally, for 45 minutes to 1 hour, depending on whether you use 2 steaks or 1 thick piece. Serve hot with eggs for breakfast, or with vegetables and potatoes as a main course. This is also good for sandwiches, made the next day.

SPANISH STEW (p. 230)

INGREDIENTS FOR 8:

3	tablespoons ham or bacon drippings, or lard
1	tablespoon flour
1	medium-sized potato cut into ½ inch cubes
	Salt and cayenne pepper to taste
½	clove garlic, mashed to a pulp with a little salt
3	cups water
2	cups chopped, cooked meat, leftover beef, veal, chicken, pork, or any combination
1	medium onion, peeled and sliced
½	No. 2 can tomatoes, or about 1 cup fresh tomatoes, peeled and chopped, or ½ cup tomato puree diluted with water to make 1 cup liquid
1	cup raw macaroni
	Tomato slices and black olives for garnish, optional

METHOD: Heat the shortening in a skillet. Add the flour and brown it. Add all other ingredients except macaroni, and over medium heat, in a covered pot, bring the stew to a boil. When boiling, add the macaroni, adjust the heat to low and simmer for 30 minutes, stirring often, or until macaroni is done. Correct seasoning and serve, decorated with fresh tomato slices and black olives, if desired.

OKRA PATTIES (p. 81)

INGREDIENTS FOR 8:

>   2 cups cooked okra, including the
>   cooking liquid
>   Salt and freshly ground black pepper
>   according to taste
>   Approximately ¾ cup cornmeal,
>   depending on the amount of liquid
>   1 egg, beaten
>   Shortening for frying, preferably lard
>   or bacon drippings

METHOD: Cut the cooked okra into small pieces. Add salt, freshly ground pepper, and the well beaten egg to okra and liquid. Sprinkle some of the cornmeal over this mixture, and fold it in with a spoon, continue to add cornmeal until the consistency of the batter is similar to that of pancake batter. Drop this by tablespoonfuls into hot shortening in a frying pan or skillet, and brown on both sides. Serve as a side dish accompanying the main course.

Favorite Recipes

of

Colfax County Club Women

Favorite Recipes

of

Colfax County Club Women

ABBOTT	JOHNSON MESA
CAPULIN	KIOWA
CHATTEAU HILL	MAXWELL
CIMARRON	MIAMI
COLMOR	MOFAX
EAGLE NEST	RATON
FARLEY	SPRINGER
FRENCH	WHEATLAND

Mrs. Lillie Mae Daughtrey
Home Demonstration Agent

1946

Foreword

THE MEMBERS OF COLFAX COUNTY HOME DEMON-
STRATION CLUBS ARE GROUPS OF ORGANIZED WOMEN
WHO ARE EAGER TO LEARN AND EAGER TO SERVE,
LIKEWISE TO SHARE THEIR SMALL MEASURE OF SUC-
CESS WITH OTHERS.

WE DESIRE TO THANK ALL WHO HAVE CONTRIBUT-
ED TO THIS BOOK.

"Born Cook"

By Miriam Clark Porter

When she was a little thing
    With flying skirts and curls,
She always loved her sand pile
    Much more than other girls.

She liked to shape a pretty cake,
    To trim a pie with clover,
Or, humming softly, to invent
    A pebble-plum turnover.

And she has her kitchen and
    Is sifting, stirring, peeling
In grown-up earnest: Still she keeps
    That lovely sand-pile feeling!!

3

Table of
Contents

BEVERAGES	4-6
BREADS, Quick, Yeast	7-14
CAKES	15-35
CAKES, FILLINGS, FROSTINGS	36-39
CANDIES	40-46
COOKIES	47-49
DESSERTS, Frozen, Gelatin, Misc.	50-64
DESSERT SAUCES	65-66
FISH	67-70
MEATS, INCLUDING POULTRY	71-81
PASTRIES	82-92
PICKLES, RELISHES AND PRESERVES	93-98
SALADS	99-105
SANDWICHES	106-108
SAUCES	109-110
SOUPS	111-112
VEGETABLES	113-120
SOAP	121-123

4

Beverages

Apple Cider:

Wash and core wind-fall apples or crabapples. Grind through cider press. Strain juice and boil for five minutes and seal.

Mrs. Zenas Curtis, Cimarron

Cocoa Egg Nog

1 egg white
1 t. sugar or honey
1 t. cocoa

¼ c. top milk (chilled)
½ t. vanilla

Beat egg white stiffly, slowly, add sugar, cocoa and salt. Beat thoroughly. Add milk, flavoring and beat well with rotary beater

— Brooks Rucker, Abbott

Cocoa Milk Shake:

3 T. cocoa
½ t. sugar or honey
pinch of salt

¼ t. vanilla
1 egg, beaten well
1 c. milk

Mix cocoa and sugar with a little milk to make smooth paste. Add remaining ingredients. Beat well. Add spoonful of whipped cream, ice cubes and serve.

— Brooks Rucker, Abbott

Grape HiBall:

Juice of 3 lemons
1½ pts. water

1 T. grape hi-ball
1 c. sugar

Mix lemon juice with other ingredients. Turn into pitcher half filled with ice and stir. Let stand 10 minutes before serving.

— Brooks Rucker, Abbott

Grape Juice:

Sterilize jar, then put in it 1 c. sugar, 1 c. grapes in ½ gallon jar. Fill with boiling water and seal while hot.
Note: Last fall, as I was short of jars, I doubled recipe, putting 2 cups of sugar and 2 c. of grapes in jar and filled with hot water. Then put in water bath and brought to boiling point. Now, when I open a jar, I add enough cold water to make 1 gallon of grape juice.

— Mrs. John Everett, Springer

Mint Raspberry Punch:

¼ c. orange juice
½ c. lemon juice
½ c. sugar

1 T. raspberry flavoring
½ doz. sprigs fresh mint
1 pint cold water

Mix fruit juices, sugar and raspberry powder or flavor. Stir well and add water. Pour over large pieces of ice. Serve with a sprig of mint in each glass.

— Brooks Rucker, Abbott

Peanut Butter Milk Shake:

Place ¼ c. peanut butter, 3 T. sugar, dash of salt and ¼ c. sweet milk in a bowl and whip with egg beater until smooth. Add 1¾ c. milk and beat until blended. Add ¼ t. vanilla. Chill until ready to use and when serving, top each glass with dash of nutmeg.

— Mrs. Lonnie Hoy, Maxwell

Saigon Tea

3 T. tea
4 c. freshly boiling water
Lemon wedges
12 whole cloves
12 all-spice berries
1 2" stick cinnamon

Put tea into heated pot; add water. Add cloves, all spice and cinnamon; let stand 5 minutes. Pour through strainer over ice in tall glasses. Garnish with lemon. Serves four.

Spiced Cocoa

¼ c. cocoa
¼ c. sugar
Pinch salt
⅛ t. cinnamon
2 c. water
1 13 oz. can evaporated milk
½ t. vanilla
Whipped cream

Mix cocoa, sugar, salt and cinnamon; add water. Bring to boiling point; boil 3 minutes. Add milk; heat. Beat with rotary beater until frothy; add vanilla. Garnish with cream. Serves 4-6.

Spiced Orange Milk

1½ c. orange juice
1 T. sugar
1½ c. evaporated milk
1 c. water
3 egg yolks and 3 egg whites
Nutmeg

Combine juice, sugar, milk and water. Beat egg yolks; add milk mixture. Beat egg whites stiff; fold in. Serve in tall glasses with ice; sprinkle with nutmeg. Serves 4.

Bread, Quick; Yeast

Apple Nut Muffins:

2 c. sifted flour
2 t. baking powder
½ t. salt
¼ c. sugar
½ c. milk

½ c. drippings or other shortening
2 eggs
¾ c. applesauce, unsweetened
½ chopped nuts

Sift flour, baking powder, sugar and salt together. Add melted drippings and mix. Add beaten eggs, applesauce and nuts. Stir only until flour is moistened. Fill greased 2½ inch tins 2|3 full. Bake in moderate oven, 375 degrees F. 20-25 minutes.

— Mrs. J. W. Ausherman, Miami

Banana Bread No. 1

½ c. shortening
1 c. sugar
1 c. sour milk
2 eggs

3 ripe bananas, crushed well
2 c. flour
1 t. soda
¼ c. chopped nuts

Cream shortening, add sugar. Cream again, then add crushed bananas to creamed shortening and cream again. Beat all ingredients together. Bake in loaf pan in slow oven.

— Ella Gillespie, Colmor

Banana Bread No. 2:

2 c. flour, sifted
1 t. baking powder
1 t. soda
½ t. salt

¾ c. sugar
1 egg
½ c. nuts
1 c. mashed bananas

Add dry ingredients. Mix egg, bananas and lemon juice to dry gredients. Bake 45 minutes.

— Frances Towndrow, Raton

Boston Brown Bread:

5 c. graham or whole wheat flour
1 c. corn meal
1 c. white flour
1 c. molasses

1 t. soda
1 t. salt
Sour milk to make a dough as for muffins

Stir all ingredients together. Put in 1 pound coffee cans or baking powder cans that have been greased. Fill 2/3 full and steam 3 to 4 hours. Then shake from the cans and put in warm oven to dry few minutes. You can add raisins if you desire. Serve with butter while hot. This makes 8 or 9 cans full.

—Mrs. G. W. Drury, Eagle Nest

Corn Bread:

1 c. cornmeal
1 c. flour
4 t. baking powder
½ t. salt

1 t. sugar
1 c. milk
1 egg, beaten
2 T. melted butter

Sift together all dry ingredients. Add milk gradually, and beat. Then add egg and melted butter. Bake in hot, well greased pan 15 to 20 minutes in hot oven, 400 - 500 degrees F.

Mrs. Vick Wilson, Eagle Nest

Farmer's Bran Bread:

2 c. flour
3 t. baking powder
½ t. soda
¼ c. sugar
¾ t. salt

1 egg
1 c. bran
2 T. melted shortening
2 T. melted butter
1 c. sour milk

Sift flour, baking powder, salt, sugar and soda in bowl. Beat egg, add sour milk and bran; stir to mix. Add melted shortening and stir into flour mixture. Place on floured board and roll to ½" thickness. Cut into rectangles 2 x 3 inches. Brush top with melted butter. Form loaf by placing rectangle on edge in pan and bake in moderate oven.

— Mrs. J. R. Black, Johnson Mesa

Georgia Sally Lunn:

½ c. shortening
½ c. sugar
2 eggs, well beaten
1 c. milk

3 t. baking powder
2 c. sifted cake flour
3|4 t. salt

Cream shortening; add sugar and cream. Combine beaten eggs and milk and add alternately with dry ingredients to mixture. Turn into a greased and floured shallow pan and bake in hot oven 450 degrees F. 25 minutes. Cut in 2" squares and serve hot with butter. Makes about 24 pieces.

— Mrs. Young, Colmor

Pancakes

2 c. flour
4 t. baking powder
2 eggs, beaten light
½ t. salt

4 T. sugar, level
1½ c. milk or more as needed
4 T. melted lard

Beat egg, add sugar, milk, then other ingredients.

— Mrs. H. A. McConnell, Springer

Hot Cakes:

Just keep in mind "one of everything" and mix in the order given:

1 c. flour
1 T. sugar
1 t. salt
1 t. soda
1 c. sour milk

1 T. melted fat
1 egg yolk
1 egg white, beaten stiff and folded in last.

The thickness of "sour" milk will sometimes cause a little variation in amount of liquid.

— Mrs. Homer Tepe, Eagle Nest

Plain Muffins:

4 T. shortening
2 T. sugar
1 egg.
3 t. baking powder

½ t. salt
1 c. milk
2 c. flour

Cream shortening and sugar, then beat in well beaten egg. Add sifted dry ingredients alternately with milk. Fill muffin tins 2/3 full. Bake in moderate oven.

— Mrs. Amos Blades, Abbott

Southern Spoon Bread:

3 c. milk
1 c. white cornmeal
1 t. melted butter
1 t. sugar
1 t. salt
3 beaten egg yolks
3 stiffly beaten egg whites

Scald milk in double boiler, add corn meal gradually, and cook 5 minutes, stirring to make very smooth. Cool slightly and add butter, sugar and salt. Add egg yolks, then fold in egg whites. Bake in greased baking dish in moderate oven about 45 minutes. Serve hot from dish in which it was baked with plenty of butter.

— Mrs. J. W. Wilferth, Springer

Steamed Brown Bread:

1 c. full graham flour, 1 c. yellow corn meal and 1 c. white flour, sifted together. Add 1 t. salt, 1 t. soda, ½ c. sugar, ¾ c. molasses and 2 c. sour milk. Put all in a pail and cover tight. Set in boiling water. Boil steadily 2½ hours. Can be put in two smaller cans.

— Daisy Diver, Raton

Yellow Biscuit:

2 c. flour
4 t. baking powder
2 T. sugar
4 T. shortening
1 egg, beaten in cup

Fill the cup with milk. Add to the dry ingredients. Roll and cut. Fold in half and butter. Let rise ½ hour and bake.

— Mrs. John Floyd, Farley

YEAST BREADS

Butterhorn Rolls:

1 cake compressed yeast
1 c. milk
½ c. shortening
½ t. salt
1 T. sugar
3 eggs, well beaten
1|3 c. sugar
3 c. sifted flour

Crumble yeast with 1 T. sugar until it goes to liquid. Add to other ingredients, stirring with spoon. Add flour, still stirring. Let raise. When light, divide in three parts. Roll to size of dinner plate. Brush with butter. Cut in pie shape (16 parts). Begin at large end, fold three times. Raise and bake carefully. Makes 48 rolls.

— Daisy Diver, Raton

Butter Milk Rolls:

Crumble into mixing bowl 1 cake compressed yeast. Add 1 c. lukewarm, thick butter milk.
¼ t. soda
3 T. shortening (melted) Stir to dissolve, and add 1 t. sugar
Sift together: 2½ c. sifted flour, 1 t. baking powder, 1 t. salt (add to first mixture). Add some flour, to keep dough from sticking. Make into rolls, let raise 30 minutes. Bake in hot oven.

— Francis Towndrow, Raton

Fleishman's Yeast Buns:

1 cake Fleishman's yeast
3 T. shortening (melted lard)
2 c. water (slightly warm)
1 egg
6 c. flour or more
½ c. sugar

Mix yeast, sugar, egg and water, then put in half of the flour, and add lard and salt; mix in rest of the flour and knead well. Put into same pan and let raise until double in bulk. Make in buns and let raise again and bake 30 minutes.

— Mrs. Lee Glasgow, Farley

Hot Rolls:

1 yeast cake
2 c. warm water
½ c. sugar
1½ t. salt
1 egg
6 c. flour
3 T. melted shortening

Mix all ingredients, knead lightly, let raise two hours. Make into rolls and let raise until light. More water may be added if desired.

— Mrs. Jessie Burris, Miami

Light Bread:

14 c. flour
2 t. salt
3½ t. sugar
6 t. melted, cooled shortening
1 cake yeast
¼ c. lukewarm water & 6 c. lukewarm water

Dissolve yeast in ¼ c. warm water, then add salt and sugar and shortening to sifted flour. Combine and knead dough until smooth. Let dough set in warm place for 2 hours and then work down. Let dough set 1 hour and mold into four 1 pound loaves. Let set for 1 hour. Bake in moderate oven 1 hour.

— Mrs. L. D. Matthews, Raton

One Hour Rolls:

1 yeast cake with 2 t. sugar. 3 eggs, beaten well
  Put in saucer, let melt   2 c. milk (room temperature)
2 T. shortening, cream with 2 2½ t. salt
T. sugar   5½ c. flour

Mix all ingredients. This makes a soft dough. Let raise for 30 minutes. Take enough dough to roll the size of a 9" pie and cut into pie shape pieces. Spread with butter. Make rolls by starting at large end and roll to the small end. Let raise for 30 minutes. Bake in quick oven for 15 minutes.

— Mrs. Davida Ross, Raton

Orange Rolls:

2 cakes compressed yeast   ½ t. salt
½ c. sugar   ¼ c. melted butter
4 c. flour   2 eggs, well beaten
½ c. milk

Scald the milk, add sugar and cool to lukewarm. Add yeast broken into small pieces. Let stand about 15 minutes. Add 1 cup flour and beat well. Add salt, butter and eggs, beating well. Gradually beat in remainder of flour. Let stand until doubled in bulk, and dough holds imprint of finger when pressed down. Keep covered during the raising and in a warm place. When light, punch down and part with hand to ¼ inch thickness. Spread orange filling over surface, roll up as cinnamon rolls, pinch edges together to seal dough and retain juice. With a pair of scissors, cut dough in 1 inch slices and place in well oiled muffin pans, with cut side down. Let raise until doubled in size and bake in moderate oven 375 degrees F for 15 minutes. Yields 3 dozen rolls. Dough may be stored in refrigerator immediately after mixing and kept for several days.

Orange Filling:

1/3 c. melted butter   2 T. orange juice
2/3 c. sugar   Grated rind of 3 oranges

Mix together and cook until thick enough to spread. Cool before spreading.

— Mrs. Glenn Matthews, Maxwell

Parker House Rolls No. 1:

½ c. milk   ½ to ¼ cake compressed yeast
1 T. sugar   1 T. lukewarm water
1 T. butter   1½ to 2 c. flour
½ t. salt

Measure the sugar, butter and salt into mixing bowl. Add scalded milk and cool to lukewarm, stirring occasionally. Soften the yeast in the luke warm water and add it to the milk mixture. Add the flour, gradually beating thoroughly, until no more can be worked in with a spoon. Cover tightly and let raise until three times its bulk. Turn onto lightly floured board, knead slightly and roll ¾" thick. Cut with a round floured cutter. Crease in the middle. rub ½ with melted butter and fold over. Place on oiled tin and let raise double size. Bake in hot oven 15 to 20 minutes.

— Mrs. Ruth James, Farley

Parker House Rolls No. 2:

1¼ c. warm water
1 cake yeast
4 c. flour, or enough to make
    soft dough

1 egg
2 t. salt
3 T. sugar
3 T. melted shortening

Dissolve yeast in ¼ c. warm water. Add remaining water, sugar, salt and 2 c. flour. Beat until smooth, add egg and shortening, and mix well. Add remaining flour to make soft dough. Let raise till doubled in bulk, about 1½ hours. Roll out ⅜ inch thick, cut with biscuit cutter. Crease through center with dull edged knife and brush with butter or oleomargarine. Fold over and place in well-greased pans. Let raise until light, about one hour. Bake in hot oven.

Parker House Rolls No. 3

2 c. scalded milk
3 T. sugar
2 T. salt

1 yeast cake dissolved in ¼ c.
    warm water

Add sugar to yeast cake and water. Add 3 T. butter and salt to milk when lukewarm, then add yeast cake, and 3 c. flour. Beat. Let raise until light. Knead down. Add 2¼ c. flour. Let raise. Roll out, cut and make rolls.

— Myrtle Durie, Johnson Mesa

Sweet Rolls Dough with Maca Yeast:

2 pkgs. Maca yeast
1 c. lukewarm water
1 c. lukewarm milk
½ c. butter
⅛ t. grated nutmeg
1 c. sugar

1½ t. salt
2 eggs, well beaten
Grated rind and juice of ½
    lemon
Sifted flour, 7 cups or more

Pour the yeast into lukewarm water, stir and let stand 5 minutes. Scald milk and cool until lukewarm. Cream together the butter and sugar and salt. Add eggs, lemon and nutmeg. Add lukewarm milk to softened yeast and blend the liquid with 3 cups flour. Beat smooth, then add butter mixture and enough more flour to make a medium soft dough. Knead smooth but keep as soft as can be handled without sticking. Let dough raise in a cozy warm place until doubled. Shape into rolls at once.

— Mrs. Frank Deacy, Colmor

Banana Bread:

Cream together, ½ c. butter or other shortening and 1 c. sugar. Add 2 eggs, beaten slightly. Sift together 2 c. flour, 1 t. baking powder, ½ t. salt and add alternately with 1 c. sour milk and 1 t. soda. Add last 3 mashed bananas and 1 c. nut meats. Pour in loaf pan and bake in a slow oven one hour.

— Mrs. William Howe, Kiowa Home Builders

Cakes

Almagated Cake:

Mix 2 c. sugar and 1 c. butter well. Sift together 2½ c. flour, ½ t. salt and 2 rounding t. baking powder. Mix with 1 c. water, add 8 well beaten egg whites.

Filling:

2 c. nuts, 2 c. raisins, 2 c. coconut. 1 c. sugar, ½ c. butter, ½ c. milk, 8 beaten egg yolks, ½ t. salt. Grated rind and juice of 1 orange and 1 lemon. Cook until thickens. Let cool.

— Mrs. Herbert Littrell

Amos and Andy Chocolate Cake:

First mix ½ c. cocoa, 1 heaping t. baking soda and 1 c. boiling water. Next, 2 c. sugar, 1 c. shortening. Cream. Add 3 eggs, 2½ c. flour, sifted three times and 1 c. sour milk, then add the chocolate and 1 t. vanilla. Bake in moderate oven.

— Mrs. Al Richardson, Cimarron

Angel Food Cake No. 1:

12 egg whites (beaten stiff)
1 t. water
1½ c. sugar
1½ t. cream of tartar
¼ t. salt
2 t. vanilla
1½ c. sifted cake flour

Bake in ungreased angel cake pan for 1 hour.

— Mrs. Lee Glasgow, Farley

Angel Food No. 2:

1½ c. egg whites (11 to 13 eggs)
½ t. salt
1 t. cream of tartar
1½ c. sugar
1¼ c. cake flour, sift once, measure and sift three times
1 t. vanilla

Beat the egg whites with the salt until frothy, add the cream of tartar, beat stiff, but not dry. Fold in the sugar, 3 T. at a time, then flour gradually and last the flavoring. Pour into angel cake pan and bake in a moderate oven until firm to touch (1 to 1¼ hours).

— Mrs. O. A. Cook, Capulin

Angel Food Cake No. 3:

Whites of 12 eggs
1¼ c. sugar
1 c. flour
½ juice of fresh lemon

Have oven hot when cake is put in. Leave open as cake raises gradually close oven. Then to finish browning, close entirely.

— Mrs. W. A. Dow, Colmor

Angel Cake No. 4:

9 egg whites (or 1 scant cup)   1 c. flour
½ t. cream of tartar   ⅛ t. salt
1¼ c. granulated sugar   1 t. vanilla

Beat the whites of eggs and salt to a froth, add cream of tartar and beat until it will bear the weight of spoon whip, add two teaspoons water, beat, then add sugar which has been sifted twice. Add vanilla and lastly fold in the flour which has been sifted several times. Bake in an ungreased angel cake tin in a slow oven, 200 degrees F. for 50 minutes. Remove from oven, turn pan upside down, let cool.

— Verma Johnston, Mills

Chocolate Angel Food Cake:

11 medium sized egg whites   (Sift this mixture 7 times)
1½ c. sugar, sifted 3 times   ¼ t. salt
¼ c. cocoa. Put in measuring   1 level t. cream of tartar
cup and fill cup level full of   1 t. vanilla and a little black
sifted cake flour.   walnut

Beat whites a little, then add cream of tartar, and continue beating until stiff, but not dry; add sugar, slowly folding in. Add flavoring, then fold in flour slowly. Put in angel cake pan and tap on table to remove air bubbles. Bake in slow oven 325 to 350 degrees for 50 minutes. Remove from oven and invert pan to cool. Make chocolate icing.

— Mrs. C. C. Lapp, Miami

Butter Cake:

½ c. butter or butter substitute 2 c. flour
¼ c. sugar   2 t. baking powder
2 eggs   ¼ t. salt
¾ c. milk   1 t. vanilla

Cream sugar and butter and add egg yolks. Beat thoroughly. Sift flour, measure and sift with baking powder and salt. Add alternately with milk to creamed sugar and butter. Beat thoroughly. Add flavoring. Fold in stiffly beaten egg whites. Pour into well oiled pans. Bake in moderate oven 25 minutes. When cool put layers together with Peach Filling.

— Mrs. V. S. Shirley, Maxwell

Carrot Cake:

2 2/3 c. sugar   2 t. shortening
2 2/3 c. water   2 c. grated carrots
1 t. salt   2 c. raisins
2 t. each of cinnamon, cloves 1 c. nuts
    and all-spice

Run carrots, raisins, 1 c. nuts through grinder. Boil above ingredients together for 20 minutes. Let cool. Add 4 c. flour, 3 t. soda, 2 eggs. Bake in moderate oven about 45 minutes.

— Mrs. C. U. Burris, Miami

Chocolate Cake No. 1:

1½ c. sugar

¾ cube butter. Cream together until light. Add beaten yolks of 3 eggs and 2 squares melted chocolate. Add 1¼ c. butter milk with 1 t. soda. Add alternately with 2 c. Swansdown flour. Beat for 10 minutes. Then add beaten whites of 3 eggs and 1 t. vanilla. Bake in two layers. Use white or chocolate icing.

— Mrs. Mary E. Peterson, Cimarron

Chocolate Cake No. 2:

¾ c. cocoa   1 t. salt
1 1/3 c. sugar   3 eggs, unbeaten
1¼ c. scalded milk   1¼ t. soda
2/3 c. Spry   2 c. sifted flour
1 t. vanilla

Sift cocoa with 1/3 c. sugar. Add scalded milk gradually and stir until smooth. Cool. Combine Spry, salt and vanilla. Add 1 c. sugar gradually and cream thoroughly. Add eggs singly, beating thoroughly after each addition. Add soda to flour And sift three times. Add flour to creamed mixture, alternately with cocoa mixture, mixing after each addition until smooth. Pour into two deep 9" layer pans, greased. Bake in moderate oven.

—Mrs. T. J. Floyd, Raton

Chocolate Cake No. 3:

1 cube butter
1 c. sugar (cream together)
3 eggs (separated) Add yolks to butter mixture one at a time, beating well.
1 c. sour milk
1 t. soda in milk

1 t. vanilla
1½ c. flour
2 t. cocoa or 2 sq. chocolate
1 egg white. Last add 3 t. boiling water. Add flour and milk alternately.

— Mrs. Robert Morrow, Raton

Devils Food Cake No. 1:

1½ c. sugar
½ c. shortening
½ c. cocoa
½ c. boiling water
2 eggs, beaten

2 c. flour
½ t. salt
1½ t. soda
½ c. sour milk
1 t. vanilla

Cream sugar and shortening well; add beaten eggs and beat well. Combine cocoa, soda and hot water well, then add to creamed mixture. Add sifted flour and salt alternately with sour milk. Add vanilla and beat well.

— Mrs. Charles Higbee

Devil's Food Cake No. 2:

1 c. sugar
1 c. butter
1 c. sour milk
1 t. soda

3 eggs, beaten separately
¼ cake chocolate
1¼ to 2 c. flour
1 t. vanilla

Beat sugar, butter, yolks to a cream. Add whites of eggs and part of the flour and the sour milk. Then the remaining flour with the soda in ¼ c. of hot water. Then chocolate and last vanilla. Bake 20 minutes.

— Lucille Nagel,

Devil's Food Cake No. 3:

1 c. sweet cream
1½ c. sugar
2 egg yolks
1 t. vanilla

1½ c. flour
1 t. soda, level
½ c. cocoa
pinch salt

Combine cream, sugar, eggs and vanilla; mix well. Then combine flour and soda and sift together well. Mix the cocoa with hot water. Combine them all together. Mix well, then bake in a 300 degree oven for about 30 or 35 minutes.

— Ethel Kuykendall, Farley

Devil's Food Cake No. 4:

1 c. sour cream
1½ c. sugar
¾ c. boiling strong coffee
3 heaping T. cocoa
2 c. flour, sifted 6 times

1 t. soda
3 eggs, separated
¼ t. salt
1 t. vanilla
½ t. almond

Pour hot coffee slowly over cocoa and soda. Mix well. Let cool while mixing the following: Cream sugar and sour cream together, add well beaten egg yolks. Add flour alternately with cocoa mixture. Add extract. Add salt to egg whites and beat stiff but not dry. Fold in last. Bake in two 9" layer pans 30 minutes in moderate oven.

— Mrs. Laura White, Farley

Devil's Food Cake No. 5:

Mix in order listed:
2 c. sugar
½ c. butter or other shortening
3 egg yolks, lightly beaten
½ c. chocolate or cocoa dissolved
in 1 c. boiling water
1 t. vanilla

1 c. sour milk in which
1 t. soda is dissolved
2 c. flour
3 egg whites, well beaten, add
last
Bake 45 minutes in moderate oven.

— Mrs. H. H. Burris, Miami

Devil's Food Cake No. 6:

4 T. cocoa
¼ c. sugar
Cook to a thick paste, beat until smooth. Cool.
¾ c. shortening (cream)
1 c. sugar or white syrup

2 eggs, lightly beaten
1 egg
½ c. sweet milk
1 c. sour milk with 1 t. soda
dissolved in milk
2 c. flour
1 t. vanilla

— Mrs. Lonnie Hoy, Maxwell

Chocolate Custard Devil's Food:

½ c. shortening
1 c. sugar
2 beaten egg yolks
2 c. flour

¼ t. salt
1 t. soda
1 c. milk
1 t. vanilla

Combine 2/3 c. sugar, 3 one ounce squares unsweetened chocolate, melted. ½ cup of milk and 1 beaten egg. Cook over low heat until thick. Cool, cream shortening and 1 cup of sugar. Add egg yolks, mix well. Add sifted dry ingredients alternately with 1 cup of milk and vanilla. Stir in chocolate mixture. Bake in 2 waxed paper lined 8" layer cake pans in moderate oven 20 to 50 minutes.

Red Devil's Cake No. 1:

2 c. cake flour
1½ t. soda
½ t. salt
½ c. shortening
1 c. sugar
2 eggs

2 sq. unsweetened chocolate
  melted and cooled
¾ c. sour milk or buttermilk
1 t. vanilla
1/3 c. boiling water

Sift, then measure the flour. Sift 3 times with soda and salt. Cream butter until light. Gradually add sugar, beating each addition until light and fluffy. Slowly add the eggs, which have been beaten until they are almost as stiff as whipped cream. Combine milk and vanilla. Alternately add dry ingredients and milk, beating after each addition until smooth. Add boiling water, beat well. Turn into greased loaf pan. Bake in moderate oven. Frost. Let stand 2 hours before cutting to allow the red color to fully develop.   — Mrs. Lonnie Hoy, Maxwell

Red Devil's Food Cake No. 2:

1 c. sugar
1 c. sweet cream
1 egg
1½ c. flour

1 t. soda
⅛ t. salt
1 T. vanilla
3 T. cocoa

Mix cake as given above; sugar, cream and egg well beaten, then add soda, salt and flour sifted together. Lastly, add cocoa melted with enough boiling water to make a medium thin paste, then add vanilla. This cake may be made in loaf or layers with Seven Minute Icing or Brown Sugar Frosting.
                                      — Brooks Rucker, Abbott

Five Minute Devil's Food Cake:

2 c. sugar
½ c. butter
2 eggs
½ c. buttermilk
3 heaping T. cocoa

1 c. boiling water
2 c. flour
1 t. soda
1 t. vanilla

Put sugar, egg and shortening in bowl and mix well. Add sour milk with soda dissolved in it. Add cocoa, flour and vanilla. Mix well. Last add boiling water and bake in two 9" pans. Bake about ½ hour in moderate oven. Makes moist red cake. Use either chocolate or Seven Minute Frosting.
                                    — Mrs. Estell Saunders, Farley

Honey Devil's Food Cake:

Cream ½ c. shortening with 1 c. honey and a pinch of salt; add 3 well-beaten eggs. Mix ¼ c. sugar with 3 heaping tablespoons of cocoa and add enough boiling water to make a smooth paste. Add this to the creamed mixture. 2/3 c. cold water with 1 t. soda and 1 t. vanilla dissolved in it. Add alternately with 2 c. sifted cake flour. Bake 25 to 30 minutes at 350 degrees.
                                     — Mrs. Harry Smith, Springer

Mrs. Young's Devil's Food Cake:

Cream ½ c. butter. Add 1¼ c. sugar. Beat well and add 3 unbeaten eggs, one at a time, beating very hard after each. Sift 1 t. soda with 2 c. flour and add alternately with 1 c. sour milk in which 1 t. soda has been dissolved. Dissolve ½ c. cocoa and 2/3 c. boiling water and add to mixture. Blend well. Bake.

— Mrs. J. C. Matthews, Maxwell

Eggless Chocolate Cake:

½ c. butter or cooking oil
1½ c. brown sugar
½ c. cocoa
1 c. hot water
1 t. soda

2 c. flour
1 t. baking powder
1 c. buttermilk or sour milk
½ t. salt
1 t. vanilla

Cream butter and sugar. Add cocoa mixed with ½ of water and soda in other half. Add flour with baking powder. Lastly beat in sour milk and vanilla. Bake.   — Mrs. Steele, Colmor

Christmas Cake:

1½ slightly warmed molasses; ½ c. butter combined with ½ c. lard; 1 cup quince or peach preserves; 1 c. finely chopped nuts; ¾ c. shredded candied orange peel; ½ c. shredded candied lemon peel; 3 c. seeded raisins. Now stir in 5 c. sifted flour, to which you have added 1 t. cinnamon, 1 t. nutmeg; ½ t. allspice; ½ t. cloves, pinch of salt, 3 level T. baking powder, 2 well-beaten eggs and last of all 1½ c. thin applesauce. Stir vigorously for 5 minutes. Bake in deep cake pan 1½ to 1¾ hours. Ice and let stand 24 hours before cutting.   — Mrs. Herbert Littrell

Coffee Cake No. 1:

1 c. molasses
½ c. sugar
3½ c. flour
1 c. strong coffee
¾ c. butter
2 eggs

1 c. chopped raisins
1 t. cinnamon
¼ t. cloves
2 t. baking soda
Pinch of salt

Sift flour once. Add baking soda and salt. Cream butter, sugar and eggs and molasses. Add coffee, raisins, cinnamon and cloves and flour and bake 50 minutes. This makes a loaf or 2 dozen cup cakes.   — Mrs. Frank Deacy, Colmor

Coffee Cake No. 2:

Soak one cake of yeast in ¼ c. of warm water. Scald 2 cups of milk. When the luke warm, cream ¾ c. sugar, ½ c. shortening, add salt and 1 egg. Add milk, yeast, raisins and flour and beat stiff. Let raise. Put in pans. Cover with melted butter, brown sugar and cinnamon. Let raise. Bake 30 or 40 minutes in moderate oven.   — Mrs. Emma Dow, Colmor

Crumb Cake No. 1:

½ c. shortening
2 c. flour
1 t. soda
1 c. sugar
1 c. sour milk

2 eggs, unbeaten
½ c. nuts, if you wish
1 t. each of cinnamon, nutmeg, cloves, allspice and ginger

Mix together except eggs, milk and soda to make crumbs. Save ½ c. crumbs to put on top of batter after putting in pan to bake. Bake in 6 x 10 inch loaf pan. The crumbs make the icing.

— Mrs. Lee Glasgow, Farley
— Mrs. Flake Fisher, Abbott

Crumb Cake No. 2:

1 lb. brown sugar, 1 c. shortening, 3 c. flour. Mix together and save out 1 cup. To the rest of the mixture add 1 egg, 1½ c. sour milk, 1 large t. soda, 1 c. raisins, 1 t. vanilla. Put in a large cake pan and place the cup of mixture saved out on top. Bake slowly.

— Mrs. Emma Dow, Colmor

Date Cake No. 1:

1 or 1½ c. dates
1 c. boiling water
1 t. soda dissolved in water
1 c. sugar
1 T. melted butter

1½ c. flour
1 egg
pinch of salt
1 c. nuts
2 t. vanilla

Add soda and boiling water to dates. Cut fine and let stand while mixing the rest of the ingredients. Add nuts and dates. Bake 50-60 minutes in moderate oven.

— Mrs. J. C. Matthews, Maxwell
— Mrs. F. A. Brookshier, Maxwell

Date Cake No. 2:

1 c. sugar
1 c. boiling water
1 pkg. dates
1¼ c. flour

1 egg
2 T. butter
1 t. soda

Sprinkle soda over dates. Pour boiling water over. Let stand while fixing nuts and creaming butter and sugar. Add egg to sugar and mix all together. Bake.

— Myrtle Durie, Johnson Mesa

Fool Proof Cake:

1½ c. sugar, ½ c. shortening (cream together), add 1 c. cold water, 2 c. flour, 4 t. syrup or honey. Beat well. Add ½ c. flour and 2 t. baking powder (sifted). Last, fold in 2 egg whites, flavor to taste.

— Mrs. Fred, Koehler, Raton

Fruit Cake Cheap and good):

1 c. brown sugar   ½ c. shortening
1 c. water   ½ t. nutmeg
1 t. cinnamon   ½ t. ginger
½ t. cloves   ½ t. allspice
2 c. raisins

Heat above ingredients and simmer for about 10 minutes. Cool thoroughly. Then add 2 c. flour, ½ t. soda, 2 t. baking powder (sifted together). Also add 1 c. dates, ½ c. nuts, ½ c. currants, ½ c. diced apples and ½ c. cut citron. Bake in a loaf pan in a slow oven about one hour. This will keep as well as any fruit cake. Other fruits may be added to batter.

— Mrs. W. C. Jenkins, Raton

Green Apple Cake:

1c. sugar   ½ t. nutmeg
½ c. butter   ¼ c. nuts
1 egg   1 c. raisins
1 t. cinnamon   1 c. chopped apples, raw
¼ t. cloves   1½ c. flour
1 t. soda in ½ c. cold coffee   1 t. cocoa

Bake in loaf and ice with chocolate frosting.

High Altitude Cake:

2 c. flour   1 c. milk
3 T. butter   3 eggs
2 T. lard   2½ t. baking powder
1 c. sugar   1 t. flavoring

Mix flour, sugar and shortening to mixture like cornmeal. Add milk and beat well. Add eggs well beaten and baking powder and flavoring. Bake.   — Marguerite M. Multz, Eagle Nest

Honey Cake:

½ c. butter, 1 c. honey, 2 eggs, 2 c. cake flour, 3 T. cream, 3 T. water, 2 t. baking powder, 1 t. vanilla, ½ t. salt. Cream honey and butter. Add well beaten eggs, water and cream. Mix well and fold in dry ingredients which have been sifted together. Bake in moderate oven about 25 minutes.

— Mrs. Hazel House, Capulin

Honey Chocolate Cake:

2 c. cake flour   1 c. honey
½ t. salt   2 eggs, well beaten
1¼ t. soda   2 sq. chocolate
½ c. lard   ¾ c. milk

Sift the measured flour. Sift 3 times with soda and salt. Cream lard, add honey gradually, slowly add eggs beaten well. Add chocolate that has been melted and cooled. Add sifted dry ingredients alternately with milk, blend thoroly. Turn into 2 greased pans. Bake.   — Mrs. Lillie Foree, Kiowa

Lady Baltimore Cake:

1 c. sugar	¼ t. salt
¾ cube butter	2 c. flour
1 c. milk	2 t. baking powder
¼ t. almond and lemon extract	Whites of 4 eggs

Cream sugar and butter. Sift and measure flour, then sift 4 times, adding baking powder and salt in last sifting. Add milk alternately with flour. Beat egg whites until stiff but not dry Fold into above mixture and bake 20 minutes in moderate oven — in layers

— Mary E. Peterson, Cimmaron

Mock Cheese Cake:

16 graham crackers	2 lemons
¼ lb. butter	1 can Eagle Brand sweetened
4 eggs	condensed milk

Roll crackers fine, melt butter, put crackers in butter, mix well and line pan. Save some for top of cake. Separate eggs, beat yolks. Squeeze lemons. Mix with yolks. Add milk. Beat whites of eggs separate. Fold in mixture. Pour over crackers. Take rest of crackers and sprinkle on top. Bake 27 minutes in 350 oven.

— Miss Rena Keenan, Springer

New Type of Cake:

½ c. sugar	4 egg yolks
1 t. vanilla	1 c. flour
3 T. milk	½ c. butter
1¼ t. baking powder	¼ t. salt

Cream butter, add sugar, eggs beaten light, vanilla. add milk alternately with flour, baking powder and salt sifted together. Spread thinly in a pan 8 x 12 or about that size. dd icing before putting in to bake, made of the 4 egg whites beaten with ¾ c. sugar, ½ t. vanilla. Spread over top of cake and bake in slow oven so the icing will be slightly brown and fluffy. Cocoanut or chopped nuts may be sprinkled on top before baking.

— Mrs. H. A. McConnell, Springer

One, Two, Three, Four Cakes:

1 c. butter	2 t. baking powder
2 c. sugar	1 c. milk
3 c. flour	1 t. vanilla
4 eggs	

Cream butter, adding sugar gradually. Add egg yolks and beat thoroughly. Sift dry ingredients and add alternately with milk. Add vanilla and fold in stiffly beaten egg whites. Bake in layers in hot oven for 25 minutes.

One Egg Cake:

¼ c. butter
2/3 c. syrup
1 egg, well beaten
1½ c. flour

2 t. baking powder
½ c. milk
½ t. vanilla

Cream butter, add syrup beating mixture hard. Then add the well beaten eggs. Sift the dry ingredients together and add alternately with the milk. Finally add the flavoring. Bake in moderate oven 30 minutes. Cover with your favorite icing. This cake can be baked as a layer cake, a loaf cake or small cup cakes.

— Mrs. Clyde Alton, Farley

Orange Layer Cake:

2 c. flour
1 c. sugar
½ c. shortening
4 t. baking powder

2 eggs (whites)
1 c. milk
Grated rind of orange

When baked, squeeze the juice of one orange on layers. **Frosting:** Use juice of one orange and yolks of eggs. Thicken with powdered sugar.

Potato Cake No. 1:

1 c. sugar
4 eggs
2 c. flour
1 c. milk
½ c. shortening
2 t. baking powder
1 t. soda

1 c. mashed potatoes
1 c. nuts
1 c. raisins
1 c. dates
2 sq. chocolate, melted
Mix as for ordinary cake.

Potato Cake No. 2:

Cream together 2 c. sugar and 1½ c. butter. Add 4 well beaten eggs. Sift together 2 c. flour, ½ c. cocoa, 1 t. cinnamon, ½ t. nutmeg, 1 t. cream of tartar and 1 t. baking powder. Add 2/3 c. sweet milk and dry ingredients to butter and sugar mixture, then add 1 c. mashed potatoes, 1 c. nuts, 1 t. almond extract, 1 t. vanilla. Beat well and bake as loaf in medium hot oven.

Powdered Sugar Filling for Potato Cake:

½ lb. powdered sugar, 1 T. butter, pinch of salt, ½ t. vanilla, 2 T. cocoa and 5 T. cream. Cream together until smooth.

— Mrs. Estell Saunders, Farley

Prune Cake:

1 c. sugar
¾ c. butter
3 T. sour cream
Salt
1 t. cinnamon
1 t. soda

1 t. allspice
2 c. flour
1 c. chopped nuts
1 c. cooked prunes
3 eggs

Put Vanilla Filling between layers.

— Mrs. W. J. Kuykendall, Abbott

Prune Loaf:

½ c. lard
½ c. sugar
2 eggs
½ c. molasses
3 c. flour
1½ c. prunes, cooked, pitted
and chopped

⅛ t. soda
⅛ t. cinnamon
⅛ t. cloves
⅛ t. nutmeg
⅛ t. allspice
Salt

Mix all and bake 1 hour in deep loaf pan. Bake slowly. Nuts and candied citrus fruits added to this, make a good fruit cake.

— Mrs. A. H. Newton, Abbott

Prune Cake:

1 c. sugar
½ c. butter
1 c. stewed prunes, seeded
1 c. prune juice
1 c. walnuts

1 t. cinnamon
1 t. nutmeg
2 eggs
1 t. soda dissolved in prune juice
2 c. flour

Cream butter, sugar and eggs. Crush the prunes and add next. Add prune juice alternately with sifted flour and spices. Add nuts. Bake in moderate oven.

— Mrs. O. A. Cook, Capulin

Quick Cake:

2 c. sifted cake flour
2 t. baking powder
¾ t. salt
1¼ c. sugar

½ c. shortening
¾ c. milk
2 eggs
1 t. vanilla

Sift flour once before measuring. Cream shortening and sugar. Add eggs. Add one half of liquid, then dry ingredients alternately. Cook in two 8" pans for about 25 minutes in moderate oven.

— Mrs. Grayson, Cimarron

Sopa Barrocha:

Make a plain cake, layer cake. When baked and cold put a layer in a pan and pour over it wine which has been diluted with a little water and add sugar. Then put another layer of cake and pour some more wine over it. Then beat the white of 3 eggs, add sugar and cover the top of the cake. Put in oven to brown as you do a pie.

— Mrs. Frank Deacy, Colmor
Miss A. Valdez

Sour Cream Cake:

Beat 2 eggs well. Add 1 c. sugar gradually. Add 1½ c. sifted cake flour alternately with 1 c. sour cream. Add 1 t. vanilla. Last add ½ t. soda dissolved in 3 or 4 T. boiling water. Bake about 25 minutes in moderate oven.

— Mrs. Davida Ross, Raton

Sour Cream Cake No. 2:

1 egg, 1 c. sugar, 1 c. thick sour cream, 1½ t. baking powder, ¼ t. soda, 1 t. vanilla, 1 t. lemon, 1½ c. flour, ½ t. salt. Oven temperature 350. Bake 25-30 minutes.

— Mrs. Ruby Davenport, Farley

Sour Cream Cake No. 3:

Mix 2 c. sugar, 2 c. sour cream. Add ½ t. soda. Separate 4 eggs. Beat yolks well and add to first mixture. Add 3 c. flour, 1 t. salt, 1 t. extract. Add well beaten egg whites. Cover with your favorite frosting.

— Mrs. M. L. Thorne, Farley

Sour Cream Spice Cake:

1 c. sugar	1¾ c. flour
3 eggs	1 t. cinnamon
1 c. sour cream	½ t. nutmeg
1 t. soda	½ t. cloves

Beat eggs, add sugar gradually, add cream. Sift flour, add spices and soda to flour. Mix.

— Mrs. Leon Johnson, Johnson Mesa

Boiled Spice Cake (eggless, milkless):

2 c. sugar	2 c. water
2 c. raisins	1 c. butter or lard
2 t. salt	1 t. nutmeg
2 t. cinnamon	½ t. allspice

Put in a stew pan and let boil. Cool and add 2 t. soda and 3 c. of flour. Bake in slow oven 45 minutes.

— Mrs. Jennie Gleaves, Cimarron

Sour Milk Cake:

1 cube butter, 1 c. sugar, creamed together. 2 eggs, beaten in one at a time. 1 cup sour milk. Alternate with 2 cups cake flour, sifted 4 times. 1 t. soda dissolved in 3 T. boiling water. Makes 2 layers or 1 medium sized loaf.

— Mrs. E. B. Majors, Raton

Sponge Cake:

Beat 4 egg yolks well, continue beating in ½ c. sugar. Beat 4 egg whites until stiff, but not dry and continue beating in ½ c. sugar. Combine the two. Add alternately 1 c. sifted flour, juice of one medium orange. Rind of orange may be grated and added. Cook in ungreased tube pan. May be served with sweetened whipped cream mixed with pineapple for strawberry shortcake or with butterscotch sauce.

— Mrs. Marian Pinson, Capulin

Speedy Sponge Cake:

2 eggs
1 c. sugar
1 c. flour
⅛ t. salt

1 t. baking powder
1 T. butter
½ c. hot milk

Beat eggs until light and thick. Slowly add sugar and beat with spoon 5 minutes or with electric mixer 2½ minutes. Fold sifted dry ingredients into egg mixture all at once. The folding in of the dry ingredients and milk should take only 1 minute. Bake in waxed paper lined 8" square pan in moderate oven for 30 minutes.

Baked-On Frosting:

Beat 1 egg white with ¼ t. baking powder. ½ c. brown sugar; spread over hot cake. Sprinkle with ¼ c. chopped nut meats. Bake in moderate oven until lightly browned, about 15 minutes.

— Martha T. Bowen, Springer

Egg Yolk Sponge Cake:

12 egg yolks
2 c. sugar
1 c. boiling water
½ t. salt

4 t. baking powder
2 t. lemon extract
3 c. sifted cake flour

Beat egg yolks until light with a beater; add sugar gradually, then hot water, beating meanwhile. Add flour, sifted with baking powder and salt, and beat thoroughly. Turn into an ungreased tube cake pan and bake in a moderate oven about one hour.

— Mrs. O. A. Cook, Capulin

Strawberry Shortcake:

1 c. sugar
1 T. butter
2 small c. flour

1 egg, beaten light
2 t. baking powder
1 c. milk

Cream butter and sugar. Add egg, add flour and milk alternately. Makes 2 layers. Bake in oven 20 minutes. Crush berries and sweeten and put between the layers. Cover top layer with powdered sugar and place whole berries on top of it.

— Mrs. Elizabeth B. Majors, Raton

Tomato Juice Cake:

1 c. sugar
1¼ t. soda
1 t. cinnamon
1 t. nutmeg
1½ c. tomato juice

½ c. lard
2 c. flour
1 egg, well beaten
¼ t. salt

Cream sugar and lard. Add beaten egg. Sift all dry ingredients and add gradually with tomato juice. Bake in two layers 15 to 20 minutes.

Treasure Chest Cake (Orange Fruit Cake)

1 large orange	¾ t. soda
1 c. seeded raisins	1 t. baking powder
1 c. walnuts	¼ t. salt
½ c. shortening	¼ t. cinnamon
1 c. sugar	¼ t. allspice
1 egg	¼ t. cloves
2 c. flour	1 c. sour milk

Squeeze juice from orange and remove white from orange peel. Put orange peel, raisins and walnut meats through coarse knife of food grinder. Add orange juice to ground fruits and nuts. Cream shortening, add sugar and cream thoroughly. Add well beaten egg. Sift flour, soda, baking powder, salt and spices together and add alternately with milk to creamed mixture. Add ¾ of the fruit and nut mixture to creamed mixture. Bake in two bread loaf pans lined with greased wrapping paper. Bake 35 minutes, at 350 degrees.   — Mrs. Lucy Holcomb, Farley

Victory Cake:

½ c. shortening	2 t. grated orange rind
1 c. syrup	2¼ c. sifted flour
2¾ t. baking powder	½ c. milk
¼ t. salt	flavoring
2 eggs	

Cream shortening and rind one minute. Gradually beat in the syrup. Beat one minute. Add ¼ sifted dry ingredients gradually. Add one egg at a time, beating one minute after each. Gradually add remaining flour and milk. Add flavoring. Bake in two 8" pans, 350 degrees for 30 minutes.

— Mrs. John James, Farley

Whipped Cream Cake No. 1:

1 c. whipping cream	2 c. cake flour
3 egg whites	1½ c. sugar
½ c. cold water	2 t. baking powder
1 t. vanilla	⅛ t. salt

Fold together whipped cream and stiffly beaten egg whites. Add water and vanilla, sift dry ingredients 3 times and mix all carefully. Bake in a 350 degree oven. Makes three layers or a loaf.   —- Mrs. Pope Gossett, Raton

Whipped Cream Cake No. 2:

1 c. whipped cream	1½ c. flour
2 beaten eggs	2 t. baking powder
1 c. sugar	pinch of salt

Mix eggs and sugar together, then fold in whipped cream. Sift baking powder and salt, then fold this in the cream mixture. Any kind of flavoring and any kind of filling. Makes three good layers.   — Mrs. Will F. Yates, Farley

Whipped Cream Cake No. 3:

1½ c. whipped cream
3 eggs
2 c. flour
2½ t. baking powder

1½ c. sugar
½ t. salt
1½ t. vanilla

Whip cream stiff, lightly fold in well beaten eggs and flavoring. Gradually fold in sifted dry ingredients, gently with flat whip. Bake 30 to 35 minutes in moderate oven.

— Mrs. Maurine Pettigrew, Mills

White Cake No. 1:

1 c. sugar and ½ c. butter. Well creamed together. Add 1 T. boiling water and beat well.

2 c. level, Swans Cake flour. 2 level t. baking powder, add to flour after sifting once. Sift 5 times. 1 full cup milk, added alternately with flour. Beat well. Whites of 5 eggs, beaten stiff and folded into mixture carefully.

— Mrs. E. B. Majors, Raton

White Cake No. 2:

1½ c. sugar
¼ lb. butter
1½ c. milk
3 c. sifted cake flour

5 egg whites
3 t. baking powder
1 t. vanilla

Cream sugar and butter, add milk and sifted cake flour alternately. Then beat egg whites (partly) add baking powder, beat until stiff. Add to mixture and pour in 3 cake pans and bake. Makes 3 large layers.

— Mrs. Fred Floyd, Johnson Mesa

White Cake No. 3:

Cream ½ c. butter with 1½ c. sugar until cream. 2 c. cake flour sifted 3 or 4 times. 1 c. cold water. Add flour and water alternately. Then fold in whites of 5 eggs, beaten, 1 t. vanilla extract. Last add 1½ t. baking powder and a pinch of cream of tartar. Mix with the hands until butter, sugar, flour and water are all mixed. Bake in layers.

— Mrs. C. C. Lapp, Miami

My Favorite White Cake:

2 c. sugar, 1 c. butter, 2 c. milk, 4 c. flour, 4 t. baking powder, 1 t. salt, 6 egg whites. Cream butter, add sugar a little at a time, beating thoroughly after each addition. Sift flour, baking powder and salt together 3 times. Add to butter and sugar mixture alternately with milk, beating after each addition. Add vanilla then egg whites, which have been beaten dry. Bake in angel food cake pan about 45 minutes, or in layers about 20 minutes.

— Mrs. Wilbur Newton, Farley

Four Cakes in One:

1 c. sugar
½ c. butter
1 c. cold water
2 c. cake flour

1½ t. baking powder
4 or 5 beaten egg whites
¼ t. salt
½ t. vanilla

Cream butter and sugar until frothy. Add water and flour alternately, beating well. Add salt, vanilla and baking powder. Fold egg whites in slowly. Makes two layers.

For Gold Cake: add egg yolks, three or four eggs.

Chocolate: Add egg yolks, and sift ½ c. cocoa with flour. Three or four eggs.

Spice Cake: Add spices to taste to the gold cake recipe. Three or four eggs.

— Mrs. Thomas Budd, Johnson Mesa

Sour Cream Cake:

1 c. sour cream
1 c. sugar
2 eggs
2 c. flour
½ t. salt

¼ t. soda
1 t. baking powder
1 t. vanilla
¼ c. milk

If cream is too thick, milk may be added to thin it. Combine cream and sugar, add eggs and beat. Measure flour, add salt, soda, baking powder and sift once. Add this to cream and sugar mixture, then add vanilla and milk. Place in a greased pan and bake 30 minutes in moderate oven. Use sweet cream if sour is not on hand, omitting soda.

Variations: A spice cake may be made by adding 1 t. cinnamon, ½ t. nutmeg, ½ t. cloves to above recipe, omitting vanilla.

— Mrs. Urma Burton, Abbott

Applesauce Cake No. 3:

2 c. flour
1 t. soda
¼ t. salt
¼ t. cloves
½ t. nutmeg
1 t. cinnamon

1 c. sugar
½ c. butter
1 egg
1 c. raisins (chopped)
1 c. coarse nuts
1 c. thick applesauce

Sift then measure flour. Sift with soda, salt and spices. Cream butter well, add sugar, gradually beating after each addition. Add egg and beat. Add raisins and nuts; then add sauce and flour alternately, beating until smooth after each addition. Bake in loaf pan 1 hour and 15 minutes in oven at 350 degrees.

— Mrs. Jim Johnston, Springer

White Cake (High Altitude—5,000 to 8,000 ft.)

Mix as **given:**
Cream with 3 T. water added (from the one cup)
½ c. fat (not butter if you want a snowy cake)
1 c. sugar
 Then add alternately, flour first
 2 c. Swansdown cake flour
1 c. water (minus the 3 T. used for creaming)
2 t. baking powder, level, in the last of the flour
1 t. extract
¼ t. salt if butter isnt used
3 egg whitee, beaten (not too stiff, and do not beat until ready to use).

 Bake in rather slow oven. Bake in two layers (makes nice ones) or in a long flat pan. Ice with favorite icing and don't remove from pan — it stays moist much longer.
       — Mrs. Homer Tepe, Eagle Nest

Plain Cake:

1 c. sugar
½ c. butter or other shortening
3 whole eggs (beat in one at a time).

2 c. cake flour
2 t. baking powder (level)
½ t. lemon flavoring
½ t. almond flavoring
1 c. milk

 Cream butter and sugar, add eggs and flavoring. Sift flour and baking powder together four times. Add flour and milk, small amount at a time. Will make two layers or a square pan.
       — Mrs. Leon Johnson, Johnson Mesa

Cocoa-Honey Divinity Cake:

 Set out all ingredients well ahead to become room temperature. Sift enriched flour once before measuring. Measure all ingredients before starting to mix.

Sift together into bowl:
1½ c. enriched flour
1 t. baking powder
½ t. soda
½ c. sugar
6 T. cocoa
¾ t. salt

Combine and cream:
½ c. shortening
½ c. honey
Add creamed mixture and
1 c. buttermilk
1 t. vanilla
  to contents of bowl.

 Mix by hand or electric mixer on slow or medium speed for two minutes by clock. Scape down sides of bowl frequently. Add two large unbeaten eggs and continue beating two more minutes, scraping bowl frequently. Pour into two well-greased and floured 8" round layer cake pans or one 8½" square pan. Bake in a moderate oven (350 degrees) 35 to 45 minutes.
       — Mrs. Isabell Ausherman, Miami

Cake:

½ c. butter
1 c. sugar
3 eggs
1 c. sweet milk

2 c. flour
1 t. vanilla
2 t. baking powder

Cream butter and sugar. Beat whites stiff. Beat egg yolks and then add to beaten whites. Fold this mixture into creamed butter and sugar. Work well. Sift flour and baking powder together. Put a little flour into egg and cream mixture first. Then alternate with milk and flour. Beat well. Add flavoring last. Bake in loaf or layers.

— Mrs. I. W. Williams, Chico

Spicy Tomato Cake:

½ c. fat
1 c. sugar
2¼ c. cake flour
2 t. cinnamon
1 t. cloves
½ t. allspice

½ t. salt
1 c. raisins
½ c. chopped nuts
1 t. soda
1 c. Libby's Tomato Juice

Cream fat; add sugar, gradually. Cream until light and fluffy. Sift flour once, measure, sift flour, spices and salt together. Add 2 tablespoons of the flour mixture to the raisins and nuts. Add soda to tomato juice. Add dry ingredients alternately with tomato juice, beginning and ending with dry ingredients. Add raisins and nuts. Pour into a greased 8-inch pan. Bake in a moderate oven (350 defrees F.) for 45 minutes. Cool and cut in squares. The cake may be iced or sprinkled with powdered sugar.

—Mrs. Carl Hennigan, Kiowa Home Builders

Pound Cake:

12 eggs
1 lb. butter
1 lb. powdered sugar

1 t. vanilla
1 lb. cake flour

Cream butter and sugar thoroughly. Add one lightly beaten egg and mix thoroughly with creamed mixture. Doing so with each until all twelve eggs have been added. Add flour, mix well; then add vanilla. Pour into funnel pan, greased and floured. Bake in slow oven, one hour and a half. This cake is not to be iced.

— Mrs. Carl Hennigan, Kiowa Home Builders

Red Chocolate Cake:

Cream 2 c. sugar and 2 heaping T. lard. Add 2 eggs, well beaten Add 2 t. soda dissolved in 1 T. vinegar to 1 c. sour milk, and add to first mixture. Do not stir. Sift together 2 2/3 cups flour and 7 heaping t. cocoa. Add to above mixture. Add 1 t. vanilla, ½ t. salt and lastly 1 c. boiling water. Mix and bake.

— Mrs. Norman Hennigan, Kiowa Home Builders

34

Applesauce Cake No. 1:

½ c. butter
1 c. sugar
1½ c. unseasoned applesauce
1-3 eggs or 1 egg plus 2 egg
    whites
2 c. flour
1 c. raisins

2 t. soda, dissolved in applesauce
2 t. cinnamon
1 t. vanilla
1 t. nutmeg
3 T. cocoa
1 c. nuts

Mix as for ordinary cake. Cook at 350 degree for about 30 min.
— Mrs. C. C. Lapp, Miami

Applesauce Cake No. 2:

1½ c. unsweetened applesauce
1 c. sugar
1 c. nutmeg
1 t. cinnamon
1½ - 2 c. flour
½ c. melted shortening
½ T. Maplene or cocoa

½ c. raisins
1 t. soda
    Dissolve soda in applesauce
and stir in other ingredients.
Bake about an hour, if baked in
a loaf pan.

— Mrs. Vera Anderson, Miami

Applesauce Cake No. 5:

2½ c. unsweetened applesauce	4 c. flour
2 c. sugar	½ c. walnuts
1 c. shortening	1 pkg. raisins
2 eggs	1 t. salt, cinnamon, nutmeg and
4 t. soda	allspice

Cream shortening and sugar; and eggs and soda to applesauce; beat well. Use 1 cup flour to dredge raisins and other mixed nuts or other mixed fruit. Add flour, and spice and mix well. Bake in loaf tins 1½ hour.

— Frances Towndrow, Raton

Applesauce Cake No. 6:

2 c. sugar	2 t. soda
¾ c. mazola	pinch of salt
2 c. unsweetened applesauce	Cinnamon, cloves, fruit or
2 c. flour	nuts as desired

Bake in loaf pan. Do not make batter too stiff.

— Daisy Diver, Raton

Comments On Applesauce Cake

This will be a Banquet,
This will be a feast;
Apples from the orchard,
Spices from the East,
Sugar from the tropics
All combine to make
A brown, delicious, fragrant
Applesauce cake.

Cakes, Fillings and Frostings

Chocolate Frosting:

2 c. sugar   1 T. Karo
1 c. cream   2 T. cocoa
Lump butter, size of an egg
  Cook until it forms soft ball when tested in cold water. Let cool. Beat until thick and spread between layers.
— Mrs. E. B. Majors, Raton

Chocolate Cream Frosting:

  2 T. Butter, creamed, blend in 1c. confectioner sugar. Add one unbeaten egg, 2 square chocolate, melted, 1 t. vanilla. Mix well with beater.
— Mary Moore, Raton

Chocolate Ligntning Frosting:

2 c. powdered sugar   3 T. hot coffee
2 T. Chocolate   2 T. butter
  Mix ingredients in order, beat until smooth and spread on cake. Rich hot milk may be used instead of coffee.
— Mrs. Frank Howell, Springer

Golden Orange Icing

  Cream 1½ T. grated orange rind and ¾ t. grated lemon rind with 1/3 c. butter. Add 2 unbeaten egg yolks, plus ¼ t. salt. Blend. Add 4½ c. powdered sugar with ¼ c. orange juice and 1 T. lemon juice.

Banana Cake Filling:

1 box powdered sugar   ¼ lb. butter, melted
3 bananas   Mix together

Ivory Frosting:

  Make Seven Minute frosting, using 5 T. water, 1¼ c. granulated sugar, ¼ c. brown sugar and 2 egg whites, add 1 t. vanilla.

Lady Baltimore Frosting:

2 c. sugar   ½ c. pressed figs
2/3 c. raisins   2/3 c. nuts
2/3 c. water   2 egg whites
  Boil sugar and water to soft ball stage. Pour slowly on well beaten egg whites, beating constantly. Put raisins, nuts and figs thru food chopper. Add to cooled icing. Spread between layers and on top of cake. Garnish with nut meats and candied cherries.
— Mary E. Peterson, Cimarron

Orange Apple Filling:

2/3 c. grated apple
¼ c. water
½ c. honey
1/3 c. orange juice

1 or 2 t. grated orange rind
2 T. cornstarch
1 egg
⅛ t. salt

Add salt to grated apple. Cook with water over low fire 5 minutes. Add cornstarch which has been thoroughly blended with orange juice and cook over water (hot) stirring frequently until thick and clear. Add honey and rind. Stir well. Add this to slightly beaten egg. Return to cooking pan and cook 2 minutes longer, stirring constantly. Cool and spread between layers of cake or split square loaf into halves crosswise and spread between sections. This is especially nice with white butter cake, plain, sponge or angel food cakes using your favorite recipes.

—Mrs. Isabel Ausherman, Miami

Honey Orange Frosting:

Butter, 2 T.
2 T. Honey
2 T. orange juice

1 t. grated rind
2 c. (approximately) confectioner's sugar

Melt butter, add strained honey, orange juice and rind, then sifted confectioner's sugar until of proper consistency to spread. Spread over sides and top of cake.

— Mrs. Isabel Ausherman, Miami

Sour Cream Icing:

1 c. sugar
1 c. thick sour cream

1 t. vanilla

Boil the ingredients until they form a soft ball in cup of water then beat until creamy and spread on Devil Food cake.

— Mrs. Alvin Rickels, Chico

38

Pastel Icing:

½ c. jelly   pinch salt
2 egg whites

Use any flavor jelly. This makes the color. Heat over hot water slightly. Remove and beat until holds shape or until stiff. Ice cake just before serving.

— Mrs. Vera Anderson, Miami

Vanilla Filling:

2 eggs   1 c. nuts
1 c. sugar   1 c. cooked prunes
½ c. sour cream   Salt
2 t. butter

Cook filling until it is thick and spread between layers (make two layers). (May be used for pie filling).

— Mrs. W. J. Kuykendall, Abbott

Seven Minute Frosting:

2 egg whites, unbeaten   ⅛ t. cream of tartar or
1½ c. sugar   1 t. light corn syrup
5 T. water   1 t. vanilla

Put egg whites sugar, water and cream of tartar (or corn syrup) in top of double boiler and mix thoroughly. Place over rapidly boiling water and beat constantly with rotary egg beater until mixture will hold a peak. Remove from fire, add vanilla.

— Mrs. T. J. Floyd, Raton

Sugarless Cake Frosting:

For sweet but sugarless cake frosting try maple whipped cream. Whip 1 cup heavy cream until it begins to thicken. Slowly add ¼ c. maple syrup and continue beating until stiff. After frosting cake, sprinkle top with 1/3 c. chopped walnuts.

— Mrs. Pope Gossett, Raton

Icing:

1 c. sugar   1 c. pecan meats
1 c. sour cream

Put on stove and let boil according to how sour cream is. If it is not very sour, it takes a little longer to boil. Remove from fire and whip. When about firm enough, add flavoring and pecans and spread on cake.

— Mrs. I. W. Williams, Chico

Candies

Best Taffy:

3 c. sugar
1 c. white syrup
2 t. granulated gelatin
1/3 c. cold water

1 T. butter
1 cu. in. parafin
Flavor

Dissolve gelatin in cold water and put all ingredients in kettle, except flavor, and stir while boiling until it threads in the water when dropped from a spoon and does not stick to the teeth when chewed. Add flavor and pour on a greased platter and pull as soon as cool and pull as long as you want to, the longer the better.

— Mrs. Faye Crawford, Springer

Black Walnut Caramels:

2½ c. sugar
¼ t. cream of tartar
¾ c. white syrup

1½ c. cream
1 T. butter

Mix 1 c. sugar, ¼ t. cream of tartar and melt over low flame. Stir while melting, then add 1½ c. sugar, ¾ c. white syrup and 1 c. cream. Stir and cook over low flame until mixture boils. Boil 5 minutes and add ½ c. cream and 1 T. butter. Cook slowly until a few drops in cold water feels hard when picked up. Remove from fire and cool a few minutes. Then add 1 c. broken walnut meats and ¼ t. vanilla. Pour in a well-buttered pan and let stand until firm. Cut and wrap in oiled paper.

— Mrs. Faye Crawford, Springer

Brown Sugar Fudge:

3 c. brown sugar
1 c. light cream or
evaporated milk

1½ T. butter or margarine
1½ t. vanilla

Combine sugar and cream. Cook slowly, stirring constantly until mixture boils. Boil slowly until small quantity dropped in water forms soft ball. Remove from heat, add butter without stirring. Cool to lukewarm. Add vanilla. Beat until mixture has creamy consistency. Pour into greased pan. Cool. Cut in squares.

— Mrs. Maurine Pettigrew, Mills

Christmas Kisses:

½ t. Knox gelatin
1 t. cold water
1 c. molasses
2 T. butter

1 c. corn syrup
1 c. sugar
¾ c. cream
Vanilla or peppermint flavor

Soften the gelatin in the cold water in a small cup and dissolve by melting over hot water. Cook corn syrup, sugar, molasses and cream until the soft ball state. Then add butter and cook until firm, hard ball stage. Pour a little of the candy over the dissolved gelatin, then return to the batch, stir, mixing it in well and pour on well-greased pan. Cool enough to handle, pull and flavor while pulling. Cut off small pieces with scissors and wrap in waxed paper.

— Mrs. Claude Click, Capulin

Date Roll:

3 c. sugar
2 T. corn syrup
1½ c. milk
2 T. butter

1 c. chopped dates
1 c. chopped nuts
1 t. vanilla

Cook sugar, syrup, milk, dates and nuts until it forms a soft ball when tested. Add butter and vanilla and beat until cool, then turn out on damp cloth and roll in cloth. Cut in slices to serve.

— Mrs. John T. Milliken, Capulin

English Toffee:

2 c. brown sugar
3 T. corn syrup
⅛ t. salt

1 1/3 can Eagle Brand condensed milk
1 T. butter
1 t. vanilla

Mix brown sugar, corn syrup, salt, Eagle Brand milk and butter together in heavy sauce pan or skillet. Gradually bring to boiling point, stirring constantly. Cook over slow flame and stir constantly until mixture reaches 212 or makes firm ball when tested in cold water. This will require about 30 minutes cooking. Remove from fire and add vanilla. Pour into buttered pan. When cold, cut in squares. May be rolled in powdered sugar to prevent stickiness.   — Mrs. Claude Click, Capulin

Honey Bittersweets:

Let section of comb honey remain in refrigerator about 24 hours before using for coating. Then dip the knife to be used for cutting in boiling water. Cut comb honey into pieces about ¾" long and ⅜" wide. Place pieces on trays covered with waxed paper and chill 30 minutes before coating. Be sure dipping chocolate is of proper temperature and then coat candy pieces just as in coating cream centers. Drop a walnut, cepan or almond on each piece.   — Mrs. C. C. Lapp, Miami

Honey Divinity

2 c. sugar
1/3 c. honey
Pinch salt

1/3 c. water
2 egg whites

Boil together the sugar, honey and water until the syrup spins a thread when dropped from a spoon. Pour syrup over well beaten egg whites, beating continuously and until the mixture crystallizes. Drop in small pieces on waxed paper.

—Mrs. C. C. Lapp, Miami

Honey Fudge No. 1:

2 c. sugar
1 sq. chocolate (cut fine)
¼ t. salt
butter size of walnut

1 c. evaporated milk
¼ c. honey
1 c. nuts

Boil sugar, chocolate, salt and milk 5 minutes. Add honey and cook to the soft ball stage. Add butter. Cool. Beat until creamy. Add nuts, pour on buttered pan and when hard, cut in squares.

—Mrs. C. C. Lapp, Miami

Honey Fudge No. 2:

2¼ c. sugar
1½ sq. chocolate (cut fine)
½ c. honey

1 c. rich milk or cream
1 c. nut meats

Cook until it forms a firm ball when tried in cold water. Take from fire, cool and beat until creamy and ready to harden. Add nuts, pour on buttered plate, mark in squares.

—Mrs. C. C. Lapp, Miami

Honey Milk Paste:

½ c. dry skim milk, ½ c. warm honey, 1 T. butter. Mix warm honey and butter and blend with dry skim milk. Allow this paste to age at least 1 week before using.

There is no end of the many fine honey cream center combinations that can be made from this basic paste. No flavor is lost by using this formula for there is no cooking of the honey. The honey and dry skim milk are blended without being heated. The secret of the flavor of this candy is in the proper aging.

Here are a few of the variety of centers that may be developed from this basic recipe:

Wrap the honey milk paste around cherries and coat with dripping chocolate. This makes a delicious Honey Cherry Cream center.

Mix shredded coconut with this honey milk paste. Roll into little balls and coat with dipping chocolate. A fine honey coconut cream centered chocolate results.

Blend chopped dates with the honey milk paste, shape and coat with dipping chocolate. Then you have a honey date cream chocolate.

Blend chopped pineapple pieces with chopped nuts. Add to the honey milk paste and shape and coat with dipping chocolate.

Chopped crystallized ginger may be added to the paste. This mixture made into little balls and coated with dipping chocolate.

—Mrs. C. C. Lapp, Miami

Honeyed Grapefruit Strips

Rind of 2 grapefruits cut in strips ⅜ inch wide and 1½ inches

long. 4 c. water and 4 t. salt. Allow grapefruit to boil in salt water
for 30 minutes. Drain and rinse. Add 2 c. hot water and then
let boil again for 6 minutes. Strain and rinse in cold water and
drain again. Mix 2 c. honey with 1 T. lemon juice and ¼ t. cinamon
2 t. vinegar. Pour over grapefruit strips and let simmer for about
one hour. Let grapefruit stand in honey syrup over night and
then carefully pick out strips. Lay on waxed paper and after 12
to 24 hours of drying, coat them with medium, bitter or milk
dipping chocolate.

—Mrs. C. C. Lapp, Miami

Honey Nougat:

⅜ c. honey

½ c. brown sugar

1 lb. almonds

2 egg whites

Boil honey and sugar together until drops of the mixture hold
their shape when poured in cold water. Add the white of the
eggs well beaten and cook very slowly, stirring constantly until
the mixture becomes brittle when dropped into water. Add the
almonds and cool under a weight. The candy can be broken into
pieces or may be cut and wrapped in waxed paper.

—Mrs. C. C. Lapp, Miami

Honeyed Orange Strips:

Cut rind of three oranges in strips (should be about 1½ c. of
strips of rind.) Boil in salt water (about 1 t. salt to cup of water)
until soft - about ½ hour. Drain, rinse in cold water and let simmer very slowly in 1 c. honey for about 45 minutes. Lay each
strip on waxed paper and let stand for day or two before coating
with dipping chocolate. These fruit strips when coated look like
green beans in shape except of course they are brown in color.
When one bites into them, he is delighted with the flavory jelly-
like center.

—Mrs. C. C. Lapp, Miami

Honey Pecan Pralines:

¾ c. evaporated milk

1 T. butter

1½ c. salted pecans

½ c. honey

1 c. maple sugar

1 c. brown sugar

Mix sugars, evaporated milk and salt together. Cook slowly for
about 5 min. Add honey. Cook until firm ball is formed when
dropped in cold water. Remove from fire, add butter and beat
vigorously until the candy is soft enough to form flat cakes when
dropped from a spoon. Arrange nut meats in groups on oiled
paper and drop candy from spoon over nuts. Let the pralines set
then wrap individually.

—Mrs. C. C. Lapp, Miami

Honey Popcorn Balls

Heat honey to about 245 degrees. Dip the popped corn into the
hot honey, shape into balls and cool. Wrap in waxed paper or
colored cellophane papers.

—Mrs. C. C. Lapp, Miami

Honey Taffy

2 c. honey   2/3 c. cold water
2 c. sugar   pinch of salt

Boil the sugar, water and honey together to 288 degrees (hard ball in cold water). Add salt. Put on buttered dish to cool, then pull until white. If the pan in which the candy is cooked is buttered around the top, it will not boil over.

—Mrs. C. C. Lapp, Miami

Kate's Candy

3 c. brown sugar   1 large lump butter
1 c. sweet fresh milk

Stir constantly until it rolls in a soft ball in ice water. Cook rather slowly. Take from fire, add 1 t. vanilla, 1 lb. English walnuts, cut fine. Beat until air bubbles form and it looks stringy and poppy.

— Mrs. Kapp, Colmor

Marshmallows:

2 level T. Knox Gelatine   ¾ c. boiling water
½ c. cold water   ½ t. salt
2 c. sugar   1 t. vanilla

Soak gelatine in cold water about 5 min. Boil sugar and boiling water together until syrup tests thread stage. Add softened gelatine and let stand until partially cooled; then add salt and flavoring. Beat until mixture becomes thick, fluffy and and cold. Pour into pans, thickly covered with powdered sugar, having the mixture 1" in depth. Let stand in a cool place (not refrigerator) until thoroughly chilled. With a wet sharp knife, loosen around edges of the pan and turn out on board lightly covered with powdered sugar. Cut in cubes and roll in powdered sugar.

Fruit juices in place of part of the water or nuts, chocolate or candied fruits, chopped, may be added. Dates stuffed with this confection are delicious.

—Mrs. Claude Click, Capulin

Minted Nuts:

1 c. sugar   ½ c. water
2 t. Karo (white)

Cook sugar, karo and water to soft ball, stir before, but not after it boils. When boiling, cover for 2 min. Remove from fire, add 6 marshmallows (cut in small pieces) ½ t. peppermint flavoring, stir around and around, but don't beat. Add nuts, any kind. Continue stirring until nuts are coated and begin to harden. Break nuts apart.

— Mrs. Fred Koehler, Raton

Nut Butter Kraunch:

1 c. butter	3 T. water
1 c. sugar	1 c. toasted nut meats
1 T. corn syrup	4 sq. unsweetened chocolate

Melt butter, add sugar and stir until dissolved. Pour in syrup and water and cook to hard crack state. Remove from fire, add half the nuts coarsely chopped, pour into shallow buttered pan and when almost at setting point, divide into squares. Dip these in chocolate, which has been melted over hot water and coat with remaining nuts, which have been very finely chopped. Makes 30 squares.

— Mrs. Claude Click, Capulin

Orange Operas

1 T. butter	½ c. English walnuts
¾ c. evaporated milk	1 T. orange juice
2 c. sugar	½ t. grated orange rind

Melt butter in pan in which candy is to be cooked. Add milk and sugar and boil to soft ball stage, stirring constantly. Cool and beat like fudge. Add nuts, orange juice and rind with the last few stirs. Makes about 120 pieces.

— Mrs. Claude Click, Capulin

Penuchi:

3 c. brown sugar	1 t. vanilla
½ c. corn syrup	2 t. butter
1 c. milk	dash of salt
1½ c. nut meats	

Combine sugar, corn syrup and milk in saucepan and cook stirring constantly until temperature reaches soft ball stage, remove from fire, add butter and set aside, without stirring, to cool. When lukewarm, add flavoring, beat until thick and creamy; stir in nuts and pour into buttered pan. Cut in squares when firm.

— Mrs. Jack George, Colmor

Peanut Brittle:

2 c. sugar	1 c. white Karo
½ c. boiling water	

Cook without stirring until it spins a long, long thread. Then add one pint or one cup "raw" Spanish peanuts and ¼ t. salt. Cook until syrup is light brown or sand color. It is necessary to stir often after peanuts are added to prevent sticking. Remove from fire and add:

2 T. butter	2 t. soda
2 t. vanilla	

Stir fast while fluffing. Spread thin on buttered table or marble slab.

— Mrs. Homer Tepe, Eagle Nest

Cookies

Ginger Cup Cakes:

2/3 c. sugar
2/3 c. molasses
½ c. lard
1 c. raisins
pinch salt

2 t. ginger
2 t. soda
1½ c. boiling water or coffee
    poured on soda

Flour for soft batter. Add 2 well beaten eggs and bake in slow oven.

— Marguerite M. Mutz, Eagle Nest

Oatmeal Cookies:

1½ c. brown sugar
1½ c. shortening
2 eggs
½ c. sour milk
1 c. chopped dates
1 c. chopped nuts
1 t. cinnamon

1 t. nutmeg
1 t. soda
½ t. salt
½ t. cloves
2 c. oatmeal
2½ c. flour

Cream shortening and sugar. Add eggs and milk. Sift flour and measure, then sift with spices. Add rolled oats. Add dates and nuts. Mix thoroughly. Drop by teaspoonfuls onto well-oiled baking sheet. Bake in hot oven 15 minutes.

— Mrs. Leon Johnson, Johnson Mesa

Rye Cookies:

1 c. butter
½ c. sugar
1 c. fine rye flour

1¼ c. white flour
1 t. baking powder

Sift flour with baking powder. Work all ingredients together into dough and set away to cool. Roll out thin and cut with round cutter. Prick cookie with tines of fork, making small holes at the sides of cookie. Bake until light brown in a slow oven about 325 degrees.

— Mrs. Vick Wilson

Pineapple Cookies:

½ c. shortening
½ c. brown sugar
½ c. white sugar
1 egg
2 c. all purpose flour
¼ t. soda

½ c. crushed pineapple
½ c. nuts, chopped
½ t. salt
1 t. baking powder
1 t. vanilla

Cream shortening and sugar, add well beaten egg. Mix well. Add pineapple and dry ingredients, then vanilla. Drop on greased cookie sheet and bake at 375 degrees.

— Mrs. Leonard Matthews, Raton

Date Bars:

4 eggs
1 1/3 c. sugar
1 1/3 c. flour
2 t. baking powder

½ t. salt
1½ c. chopped dates
1 c. nuts

Beat egg whites stiff, add beaten yolks, then sugar. Dredge fruit in part of flour, add plain flour, baking powder and salt and extract to egg mixture. Then add fruited flour and fruit and nuts. Bake in buttered pan 11" x 14" until brown and firm to touch. Cut in squares. Dust with powdered sugar. Put in tight container while still warm.

— Mrs. Leonard Matthews, Raton

Desserts, Frozen

"A good meal makes a merrier heart
Than all your high aesthetic art."

Apricot Mousse:

Drain the contents of one large can of apricots through sieve. Add one cup honey and juice of lemon. Fold in 2 stiffly beaten egg whites and then 1½ cups cream, whipped. Pour into refrigerator tray and freeze without stirring.

— Mrs. J. W. Ausherman, Miami

Buttermilk Ice Cream:

2 c. buttermilk
1 c. sugar
pinch salt

1 t. vanilla
1 c. or 1 can crushed pineapple
2 egg whites

Mix well and freeze to mush. Add well beaten egg whites. Freeze until hard.

— Mrs. M. F. Howland, Raton

Butterscotch Toffee Ice Cream:

2 c. sweet milk
30 butterscotch toffee caramels

2 eggs
1 c. cream, whipped

Let milk come to a boil and dissolve the caramels in it. Beat the eggs and add to milk. Let cool. Add the cream; place in two trays and freeze.

— Mrs. Bob Buttram, Maxwell

Corn Syrup Vanilla Ice Cream:

2 eggs
1 c. crystal corn syrup
1 c. milk

1 t. vanilla
1 c. heavy cream

Beat eggs until thick and lemon colored. Stir in syrup, then milk and flavoring. Whip cream and add to egg mixture. Pour into freezing tray of refrigerator and freeze until a one-inch layer of mixture is frozen around sides. Remove from tray and beat mixture until smooth. Return to refrigerator and continue freezing until firm.

— Mrs. Ruth James, Farley

Ice Cream:

½ lb. marshmallows
1 can pineapple
½ c. sugar
juice from ½ lemon

1 c. milk
2 c. cream
3 egg whites

Melt marshmallows, add pineapple, sugar and lemon juice and milk. Put in the freezing tray and freeze solid. Whip cream (not too thick), beat egg whites. Add this to the frozen mixture and stir well. Return to refrigerator and stir several times.

— Mary Moore, Raton

2 Quart Freezer of Ice Cream:

1 pint heavy cream; enough thin cream is added to make the 2 quart freezer ⅞ full. To the heavy cream that has been whipped, add 2 eggs; beat. Then add a scant cup sugar (during this war time use part sugar and corn syrup or honey). Flavor to taste. Turn in the freezer and store in mechanical refrigerator.

— Martha T. Bowen, Springer

Fruit Sherbet:

The juice of 4 oranges
   and 2 lemons
3 c. sugar
1 small bottle marachino
   cherries

1 small can crushed pineapple
½ c. pecans
1 pint cream
1 qt. milk
Eggs, if you like

— Mrs. Leon Johnson, Johnson Mesa

Lemon Cream Sherbet:

1 pint milk
1 c. sugar
Juice of 2 lemons

Grated rind of 1 lemon
2 egg whites 2 t. sugar
½ pint whipping cream

Add sugar to milk, allow to dissolve, add lemon juice and grated rind, stirring constantly. Turn into freezer, let freeze one hour. Beat egg whites and 2 t. sugar, whip cream and add to eggs, etc. Last stir in frozen mixture. Finish freezing.

— Mrs. Fred Koehler, Raton

Peppermint Ice Cream:

Beat 2 egg whites stiff, 1 c. heavy cream until thick but not stiff, 2 egg yolks until lemon colored. Dissolve ¾ c. ground peppermint candy in 1½ c. top milk, add pinch of salt. Stir twice while freezing.

— Mrs. W. C. Jenkins, Raton

Rhubarb Conserve Ice Cream:

3 eggs
1½ pint cream

2 c sugar
1 qt. rhubarb conserve

Finish filling freezer with enough milk for one gallon of ice cream. Freeze.

— Mrs. Pleasant Smith, Springer

52

Spring Creme Freeze

2 c. diced rhubarb, 2 beaten egg yolks, 2 egg whites, ½ c. sugar,
1 T. lemon juice, ½ c. sugar ,few grains salt, 1 c. top milk, ¼
t. vanilla. **Select tender, rosy rhubarb.** Do not peel. Combine
rhubarb, ½ c. sugar and salt, no water, cover and simmer. When
tender, cool. Combine milk, egg yolk, lemon juice and vanilla.
Add rhubarb; mix thoroly. Freeze   in automatic refrigerator
tray—at coldest setting of control—until firm. Beat egg whites;
gradually add the ¼ c. sugar; continue beating until stiff and
sugar dissolved. Now turn frozen mixture into chilled bowl;
break in chunks. Beat until fluffy-smooth, but not melted with
electric beater. Fold in egg white mixture. Return quickly to
tray; freeze firm. Serve 6. Substitute other fruits. For variation, use honey or corn syrup for part of the sugar.

— Mrs. J. W. Ausherman, Miami

Desserts, Gelatin

Fruit Juice Cream:

Save the juice from the canned fruit until you have 2 c. full.
Bring this juice to a full rounding boil. Pour over raspberry or
strawberry gelatin. Whip ½ c. cream and pour the gelatin mixture
into it (if it is combined with cream while hot, it will set in 2
or 3 layers). Serve with whipped cream.

— Mrs. E. B. Majors, Raton

Heavenly Hash:

Soak 1 T. gelatin in ¼ c. cold water. Dissolve in 1/3 c. boiling
water. Cool but not congeal. 3 egg whites beaten stiff, ½ pt.
whipped cream, add ½ c sugar, 1 t. vanilla. Fold beaten egg whites
and whipped cream together ,add gelatin slowly. Roll ½ lb. chocolate cookies into crumbs. Butter a square pan, line with
crumbs. Pour in mixture, sprinkle top with crumbs. Set in ice
box over **night.**

— Myrtle Durie, Johnson Mesa

Pear Bavarian:

1 pkg. strawberry Jello
1 c. boiling water
1 c. canned pear juice
1 c. canned pears, crushed

1 c. cream, whipped
½ c. sugar
½ t. salt
½ t. vanilla

Dissolve Jello in boiling water. Add pear juice. Chill. When slightly thickened beat with rotary egg beater until consistency of whipped cream. Fold in pear pulp. To whipped cream, add sugar, salt and vanilla and fold into Jello. Chill. Serve in sherbet glasses and garnish with chopped nuts. Chill before serving.

Follow same directions; using lemon juice and peaches for peach Bavarian.

—Mrs. J. W. Ausherman, Miami

Pecan Charlotte:

1 pkg. orange Jello
1½ c. boiling water
¼ t. salt

½ c. honey
1 c. whipped cream
1 c. chopped pecans

Dissolve jello in boiling water. Add salt and honey. Chill. When slightly thickened, beat with rotary egg beater until like whipped cream. Fold in whipped cream and nuts. Serves 8.

— Mrs. J. W. Ausherman, Miami

Pineapple Dessert:

1 No. 2½ can pineapple
½ c. sugar
1 c. whipping cream

2 T. sparkling gelatin
2 T. lemon juice
½ c. water

Soak gelatin in water. Drain juice from pineapple, heat with sugar. Add gelatin and stir until dissolved, add lemon juice; let cool until thick. Beat until fluffy with egg beater. Fold in whipped cream, pour into mold and chill. ½ c. nuts or cocoanut may be added.

— Mrs. Hazel House, Capulin

Chocolate Sponge Pudding:

1 T. Knox Sparkling Gelatine
    (level)
¼ cold water
¼ c. boiling water
1 t. vanilla

1/3 c. sugar
3 eggs and a few grains of salt
1½ squares of chocolate or
    4 T. of cocoa

Soak gelatine in cold water five minutes. Then dissolve in boiling water. Add cocoa or melted chocolate. Beat egg whites until stiff, and add well-beaten egg yolks to whites. Add sugar dissolved gelatine which has been beaten well; then beat and add flavoring and 1 cup of chopped pecan meats. Pour into wet mould and chill. Serve plain or with whipped cream. This is very nice.

— Mrs. I. W. Williams, Chico

Desserts, Miscellaneous

Apples:

6 apples, sliced   1 c. sugar
Butter size of an egg
     Put butter in baking dish. Get hot, put in apples, pared and sliced. Sprinkle sugar over them. Mix batter of one cup of thin sour cream, 1 small spoonful of soda and enough flour to make a thin batter and pour over apples and bake.
                     — Mrs. Pleasant Smith, Springer

Fried Apple Circles:

Cooking apples   Crisco
Powdered sugar
     Wash cooking apples, cut crosswise into slices ½" thick. In a heavy frying pan melt enough Crisco to cover the bottom. Place the apple circles in the hot fat, cooking until tender and brown on both sides. A broad bladed spatula or pancake turner is a good utensil to use for turning the slices. Remove from frying pan to a heated serving dish. Sprinkle circles with powdered sugar and serve hot. These are nice served with broiled ham, baked ham or braised pork chops.
                     — Mrs. Sneed, Capulin

Apple Crisp:

     Cut 4 apples up as for pie; put in pyrex pie plate and cover with 2/3 c. flour, and 1 c. sugar; 1 t. cinnamon, ½ c. melted butter poured over flour sugar and cinnamon after they have been mixed. Mix well and pat over top of apples like crust. Cook like apple pie until apples are done.
                     — Mrs. C. U. Burris, Miami

Apple Goodie:

½ c. sugar   ½ t. cinnamon
2 T. flour   4 c. chopped apples
     Mix apples with dry ingredients and place in greased baking dish.
¾ c. uncooked oatmeal   ¼ t. soda
¾ c. brown sugar   ¼ t. baking powder
¾ c. flour   shortening
     Mix dry ingredients and crumb in the shortening as for pie crust. Never melt shortening. Pat well blended mixture on top of apples and pat down firmly. Bake in moderate oven until apples are tender. Serve with whipped cream.
                     — Mrs. M. F. Howland, Raton

Carnival Dessert:

1/3 c. shortening   ½ t. soda
1½ c. sugar   ½ t. salt
2 eggs   1 c. milk
2¼ c. flour   2 c. sour cherries, drained
1½ t. baking powder   ½ c. chopped nuts.

Cream sugar and shortening. Blend in well beaten eggs. Sift flour, baking powder, soda and salt and stir in creamed mixture, alternately with milk. Blend in cherries and nuts. Pour into greased and floured 8 x 12 pan. Bake 50 minutes in moderate oven. Serve with Hot Cherry Sauce.
— Mrs. Maurine Pettigrew

Celestine Crust:

3 eggs, beaten   ½ c. sweet milk
3 T. sugar   1/3 t. salt
1 T. butter

Mix all well. Add enough flour to make a dough almost as thick as for noodles. Knead well. Roll out thin and punch holes in it with a form as for pie crust. Cut in pieces 3 x 5" long or square. Fry in hot fat. Put large quantities in large paper sack. Pour powdered sugar over them and shake well.
— Mrs. Charlie Bada, Jr., Springer

Cream Puffs:

1 c. boiling water   ⅛ t. salt
½ c. shortening   3 eggs
1 c. flour   2 t. baking powder

Heat water and lard in pan until it boils up well. Add all at once flour and salt, stir well. Remove from fire as soon as mixed and cool. Stir in unbeaten eggs, one at a time. Add baking powder and mix. Drop by spoonfuls 1½ inch apart on greased pans, keeping them higher in the middle than on the sides. Bake about 30 minutes. Split and fill each with whipped cream.
— Mrs. Charlie Bada, Jr., Springer
— Mrs. Maurine Pettigrew, Mills

Filling for Cream Puffs (fresh fruit):

¼ - ½ c. sugar   1 c. whipping cream
1 c. fresh fruit

Sprinkle sugar over cut up fruit and let stand while whipping cream. Fold fruit mixture into whipped cream. Place in cream puffs.

Custard Filling:

Mix 6 T. sugar with 3 T. flour and ⅛ t. salt in top of double boiler. Beat 2 egg yolks slightly and add 1 c. top milk or cream. Add slowly to flour and sugar mixture. Cook over hot water, stirring constantly until thick. Cool. Add 1 t. vanilla. Place in cream puffs.   — Mrs. Maurine Pettigrew, Mills

A Good Dessert:

1 lb. marshmallows   pinch of salt
1 small can pineapple   1 c. cream
1 c. milk

Melt milk and marshmallows in double boiler. Cool, add pineapple and whipped cream. Let stand awhile before serving. Serve vanilla wafer crumbs on top.   — Mrs. Young, Colmor

Doughnuts:

3 eggs, beaten   1½ c. sweet milk
3 T. melted lard, not hot   ½ t. nutmeg or 1 t. vanilla
1 c. sugar   (both may be used)
2 T. baking powder
Roll to ½ inch thick, cut and fry in deep fat.
                                        — Mrs. Mary Powell

Doughnuts:

4 c. flour   1 t. cinnamon
4 t. baking powder   ½ t. nutmeg
1 c. sugar   2 eggs
½ t. salt   1 c. milk
1 t. vanilla   3 T. fat, melted
  Mix ingredients lightly. Toss soft dough onto floured board
and roll out dough until 1/3" thick. Cut out doughnuts with cutter and fry in deep hot fot. Let doughnuts cool and then cover
with confectioner's sugar or dip in icing.
                                        — Mrs. W. P. Rogers, Springer

Doughnuts:

1 qt. yeast   2 or 3 eggs well beaten
1 c. sugar   1 qt. milk, scalded
1 t. salt   1 t. vanilla
  Set yeast the night before. Next morning mix a stiff dough.
Let raise, work down, let raise again and roll out ¼" thick. Let
raise. Fry in deep fat until a golden brown. Makes 150 doughnuts.   — Cremilla Johnston

Potato Doughnuts:

3 eggs   ¾ c. milk
1 c. sugar   2 t. baking powder
2½ lbs. lard   2½ c. flour
1 c. mashed potatoes, warm   vanilla and salt
  Mix in order named. Add more flour if needed. Roll, fry in
hot fat.   — Myrtle Durie, Johnson Mesa

Raised Doughnuts:

1 pint scalded milk   1 c. sugar
½ c. butter   1 cake yeast (soaked in water)
½ t. salt   ½ t. nutmeg
2 or 3 eggs
  Let raise until double in bulk, punch down and let raise again.
Roll and cut out doughnuts and let raise a short time and fry
in deep hot fat.

Glase for Doughnuts:

  5 T. cream, scalded. Add 1 c. powdered sugar and dip doughnuts in mixture.   — Mrs. Lee Glasgow, Farley

Apple Dumplings:

1 c. sour cream, 1 egg, 2 c. flour or enough for stiff dough, 2 t. baking powder, ½ t. soda, ¼ t. salt and 1½ T. sugar. Slice 5 large tart apples, sprinkle with nutmeg and cinnamon and sugar. Spread on dough rolled like cinnamon rolls and cut in slices and put in greased pan. Now pour over the following: 1 c. sugar, 2 T. butter and 1 c. hot water. Bake 1 hour in slow oven.

— Mrs. J. H. Littrell

Burnt Sugar Dumplings:

1 c. burnt sugar, 3 c. water. Mix boiling water, burnt sugar and 1 T. butter and put in a skillet, which you burnt the sugar in and let boil until all is dissolved. Mix stiff: ½ c. sugar, 1 t. baking powder, ½ c. sweet milk and 1 pinch salt. Drop batter in boiling liquid, a teaspoonful at a time. Then put skillet in the oven and bake 30 minutes.

— Mrs. Lee Glasgow, Farley

Caramel Dumplings:

½ c. sugar, browned	1 T. butter
2½ c. boiling water	1 T. vanilla
1 c. sugar or syrup	

Boil above ingredients ten minutes.

Dough:

½ c. sugar or syrup	1 t. vanilla
½ c. sweet milk	1 t. baking powder
pinch of salt	Flour to make stiff dough

Drop by spoonfuls into boiling caramel and bake 10 minutes or longer, if needed.

— Mrs. W. C. Halferty, Abbott

Cherry Dumplings (sugar saver):

2½ c. sour cherries	3 t. baking powder
½ c. sugar	½ t. salt
¾ c. honey	4 T. shortening
2 c. flour	¾ c. milk

Place cherries and juice with honey in a covered sauce pan. Bring to simmering point and simmer for 2 minutes. Sift flour, measure and sift again with baking powder and salt. Cut in lard until mixture has a fine even crumb. Add the sugar and enough milk to make a soft dough. Drop by tablespoons over the cherry sauce. Cover and allow to steam for 25 minutes without removing cover. Serve hot or cold with cream.

— Mrs. Walden Ingram, Springer

58

Gingerbread:

2 c. flour, sifted with ¼ t. cloves, cinnamon, nutmeg and 1 t. ginger. Cream ½ cup sugar with ½ c. shortening. To this, add 2 well beaten eggs and ½ c. dark molasses. Mix well. Add flour mixture and last beat in quickly 1 c. boiling water to which has been added 1 t. soda, well dissolved. Beat hard and add ½ c. nut meats or raisins if desired. Bake in loaf pan 45 minutes in moderate oven or in two layers and put together with cream cheese or whipped cream slightly flavored with lemon juice.

— Rena Keenan, Springer

Best-Ever Gingerbread (with honey)

½ c. butter or vegetable shortening, ½ c. sugar, 1 egg, 1 c. honey 2½ c. sifted flour, 1½ t. soda, 1/2 t salt, 1 t. cinnamon, 1|2 t. cloves, 1 t. ginger and 1 c. boiling water. Cream shortening, adding sugar gradually and cream thoroughly. Add well beaten egg honey and then dry ingredients sifted together. Stir in boiling water last and beat until smooth. Bake in a greased, shallow pan about 35 minutes in a moderate oven.

— Mrs. C. C. Lapp, Miami

Granny's Gingerbread:

1 egg	1 t. soda
⅛ c. sugar	¼ t. salt
½ c. molasses	1¼ c. flour
¼ c. melted fat	½ c. boiling water

Stir in ingredients as they are named. This cake is excellent in loaf or layer form. For a layer cake, double the recipe. Grease the pan and bake in a moderate oven. You may use any kind of frosting. This cake is soft and is fine for picnics and lunch pails, because it will not dry and become hard.

— Mrs. Arthur L. Smith, Springer

Pineapple Honey:

2 qts. sweetened pineapple juice or 2 qts. unsweetened and 1 pint honey. 1 gallon shredded ripe delicious apples, peeled and cored - fresh from tree. Bring juice and honey to boil, add one qt. apples at a time, which have been shredded on a medium salad grater. Continue to boil, stirring constantly until thick and clear. Well ripened sweet pears may be used instead of apples.

— Mrs. Patterson, Cimarron

Apple Crumb Pudding

6 - 8 medium size cooking apples   ½ c. flour
½ c. butter or margarine

Wash, pare and slice apples. Place in buttered shallow baking dish. Combine butter, sugar and flour and mix with a pastry blender or two knives until it forms coarse crumbs. Sprinkle this mixture over sliced apples and bake in a moderate oven for 30 to 35 minutes or until done. Serve warm or cold with cream or lemon sauce.

— Mrs. Coy Maxwell

Caramel Pudding:

Place a can of Eagle Brand sweetened condensed milk (unopened) in a kettle of boiling water. Let boil for 2½ hours. Keep the water over the can all the time. Chill thoroughly. Cut the can at both ends and slice the contents onto a plate. Dip a knife in hot water and slice. Serve with whipped cream topped with nuts.

— Mrs. E. B. Majors, Raton

Chocolate Pudding:

Forms its own sauce and serves 8.

¾ c. sugar   1 c. flour
2 level t. baking powder   1½ T. cocoa
½ t. salt

Mix dry ingredients together then add ½ c. milk, 1 t. vanilla and 2 T. butter. Pour batter in greased pan and pour over it the following for the sauce.

1 c. boiling water, 1 c. sugar and 5 small T. cocoa mixed together. Nuts may be added. Sauce will be at bottom. 1 can syrup in the sauce and ½ c. sugar in the batter does very well.

— Mrs. H. A. McConnell, Springer

Date Pudding No. 1:

¼ c. butter, creamed with 1 c. sugar. Add 2 well beaten eggs, 1 T. flour and beat well. Add 1 c. milk, 1 t. vanilla, 1 c. dates and 1 c. nuts. Bake 30 minutes.

— Mrs. Young, Colmor

Date Pudding No. 2:

1 c. dates, chopped   1 c. sugar
1 t. soda sprinkled over dates   1½ c. flour
add 1 c. hot water, let stand un-   ½ c. nut meats
til cool.   1 egg
1 T. butter   Bake in moderate oven.

—Mrs. V. S. Shirley, Maxwell

Date Nut Pudding:

1 c. dates   1 c. sugar
½ c. nut meats   2 t. baking powder
3 eggs   4 T. cracker crumbs
4 T. pastry flour

Combine sugar, baking powder and cracker crumbs. Add beaten egg yolks, dates and nuts. Fold in stiffly beaten egg whites and pour in buttered loaf tin. Bake 40-60 minutes in moderate oven.

— Mrs. Glenn Matthews, Maxwell

Graham Cracker Pudding:

18 graham crackers, ½ c. melted butter and ½ c. sugar. Roll crackers into crumbs and mix butter and sugar in them. Then line a pie plate or a baking dish with the crumbs and put in oven and bake until brown. Then add pudding of

5 T. cornstarch	2 eggs
1 c. sugar	2 T. butter
3 c. milk	1 t. vanilla

Mix cornstarch and a little salt and sugar, then add milk and cook until thick, then add egg yolk one at a time and stir fast. Add butter and remove from fire and add vanilla and put in crust. Put meringue over top and brown.

— Mrs. Phil McConnell, Springer

Holiday Cranberry Pudding:

2 c. raw cranberries	½ c. sorghum or molasses
1½ c. flour	1/3 c. warm water
1 t. baking powder	2 T. melted shortening
¼ t. salt	2 t. soda

Sift flour, baking powder and salt together. Add washed cranberries. Mix syrup, water, shortening and soda; and add to cranberry-flour mixture. Pour into greased mold and tie waxed paper loosely over top. Steam 2 hours. Unmold into serving platter. Serve hot with hot Vanilla Sauce.

— Mrs. Maurine Pettigrew, Mills

Hot Fudge Pudding:

1 c. flour	½ c. milk
2 t. baking powder	2 T. melted shortening
¼ t. salt	1 c. chopped nuts
¾ c. sugar	1 c. brown sugar
2 T. cocoa	4 T. cocoa

Sift dry ingredients together, stir in milk and shortening. Mix until smooth. Add nuts, spread in pan. Sprinkle with brown sugar and cocoa mixture. Pour 1¾ c. hot water over entire batter. Bake. Invert squares on plates, dip sauce from pan over each. Bake 40-45 minutes in moderate oven.

— Mrs. Maurine Pettigrew, Mills

Ice Box Pudding:

1 box vanilla wafers (20 cookies)	1 c. sugar
	½ c. English walnuts
1 egg	½ c. butter or oleo
1 c. diced pineapple	

Cream butter and sugar, add egg beaten separately. Crumble the wafers, then add pineapple. Let stand 24 hours in ice box.

— Marie Townsley, Springer
— Mrs. Cockriel

Lemon Pudding No. 1:

1 c. sugar and 2 T. butter creamed together. 2 egg yolks, 3 T. flour, juice and rind of 1 lemon, 1 c. milk. Mix. Beat egg whites stiff and mix in lightly. Bake in a dish or custard cups set in a pan of hot water until cake is brown on top, about 45 minutes, in a moderate oven.

— Mrs. Ellis Littleton

Lemon Pudding No. 2:

1 c. sugar	1 lemon, grate the rind and the
lump of butter size of an egg	juice
1 egg	1 qt. boiling water

Mix all and pour the quart of boiling water over the mixture. Make rich biscuit dough and roll out about six biscuits.

— Mrs. Frank Howell

Lincoln and Lee Pudding:

1 c. brown sugar	2 c. water
1 T. butter	

Cook together only until mixture boils. Cool slightly.

1 c. flour	⅛ t. baking powder
½ c. sugar	½ c. milk
½ c. chopped nuts	½ c. raisins

Mix quickly. Drop in first mixture and bake 30 minutes in hot oven.

— Mrs. M. F. Howland, Raton

Marshmallow Pudding:

Dissolve 1 heaping T. gelatine in ½ c. cold water. Place over the fire and stir until thoroughly dissolved. Add ½ c. of cold water and let stand to cool. Take the whites of 4 eggs beaten very light and stiff and pour over the gelatine slowly, beating all the time while pouring in. Sprinkle in 1 cup white sugar and beat while adding. Add 1 t. almond or lemon extract and beat again. Take 1/3 of mixture and color pink. Then spread one layer of the white in the pan and sprinkle with chopped nuts; then the pink layer and chopped nuts and the rest of the white for the top layer. Let cool and serve with whipped cream. Cut in squares.

— Mrs. C. C. Lapp, Miami

Orange Pudding:

1 pt. milk	salt
3 oranges	2 egg yolks
1 large T. cornstarch	½ c. sugar
vanilla	

Cut oranges in small pieces, add sugar and let stand until custard is made. Then pour over oranges and sugar while hot.

— Daisy Diver, Raton

Butter Scotch Cake Pudding (A hurry-up dessert)

First part:
1 c. brown sugar
1 T. butter
1¾ c. boiling water
Cake part:
½ c. sugar
1 T. butter

1 c. flour
2 t. baking powder
½ c. milk
If desired, add:
(1 t. cinnamon
(½ t. nutmeg
(½ c. raisins

Bring first part to boil. Pour into casserole. Pour cake batter into it and bake in moderate oven about twenty minutes. Spices and raisins may be left out for variation.

— Mrs. C. V. Coulter, Springer

Amber Steamed Pudding:

½ c. butter
1¼ c. sugar
2 c. finely grated raw carrots
2 eggs, beaten
1 c. finely grated raw potatoes
3 c. all purpose flour
3 t. baking powder
2 t. cinnamon
1 t. salt
1½ t. allspice

¼ t. cloves
1 t. nutmeg
1 c. raisins
½ c. chopped nuts
½ c. chopped dates
1/3 c. mixed fruit (fruit cake type)
1/3 c. water (if necessary to make batter moist)

Cream butter and sugar, add eggs and vegetables. Sift flour, spices, salt, baking powder and dredge fruit and nuts in it. Add to first mixture and add water if necessary. Put in buttered mold and steam three hours. Serve with any hard sauce recipe. Makes twenty medium servings.

— Mrs. Leonard Matthews, Raton

Grape Tapioca:

1/3 c. quick tapioca
½ c. sugar
¼ t. salt
¼ t. cinnamon
⅛ t. allspice

⅛ t. nutmeg
1½ c. water
1 c. grape juice
½ t. grated orange rind
¼ t. grated lemon rind

Cook tapioca, sugar, salt, spice and water together and boil for five minutes. Add grape juice, grated rinds and chill. Serve with whipped cream.

— Mrs. I. W. Williams, Chico

Plum Pudding No. 1:

1 c. raisins
1 c. currants
1 c. mixed candied fruit
1 c. ground suet
1 c. brown sugar
1 c. sour milk

1 t. nutmeg
½ c. molasses
½ t. soda dissolved in
1 T. hot water
3 c. flour or enough to make a
rather stiff dough.

Mix well and steam 3 hours. Serve with hard sauce.

— Mrs. E. B. Majors, Raton

Plum Pudding No. 2

1 c. suet
1 c. currants
1 c. nuts
3 c. bread crumbs
1 t. soda
1 t. allspice

¼ t. nutmeg
1 c. Raisins
1 c. sugar
1 c. sour milk
2 eggs, beaten
1 t. cinnamon
½ t. cloves

Steam 3 or 4 hours in a double boiler or in tins. Have water boiling constantly.

— Mrs. Leon Johnson, Johnson Mesa

Steamed Carrot Pudding

1 c. grated carrots
1 c. grated potatoes
1 c. brown sugar
½ c. white sugar
½ c. melted shortening
1 c. raisins
1 c. nuts

½ t. soda
1 t. baking powder
1 t. cinnamon
¼ t. cloves
¼ t. nutmeg
3 c. flour

Mix potatoes with soda, add carrots melted shortening and sugar, add dry ingredients and nuts and raisins, flour and cover. Steam 2 hours at 15 lbs. pressure.

— Mrs. W. A. Dow, Colmor
— Mrs. Frank Deacy, Colmor

Dessert Sauces

Sauce:

1 cube butter   ½ c. cream
1 c. sugar
Melt. Whip until foam and serve hot
— Mrs. W. A. Dow, Colmor
— Mrs. Frank Deacy, Colmor

Butterscotch Sauce:

2/3 c. light corn syrup   2 T. butter
1 c. brown sugar   ¾ c. cream or evaporated milk
¼ t. salt
Cook sugar, salt and syrup until it forms a soft ball in cold water. Remove from fire; add the butter and as soon as it is melted beat in cream or evaporated milk and nuts. Keep warm over water. May be served on pudding, cake or ice cream.
— Marian Pinson, Capulin

Easy Vanilla Sauce:

¼ c. sugar, ¾ c. Karo, ½ c. cream, 2 T. butter, 1 t. vanilla.
Mix sugar, syrup and cream. Heat, but do not boil. When ready to serve, beat in butter and vanilla.
— Mrs. Maurine Pettigrew, Mills

Hot Cherry Sauce:

½ c. sugar   2 T. cornstarch
¾ c. cherry juice   1 c. water
¼ t. almond flavoring
Mix sugar, salt and cornstarch together in saucepan. Blend in cherry juice and water. Boil until mixture thickens. Blend in almond flavoring. Serve hot over Carnival Dessert.
— Mrs. Maurine Pettigrew, Mills

Lemon Sauce for Carrot Pudding:

3 eggs, beaten   ¼ c. lemon juice
½ c. sugar   ⅛ t. salt
½ c. orange juice   ½ c. water
2 T. butter
Beat eggs and add rest of ingredients. Cook in double boiler until slightly thickened. Do not over cook. It may curdle.
— Mrs. W. A. Dow, Colmor

Foamy Sauce for Steamed Pudding:

¼ c. butter   2 egg yolks well beaten
1 c. brown sugar   1 c. milk
½ T. flour
Cook in double boiler until thickened. Cool slightly and pour over stiffly beaten egg whites. Use vanilla or rum for flavoring. Mix well.
—Mrs. Marshall Howland, Raton

Fish

Baked Halibut:

3 lbs. halibut (in piece)
1 small jar stuffed olives, sliced.
6 dill pickles
Salt, pepper and ½ cube butter
pour 1 can tomatoes over this
Bake 1½ to 2 hours in medium oven

— Mrs. Mary E. Peterson, Cimarron

Baked Halibut Steak:

1 halibut steak
4 slices bacon
1 onion
½ c. cornmeal
3 T. butter
3 T. flour

Place bacon in bottom of dipping pan and cover with thin slices of bacon. Place steak on top of bacon and onion and mask with a mixture of butter and flour. Sprinkle with cornmeal. Cover with oiled paper and bake at 350 degrees for 1 hour. Remove paper at end of 45 minutes to brown. Garnish with thin slices of lemon and parsley.

Baked Tuna and Noodles:

1 4 oz. pkg egg noodles, cooked
1 can condensed mushroom soup diluted with equal quantity of evaporated milk
½ t. celery salt
2 t. grated onion
1 c. canned peas, drained
1 pimiento, chopped
1 7 oz. can tuna fish
fine buttered crumbs

Cook noodles in boiling salted water, drain and blanch with cold water. Add to cream of mushroom soup, diluted, celery salt, pimiento and onion (to soup). In a buttered casserole, alternate layers of noodles, tuna and peas, adding a layer of noodles last. Bits of mushrooms, fresh green or red peppers may be added to each layer of tuna. Pour soup mixture over top. Cover with buttered crumbs. Bake 30 to 40 minutes.

— Mrs. W. C. Jenkins, Raton

Baked Tuna Fish:

1½ pt. noodles, well cooked in double boiler. Drain. Alternate layers of noodles and tuna fish until all is used. Then pour one can mushroom soup over it and sprinkle with salt and pepper. Bake 10 minutes.

— Mrs. Zenas Curtis, Cimarron

Clam and Tomato Bouillon :

2 cans of minced clams and add 1 qt. tomato juice and 1 pt. beef stock made from bouillon cubes, paste or powder. Season with salt and pepper, 1 t. grated onion and a few slices of lemon. Simmer until flavor suits your taste. — Mrs. Ellis Littleton

Fish Chowder, (catfish):

2 c. soup or fish stock	¼ t. pepper
1" cube fat salt pork, diced	1 lb. fish, cut in small pieces
3 slices onions	2 T. fat
2 c. potatoes diced	2 T. flour
1 t. salt	2 c. scalded milk

Place the fat pork in a frying pan with the onions and cook for five minutes until brown. Strain into a saucepan and add the fish stock, potatoes, salt, pepper and the fish. Cook until the potatoes are soft. Melt fat, add flour and when smooth, add the scalded milk. Stir until the sauce boils and then add to the soup stock.

— Mrs. Ruth Wilferth, Springer

Fried Oysters:

24 large oysters	½ t. salt
2 eggs	⅛ t. pepper
2 T. cold water	1 c. bread crumbs

Wash and drain oysters. Beat the eggs with the seasoning and add water and mix. Dip oysters into the egg mixture, then into the crumbs. Let stand 5 minutes before frying. Fry in hot fat until golden brown. Serve at once.

— Mrs. Ruth Wilferth, Springer

Oyster Soup:

1 qt. oysters	2 T. flour
3 c. milk	1½ t. salt
1 c. cream	¼ t. pepper
3 T. butter	1 T. grated onion

Melt the butter and stir in the flour and blend well. Slowly add the milk, stirring at the same time, then the cream and seasoning and onion. Keep hot over a low flame. Bring the oysters to a boil in their own liquid. Cook about 5 minutes or until the edges curl. Strain. Add oysters to the milk stock, heat about 5 minutes without boiling. Serve immediately.

— Mrs. Ruth Wilferth, Springer

Salmon Green Bean Casserole:

Can one lb. salmon	½ t. salt
1 No. 2 can string beans	¼ t. pepper
¼ c. pickle relish	1½ c. milk
3 T. butter	½ c. soft buttered bread crumbs
3 T. flour	

Remove bones and skin from salmon. Arrange salmon, string beans and pickle relish in alternate layers in greased casserole. Melt butter, add flour and seasoning and blend well. Add milk gradually. Cook, stirring constantly until thick and smooth. Pour over salmon mixture. Top with buttered bread crumbs. Bake in a moderately hot oven 30 minutes.

— Francis Towndrow, Raton

Salmon Patties:

To use leftover salmon: To salmon, add equal amount of mashed potatoes at least one beaten egg. Make in patties, roll in cracker crumbs and fry until nicely browned.

Tuna Supreme:

1 can Tuna	salt
1 small package noodles	1 T. flour
½ cube butter	½ pt. milk
½ lb. cream cheese	1 pimiento cut fine
salt, pepper, onion salt, garlic	½ green mango, cut fine

Cook noodles in salt water until tender. While the noodles are cooking, mix butter in sauce pan with flour and part of milk. Cook, stirring constantly, until it begins to thicken, add grated cheese. Add the rest of the milk. Stir until a smooth sauce. Drain noodles, place layer in greased baking dish. Add part of tuna, pimiento, mangoes and seasoning. Continue until the dish is filled. Add cheese sauce and bake in moderate oven ½ hour.

— Mrs. E. B. Majors, Raton

Meats, including Poultry

Camouflage Loaf:

One way to make leftover meat go big.

2 c. cooked chicken, lamb or pork chopped.
¼ c. cracker crumbs
2 t. onion juice
5 - 6 T. liquid, stock or water

3 c. rice, hot, cooked
2 t. lemon juice
½ t. celery salt
1 t. salt
1 egg, slightly beaten

Combine meat, crumbs and seasoning. Add egg, mix well; add liquid to moisten. Line bottom and sides of greased loaf pan with 2 c. of the rice, fill center with meat mixture, cover with remaining rice. Tie greased heavy paper over pan, steam 45 minutes. Turn out on platter. Serve with appropriate sauce-chicken, tomato, mushroom or curry.

Cabbage Piglets:

4 large white cabbage leaves
½ lb. sausage meat
1 c. cooked rice
1 egg
½ t. salt
½ t. pepper

1 small onion
1 can cream of tomato soup or
2 c. tomato juice
1 bay leaf
½ c. water

Mix the meat, rice, egg, salt and pepper thoroughly. Put spoonfuls of the meat mixture on each of the cabbage leaves, roll and fasten with toothpicks. Place in frying pan. Mix the contents of the can of cream of tomato soup or tomato juice, bay leaf, onion and water; pour over the cabbage rolls; simmer one hour.

— Mrs. Jenny Gleaves, Cimarron

Chicken with Rice:

Dress chicken for baking. Put in baking dish, put 2 cups rice in and around chicken, season with salt, pepper and a bit of curry powder; cover with water, add 2 cups of tomato pulp, cover and do not open until ready to serve. Garnish with parsley Bake 2½ to 3 hours.

— Mrs. C. U. Burris, Miami

Special Chicken:

1 large frier cut up as for frying. Salt and roll in flour. Put 2 cups of sour cream in roaster and get hot. Put in chicken and put in oven and cook until tender and brown.

— Mrs. Pleasant Smith, Springer

My Mother's Chicken Pie:

Dress chicken and cut as for frying. Salt and cook in plenty of water until done. Put pieces of chicken in bottom of pan. Make gravy with broth and season with salt and pepper. When medium thick, pour over pieces of chicken in pan. Have ready rich biscuit dough made with 2 c. flour, ½ c. fat, 2¾ t. baking powder, ¾ c. sweet milk, ½ t. salt. Roll dough about ½" thick and cut in about 1¼ inch squares. Have gravy and chicken boiling hot. Lay biscuit squares carefully on top of gravy and bake in oven at 400 degrees until biscuits are a nice brown. Serve from baking container. When properly made, this is very delicous.

— Mrs. C. C. Lapp, Miami

Chicken Mexicana:

3 lbs. chicken	1 No. 2 can tomatoes
3 T. fat	1 t. salt
1 T. flour	pepper
1 medium onion	1 t. chili powder
Hot cooked rice	

Brown chicken (cut in pieces) in fat. Remove chicken. Blend flour with fat in pan, slice onion; add with tomatoes, salt, pepper and chili powder; heat. Add chicken. Cover; simmer one hour 15 minutes. Serve on rice.

— Mrs. Maurine Pettigrew, Mills

Chicken A La King:

½ c. mushrooms	2 T. chopped pimiento
¼ chopped green pepper	1½ c. diced cooked chicken
2 T. butter	salt
1½ c. medium white sauce	pepper
½ c. cream	1 egg yolk

Bake pastry shell or individual shells. Brown mushrooms and green pepper in butter. Combine with sauce, cream, pimiento and chicken. Season with salt and pepper. Heat over hot water. Beat egg yolks. Add sauce mixture. Heat, stirring constantly one minute. Serve in pastry shell.

— Mrs. Maurine Pettigrew, Mills

Chili:

2 lbs. meat	2 c. tallow
2 large onions	1 gallon broth or water
3 bunches garlic	1 T. salt
2 t. cummin seed	Tomatoes and beans, if desired
2 T. chili powder	

Cut onion and garlic fine and put in skillet with tallow. Add ground meat in skillet with tallow. Add chili powder and cummin seed (ground fine). Cook until meat is done. Put into a big stewer where bone has been boiled.

— Mrs. Tenna Luellen, Farley

Chili Con Carne (Spanish style):

Boil 1½ pounds of meat about 1½ hours or until tender. Place lard or shortening in skillet and add two heaping tablespoons of flour and two teaspoons of chili and fry just a little. Add soup stock and meat. Season with salt and add garlic if desired.

Chili Con Carne:

3 lbs. lean beef (round or neck meat) cut in small pieces or grind through meat chopper.
1 lb. fresh kidney suet, chopped fine

8 level T. chili powder
3 pints boiling water
Salt to taste

Render suet in agateware kettle, then add chopped meat and steam until half cooked. Salt, add water and chili powder and cook slowly about two hours. Flour may be added for thickening if desired. Tomatoes and beans may be added if desired.
— Helen McCarty, Mills

Chipped Beef Casserole:

1 c. cooked rice, blanched
¼ lb. dried beef, mince and fry in butter

1 c. grated cheese
2 c. tomatoes

Add as much water as necessary and bake one hour. Keep adding water as needed while baking.
— Mrs. M. F. Howland, Raton

Dinner—In-A-Roll:

1½ c. ground beef; 1 t. salt; ¼ t. pepper; 1/3 c. chopped onion; ½ c. chopped celery or carrots; 2 T. melted butter; 1 egg, unbeaten; 1 T. chopped green pepper; 1 c. mashed sweet potatoes or Irish potatoes.

Make a regular biscuit dough using 2 c. flour. Combine meat, salt, pepper, onion, celery or carrots. Add ⅛ t. pepper, ¼ t. salt, 1 T. butter, green pepper to potatoes. Mix well and spread on biscuit dough which has been rolled out to 10 x 15 inches. Roll dough enough to enclose potatoes. Spread meat mixture on remainder of dough and continue rolling. Seal edges, brush top with milk, gash top in a few places. Place in well greased pan and bake in hot oven. Serve with tomato sauce.
— Emma Orin

Barbecued Frankfurters:

To make sauce melt, 1 T. butter, add ½ c. chopped onion and cook until clear. Add 1 t. paprika, ¼ t. pepper, 4 t. sugar, 1 t. mustard, 4 t. Worchestershire sauce, ¼ c. catsup, and 3 t. vinegar Slit 10 frankfurters lengthwise, but not to the ends. Place in shallow baking pan, slit side up. Cover with sauce. Bake 20 minutes.
— Mrs. Rose L. Gillespie, Raton

Frankfurter Creole:

3 medium sized onions	1 lb. frankfurters
3 green peppers	3 T. fat (or more as needed)
Med. size can of tomatoes	Salt and pepper to taste

Melt fat in large frying pan (bacon fat is best), add onions (sliced thin), frying slowly while cutting green peppers in thin strips. Add to onions and cook about 10 minutes. Onions should be golden brown and peppers soft. Add tomatoes and simmer another 10 minutes before adding franks, cut in slices. Put cover on frying pan and cook another 10 or 15 minutes, adding salt and pepper. Fresh tomatoes may be used in summer.

— Mrs. Chas. Griffith

Ham Loaf:

2/3 lb. cured ham, ground	1 c. milk
1 1/3 lb. fresh pork, ground	1/3 c. brown sugar
1 c. fine cracker crumbs	1 T. dry mustard
¼ t. pepper	¼ c. vinegar
2 eggs, beaten	

Combine meat, crumbs, pepper, eggs and milk. Mix thoroly, form into loaf and place in baking pan. Mix sugar, mustard and vinegar and pour over meat. Bake in moderate oven one hour. Use mushroom soup for sauce.

— Mrs. J. W. Wilferth, Springer

Ham Roll:

12 slices baked ham	1 lb. asparagus, cooked

Place 3 or 4 stalks of asparagus on slice ham and roll up. Place in greased baking dish, open side down. Cover with the following cheese sauce: 2 T. butter, melted, mixed with 1 T. flour. Add milk to make smooth paste. Add ½ lb. grated cheese and 1 cup more of milk. Cook until thickens. Pour over ham rolls and bake ½ hour in moderate oven.

— Mrs. E. B. Majors, Raton

Ham and Chicken Mousse:

1 c. finely ground cooked ham	3 T. cold water
1 c. finely ground cooked chicken	¾ c. whipping cream
	1 c. mayonnaise
1 t. prepared mustard	¼ c. whipping cream
1 bouillon cube	1 T. horse radish
1 c. hot water	6 chopped olives
1 T. gelatine	Tomato slices
water cress	

Mix ham, chicken and mustard; dissolve bouillon cubes in hot water; add gelatine softened in cold water and stir until gelatine is dissolved. Cool, add ¾ c. cream, whipped and chill in a ring mold. Unmold on a large platter; fill center with a mixture of the mayonnaise, ¼ c. cream, whipped, horse-radish and olives. Garnish with water cress and tomatoes. Serves 6.

— Mrs. J. W. Wilferth, Springer

Baked Hash Loaf:

Put through the food chopper 2 c. of any cooked meat, ½ c. each carrots, string beans and potatoes and 1 small onion. Make a white sauce of 2 T butter, 2 T. flour and ½ c. milk or water in which the carrots were cooked. Stir the chopped mixture in the white sauce and mix. Salt and pepper. Grease a baking dish and pack in hash. Bake 1 hour. Turn out on platter and garnish with sliced boiled eggs. Serve hot or cold. Good for supper.   — Mrs. Herbert Littrell

Breaded Brains:

Remove the skins that cover the brains and the fibers. Place brains in a dish. Add 1 T. vinegar and cover with cold water for 2 hours. Place the brains in a saucepan, adding sufficient boiling water to cover. Bring to a boil and cook slowly for 15 minutes. Drain and cool. Then quarter each brain. After preparing as directed, divide them into small pieces which are not too thick. Dip in seasoned cracker crumbs, into slightly beaten eggs, into cracker crumbs again and then fry in hot fat until a golden brown. Serve with cole slaw or chili sauce. Garnish with parsley.   — Mrs. Vera Anderson, Miami

Heart (calf, lamb, beef):

Wash thoroughly, remove arteries, veins, etc. and wipe with damp cloth. Chicken fried heart: ½" slices. Dip in flour, salt and pepper. Brown in hot fat. Add little hot water. Cover. Simmer 30 to 45 minutes.

Stuffed Heart: Fill heart cavity with well seasoned bread dressing. Fasten with skewers and string. Roll in flour, salted and peppered. Brown in hot fat. Add ½ c. water. Cover. Simmer until tender, 3½ hours for beef heart; 2 to 2½ hr. for veal or lamb heart. Make brown gravy with juices in pan.

Kidney (veal, lamb, pork, beef):

Wash, remove outer membrane, split through center lengthwise, remove fat and heavy veins. Soak in cold salted water 45 minutes before cooking. (Precook beef kidneys 1 hour, pork kidneys 20 minutes. Change water.)

1. Dip in melted fat and season. Broil 5 minutes until tender, turn often. Brush with melted fat, sprinkle with lemon juice. Serve on toast.

2. Dip in egg, roll in crumbs, fry in melted fat. Serve with creole sauce.

Liver (calf, lamb, beef, pork):

Remove skin and tough fibers with a knife or scissors. Wipe with damp cloth.

1. Brush ½" slices with melted fat. Broil about 5 minutes on each side.

2. Thread alternate slices of bacon and cubes of liver on skewers. Broil.

3. Panbroil liver. Save drippings in pan. Make creamy gravy in it. Add chopped cooked liver. Serve on toast.

Sweetbreads and Brains:

Use immediately after purchase, or precook and refrigerate. Precooking: Cover with cold water, soak ½ hour. Drain. Remove loose membranes. Simmer 20 minutes in salted hot water to which lemon juice or vinegar (1 T. to 1 qt. water) has been added. Drain. Plunge in cold water. Remove membrane. Cover and cool.

1. Dip in melted fat. Broil or pan fry until brown (about 10 minutes) serve hot with mushroom sauce.

2. Sweetbread Brochettes: Thread alternate pieces parboiled sweetbreads with bacon on skewers. Brush with melted fat. Broil.

3. Serve creamed sweetbreads on toast, in patty shells or over rice. Combine with any of the following: leftover ham, chicken, veal, peas, mushrooms, asparagus tips or oysters.

4. Crumble and scramble with eggs.

Tongue (beef, calf, pork):

Wash. Cover with hot salted water. Cook until tender (about 2 hrs. for pork and veal tongue, 3 hrs. for beef tongue.) Allow tongue to cool in liquid. Remove connective tissue, roots and skin.

1. To serve hot; skin and slice. Serve with horseradish sauce (½ c. whipped cream, 2 T. drained horseradish, 1 T. salad dressing).

2. Bake sliced cooked tongue with diced carrots, celery and onion, adding some of stock in which tongue was cooked.

3. Slice cold tongue and serve with potato salad or cole slaw.

Crown Roast of Lamb:

Have a crown roast of lamb prepared at market. Wipe meat carefully and rub over with flour mixed with salt and pepper. To keep ends of bones from burning, cover with stiff dough of flour and water or put cube of salt pork on each side. Put in baking pan and roast in moderate oven according to general rules.

Stuffed Lamb Chops:

Have chops cut an inch or more thick with a deep pocket cut in each. Fill the pockets with a bread stuffing, close opening with strip of bacon and fasten with a tooth pick. Bake one hour.

— Frances Towndrow, Raton

Stuffed Lamb Shoulder Roast:

1 lamb shoulder with blade removed; 1½ t. salt; ¼ t. pepper; 1 c. diced celery; 2½ c. soft bread crumbs; 1. T. minced onion; 1 T. minced parsley; 1 T. butter; ¼ t. celery seed and marjoram mixed; 2 T. water or meat stock. Sprinkle meat inside and out with 1 t. salt and ⅛ t. pepper. Meanwhile, cook celery, onion and parsley in butter 5 minutes. Add remaining salt and pepper and other ingredients. Fill pocket in roast loosely with

stuffing, skewer or side opening. Place on wire rack in open roaster, fat side up. Roast without water in a slow oven of 300 degrees, allowing 50 minutes per pound of roast. Make gravy of drippings. — Mrs Pearl Crowder, Colmor

Meat Loaf:

1 lb. ground beef	2 eggs, unbeaten
1 c. ground raw carrots	1 c. tomato sauce (milk may be
2 c. corn flakes	used)
1 sweet green pepper	½ t. poultry seasoning or sage
1 medium sized onion	1 t. salt

Mix thoroughly. Form in loaf 2 inches thick. Bake in medium hot oven one hour. — Mrs. Henry Floyd, Johnson Mesa

Western Ranch Meat Loaf:

2 lbs. ground beef or 1 lb. each	½ t. pepper
beef and lamb	2 t. salt
1 medium onion	2 eggs
¾ c. diced celery or ground	3 c. soft bread crumbs
carrot	½ c. water
¼ c. lard or shortening	½ c. tomato juice
1/3 c. diced green peppers or	2 T. melted butter or margarine

Chop onion. Brown onion and celery or carrots in lard. Combine with green pepper, salt, eggs, bread crumbs and water to make a dressing. Add half the dressing (1½ c.) to the meat, mixing well. Pat out half the mixture in a 2 qt. loaf pan. Cover with the remaining dressing, then top with remaining meat mixture. Bake in moderate oven 1¼ hours. Baste twice with tomato juice and butter to keep loaf moist. — Mrs. Sneede, Capulin

Pork Chops with Prunes:

6 - 8 pork chops	2 T. perrin sauce
1 c. chili sauce	1 c. catsup
1 t. grated onion	½ c. dried prunes
1 T. mustard	

Have pork chops cut thick. Brown slightly, place in pan, cover with sauce and cook until tender.

— Frances Towndroy, Raton

Prime Rib Roast:

Select a 5 lb. rib standing roast, wipe off with a cleam damp cloth. Sprinkle with salt, pepper and flour. Place in pan without water. Roast at 350 degrees. Roast 30 minutes per pound.

Baked Sausage:

Place sausage patties in casserole, put 1 c. rice, 1 c. peas, 1 small onion, diced, 1 c. tomato pulp, cover with water. Bake until rice is done. Fresh or canned sausage may be used.

— Mrs. C. U. Burris, Miami

"A steak is grander, it is true, yet needs
  No special skill to brew.
It is an art a stew to make, but
  Anyone can broil a steak!" — Joseph Alger, Jr.

Cowboy Stew:

2 lbs. lean meat, cut in 1" cubes 1 t. salt
1 t. ground onions   ¼ t. pepper
1 t. ground green peppers   ½ - 1 c. canned tomatoes

Flour meat and sear in lard. Place onions and green peppers in hot fat and cook for a few minutes. Add meat, seasoning, tomatoes and a little water. Place in can and process one hour at 15 pounds pressure.   — Mrs. O. M. Horn, Abbott
    — Mrs. John Anderson, Abbott

Hamburg Dumpling Stew:

1½ lb. ground chuck beef   1 T. chili sauce
⅛ t. pepper   1 c. canned tomato soup
1 small onion, chopped   2 c. hot water
2 t. prepared mustard   4 t. baking powder
1/3 c. fat   ⅞ c. milk
2 c. and 1 T. sifted flour

Mix thoroughly beef, ½ t. salt, pepper, onion and mustard and shape into 15 small cakes. Brown on both sides in fat in a deep kettle. Lift out meat cakes. Put 1 T. flour in kettle and blend with fat; add chili sauce, tomato soup, ½ t. salt, hot water; replace cakes in kettle and bring to the boiling point. Make dumpling mixture as follows: Sift 2 c. flour with the baking powder and ½ t. salt; add milk gradually, beating until smooth. Drop mixture by spoonfuls on top of boiling hamburg mixture. Cover closely and steam for 15 minutes. Serve at once.   — Mrs. Ellis Littleton

John Marzeth Stew:

1½ lbs. ground , lean pork   1 can mushrooms
2 boxes wide noodles   1 red sweet pepper
2 stalks celery   6 onions
1 qt. tomatoes   1 lb. cheese

Cook pork, celery, tomatoes, mushrooms and peppers together. Grind onions through vegetable grinder. Fry in salad oil until light brown. Add mixture. Cut cheese into small pieces and add. Cook noodles in boiling water twenty minutes and add. Serve with lettuce dressed with sharp salad dressing.   — Mrs. William Neish, Johnson Mesa

Lamb Stew:

2½ lbs. cubed lamb   1 can peas
2 c. carrots   1 onion
salt and pepper

Brown lamb and add vegetables plus 1 c. water. Boil about 2½ hours. Top with small biscuits and bake in oven until biscuits are done.   — Mrs. Violet Godfrey

Quick Skillet Stew:

Brown 1 lb. or more ground beef (made into small meat balls) in 4 T. fat. Stir in 3 T. flour. Add 3 c. hot water, 1 large onion, 3 medium carrots (sliced), 1 t. salt, ½ T. vinegar and 1/3 c. catsup. Simmer until carrots are half done. Add four potatoes (diced). Cook until tender. Note: 2 c. cooked left over diced beef may be used as meat if desired.

Stuffed Flank Steak:

2 flanked steaks   1 minced onion
2 c. bread crumbs   ½ t. poultry seasoning
3 T. crisco

Score the steaks in criss-cross fashion. Make a dressing by blending bread, onion, crisco and seasoning. Moisten it with a little boiling water and spread on one flank steak. Roll and secure with toothpicks. Sear well in hot crisco put in casserole or baking dish, add 1 c. boiling water and cook slowly, covered, until tender; about 2½ hours. — Mrs. Rose L. Gillespie, Raton

Stuffed Green Peppers:

6 large green peppers   ½ t. salt
1 lb. pork sausage or hamburger ¼ t. pepper
¼ c. chopped onion   1½ c. cooked rice
½ c. diced celery or   ½ c. cracker or bread crumbs
1 t. celery seed   1 egg, well beaten

Cut off tops of green peppers at stem end, remove seeds and fibrous portion and wash. Drop into boiling salt water and cook about 3 minutes. Combine meat, onions and all other ingredients and fry over moderate heat until meat is thoroly done, (about 15 minutes), then add rice, cracker crumbs and well beaten egg. Stuff peppers and place in upright position in greased baking dish and bake in moderately hot oven 30 to 40 minutes. Makes 6 servings. — Brooks Rucker, Abbott

Stuffed Spare Ribs:

2 c. hot mashed potatoes   1 egg
1½ c. softened stale bread   1½ t. salt
     crumbs   1 t. sage
1/3 c. melted butter   1 onion, chopped fine

Mix all ingredients thoroughly, remove the extra fat from the strip of spareribs which have been broken through the center, spread the potato mixture on the inside of ribs, fold on broken line, place the roast in a baking pan, heavy meat side on top. Dredge with salt, pepper and flour. Cover the bottom of pan with boiling water. Cook in a moderate oven.
— Mrs. Chas. Short, Johnson Mesa

Tamale Pie:

½ lb. hamburger   1 c. milk
½ lb. sausage   1 can tomato juice
chili powder   2 eggs
garlic   salt
½ c. corn meal

Fry hamburger, sausage, chili powder and garlic until brown. Beat eggs in milk, add corn meal and tomato juice. After meat is fried, pour cornmeal mixture over meat. Bake 30 minutes.

— Myrtle Durie, Johnson Mesa

Vegetable Meat Patties:

¾ lb. ground round steak
1 c. mixed, cooked vegetables
1 egg
¼ c. milk
¾ t. salt
½ c. buttered bread crumbs

¼ t. pepper
1 c. dry bread crumbs
4 T. butter
4 T. flour
1 large can onion soup

Mix meat and drained vegetables. Add beaten egg, milk, salt, pepper and ½ c. dry bread crumbs to meat and blend well. Shake into 6 patties. Roll in remaining dry bread crumbs and saute in 2 T. of butter. Melt the remaining 2 T. butter. Add the flour and blend well. Add the onion soup and cook until thickened. Place browned patties in a casserole. Cover with soup and top with buttered crumbs. Bake in a moderate oven for 30 minutes. Serves six.

— Frances Towndrow, Raton

Venison or Elk Roast:

4 lbs. or venison or elk
1 can of tomato sauce
Salt and pepper
1 large onion

½ c. water
1½ T. Worcestershire sauce
Flour

Rub meat with flour, salt and pepper. Then brown meat in cooking fat. Put in heavy kettle or Dutch oven. Add water and cover tightly. Cook slowly about 4 hours or until tender. More water may be used if necessary.

— Mrs. Leon Johnson, Johnson Mesa

Victory Meat Dish:

¼ c. Wesson oil
2 onions cut and cooked with the oil
2 lbs. ground steak
1 qt. tomato juice

1 can green chili
1 lb. cheese
1 small can corn
1 box spaghetti
2 T. Wesson sauce

Mix all ingredients. Put cheese on top. Bake 1 hour. Hamburger may be used instead of steak.

— Mrs. Mae Black, Raton

Enchiladas:

2 lb. ground beef with beef suet
3 cloves of garlic
2 T. chili powder

2 t. comino seed
2 t. salt
1 t. black pepper

Brown all these ingredients in a skillet, cook until well done, adding a little water from time to time. Then using tortillas, dip each one in hot fat and serve this on a plate covered with the meat mixture and on this put grated cheese, chopped onions, lettuce and tomatoes.

— Mrs. Famie Richardson, Cimarron

Pastries

Angel Food Pie No. 1:

1 c. sugar, 2 heaping t. cornstarch, 1½ c. boiling water. Cook until thick and clear. Whip whites of 4 eggs, add above mixture while hot, spoonful at a time, and beat vigorously. Use any extract desired. Put in baked pie shell and top with whipped cream. Above mixture is for 2 pies.　　— Mrs. J. H. Littrell

Angel Food Pie No. 2:

1¼ c. sugar　　　　　　　　2 c. boiling water
2 heaping T. cornstarch　　2 egg whites
¼ t. salt　　　　　　　　　1 t. vanilla

Sift sugar, cornstarch and salt together three times. Add boiling water. Cook until thick. Fold into stiffly beaten egg whites. Pour in pie shell and cover with whipped cream. Bake pie shell first.　　　　　— Mrs. Al Richardson, Cimarron

Dutch Apple Pie:

Prepare plain pastry for one 9" crust.

6 medium sized apples, pare　　¼ t. cloves
　and slice thin　　　　　　　½ t. cinnamon
1 c. sugar　　　　　　　　　1 c. sour cream
3 T. flour　　　　　　　　　1½ T. sugar

Mix sugar, flour and cloves. Add sour cream. Mix thoroughly. Pour over apples. Put all into crust. Combine cinnamon and 1½ T. sugar. Sprinkle over top. Use trimmings of crust to decorate with any desired cut outs. Bake in hot oven 450 degrees for 10 minutes. Continue at 350 degrees for about 35 minutes. Serve warm or chilled.　　　— Mrs. J. W. Ausherman, Miami

French Apple Pie No. 1:

6 c. tart apples　　　　　2 T. flour
½ to 2/3 c. sugar　　　　½ c. brown sugar
1 t. cinnamon　　　　　　1 c. flour
½ c. butter

Line 9" pie pan with pastry. Chill. Mix together sliced apples, sugar, cinnamon and flour. Cream together the butter and brown sugar. Work in 1 c. flour to make a crumb mixture. Sprinkle the crumbs over the apples. Bake 15 minutes in hot oven, then reduce temperature to moderate and bake 20 to 30 minutes longer. Serve with plain or whipped cream if desired.

　　　　　　　　　— Mrs. Maurine Pettigrew, Mills

French Apple Pie No. 2:

Peel and slice 6 to 8 apples. Mix together ½ to 2/3 c. sugar, 1 t. cinnamon or nutmeg, 2 t. flour and mix with apples. Place in pan with crust and dot with butter. Then mix ½ c. butter, ½ c. brown sugar in 1 c. flour. Sprinkle crumb mixture over apples and bake.　　　　　　　— Mrs. Lee Glasgow, Farley

Banana Pie:

Slice 2 large bananas in baked pie shell. Make a custard of 2 egg yolks, 2 c. milk, ½ c. sugar, 2 T. flour, small piece of butter, pinch of salt. Boil until thick, cool over bananas and add meringue and brown. — Mrs. Ora House, Capulin

Bean Pie:

2 c. beans, cooked and salted	1 t. vanilla
3 egg yolks	1 t. cinnamon
1 t. cloves	1 t. allspice
Sugar	

Be sure all water is drained from beans, mash until smooth, add sugar and egg yolks, beating well. Add flavoring, and beat again. Pour into two pie pans lined with uncooked pie crust. Bake in hot oven until filling is firm but not dry. Make a meringue of egg whites, cover each pie, return to oven and brown lightly. — Mrs. John Everett, Springer

Buttermilk Pie:

3 c. thick buttermilk	1½ c. sugar
3 T. flour or cornstarch	3 eggs
butter size of egg	1 t. lemon extract

Mix well. Pour into unbaked pie crust and bake until filling becomes solid. Makes 2 small pies.
— Mrs. Jim Johnston, Springer

Butterscotch Pie No. 1:

1 egg	2 T. flour
1 c. brown sugar	2 T. butter
¼ c. milk	1 t. vanilla
¼ t. salt	3 T. water

Put egg yolks in sauce pan, add brown sugar and flour, milk, water, butter, salt and vanilla. Stir over fire until thick. Pour into baked crust. Add meringue and brown in oven.
— Mrs. Robert Morrow, Raton

Butterscotch Pie No. 2:

1 c. dark brown sugar	2 eggs
4 T. butter	2 T. powdered sugar
1½ c. milk	½ t. vanilla
3 T. flour	

Measure sugar and butter together into a heavy frying pan slightly heated, caramelizing them together until a thick brown syrup is formed. To this, add 1 c. milk and the vanilla. Separate eggs, beating yolks lightly and combine with remaining milk and flour beaten together until smooth. Pour this into caramelized mixture and stir until thick and creamy. Pour into baked pie shell. Cover with meringue and bake in a very slow oven until meringue is browned.
— Mrs. Everett Kulhman, Springer

Chocolate Pie:

¾ c. sugar	Butter size of egg
3 T. cocoa	3 T. flour
2 c. sweet milk	1 t. vanilla

Melt butter in heavy iron skillet, add cocoa and work smooth. Add milk and bring to boil. Combine flour and sugar, add to milk, stirring continually until smooth, adding vanilla last. When cool, top with whipped cream.

— Mrs. Tomas F. Simons, Johnson Mesa

Chocoate Chiffon Pie No. 1:

1 envelope Knox Sparkling gelatin	4 eggs
½ c. boiling water	1 c. sugar
¼ c. cold water	¼ t. salt
4 level T. cocoa	1 t. vanilla
	1 8" baked crust

Soften gelatin in cold water. Mix cocoa and boiling water until smooth. Add gelatin to hot chocolate mixture, stirring thoroughly. Add egg yolks, slightly beaten, ½ c. sugar, salt and vanilla. Cool and when mixture begins to thicken, fold in stiffly beaten egg whites to which the other ½ c. of sugar has been added. Sprinkle baked shell with broken nut meats, pour in filling and let chill several hours. Serve with whipped cream.

— Mrs. E. B. Majors, Raton

Chocolate Chiffon Pie No. 2:

1 T. gelatin	9" baked pastry shell
¼ c. cold water	¼ t. salt
½ c. boiling water	3 egg yolks
2 sq. unsweetened chocolate	1 t. vanilla
1 c. sugar	3 egg whites
Whipped cream	

Soften gelatin in cold water; add boiling water, stir until gelatin is dissolved. Melt chocolate over hot water. Add gelatin mixture. Add ½ c. sugar and salt. Cook 2 minutes. Beat egg yolks; add chocolate mixture; cook over hot water 2 minutes. Cool. Add vanilla. Beat egg whites stiff; gradually add remaining sugar, beating constantly. Fold into chocolate mixture; pour into pastry shell. Chill until firm. Serve with whipped cream.

— Mrs. Maurine Pettigrew, Mills

Magic Chocolate Pie:

2 sq. unsweetened chocolate	
1 1/3 c. Eagle Brand sweetened condensed milk	¼ t. salt
½ c. water	½ t. vanilla
	Baked pie shell

Melt chocolate in top of double boiled.Add Eagle Brand sweetened condensed milk and stir over rapidly boiling water 5 minutes until thick. Then remove from heat. Add water and salt and mix well. When cool, add vanilla. Pour into baked pie shell. Garnish with whipped cream. Chill.

— Mrs. W. M. Coleman, Farley

Nestles Chocolate Cream Pie:

2 c. milk
3 T. cornstarch (heaping)
1/3 c. sugar
⅛ t. salt
1 t. vanilla

1 T. butter
1 egg yolk
½ of an 8 oz. box of chocolate
   chips

Mix cornstarch and sugar and salt together. Add milk. Stir. Cook until thick, stirring all the time. When thick, add egg yolks and beat well. Add butter and chocolate chips. Take off stove and cool a little. Add vanilla. Pour into baked pie shell. When cool, spread whipped cream over top. Meringue may be used. — Mrs. Morris McConnell, Springer

Corn Meal Pie:

2 c. brown sugar or 1 c. Karo
  and 1 c. brown sugar
2 eggs
2 T. milk

2 T. cornmeal
2 T. butter
1 c. coconut
1 t. vanilla

Mix together and bake in unbaked crust until done in slow oven. — Mrs. Iva Zimmerman, Colmor

Cream Pie with Syrup:

3 eggs, separated
2 T. flour
2 T. butter

1 t. grated nutmeg
1½ c. cream
1 c. syrup

Beat yolks of eggs. Add syrup and flour mixed together. Then cream and butter. Put in double boiler. Stir constantly until ready to boil, then put in crusts and bake. Make meringue of whites. — Mrs. Clyde Alton, Farley

Lemon Pie No. 1:

1¼ c. sugar
½ c. cake flour
1½ c. water

3 egg yolks, slightly beaten
½ c. lemon juice

Mix sugar and flour together, then add water and lemon juice, retaining 6 T. sugar for egg white topping. Cook above ingredients until desired thickness is attained. Pour in shell and cover with topping. — Mrs. H. H. Burris, Miami

Lemon Pie No. 2:

1 c. sugar
5 T. cornstarch
2 egg yolks

3 T. butter
1½ c. boiling water
2 lemons

Mix sugar and cornstarch. Stir in boiling water and cook over direct heat, stirring constantly until thick; then add egg yolks, one at a time and stir fast. Cook for a few minutes longer then remove from fire and add lemon juice and butter. Pour in pie shell and cover with meringue.

— Mrs. Phil McConnell, Springer

Lemon Pie No. 3:

1 c. sugar
2½ c. boiling water
3½ T. cornstarch
2 eggs

juice of 1 lemon
½ t. butter
grated rind ½ lemon

Combine cornstarch and 1 c. sugar. Add water slowly, stirring constantly. Cook over hot water, stirring constantly until thick and smooth. Add beaten egg yolks, butter, lemon rind, a few grains salt. Add lemon juice last. Cook 2 minutes. Pour into baked pastry shell. Cover with meringue made of egg whites and 2. T. sugar.

— Mrs. Leon Johnson, Johnson Mesa

Angel Lemon Pie:

Beat 4 egg yolks until light. Add ½ c. sugar, blend well; add juice and rind of 1 large or 1½ small lemons and lump of butter size of an egg. Cook in double boiler until thick. Beat whites stiff. Add ½ c. sugar. Beat again. Take half and fold with lemon mixture and put other half on pie. Put in crust that has been baked and cooled.

— Mrs. Tenna Luellen, Farley

Lemon Chiffon Pie:

4 egg yolks
¾ c. sugar
¼ c. water
1 envelope gelatin
½ c. lemon juice
3 T. orange juice

½ c. sugar
4 egg whites
½ t. orange rind
½ t. lemon rind
¼ t. salt

Beat egg yolks well, add lemon juice, orange juice and salt and cook until thick. Dissolve gelatin in ¼ c. cold water and add to hot mixture. Let cool. Beat egg whites and add ¼ c. sugar, orange rind and lemon rind, and fold into mixture. Pour in pie shell.

Pie Shell of Graham Crackers: add ¼ c. sugar, ½ c. butter to graham crackers. Serve with 1 c. whipped cream.

Lemon Cream Pie:

4 egg yolks beaten very
    lightly.
½ c. sugar

Grated rind of 1 large lemon
6 T. lemon juice

Cook in double boiler until thick. Beat 2 egg whites until light and add ½ c. sugar. Fold into cooked part. Pour into baked shell and frost with remaining 2 whites, beaten light with 2 T. sugar.

— Mrs. Mary E. Patterson, Cimarron

Lemon Meringue Pie:

1 1/3 c. Eagle Brand   2 eggs
  sweetened condensed milk   2 T. granulated sugar
½ c. lemon juice   1 baked crust
Grated rind of lemon
  Blend together milk, lemon juice, grated rind and beaten egg yolks. Pour into baked crust. Cover with meringue made from 2 egg whites and 2 T. sugar. Brown.
               — Mrs. E. B. Majors, Raton
            — Mrs. Maurine Pettigrew, Mills

Million Dollar Pie:

3 eggs   ¾ c. nuts
1½ c. sugar   ¾ c. raisins
2 T. butter   2 T. water
½ t. spice   1 T. vinegar
  Mix well and place in pie shell. Bake in moderate oven.
             — Mrs. Tenna Luellen, **Farley**

Mince Meat:

3 lbs. chopped lean beef   4 c. raisins
½ lb. chopped suet   1 T. salt
8 c. chopped apples   2 t. cinnamon
6 c. sugar   1 t. cloves
1/3 c. molasses   1 t. nutmeg
2 qts. cider   ½ c. chopped candied orange
½ c. chopped citron   peel
  Mix and cook slowly 1½ hours. Pour into jars and seal at once. Spiced fruit juices are good to add to the mixture when ready to place in the pies.

Pecan Pie No. 1:

1 unbaked pastry shell   2 c. light corn syrup
1 beaten egg white   1 t. vanilla extract
3 eggs   ¼ t. salt
1 T. sugar   1 c. whole pecan meats
2 T. flour
  Brush unbaked shell with egg white and put in hot oven 3-5 minutes to set crust. Beat eggs until light. Mix sugar and flour and add to eggs, beating well. Add syrup, vanilla and salt. Sprinkle nut meats in pastry shell and add filling. Bake in moderate oven about 45 minutes.
             — Mrs. Claude Click, Des Moines

Pecan Pie No. 2:

4 egg yolks, unbeaten   ½ c. pecan meats
1¼ c. dark Karo
  Mix egg yolks and Karo well (don't beat). Pour in unbaked pie shell. Arrange nut meats on top and bake in moderate oven until well browned.
             —Mrs. Tom Novinger, Springer

Pineapple Chiffon Pie:

1 level T. gelatin	¼ t. salt
½ c. cold water	1 T. lemon juice
1¼ c. crushed pineapple	½ c. sugar
4 eggs	

Soak gelatin in cold water. Beat egg yolks slightly. Add ¼ c. sugar, pineapple, lemon juice and salt. Cook over boiling water until of custard consistency. Add softened gelatin, stir thoroly and cool. When mixture begins to thicken, fold in stiffly beaten egg whites, to which have been added the other ¼ c. sugar. Fill baked pie shell and chill. Serve with whipped cream flavored with pineapple juice and a little sugar.

— Mrs. W. C. Jenkins, Raton

Two crust Pineapple Pie:

1 can pineapple	1 c. sugar
2 eggs	2 T. flour
	Butter

Mix sugar and flour together. Mix all together and put in unbaked crust. Put butter on top of pineaple before the last crust.

— Mrs. Ruby Davenport, Farley

Pumpkin Pie:

1 c. pumpkin	1 pinch cloves, allspice, ginger
1 c. sugar (brown preferable)	and nutmeg
½ c. milk	1 or 2 T. melted butter
½ c. cream	1 t. vanilla
2 eggs	½ t. lemon juice
1 t. cinnamon	½ c. walnuts

Bake in oven about one hour.

— Mrs. Jennie Gleaves, Cimarron

New England Pumpkin Pie:

Use baked or stewed pumpkin browned in a pan. Thicken 1 c. boiling milk with flour and cook until smooth and add: yolks of 2 eggs, beaten; 1 c. sugar; 1 c. pumpkin; ¼ t. salt; ¼ t. cinnamon; ¼ t. nutmeg; ¼ t. ginger. At last add beaten egg whites, put in crust and bake until it puffs and is brown.

— Mrs. Ora House, Capulin

Raisin Pie:

1 c. sour cream	¼ t. cloves
1 c. sugar	½ t. cinnamon
½ c. raisins	¼ t. nutmeg
2 egg yolks	1 beaten egg white

Bake in uncooked shell and cover with meringue of egg whites.

— Mrs. Maurine Pettigrew, Mills

Rhubarb Pie:

1 qt. rhubarb, cut fine	3 T. flour
3 egg yolks	¼ lemon and small amount of
2 T. butter	rind
1 c. sugar	

Let rhubarb stand in hot water 10 minutes and drain. Mix other ingredients thoroughly and bake. Put meringue on top.

— Francis Towndrow, Raton

Sour Cream Pie:

Soak 1 c. raisins in hot water. Mix together:

1 c. sugar	½ t. cloves
½ t. cinnamon	½ t. allspice
2 T. flour	

Add 1 c. sour cream or 1 c. sweet cream plus 2 T. vinegar, 3 egg yolks beaten, then add raisins and lastly fold in stiffly beaten whites of 3 eggs. Pour in unbaked pie shell and bake in very moderate oven 1 hour or until brown and set.

— Mrs. Hazel House, Capulin

Sour Cream Pie No. 2:

1 c. sour cream	2 egg whites
¼ t. salt	½ t. cinnamon
½ c. sugar	¼ t. cloves
½ c. raisins	2 T. vinegar
2 egg yolks	6 t. sugar

Combine cream and ½ c. sugar, add yolks beaten well, add spices, vinegar and raisins. Line pie plates with pastry and pour in mixture. Bake in hot oven long enough to set pastry. Meringue made of egg whites and 6 t. sugar and ½ t. vanilla.

— Marie Townsley, Springer

Sour Cream Upside Down Pie:

1 c. sour cream	Pinch of salt
1 c. sugar	1 level t. soda
2 eggs	1 t. vanilla
2 c. flour	

Mix batter and pour in a shallow pan and add 1 qt. of any kind of fruit sweetened to taste on top. Cook until brown on top. Don't cook too fast.

— Mrs. W. P. Rogers, Springer

Sour Cream Raisin Pie:

1 c. raisins	2 eggs
1 c. sour, thick, cream	1 t. cinnamon
1 c. sugar (brown is best)	½ t. nutmeg
1 T. flour	1 t. vanilla (optional)

Mix sugar and flour. Beat eggs slightly. Add to flour and put in all the others and stir until flour and sugar is smooth. Pour in pie crust and bake until when tested with a knife, it comes out clean.

- Mrs. Fred Floyd, Johnson Mesa

Syrup Pie:

2 c. white syrup	1 c. cream or butter
3 eggs	pinch salt
2 T. flour	dash nutmeg or vanilla

Cook in unbaked pie crust. Makes 2 pies.

— Mrs. W. C. Fielden, Farley

Magic Lemon Filling Without Cooking:

1 1/3 c. Eagle Brand sweetened milk; ½ c. lemon juice; grated rind of 1 lemon or ¼ t. lemon extract. 2 eggs, separated; 2 T. sugar. Baked 8" pie shell. Blend Eagle Brand sweetened condensed milk, lemon juice, grated lemon rind or lemon extract and egg yolks. Pour into baked pie shell. Cover with meringue, made by beating egg whites until foamy, then adding sugar, gradually, beating until stiff. Bake in moderate oven 350 degrees ten minutes or until brown. Chill.

— Mrs. W. M. Coleman, Farley

Orange Filling:

5 egg yolks, beaten light	Juice of ½ lemon
½ c. sugar	5 T. orange juice
lump butter size of small egg	Grated rind of orange

Cook in double boiler until thick.

— Mrs. E. B. Majors, Raton

Cream Pie:

1 ¾ c. sweet milk   ¼ t. salt
¼ c. sweet cream   4 T. flour
½ c. sugar   ½ t. vanilla
2 eggs

Place milk in double boiler, scald. Beat egg yolks, add flour, sugar and salt which has been mixed together with cream. Add to milk and cook until mixture is thick, stirring occasionally. Then remove from fire, add vanilla and beat until smooth. Pour in baked pie shell. Cover with meringue. Bake in hot oven until brown. Makes one 9" pie.

— Mrs. Urma Burton, Abbott

Pineapple Cream Pie:

Use the recipe for cream pie, using pineapple juice for part of milk. Add 2 T. more flour, omitting vanilla. Add pineapple from No. 1 can crushed pineapple.

— Mrs. Urma Burton, Abbott

Lemon Chiffon Pie:

1 T. gelatin   1 c. sugar
¼ c. cold water   ¼ t. salt
6 T. lemon juice   4 eggs
½ grated lemon rind   ½ t. vanilla

Blend gelatin and water. Beat egg yolks, one half of sugar, lemon juice, rind and salt. Cook until thick. Stir in gelatin, mix well, cool, stir in stiffly beaten egg whites with remains of sugar and vanilla. Pour into baked pastry shell.

— Mrs. Lillie Foree, Kiowa Club

Sour Cream Pie:

1 c. white Karo syrup 1 c. sour cream
½ t. cinnamon   ⅛ t. salt
½ t. cloves   2 T. vinegar
2 eggs   1 c. raisins

Beat the eggs, mix syrup and spices and add to the eggs; then add the raisins, salt and vinegar. Beat well. Pour into the raw crust and bake at 350 degrees F. until an inserted knife comes out clean.

— Mrs. Lillie Foree, Kiowa Club

Fool Proof Pie Crust:

3 c. flour   1 c. lard or shortening
1 t. salt   2/3 c. cold water

Cream flour, salt and lard together until soft and creamy. Add water and work until soft and creamy again and doesn't stick to your hands. Use immediatly or store in refrigerator. Will keep several weeks in refrigrator.

— Mrs. J. D. Cheney, Springer

Pickles, Relishes and Preserves

Celery Relish:

1 qt. celery, chopped	1 t. salt
1 c. white onions, chopped	2 c. vinegar
2 large red peppers	½ c. sugar
2 large green peppers	1 t. pepper

Let vegetables and salt stand 30 minutes. Add other ingredients and pack in sterilized jars and seal.

— Mrs. Jo McKee, Springer

Cranberry Apple Relish:

1 qt. cranberries	1 c. sugar
2 c. apples	

Grind cranberries and apples and add sugar. Delicious with fowl or lamb. — Mrs. Kathryn Smith, Springer

Fresh Garden Relish:

1 lb. cabbage (12 c. chopped)	12 small onions
6 green peppers	10 medium carrots
2 sweet red peppers	

Force ingredients through food chopper. Add ½ c. salt and let stand 2 hours. Drain thoroughly and add:

6 c. vinegar	1 T. celery seed
6 c. sugar	Pack in sterilized jars and seal.
1 T. mustard seed	

— Mrs. Jo McKee, Springer

Uncooked Mixed Relish:

9 green sweet peppers	7 red peppers
8 onions	8 carrots
2 medium cabbage	

Grind all together and pour ½ c. salt over all and let stand 3 or 4 hours. Then drain through sack, squeezing dry. Add 3 pints vinegar, 2 t. mustard seed, 2 pints sugar and 2 t. celery seed. Seal without cooking. Good to eat in about 10 days.

— Mrs. Lee Glasgow, Farley

Bread and Butter Pickles:

4 qts. cucumbers, sliced thin   8 small onions, sliced thin

Mix all together with 1 qt. ice cubes and ½ c. salt. Let stand 3 hours. Drain well and have prepared 5 c. vinegar, 1½ t. turmeric powder, 5 c. sugar, 2 T. mustard seed, 1 t. celery salt. Cook slowly but not boil. Seal hot. — Mrs. Steele, Colmor

"Down Cellar"

See the boxes of potatoes,
See the jars of canned tomatoes,
See the rows and rows of berries,
Peaches, plums and bright red cherries,
Pickles sour and pickles sweet,
Piles of apples — good to eat —

Catsup, jam and marmalade.
  When the garden things were here
In the summer of the year,
  Crocks of lard and jars of meat
And other things we used to eat —
  Makes me glad there's food for all
In rows around the cellar wall.

Chunk Pickles:

7 lbs. cucumbers, soaked in salt water strong enough to float an egg. Soak 3 days. Take from brine and soak in clear water for 3 days, changing water each day. Cut into chunks, put into 2 qts. water, 1 qt. vinegar and alum the size of a walnut. Simmer for 2 hours. Take out and drain well. Boil the following for 3 minutes: 3 lbs. sugar, 1 ounce celery seed, 1 ounce whole allspice, 1 ounce stick cinnamon and 3 pints vinegar. Fill jars with the hot cucumbers, cover with the hot spiced vinegar and seal while hot. — Mrs. George Shultz, Miami

Chunk Pickles (sweet)

Cut medium cucumbers in chunks. Soak in brine (to float an egg) for 3 days. Drain and leave in clean water 3 days. Drain again, then cover with the following solution 3 days: ½ pt. vinegar, 1 t. alum, 2 c. sugar. Simmer pickles 30 minutes. Reheat solution each day for 3 days. Discard last solution, pour over pickles 3 pints vinegar, 2½ pts. sugar and 3 t. pickling spices. Store in jars. Cover well. Do not have to be sealed.

— Mrs. Fred Koehler, Raton

Dill Pickles:

12 c. water   1 c. vinegar
1 c. salt
Bring to boil. Wash dill and put in jar. Wash cucumbers and add to jar. Pour in boiling solution and seal.

— Mrs. W. P. Rogers, Springer

Dill Pickles:

Place medium sized cucumbers in clear water, for two hours. For solution, add one quart vinegar to one gallon water. Add one cup salt to vinegar and water solution and bring to a boil. Place cucumbers in sterilized jars. Place cucumbers in jars and pour hot solution over them and seal. Add dill and some garlic if desired. — Ella Gillespie, Colmor

Dill Pickles in Jars:

Pack pickles into jars and pour over the following: ½ gal. water, 1 c. vinegar, ½ c. salt and dill. Mix water and vinegar and salt and pour over the pickles cold. Seal. Set away to ferment. This is enough brine for 6 quarts.

— Mrs. Charlie Bada, Jr., Springer

Heinz Sweet Pickles:

Wash cucumbers and put in stone jar in brine (1 pt. salt to 1 gal. water). Let stand 5 days, then wash off brine with water and drain. Then cover with boiling hot alum water (1 scant T of alum to 1 gal. water). Let stand 24 hrs. Wash and drain. Split each pickle and again cover with alum water. Let stand 24 hours, wash and cover with the following:

5 pts. vinegar, 5 pts. sugar, ½ c. celery seed and mixed spices to suit taste. Drain each morning for 3 mornings and reheat vinegar etc. Add 1 c. sugar each morning and can the third morning.

— Mrs. Lee Glasgow, Farley
— Mrs. Charlie Bada, Jr., Springer

Ice Box Pickles (sweet):

Use fresh cucumbers, preferably small ones. However, large ones may be sliced the round way and do nicely. Bring to a boil brine that will float an egg. Let cool. Pour brine over cucumbers and let stand 10 to 15 days. Remove from brine, cover with cold water and let stand 24 hrs. Cut in pieces ½" thick. Cover with alum water, made with 2 t. powdered alum to 1 qt. water and bring slowly to a boil. Let stand 2 hrs. Drain. Cover with ice and allow to stand until thoroughly chilled. Boil syrup five minutes and pickles and boil gently for eight minutes. Pour off syrup and bring it to a boil and pour it back on the pickles every day for three days. The third day pack cucumbers in jars and seal. These pickles keep nicely in a stone jar not sealed.

For the Syrup: 1 pt. sugar, 1 pt. vinegar, 1½ T. whole cloves, 2 sticks cinnamon, 2 T. powdered cinnamon. Tie spices in a cloth. Make as many recipes of the syrup as necessary to cover the pickles and add an extra pint of sugar.

— Mrs. Harry Smith, Springer

Mustard Pickles:

1 qt. large cucumbers, cubed	coarse
1 qt. small cucumbers, whole	2 red sweet peppers, chopped
1 qt. silver skilled small o-	fine
nions	1 large cauliflower broken in
1 qt. green tomatoes, chopped	small pieces

Wash vegetables, cover with brine solution of 1 qt. water and ½ c. salt; let stand 24 hours. Bring to boil in same solution. Drain and make following dressing:

6 T. powdered mustard	2 c. sugar
1 T. turmeric	2 qts. vinegar
1 c. flour	

Mix thoroughly and cook until thick. Stir in pickles, heat thoroughly. Empty into sterilized glass jars; seal. Makes 6 quarts.

— Mrs. Morris McConnell, Springer

Sweet Dill Pickles:

1 gallon dill size cucumbers	2 T. salt
3 c. sugar	2 T. dill seed
1 qt. vinegar	2 T. mustard seed

Combine and let come to a boil. Add cucumbers; let simmer until heated well, but do not boil. Seal.

— Mrs. Sam Pompeo, Maxwell
— Mrs. M. E. Hardway, Maxwell

Seven Day Pickles:

Put cucumbers, preferably about 3" long in stone jar or enameled container. Pour boiling water over them every day for six days. Add salt 7th day to take care of freshness, 8 th day, cut in chunks, put in jars, drain what liquid may form in jars, then cover with syrup. Proportions as follows: 1 c. vinegar, ¼ t. turmeric, 1 t. celery seed, 2 c. sugar, 1 t. mustard seed.

— Mrs. H. A. McConnell, Springer

Spiced Pickles:

Wash medium sized cucumbers and slice about 1" thick. Mix 1 c. vinegar, 1 c. sugar, ½ t. salt, ½ t. mustard seed, ½ t. celery salt or seed, ½ t. turmeric and bring to boil. Add cucumbers and put in jars. Add whole cloves and cinnamon sticks in small amount. Seal.

— Mrs. J. M. McCallister, Colmor

Split Pickles:

Soak cucumbers in salt water: 1 pt. salt to 1 gal. boiling water for 1 week or as long as you like; drain and cover with alum solution. 2 T. powdered alum to 1 gal. boiling water. Let stand 24 hours. Then drain and cover with fresh alum solution and let stand 24 hrs. Drain and cover with syrup, using 1 c. sugar and 1 c. vinegar. Bring to a boil and cover pickles, let stand 24 hrs. Drain and reheat and cover and let stand 24 hrs. Then drain off and add the same amount of sugar. Bring to a boil and cover pickles. You may seal or leave in open crocks. Add pickling spices, 1 t. to gallon pickles. These pickles must be split. The best time is after the first alum solution.

— Mrs. Zenas Curtis, Cimarron

Sweet Pickles:

Cut cucumbers in chunks and soak in salt water for 3 days. (brine strong enough to hold up an egg). Then put in clear water for 3 days. Make a solution of ½ pt. vinegar, 1 T. alum and enough water to cover pickles. Simmer pickles for 30 min. (do not let boil). Drain. Take: 3 pts. vinegar, 2½ lbs. sugar and ½ box pickling spices. Heat and pour over pickles next day heat solution. Do this for three days, then seal.

— Mary Moore, Raton

Sweet Pickles:

Soak 2 gal. of cucumbers in brine that will soak an egg for 1 week. Drain. Cover with boiling water and let stand 24 hrs. Drain. Soak 24 hrs. in water with a piece of alum size of a walnut. Drain. Cover with boiling water and let cool. (split each cucumber) Heat 2½ qts. good vinegar, 4 c. sugar, 1 T. celery seed, 2 T. mixed spices and piece of cinnamon bark and pour over pickles. Heat for 3 successive mornings the vinegar solution and each morning add 1 more cup sugar. Seal or not as desired. Will keep indefinitely in stone jar.

— Mrs. Hazel House, Capulin

Strawberry Preserves:

Take 4 c. strawberries which have been washed and hulled and 5 c. sugar. Place 1 c. of berries in a heavy saucepan and cover with 1 c. sugar and continue until all of the berries and sugar have been placed in the saucepan layer by layer. Bring slowly to a boil and boil gently for 9 minutes. Remove from fire and add 3 T. lemon juice. Let stand over night. Next day bring to a boil and let boil gently an additional 9 minutes. Remove from fire, skim and let stand in saucepan until thoroly cold, then seal in hot sterilized jars. The berries remain whole and retain their natural flavor and color.

— Mrs. Leon Johnson, Johnson Mesa

Pickled Beets, Carrots or Cauliflower:

Cook small vegetables until tender. Cold dip and slip skins off beets. Make a pickling syrup of 2 c. sugar, 2 c. water, 2 c. vinegar, 1 lemon sliced thin, 1 T. cinnamon, 1 t. cloves, 1 t. allspice. Tie spices in a cloth or omit them and lemon. Cover mixture and simmer 15 minutes. Seal.

— Mrs. Mary Kulhman, Springer

Pickled Beets:

2 c. water to 1 c. and a little over of vinegar
1 c. sugar

Fix what amount you think it will take to cover your beets and let it come to a boil. Then put in your beets which have been boiled and peeled, and let boil up again. Put in jars and seal while hot.

— Mrs. I. W. Williams, Chico

Apple and Pineapple Jam:

Grind 3 gallons of apples and add 1 gallon of crushed pineapple and half as much sugar as fruit. Bake in the oven.

— Mrs. Alvin Rickels, Chico, New Mex.

Salads

Apple and Carrot Salad:

4 large apples	½ t. salt
4 medium carrots	1 T. sugar
1 c. raisins	Salad dressing

Grate apples and carrots, add raisins that have been softened in boiling water. Add salt and sugar and moisten with salad dressing. — Mrs. John T. Milliken, Capulin

Cabbage Slaw:

½ c. vinegar, 3 T. sugar, butter size of walnut, 1 egg beaten to a cream, ½ c. sweet milk, 2 T. flour. Bring vinegar with sugar and butter to a boil. Pour in milk, egg and flour beaten smooth and cook carefully until a thick custard. If it should curdle beat quickly with egg beater until smooth. Pour over finely cut cabbage. — Daisy Diver, Raton

Cranberry Salad:

2 c. cranberries, ground	1 pkg. lemon jello
1 1/3 c. sugar	½ c. hot water
2 large oranges	1 c. nut meats

Combine jello, hot water, sugar, ground cranberries and oranges, leaving rind on ½ orange, but peeling the rest. Add to jello. Add nuts. Chill until firm. — Mrs. Rose Gillespie, Raton

Cranberry Salad:

1 pkg. cherry jello	¾ c. celery
1 c. cranberry sauce	½ to ¾ c. nuts
1 c. shredded pineapple	

Make jello and when it begins to thicken, whip with egg beater. Add cranberry sauce, pineapple, celery and nuts.
— Marian Pinson, Capulin

Raw Cranberry Salad:

1 qt. fresh cranberries	¼ lb. marshmallows
1½ c. sugar	½ c. whipping cream
1 c. chopped nuts	1 c. chopped seeded fresh grapes

Run cranberries through food chopper. Put sugar on cranberries and let stand one or two hours. Put in colander and let drip for several hours (over night). Mix grapes, nuts and marshmallows which have been cut in small pieces with scissors with cranberries that have dripped. Set in cool place and add whipped cream just before serving. — Mrs. Florence Patterson, Abbott

Cabbage Salad:

1 small firm head of cabbage shredded or chopped	1 t. sugar
½ c. chopped walnut meats	Sprinkle lightly with cinnamon
salt to taste	Mix with four T. of dressing.

— Mrs. Henry Floyd, Johnson Mesa

100

Easter Salad:

1 pkg. lemon jello   Green fruit coloring
1 T. vinegar   6 eggs, hard boiled

Dissolve jello in boiling water. Add vinegar and enough of the green coloring to make an emerald green. Mold in a deep pan. Peel the eggs, cut in halves, take yolks and mash up. Add 1 T. mayonnaise, a little vinegar, salt and pepper and mustard, ½ t. Mix well and stuff the eggs. When the gelatin is cold, just ready to set, put 1 deviled egg for each square, place thin slices of stuffed olives around the eggs. Let set overnight. Cut one square with the egg, put on lettuce and place a spoon of mayonnaise on each to one, to one side letting it tumble off. This is a very pretty and appetizing salad.

Mrs. E. B. Majors, Raton

Frozen Salad:

Pack cans of fruit salad in freezing compartment of ice box 24 hrs. To open can, put a hot cloth, and then a cold one around can for 1 minute, after having taken top off can. Slice and serve on lettuce leaf.

— Daisy Diver, Raton

Fruit Salad:

1 pt. pineapple, drained and   2 bananas
   cut into small pieces   Mix fruit and pour sweet
1 pt. apricots, drained and cut   dressing over it
   into small pieces

— Mrs. Pittard, Capulin

Green Pepper and Cheese Salad:

A salad chuck full of vitamins. Three large green peppers, ½ lb. cream cheese, ¼ lb. chopped nuts, 1 T. minced parsley. Blend the cheese, nuts and parsley and stuff the peppers with the mixture. Chill thoroly and when ready to serve, slice in rounds with a sharp knife and arrange on beds of lettuce. Mayonnaise or French dressing may be served separately.

— Mrs. Jack George, Colmor

Little Pig Salad:

Take as many halves of pears as required for the table, one for each guest. Stick ½ of a blanched almond or pecan nut in the small end for ears, one whole clove for nose and tail. Arrange on a lettuce leaf on plate, 2 stalks of cooked asparagus and a strip of pimento. Now place your pig as if he were eating the asparagus. Dust with paprika and place a spoon of salad dressing to one side. A surprise for the guests and a very tasty salad.

— Mrs. E. B. Majors Raton

Macaroni Salad:

1 box macaroni. Cook in salty water until tender put in colander, pour cold water over them. Grate ¼ lb. yellow cheese, 4 hard boiled eggs, chopped fine, 2 small onions and can of pimentos mashed. Add salad dressing. Mix well.

— Mrs. T. J. Floyd, Johnson Mesa

Orange and Prune Salad:

Steam 1 lb. of prunes and when tender, let cool. Remove seeds and put on lettuce leaf with either sliced oranges or the cloves of the orange. Put a little salad dressing and sprinkle grated cheese or shredded coconut on top. Makes a pretty appetizing salad.

— Mrs. G. Drury, Eagle Nest

Overnite Salad:

1 No. 2 can Queen Anne cherries or grapes
3 c. pineapple tidbits
1 c. blanched almonds or walnuts
2 c. marshmallows
1 c. cream, whipped

Remove seeds from cherries or grapes and combine pineapple, nuts and marshmallows. Next add a salad dressing, made as follows:

2 eggs, beaten, 1c. sugar into which has been blended 2 T. flour, 1½ c. liquid (juice from cherries and pineapple) Cook above ingredients until thick. After salad dressing has been blended with fruit mixture, add cream which has been whipped. Let stand in cool place 24 hours, stirring lightly 3 different times.
— Helen Jeffers, Farley

Party Potato Salad:

2½ c. diced hot cooked potatoes
2 t. grated onion
3 T. vinegar
2 T. salad oil
1¾ t. salt
1 pkg. lemon or lime jello
1¼ c. hot water
3 T. vinegar
dash of salt
5 T. mayonnaise
½ c. diced cucumbers
¼ c. sliced radishes
½ c. chopped celery
2 T. green pepper strips

Combine potatoes, onion, vinegar, salad oil, salt, pepper. Let stand 25 min., stirring occasionally. Dissolve jello in hot water, add vinegar and salt. To 2|3 c. jello mixture, add 3 T. water. Turn into mold. Chill until syrupy. Arrange cucumber and radish slices in mixture. Chill until firm. Chill remaining jello until syrupy. Place in bowl on ice and whip with rotary beater until fluffy. Fold in mayonnaise, potato salad and other ingredients. Chill until firm. Garnish with lettuce and hard cooked deviled eggs.
— Mrs. Maurine Pettigrew, Mills

Salad:

1 c. ground cranberries   ½ c. nuts, chopped
1½ c. diced apples   mix with whipped cream
   Place in refrigerator for 1 hour.
                — Mrs. Mary E. Patterson, Cimarron

Vegetable Salad:

4 tomatoes   ½ onion, minced
1 cucumber   ¼ cabbage, shredded
1 green pepper   Salt
1 stalk celery   Pepper
3 radishes, sliced   Mayonnaise
   Peel and slice tomatoes and cucumbers. Cut pepper and celery into ¼" pieces. Mix all ingredients together. Serve with mayonnaise in bowl lined with lettuce.

Spinach Salad:

   Take about 1 lb. of young spinach crisp cut fine. Cut up three hard boiled eggs, 1 small can pimentoes, 1 green sweet pepper and 3 pieces celery and mix salad with salad dressing and chill.
                — Mrs. T. J. Floyd, Johnson Mesa

Tomato Aspic Salad:

   2 c. tomato juice, 1 bay leaf, dash nutmeg and 3 or 4 whole cloves. Let come to a good boil. Strain and pour over 1 pkg Lemon jello. Stir well, add 1 T. vinegar. When cold, but not set, put into individual molds, placing 3 shrimps in the mold. If you use Mary Ann molds, after unmolding to serve, place the salad dressing in the depression the mold makes. Dress it up with slices of avocado or artichoke hearts. This is such a pretty salad. To make a Christmas salad of this, make another thick mold of lime jello and cut or mold in small cylinders and one in the depression. This gives the red and green and builds it up in the center. Place dressing over top, so it will run down on side.
                — Mrs. E. B. Majors, Raton

Turnip Slaw:

   Grate the desired amount of raw turnips, using a coarse grated blade, in a salad bowl. Sprinkle with 1 t. sugar and salt and pepper to taste. Moisten with Miracle Whip or any good salad dressing.
                — Mrs. John T. Milliken, Capulin

Vegetable Salad:

1 pkg. jello (lemon or lime)   1 medium carrot, shredded
1 c. shredded cabbage   1 tart apple, shredded
   Mix jello, add other ingredients and chill. Will serve six.
                — Mrs. Mary Powell, Gladstone

Cooked Salad Dressing:

1 t. salt	2 eggs or 3 yolks
¾ t. dry mustard	2 T. butter
2 T. sugar	¾ c. water
2 T. flour	½ c. mild vinegar

Mix dry ingredients. Beat eggs thoroughly, add vinegar and water and beat again. Combine with dry ingredients and cook over hot water until thick and smooth, stirring constantly. Add butter and cool. When serving, thin with plain or whipped cream.

— Mrs. John T. Milliken, Capulin

Salad Dressing:

Heat 7 T. vinegar. Take off fire, add 1 box of marshmallows. Beat well and set aside to cool. Pour vinegar and marshmallows into 1 pt. cream that has been whipped. Add nuts. Serve on slices of frozen salad.

— Daisy Diver, Raton

Mayonnaise:

½ T. flour	¼ c. cream
½ c. sugar	1 egg
¼ t. salt	¾ c. vinegar
½ t. mustard (dry or prepared)	butter

Sift dry ingredients and mix with cream. Add egg and beat, then add vinegar and butter and boil.

— Mrs. Faye Crawford, Springer

Russian Salad Dressing:

3 T. flour	2 egg yolks
2 T. dry mustard	½ c. milk
½ t. salt	2 egg whites
1 T. sugar	½ c. vinegar

In top of double boiler, mix flour, mustard, sugar and salt. Beat egg yolks slightly, add milk and beat into flour mixture until smooth. Add vinegar and cook until it thickens. Beat egg whites stiff and fold into dressing. Place in jar and keep cool. It will keep for several days. If too thick, thin with cream.

— Mrs. Fred Floyd, Johnson Mesa

Salad Dressing:

Cut 2 cloves of garlic	1/3 c. vinegar
¾ c. catsup	4 T. sugar
¾ c. salad oil	dash of paprika

— Mrs. J. H. Steele, Colmor

Salad Dressing for Fruit Salad:

½ c. milk   ¼ c. vinegar
1 egg   1/3 c. sugar
1 T. flour   Salt to taste
    Cook until thick and add 1 T. butter.

                 — Mrs. Kathryn Smith, Springer

Sweet Dressing:

1 c. sugar   1 well beaten egg
1 c. sweet cream   pinch of salt
    Cook until thick, cool and pour over fruit.

                 — Mrs. Pittard, Capulin

Sandwiches

Baked Sandwiches:

2 3 oz. cans of ham or liver   1 can condensed tomato soup
8 slices enriched bread   ½ c. milk
1 c. condensed mushroom soup
  Spread ham or liver on 4 slices of the bread and cover with the remaining bread. Place sandwiches in a shallow greased casserole, pour soup which has been diluted with milk over sandwiches and bake in a moderate oven 350 degrees for 30 minutes.
         — Mrs. Grayson, Cimarron

Broiled Meat Sandwiches:

1¾ lbs. lean beef   1½ t. salt and black pepper
1 egg   Red pepper and onion seasoning
1 T. butter   mustard to taste
  Grind meat through chopper real fine. Add beaten egg, melted butter and seasoning. Spread sandwich bread with creamed butter. Cover one side with meat mixture. Cook open sandwich under broiler. Cover with piece of buttered bread. Toast to a light brown. Turn, toast bread on other side. Cut in diagonal pieces. Serve on hot plate.   — Brooks Rucker, Abbott

Egg Sandwiches:

6 hard cooked eggs (boiled)   Mustard and mayonnaise to
dash of salt and pepper   make a smooth paste
  Put hard boiled eggs through ricer. Add the salt and pepper, then mix with mustard and mayonnaise and spread between whole wheat or white bread.
         — Brooks Rucker, Abbott

Fruit Sandwich Filling:

  1 c. figs and 1 c. hot water cooked to a paste. Add 1 T. lemon juice and cool. Spread on bread and dust with chopped nuts.

Ham Sandwiches:

  Make sandwiches of whole wheat bread. Spread with canned deviled ham and horse radish mustard. Dip in:
1 c. milk and 2 eggs. Brown both sides on griddle.
         — Mrs. Grayson, Cimarron

Picnic Sandwiches:

Crisp bacon   Ripe banana
Whole wheat bread   Peanut butter
  Cut crisp bacon fine, add mashed ripe banana. Butter thin slices of bread, spread one side with peanut butter. Add banana-bacon mixture. Cover with slices of bread. Spread top with butter and toast.   — Brooks Rucker, Abbott

Pinwheel Sandwiches:

Remove crusts from loaf unsliced bread. Cut in thin lengthwise slices. Soften cream cheese, tint pink, green or yellow with vegetable coloring. Spread on bread slices; roll up jelly-roll fashion. Wrap in waxed paper. Cover with damp towel. Chill thoroughly. Cut in thin slices.

Sandwiches:

Cook prunes until very soft. Fry bacon very crisp. Grind together. Moisten with salad dressing and spread on whole wheat bread.

— Daisy Diver, Raton

Sandwich Spread:

1 pint green tomatoes   ½ c. water
4 sweet green and red peppers   2 t. salt

Put all through food chopper. Let stand a few minutes, then simmer 15 minutes. Drain. Add ¾ c. sugar (can be omitted) ½ c. sour cream, ½ c. vinegar, 3 eggs (beaten), 2 t. flour, 1 t. powdered mustard and 1 gallon sweet pickles. Add altogether, cook until thick, about 30 minutes. Seal in glass jars.

— Mrs. Lonnie Hoy, Maxwell

Victory Sandwich:

2 med. sliced carrots   ½ c. chopped nuts
10 stuffed olives   2 T. mayonnaise
¾ c. chopped raisins

Clean and scrape the carrots. Run through food chopper, together with the olives and raisins. Add nuts mixed with mayonnaise and mix well. Use as a spread on dark bread with crisp lettuce. It is best to be used right away, but can be kept in a covered jar in refrigerator.

— Brooks Rucker, Abbott

Sauces

Barbeque Sauce:

½ c. ground onions
¼ c. ground green peppers
2 c. tomatoes, cut up fine
¼ c. water
2 T. catsup
2 T. Worcestershire sauce
½ T. vinegar
1 t. onion salt
1 t. nutmeg

½ T. brown sugar
1 t. Salt
½ t. black pepper
1 t. chili pepper
3 bay leaves
1 t. paprika
1 t. dry mustard
1 t. garlic salt
½ t. cloves

Mix all and let simmer for one hour. Taste and if too strong, add more water. Cover almost any kind of meat and cook. Gives a grand flavor.

— Mrs. E. B. Majors, Raton

Catsup:

Wash and cut into pieces 1 bu. ripe tomatoes and 1 doz. medium sized onions. Cook tomatoes and onions together until soft, then press through a sieve. Let stand overnight and then pour off the clear liquid that comes to the top. Place the remaining tomato pulp in large kettle and add the following: 2½ qts. sugar, 2 qts. cider vinegar (save out 1 c. and add when catsup is partly cooked down) 2 t. red pepper, 4 T. salt, 1 t. mixed pickling spices, 1 t. cinnamon, 1 t. cloves, 1 t. mustard, 1 t. celery seed, 1 t. allspice. Tie spices in small bag and add to tomato pulp. Boil slowly until thick, stirring occasionally. Remove spice bag and seal catsup in hot sterilized jars. (makes 15 pts.).

— Mrs. Geo. Shultz, Miami

Meat Sauce for Spaghetti or Macaroni:

½ c. oil, 1 lb. beef stew meat, cut in small pieces, 1 large onion, chopped; 1 clove garlic cut fine; 1 T. chili powder, ¼ t. each of marjoram, thyme and allspice; 3 bay leaves; 1 large No. 2½ can of tomatoes; salt and pepper; 1 large can of mushrooms with liquid; 1 small can of ripe olives with liquid; ½ to 1 lb. of uncooked spaghetti; grated parmesan cheese. Heat the oil in a large frying pan or dutch oven and in it brown the cubes of meat nicely, (they may be rolled in flour first, if you wish). When browned, add the minced onion and garlic, the spices, tomatoes and salt and pepper to taste. Let cook 2 or 3 hours, adding water as needed. When the meat is tender, add the liquid from the mushrooms, ripe olives, plus enough more water to make about 1 to 1½ qts. sauce. Thicken slightly with flour and water paste. Add the mushrooms and olives, heat thoroughly again. Cook the spaghetti tender in plenty of boiling salted water, about 20 minutes. Drain, turn into a deep platter, pour the sauce over it and serve passing a bowl of grated parmesan cheese. The meat sauce as described may be stretched to be sufficient for a lb. of spaghetti, serving 8 or 10 generously, or it can be cooked down into a thicker, richer sauce for ½ lb. of spaghetti, serving 4 or 5.

— Mrs. Rose L. Gillespie, Raton

Tarragon Vinegar:

Tarragon before it blooms, fill jar with tarragon mashed. Cover with vinegar, let stand 4 weeks. Drain. Strain and bottle. (Mint can be used the same way).

— Mrs. Ruth Wilferth, Springer

Tartar Sauce for Fish:

½ c. mayonnaise
2 T. dill pickles, grated
1 T. grated onion

1 T. minced parsley
lemon juice or vinegar to taste

— Mrs. Ruth Wilferth, Springer

Ten Minute Cranberry Sauce:

1 qt. cranberries (4 c.)
2 c. water

1½ to 2 c. sugar

Boil sugar and water together five minutes, add cranberries and boil without stirring five minutes, until all skins pop open. Remove from the fire when the popping stops and allow the sauce to remain in the vessel undisturbed until cool.

— Mrs. Davida Ross, Raton

Soups

"The turnpike road to people's
hearts we find,
Lies thru their mouths, or we
mistake mankind."

Peanut Butter Soup:

Place a quart milk in sauce pan, heat until nearly boiling.
While it is coming to boiling point, add 2 T. (heaping) peanut
butter, pinch salt, amounting to ⅛ t. Dissolve peanut butter in
milk by leaving on stove for few minutes longer and cooking at
boiling point. Serve with crackers.

— Mrs. Urma Burton, Abbott

Vegetables

Asparagus:

Cook asparagus until tender. Put in shallow dish, top with sliced hard boiled eggs and cover with cooked dressing.

— Mrs. T. J. Floyd, Johnson Mesa

Asparagus Au Gratin:

2 lbs. asparagus (cooked)
2 sliced hardboiled eggs
¼ lb. ground cheese
salt
1½ c. white sauce
paprika

Alternate layers of asparagus, sliced eggs and ground cheese. Pour over this the thick white sauce which have been well salted. Top with a little more grated cheese and sprinkle with paprika. Bake in moderate oven 20 to 30 minutes.

— Janet Bartlett, Eagle Nest

Beanburgers:

1 c. beans
½ c. dry bread crumbs
Salt
Pepper
½ c. grated raw carrots
1 onion, chopped

Mash cooked beans in bowl, add remaining ingredients with additional sauce from beans, if necessary, to moisten. Shape into "burgers." Then coat with extra bread crumbs and saute to a delicate brown. If you wish to substitute with sausage, add about ½ t. sage or poultry seasoning.

— Mrs. C. U. Burris, Miami

Beets in Jelly:

4 T. sugar
½ c. vinegar
3 t. cornstarch
½ c. water in which beets were cooked

Mix sugar and cornstarch; add vinegar and water and cook until thick, stirring constantly. Add a lump of butter and pour over beets.

— Mrs. Geo. Abdalla, Springer

Cauliflower Mexican:

1 medium head cooked cauliflower
1 t. salt
Few grains pepper
No. 2 can tomatoes
1 c. grated American cheese
Soft bread crumbs
Butter or margarine

Place cauliflower in greased casserole. Add salt and pepper to tomatoes. Cook rapidly until most of liquid has evaporated. Pour over cauliflower. Top with cheese and crumbs. Dot with butter. Bake in moderate oven 15 minutes.

— Mrs. Maurine Pettigrew, Mills

Celery Beans:

1 qt. navy beans, 1 qt. can tomatoes or tomato soup, 1 small onion, chopped fine, 2/3 c. molasses, ½ c. sugar, ½ c. vinegar, 1 t. cinnamon, 1 T. celery salt or 1 c. chopped fine celery. Salt and pepper to suit and 1 t. mustard. Soak beans overnight in water in which 1 t. soda has been dissolved. Next morning, drain and cook until tender in clear water. Add all ingredients and bake two or three hours. After putting slices of uncooked bacon over top, add water as needed.　　　　　— Mrs. Dow, Colmor

Cheese and Corn Souffle:

2 T. fat	1 c. grated cheese
4 T. flour	3 eggs
2 c. milk	1 c. corn cut from cob or canned
½ t. salt	1¼ T. green pepper or pimientos
¼ t. paprika	cut fine

Melt butter, add flour, salt, paprika and mix well. Add milk slowly and constantly. Remove from fire, stir in cheese. When melted, add egg yolks well beaten, corn and chopped pepper. Beat egg whites and fold into mixture. Put into well greased baking dish and bake in pan of hot water in a moderate oven 45 to 50 minutes, until firm. The pepper may be omitted if desired. If can corn is used drain off liquid, measure and decrease milk by that amount. This makes 6 servings.

　　　　　— Mrs. Pope Gossett, Raton

Chili Con Carne and Green Beans:

1 pt. green beans	½ lb. chili con carne

Pour green beans into a greased baking dish. These may be canned or freshly cooked. Over the beans pour the chili con carne and bake a few minutes.

　　　　　— Mrs. Pleasant Smith, Springer

Colorado Brown Beans:

Put a layer of brown beans and mince 1 T. onion. Repeat layers. Top with bacon or ham and pour sweet milk to cover. Simmer in oven 1 hour.　　　　　— Mrs. Jennie Gleaves, Cimarron

Corn and Oyster Casserole:

1 No. 2 can corn	Pepper
1 small can oysters	Butter
Cracker crumbs	Milk or cream
Salt	

Arrange a layer of corn and a layer of oysters in casserole, using half of each. Sprinkle with cracker crumbs, salt, pepper and dot generously with butter. Repeat each layer. Moisten with milk or cream poured over the top. Bake in a moderate oven until brown.　　　　　— Mrs. O. A. Cook, Capulin

Corn and Tomatoes:

1 pt. corn
2 T. green pepper
2 T. meat fryings

1 pt. tomatoes
1 small onion, sliced

Put in baking dish and cover with bread crumbs and bake one hour. — Mrs. Pleasant Smith, Springer

Egg Plant Columbia:

1 small egg plant
1¾ c. medium white sauce

¾ c. chopped ripe olives
½ c. grated American cheese

Pare eggplant, quarter, cover with boiling salted water. Cover. Boil 15 min. Combine sauce and olives, pour over egg plant, top with cheese. Bake in moderate oven 10 minutes.
— Mrs. Maurine Pettigrew, Mills

Fried Carrots:

Wash carrots clean. Slice lengthwise. Boil. While still firm strain off water and let dry. Roll in a beaten egg, then cracker crumbs. Fry until cooked and brown.
— Mrs. Walden Ingram, Springer

Harvest Beets:

1 qt. beets
½ c. sugar
1 T. cornstarch

½ t. salt
½ c. vinegar
2 T. butter

Let boil 5 minutes and add beets. Let stand for few minutes to absorb flavor
— Frances Towndrow, Raton

Hominy:

Dissolve 10 scant T. of lye in 6 qts. water. Stir in 5 qts. corn, preferably white, and let stand for 15 hours. (Use stone jar for this soaking, if possible; do not use aluminum.) Pour off the lye water and discard, preferably pouring it on to bare ground and add fresh water to wash the grain thoroughly. (In washing some of the hulls will be removed, but if all are not loosened, pour the corn into bleached flour sack and rub between hands. Then rinse again.) By this time, black tips and hulls should be off and the kernel should look clean. Soak in water to which a little salt has been added to remove any discoloration that the lye may have caused. Then boil in covered kettle for 3 or 4 hours or until thoroughly cooked, making sure that the grain remains covered, with water during the cooking. Change water 2 times during the process of cooking. Five quarts of corn will make 15 to 20 quarts of hominy. Hominy will keep well in an open covered container, if kept very cold (near freezing point).
— Mrs. Walden Ingram, Springer

Italian Spaghetti:

1½ lb. beef
2 small pieces garlic
1 small onion
1 can tomato paste

1 small can tomatoes
½ c. grated cheese
salt to taste
Spaghetti

Brown beef, chopped in small pieces, add garlic and onions and brown. Add tomato paste and tomatoes with a cup or so of water. Simmer until it is about as thick as tomato catsup. Cook spaghetti, until tender in salted water. Drain. Pour cheese over spaghetti, then add the sauce. A pinch of allspice may be added if desired.

— Mrs. Viola Munden, Capulin

Italian Spaghetti:

½ c. butter or shortening
1 can tomato paste
1 onion

1 clove garlic
cheese of desired flavor
spaghetti

Brown onions and garlic in butter. Add tomato paste and e-nough water to keep it from burning. Simmer for several hours. Cook spaghetti. Strain the sauce and all. Sprinkle with cheese and bake in oven until flavor is blended.

— Mrs. John Floyd, Farley

Left Overs Pie:

1 c. chili con carne
1 c. carrots
1 c. green beans
1 c. tomatoes

2 c. diced potatoes
½ c. diced onion
salt
pepper

Cover with a rich biscuit dough and bake until potatoes and onions are done and crust is brown.

— Mrs. Flake Fisher, Abbott

One Meal Altogether:

1 lb. steak
2 carrot tops

1 lb. salt pork
1 onion

Grind altogether and fry. Add 1 can tomato sauce. Cook one pack of noodles and drain. Put the meat sauce over and add grated cheese and serve hot.

— Mrs. Al Richardson, Cimarron

One Dish Meal:

1 lb. hamburger	1 green pepper or chile
2 T. fat	2 c. corn
2 c. tomatoes or paste	salt

Carrots and rice may be added. Cook rice and carrots before adding. Fry onion and pepper in fat to light brown. Remove from fat, add hamburger, fry until brown. Place in bake dish in layers with other ingredients until dish is full. Cover with crumbs. Bake ½ hour. Do not cook to dry as rice thickens. Omit rice and carrots if you do not care for them. — Mrs. Rinehart, Colmor

Five Layer Vegetable Dish:

1 c. potatoes	1 c. sweet peppers
1 c. onions	Hamburger meat or other
1 c. tomatoes	ground meat

Place potatoes in bottom of casserole. Add layer of onions, then tomatoes, next peppers. Cover the whole with the meat.
— Mrs. John Anderson, Abbott

Six Layer Dinner:

Place in buttered casserole:

Layer of rice	Layer of diced potatoes
Layer of carrots, diced	Layer of hamburger (1 lb.)
Layer of chopped onion	

Over this pour 1 large can tomatoes that have been run through strainer. — Mrs. Mae Burnette, Colmor

Minted Carrots:

Cook carrots until done. Then remove and turn over and over in 2 T. granulated sugar and just a little bit of dried mint.
— Francis Towndrow, Raton

Scalloped Corn:

When canning corn, put about 2 T. of ground green sweet peppers to each can of corn. Scallop as usual.
— Mrs. Pleasant Smith, Springer

Something Good:

Take yellow summer squash and okra. Cube squash and slice the okra into mixing bowl. Add salt. Sift corn meal over contents, mixing thoroughly. Have grease hot and add squash and okra. Cook until done and brown. If okra is omitted, add a little sugar to the squash and cook as above.
— Mrs. Otto Carr, Des Moines

Squash Souffle:

3 slices bread crumbs	1 t. salt
2 eggs	1 T. sugar
5 T. butter	1 white onion
1½ lbs. yellow squash	

Cook squash and onion together until done. Beat egg whites

stiff, blending in the sugar. Use beater to whip squash mixture smooth. Add egg yolks, salt, bread crumbs and part of melted butter. Fold in egg whites and pour mixture into buttered casserole. Use rest of butter to lightly brown 2 or 3 T. bread crumbs. Spread these lightly over the top and cook in moderate oven 30 to 40 minutes.   — Janet Bartlett, Eagle Nest

Stuffed Cabbage:

1 medium onion
1 medium head cabbage
6 strips bacon
1 lb. ground meat

1 t. salt
few grains pepper
3 T. catsup
¼ t. Worcestershire sauce

Cover cabbage with large amount of boiling water; boil 30 min. Drain, cool. Carefully remove center. Mince onion. Dice 2 strips bacon. Cook together until brown. Add meat. Cook 5 minutes. Add salt, pepper, catsup and Worcestershire sauce; stuff cabbage. Place in greased baking dish. Cover. Bake in moderate oven 35 minutes. Fry remaining bacon. Use to garnish.
                          — Mrs. Maurine Pettigrew, Mills

Stuffed Celery:

Prepare celery stalks (well curved stalks stuff better). Mix ½ c. cheese with 2 T. cream (or mayonnaise), 6 or 8 chopped olives and ½ c. broken nutmeats. Mix well and fill celery stalks. Chill until served.
                          — Mrs. Tom Novinger, Springer

Succotash:

Ten ears green corn, 1 pt. lima beans; Cut the corn from the cob and stew gently with beans until tender. Use as little water as possible. Season with butter, salt and pepper. Milk also if you choose.
                          — Mrs. Kapp, Colmor

Sweet Potatoes and Apples:

2 lbs. sweet potatoes
6 apples
½ lb. sugar
2 T. sausage drippings

¼ c. water
1 t. salt
1 t. nutmeg

Cook potatoes and peel. Cut in slices ½" thick, lengthwise. Alternate in casserole with layers of peeled, sliced apples. Season each layer with sugar, salt and nutmeg. Pour over drippings (or sausage patties can be broiled on top). Last pour over water in which sugar has been dissolved. Roman Beauty apples do not need to be pre-cooked but some apples need to be cooked for ten minutes before being used in the casserole. Be sure to use water in which apples were cooked.
                          — Janet Bartlett, Eagle Nest

Tomato Bisque:

3 c. fresh milk
2 T. butter
1 heaping T. flour

¼ t. soda
1 can tomatoes
pinch of salt

Mix butter, soda and flour together until smooth. Put milk in kettle, add butter and flour mixture. When it boils up, add pre-heated tomatoes. Good served on buttered toast.

— Mrs. Lucy Holcomb, Farley

Spinach Mold:

4 c. cooked spinach (canned or fresh)
3 eggs, beaten
½ c. finely rolled bread crumbs
3 slices bacon cut into small

pieces and fried brown
1 8-ounce can mushrooms, sliced
1½ t. salt
¼ t. pepper
Bacon fat

Chop spinach, add eggs, bread crumbs, fried bacon, bacon fat and mushrooms. Season, turn into a greased 7½ inch, round Pyrex casserole or ring mould. Into a covered utensil pour 1½ cups water, place a trivet in the bottom, then place the spinach mold on this. Cover. Place on the large Economizer speed unit, turn switch to "high" until the steam escapes; then turn switch to "simmer." Steam 45 minutes. Turn out on a hot serving plate, then garnish with hot shredded beets, hard cooked eggs, and parsley.

2

Soap

(Equipment Needed)

A two quart enamel pan or pitcher should be used for mixing the lye solution. A six quart enamel pan, earthernware dish or crock should be used for mixing the soap ingredients. Use a wooden paddle or spoon or an enamel spoon for stirring. Molds for the soap can be made from common boxes which have been lined with waxed paper. A dairy thermometer is a useful part of the equipment. Household scales are useful.

(Wash Grease for Making Cold Soap)

The grease should be cleaned by adding twice its bulk of boiling water. Stir the grease until it is dissolved and then let it stand until it hardens.

If the grease has a strong odor melt it in the top of a double boiler and cook it with clabbered milk — one cup of milk to a pound of grease. A sliced medium sized potato added for each three pounds of grease is another good method for combatting odors in grease.

(Cold Soap Recipe)

6 lbs. fat (tallow, lard or com-   1 can high-test lye (about
bination)   13 oz.)
2½ pts. cold water

(6 lbs. fat equals 6¾ pints or 13½ standard measuring cups of liquid fat)

Add the lye to the water. (This will prevent boiling action.) Cover lye as you stir with wooden or enamel spoon to prevent fumes irritating nose and throat. Cool to correct temperature. Melt fat to clear liquid. If different kinds of fat are used, mix thoroughly. Cool until the fat reaches the right temperature. Pour the lye solution into the fat in a thin steady stream, stirring the fat and lye solution slowly, steadily, and in one direction. Stir until the mixture becomes thick like honey. This will take about 10 or 20 minutes. When spoon leaves a decided tract in the thick mixture it is ready to pour.

If you want to make soap float, gently fold in air before it sets.

If the mixture of lye and fat does not become thick within a reasonable time and there is a greasy layer on top, the mixture is too warm. Set container in a pan of cold water for a short time and keep mixture stirred from sides and bottom or simply leave mixture standing in the room and give it an occasional stir. If, on the other hand, there are lumps in the mixture, it is doubtless too cool; so place container in a pan of warm water for a short time and continue stirring to remove lumps. All this can be avoided if a thermometer is used.

When the soap is thick, pour into box that has been lined with waxed paper. Cover soap to retain heat. Let it remain undisturbed for 24 hours in a warm place. When there is neither grease on top nor liquid at the bottom, it is ready to cut. Stack in log cabin fashion to harden. The soap should be allowed to stand from three to six months before using. It will then be perfectly dry.

Watch temperature in Soap Making)

If you use a thermometer, the following guide will help: (Fahrenheit)

Kind of fat:	Temperature of fat:	Temperature of lye solution:
Sweet lard or other soft fat	80-85	70-75
Lard & tallow (half and half)	100-110	80-85
All tallow	120-130	90-95
Soft rancid fat	97-100	75-80

If at the end of 24 hours there is a film of grease on top of the soap, leave it for 48 hours or until all the grease disappears, then cut the soap. If 24 hours after pouring the soap, a liquid is found in the bottom of the pan, cut soap in small squares and let it stand until all the liquid is absorbed.

(Imperfections in Soap)

Hard, crumbly soap is caused by excess lye or too vigorous stirring.

Hard, brittle soap is caused by too low a temperature while stirring.

Greasy layer on top of the soap indicates too little lye for the amount of fat used.

Streaked soap shows that fat and lye solution were not thoroughly mixed.

Clear layer on the bottom of the soap may be due to a partial separation of fat and lye.

White deposit on soap may be due to use of hard water in making lye solution; a little free lye; addition of too much borax.

Cracks in the soap may be due to too much stirring; too much free lye; drying too quickly.

A neutral soap will not "bite" the tongue or smart the skin; it will not feel greasy to the hands; it will be ororless; and it will have a uniform attractive appearance.

(Variations in Homemade Soaps)

Soap Flakes. Flake soap that is about three days old with soap chipper or slaw cutter. Stir occasionally while drying. This is convenient because it dissolves so readily, and is economical in use as well as convenient.

Soap Jelly. Cut 1 pound of hard soap into fine shavings and add 1 gallon of water. Boil slowly for about 10 minutes, then cool. Keep covered to prevent drying out.

Borax Soap. Two tablespoons borax may be added to the recipe for quickening the sudsing action of the soap.

Scouring. To the soap recipe add 4 pounds of pumice stone OR whiting when the mixture thickens, and stir until it is thoroughly blended. Pour into mold and cover.

Abrasive Soap Paste:

1 lb. homemade or 1 large cake of neutral soap cut or shaved in
   pieces
1 pt. hot water
2 oz. light mineral oil   1 lb. powdered pumice stone

Melt the soap in hot water, add mineral oil and mix well. When mixture is cool enough to handle, combine with pumice stone. Store paste in glass jars tightly covered to prevent drying out.

Glycerine Soap: Add 4 to 6 ounces of glycerine to the soap shortly after the lye solution has been added. This is especially good for dry, sensitive skins.

Colored and Perfumed Soaps: No soap should be deeply colored or of strong odor. Oil of perfumes and not essence should be used in small amounts. Perfume and vegetable coloring matter should be added and mixed with the soap. This should be stirred evenly throughout the soap before pouring into the mold.

(Helpful Hints for the Soap Maker)

Save the grease. It is surprising how the small bits mount to six pounds. Care should be used in collecting grease to avoid rancidity. Salt should be washed from fat because rancid fat and salt may cause the fat and lye to separate. Use soft water to make soap. (Rain water is soft).

Caution: Lye burns! If it should spatter on hands or clothes sop the area with vinegar. The vinegar will neutralize the action of the lye.

Melt fat in double-boiler. To make a large double-boiler use a dish pan to hold the water and set the large kettle that holds the grease into it. Don't use aluminum for soap making. Strong alkalis (lye) turn the aluminum black.

When you find it necessary to buy soap know what you are getting. Know the weight of the soap; know the composition of the soap; and from this knowledge determine if it is the kind of soap for the work you want to do with it.

Buy good soap for cleaning purposes. Adding borax or kerosene to the water when cleaning will make the soap more effective. Water glass can also be used with soap and water as it has detergent qualities.

Cooked Soap:

2 Gallons cracklings (scant)   2 Cans lye
3 Gallons water

Cook all ingredients about 30 minutes. Let boil gently. Stir until cold. Soap will float.

124

Finis

A kitchen is a friendly place,
  Full of living's daily grace;
And rich in dignity is she
  Who shares its hospitality.

THE GARFIELD WOMAN'S CLUB

COOK BOOK

"If food no longer tastes the same,
  Whatever care they take,
If you are longing for the things
  That mother used to make,
Arise at four and milk the cows,
  Go out and feed the hogs,
Then just to while the time away
  Split up some hickory logs.
So stop before you kick about
  The biscuit and the cake,
And get the kind of appetite
  Your mother used to make."

THE GARFIELD WOMAN'S CLUB

COOK BOOK

A collection of Tested and Tried Recipes contributed and vouched for by
the Women and Friends of the Garfield Woman's Club
of Garfield, Utah.

Dedicated to Our Husbands

Compiled and Published by
The Garfield Woman's Club
1916

Preface

The primary purpose of publishing this little book is to raise funds for purchasing books for the Garfield Woman's Club's Free Public Library; and all money derived from its sale will be used to that end.

We have endeavored to secure the best recipes from as many contributors as possible, and we feel that this collection is truly cosmopolitan, the cookery of every section of our own nation being represented, as well as many favorite dishes from across the seas.

We do not claim originality for these recipes, but the worth of each one is attested by its contributor, and as you try them one after another you will find "the proof of the pudding is in the eating thereof."

A Word To Our Subscribers

The publication of this book has been made possible by the assistance of our advertisers.

The professional and business men and firms here represented are reliable, and we bespeak for them the loyalty and patronage of every home in which the Garfield Woman's Club Cook Book finds a place.

We hope you will use your copy as an advertising guide as well as a culinary help.

We wish also to thank the ladies who, by contributing their choicest recipes, have made our book a success.

MRS. T. F. MAHER.
Pres. Garfield Woman's Club
MRS. GILBERT PALMER,
Chairman Library Committee

SOUPS

Compiled by Mrs. W. Boucher.

"Now good digestion wait on appetite and health on both."—Shakespeare.

Cream Corn Soup.

1 Can Corn	4 Tablespoons Flour
2 Tablespoons Onion	1 Quart Milk
1 Pint Water	2 Teaspoons Salt
4 Tablespoons Butter	

Boil corn and onion in water, press through sieve, add milk, heat and thicken with flour and butter blended together. Season just before serving, add yolks of two eggs well beaten.—Mrs. D. L. Barnard.

Celery Soup.

Use the outside pieces of celery, cut in small pieces, cover with cold salted water, boil until tender. Press through sieve, add milk and let come to a boil. Serve with a little ground fresh parsley sprinkled on top.—Mrs. R. B. Tempest.

Cream Tomato Soup.

½ Can Tomatoes	1 Pint Milk
1 Pint Water	Pinch of Soda

Bring tomatoes and water to boil, add soda, butter and seasoning, add boiling milk just before serving.—Mrs. A. M. Henderson.

Vegetable Soup.

1 Carrot	1 Onion
1 Potato	1 Tablespoon Butter
1 Teaspoon Salt	½ Teaspoon Pepper
1 Turnip	½ Pint Tomatoes
1 Parsnip	2 Quarts Water
1 Tablespoon Flour	

Chop vegetables fine, add water, cook slowly ½ hour, press through colander, return pulp to kettle, add tomatoes, salt and pepper, stir flour in melted butter, add to liquid, serve with cretons.—Mrs. R. M. Hawley.

Vegetable Soup.

1 Soup Bone	½ Cup Pearl Barley
1 Cup Chopped Cabbage	1 Onion
1 Carrot	1 Cup Chopped Celery

Boil soup bone, skim, add barley and ½ hour before serving add chopped vegetables and seasoning.—Mrs. Fred Barton.

Southern Gumbo

¾ lb. veal, or	1 large tablespoon crisco
1 small chicken	1 Onion
½ lb. ham	1 quart water
1 can tomatoes	1 lb. fresh Okra, or
1 pint fresh oysters, or	1 can okra
1 can shrimps	

Cut meat in small pieces and fry in crisco until nicely browned, add salt and pepper to taste, one sliced onion, one quart of water, one lb. of fresh okra, cook one hour. If canned okra is used, add after meat is thoroughly cooked, then can tomatoes. Just before serving, add one can shrimps or 1 pint fresh oysters, cook for six minutes and serve with boiled rice.—Mrs. R. H. Hawley.

Clam Broth

1 pint sego milk	1 7-oz can minced sea clams
2 pints water	Salt and Pepper to taste
1 tablespoon butter.	

Heat milk and water nearly to boiling point, add contents of can clams, let come to boil. Serve.—Mrs. J. E. Brinkman.

Italian Soup.

1 can Tomatoes	2 tablespoons flour
¼ cup each of onion, carrot, celery	½ teaspoon black pepper
	1 teaspoon salt
1 cup macaroni	3 tablespoons butter
1 quart water	1 small bay leaf

Cook onions, carrots and celery in butter for 5 minutes; add flour, seasoning, then 1 quart water and can tomatoes. Cook slowly 1 hours, press through colander and add macaroni that has been cooked separately.—Mrs. R. H. Hawley.

Jewish Chicken Soup.

½ chicken	A little celery, parsley,
½ pound beef (brisket)	onion, carrot
¼ cup navy beans	

Boil chicken and beef in enough water to cover until half done, then add beans, boil until well done, salt vegetables and add them ½ hour before serving.—Mrs. Axelrad.

Tomatoe Soup.

1 can tomatoes	1 tablespoon flour, mixed with
1 stalk celery	butter, salt and pepper
1 onion	to taste

Cook tomatoes, celery and onion until tender, add flour and butter, salt and pepper. Strain and serve.—Mrs. B. W. Day.

Noodle Soup

Boil a chicken until tender. Take chicken from kettle, leaving 1 quart of soup. After skimming the fat, bring to boil and add noodles. Cook for 25 minutes. The noodles are made as follows:

1 egg	½ egg shell water
½ teaspoon salt	Flour to make stiff dough

Beat egg, add salt and water, flour. Knead; roll as thin as possible. Cover with a towel until surface is dry, then roll like a jelly roll and cut off in thin slices, which will break in small pieces.—Mrs. R. C. McLeise.

Lobster Bisque

1 can lobster	2 cups milk
3 pints boiling water	½ cup fine cracker crumbs
Salt and pepper	1 tablespoon butter

Chop lobster rather coarse, taking care not to tear it. Put boiling water, salt, pepper and lobster into a soucepan and cook gently 40 minutes. Have ready scalding milk in which the crumbs have soaked 20 minutes. Stir in butter, then milk and crumbs; set saucepan in hot water 5 minutes and serve.—Mrs. G. H. Paddock.

MEATS

Compiled by Mrs. J. McLachlan.

"Jack Sprat could eat no fat, his wife could eat no lean—
And so between them both, they licked the platter clean."

Wild Rabbit Friscassee.

Take young rabbit, cut up and place in salt water over night. Cook until tender, when nearly done have one large carrot and turnip cut in oblong pieces, also small onion sliced and a few whole cloves, 2 slices of bacon diced, season to taste, just before taking off fire add ½ glass port wine, 2 tablespoons red currant jelly and thicken.—Mrs. J. McLachlan.

Smothered Chicken.

Take young chicken, have flattened as for broiling, put breast up in double roaster, sprinkle with salt and pepper, put in 1 cup boiling water in which a tablespoon of butter has been dissolved. When half done turn chicken and bake until nearly done, then turn again, remove cover and lay thin strips of fat bacon across breast and bake until brown. Thicken gravy with flour and butter and turn over chicken, garnish with parsley or watercress.—Mrs. J. McLachlan.

Curried Lamb

2 cups cold meat cut in dice	1 quart tomatoes
1 teaspoon curry powder	1 slice onion
1 cup meat gravy, salt	1 bay leaf

Stew tomatoes with onion and bay leaf for ten minutes then strain and add to meat and gravy with curry powder. Season to taste with salt and serve on boiled rice. A little thickening may be added if desired—Mrs. E. E. Nelson.

Individual Meat Pies.

Filling.

1½ pound round steak	3 tablespoons good meat dripping
2 cups mashed potatoes	2 cups water or milk
2 tablespoons flour	Salt, pepper, parsley and celery to taste

Put steak, celery and parsley through chopper; put drippings in frying pan; add ground meat and flour (an onion may be used and should be chopped with meat); brown all well, add water, let boil until thick, add potatoes. Line Gem pans with good pie crust. Fill with meat mixture, put crust on top, bake 20 to 30 minutes. Will make 12 pies.—Mrs. H. R. Allen.

Sausage

To 50 pounds meat add	1 heaping pint powdered sage
1 pint fine salt	
½ pint ground pepper	

—Mrs. A. E. McArthur.

Meat Pie

1½ pounds raw hamburger   Salt, pepper and sage to
1 large onion   taste

Chop onion and boil with meat for two hours; thicken with one tablespoon flour. Fill rich pie crust with mixture and bake.—Mrs. George Pugsley.

Meat Patties

2 pounds hamburger   ½ pound cheese
2 green peppers

Mince the peppers and cheese fine, mix with hamburger, make in little patties. Fry in hot lard.—Mrs. Frank Avis.

Steamed Wild Duck

Prepare ducks as for roasting, using good sage dressing. Place ducks in double steam cooker without water or butter, steam four or five hours or until tender. Before serving put in hot oven to brown. Serve with giblet gravy made from the liquor in steaming pan.—Mrs. T. F. Maher.

Baked Lamb Hearts

Soak four lamb hearts in cold water two hours, remove muscles from inside. Stuff hearts with good sage dressing, sew or tie hearts to keep dressing in place. Place in steamer with salt, pepper and butter and steam for two hours. Place in hot oven and bake 30 minutes, basting often with liquor in pan. Very nice sliced cold.—Mrs. C. F. Anderson.

Spanish Stew

Cut 1 pound round steak in cubes and let stand in two quarts of cold water for one hour. Slice 2 onions and fry golden brown in three tablespoons of drippings. Add onions to stew and let simmer till quantity is about four or five cups. Then thicken with two tablespoons flour blended with water enough to make smooth paste. Season with salt and pepper to taste. Cook cup macaroni and place on a platter and pour stew over same. Serve six people.—Mrs. H. F. Snyder.

Pork Tenderloin Roast

Split pork tenderloin lengthwise on the side, put layer of dressing between the two pieces, and sew together. Cut small carrot and small onion in pieces and lay in bottom of baking pan and put meat over this. Put slices of bacon or fat pork over tenderloin. Put small potatoes around meat and bake for about 1 hour.—Mrs. T. F. Maher.

VEGETABLES

Compiled by Mrs. C. F. Anderson.

"Herbs and other country messes
Which the neat handed Phyllis dresses."

Mushrooms and Peas.

1 can peas	½ cup milk
1 can mushrooms	2 tablespoonsfuls butter
1 cup cracker crumbs	1 Tablespoonfuls flour

Cook peas until well done in own juice. Pour juice off mushrooms and cook in milk until tender, or well done. Put butter in small skillet, thicken with the flour and brown as if for gravy. Then mix peas, mushrooms, browned flour, salt and pepper together and put in baking dish and cover with cracker crumbs. Bake 30 minutes.—Mrs. C. F. Anderson.

Hominy French Style.

½ pound hominy	½ pound grated cheese

Soak hominy in cold water over night; next morning boil till soft; when cooked add grated cheese, put into dish and bake 20 minutes. Very good with salad.—Mrs. B. Call.

Boston Baked Beans.

1 quart navy beans	½ pounds salt pork.

Pick over beans, cover with cold water, soak over night; drain in the morning, cover with fresh water, heat slowly (keeping water below boiling point), cook until skins will burst, which is best determined by taking a few beans on trip of spoon and blowing on them, when skin will burst is sufficiently cooked. Drain beans Scald rind of pork, scrape, remove ¼ inch slice and put in bottom of bean pot. Cut through rind of remaining portion every ½ inch, making cuts 1 inch deep. Put beans in pot and bury pork in beans leaving rind exposed. Mix 1 tablespoon salt, 1 tablespoon molasses, 3 tablespoons sugar, add 1 cup of boiling water and pour over the beans. Add enough more boiling water to cover beans. Put in oven with cover on bean pot and bake at least 12 hours, adding water as needed. Leave cover off the last hour of baking that rind may become brown and crisp. Served with Boston Brown bread.—Mrs. E. E. Nelson.

Scalloped Asparagus.

1 bunch asparagus	5 hard boiled eggs
1 pint milk	Bread crumbs
2 tablespoons butter	Salt and pepper
2 tablespoons flour	

Wash and cut asparagus in small pieces, cook till tender, adding the tips a little later then the stalks. Make a white sauce of the milk, butter, and flour; season to taste with Salt and pepper, cut the hard-boiled eggs in pieces and add to sauce. Cover the bottom of a baking dish with asparagus, add some of the sauce, then cover with a thin layer of bread crumbs and repeat until the dish is full. Bake in a quick oven until brown.—Mrs. A. McArthur.

Spinach Rice.

2 slices bacon, diced small 1 can tomatoes
1 small onion   1 cup cold boiled rice

Put bacon and onion in a frying pan and brown, add tomatoes, then the rice, season to taste with salt and pepper and 1 teaspoon of Chile powder. —Mrs. H. E. Atchinson.

Stuffed Tomatoes.

Select smooth skinned tomatoes, cut a slice off the stem end, take out inside carefully, salt it and turn up side down to drain.

Bread Crumb Filling.

Cook pulp, add ½ cup bread crumbs, 1 teaspoon of melted butter, salt and pepper, add chopped onion, or ½ cup boiled rice, stuff tomato with either filling and bake 15 minutes.—Mrs. Chas. H. Rees.

Baked Tomatoes.

6 tomatoes   Bread crumbs
6 shelled walnuts Pepper
small onion   Salt

Remove thin slice from stem end of smooth medium size tomatoes. Take an equal quantity of bread crumbs, season with salt, pepper, a little finely chopped onion, and walnuts chopped fine, fill tomatoes with mixture. Place in a buttered pan, sprinkle with buttered crumbs and bake 20 minutes in hot oven.—Mrs. Harry Bible.

Scalloped Cabbage.

Cook cabbage, chop and mix with white sauce in a baking dish and cover with cracker crumbs and pieces of butter; put in oven long enough to brown crumbs.

White Sauce.

2 tablespoons butter   1 cup milk
2 tablespoons flour   Salt and pepper

Mrs. Chas. Rees.

Spanish Beans

1½ cups small red beans 2 whole chile peppers
½ can tomatoes   Salt
1 large onion   Pepper

Soak beans over night. After cooking 2 hours, take tomatoes, strain through sieve and add to beans, fry onion a delicate brown, in a ½ cup of butter or lard, add chile peppers, salt to taste, turn into the beans and cook 1½ hours.—Mrs. B. Cail.

Cauliflower and Cheese.

Remove leaves, cut off stem and cook until soft in boiling salted water; then drain, separate flowerets and put layer of cauliflower sprinkled with flour, salt, pepper and layer of grated cheese, fill casserole with these layers, then cover all with milk. Bake until cheese is melted or about 30 minutes.—Mrs. D. L. Barnard.

Potato Puffs

2 cups mashed potatoes 1 cup milk.
2 eggs   1 teaspoon butter

Mashed potatoes, add beaten eggs, then milk, salt and pepper to taste; then melted butter. Bake in well-greased gem tins.—Mrs. J. T. Miller.

Mock Crab.

1 cup corn, canned or fresh	½ cup flour
1 cup buttered bread crumbs	4 tablespoon butter
1½ cup hot milk	¾ teaspoon mustard
1 egg	Salt

Melt butter, add flour, mix dry seasoning, add milk and boil till thick; add corn and egg, cover with crumbs and bake.—Mrs. Chas. Goodman.

Scalloped Potatoes and Cheese

Pare the potatoes, cover the bottom of baking dish with bread crumbs; then add a layer of sliced potatoes, bits of butter, salt and pepper, then a layer of grated or thinly sliced cheese; fill the dish with alternate layers; wet the whole with milk and bake 1½ hours.—Mrs. Goodman.

Potatoes on Half Shell.

Bake nice large potatoes, cut a slice from top, take inside out carefully with a teaspoon, and avoid breaking shell. For six potatoes add 2 tablespoons melted butter, salt and ½ cup hot milk. Beat till fluffy, refill shells, brush with beaten egg and place in oven to brown. To improve, add whites of two eggs beaten.—Miss Ruth Rees.

Baked Eggplant

Boil the whole eggplant in salted water for 20 minutes; half it with a sharp knife, scoop out the center, chop and mix with bread crumbs, a little finely cut raw tomato, chop parsley, onion juice or small onion chopped fine and seasoning. Refill the shells with mixture, cover them with buttered crumbs and bake for ½ hour in hot oven.—Mrs. C. F. Anderson.

Potato Balls

Take four cold boiled potatoes, rub through a wire sieve, put into a stewpan with ½ ounce of butter and a dessert spoonful of milk; beat over the fire till smooth. Add pepper and salt, the yolk of an egg and chopped parsley. When cold form into balls, brush over with the white of egg, roll in bread crumbs and fry in hot fat.—Mrs. E. L. McQuawn.

Baked Stuffed Summer Squash

2 medium sized summer squash	2 teaspoons salt
4 teaspoons melted butter	½ teaspoons pepper
½ cupful milk	1 large green pepper, minced
1 cupful soft bread crumbs	½ can tomatoes

Scoop out the centers of the squashes, leaving thin shell, chop the squash fine, add the other ingredients well mixed, put into a hot skillet and cook for about 10 minutes. Refill shells with this; sprinkle top with cracker or bread crumbs; set in a baking pan with a little water in bottom and bake slowly for 45 minutes.—Mrs. R. B. Tempest.

Sweet Potato Balls

Steam and peel the potatoes and mash. Add a little milk, salt and butter; mix thoroughly, roll into balls, dip in eggs and cracker crumbs and fry in deep fat.—Mrs. R. S. Hales.

Baked Mashed Potatoes.

Place a layer of cold mashed potatoes in a baking dish; then slices of hard boiled eggs; then a layer of potatoes, and lastly buttered bread crumbs. Bake till brown.—Mrs. R. S. Hales.

SALADS and SALAD DRESSINGS

Compiled by Mrs. R. H. Hawley.

"To make a perfect salad there should be a spendthrift for oil, a miser for vinegar, a wiseman for salt and a madcap to stir the ingredients up and mix them well together."—Spanish Proverb.

Mayonnaise.

Yolks of 2 eggs
1 cup olive oil
½ teaspoonful salt

¼ teaspoonful paprika or black
  pepper
Juice of 1 lemon
Few drops of tabasco

Beat eggs, add oil drop by drop until thick, add seasoning and last the lemon.—Mrs. R. H. Hawley.

Thousand Island Dressing

1 cup mayonnaise
2 tablespoonfuls tomatoe
  catsup
½ cup ground pimentos

½ cup India relish
2 tablespoons ground green
  peppers
1 cup or more of
  whipped cream

Mix well with mayonnaise.—Mrs. W. D. Leonard.

Worcestershire Sauce Dressing.

¾ cup olive oil
2 tablespoonfuls celery
  salt

¼ teaspoon salt
2 tablespoonfuls
  Worcestershire sauce

Beat until thick, serve on tomatoes, lettuce endive or cucumbers.—Mrs. O. W. Kumrow.

French Dressing.

½ teaspoonful salt
¼ teaspoonful black
  pepper or paprika

1 tablespoonful vinegar
1 cup olive oil, few drops
  of tabasco

Mix salt and pepper with vinegar, add oil slowly and beat until thick. For Roquefort cheese dressing add one-quarter pound grated cheese to above recipe. One teaspoonful of mayonnaise added to French dressing improves it.—Mrs. R. H. Hawley.

Boiled Salad Dressing.

2 heaping tablespoons sugar
1 teaspoon mustard
1 teaspoon cornstarch

¼ teaspoon salt
2 eggs
½ cup vinegar

Mix dry ingredients. Add eggs and vinegar; cook in double boiler until thick, when cool add one cup cream, or one small can Sego condensed milk. —Mrs. H. C. Smith.

Salad Dressing Without Eggs.

¼ cup vinegar
1 teaspoon mustard
1 teaspoon sugar

½ teaspoon salt
1 teaspoon flour
½ cup cream

HERE IT IS—

An Electric Range. Economical in Operation. Ovens properly ventilated. No disagreeable odors. No dirt, soot or fumes as when fuel is used.

Yes, the Electric Range is cheaper to operate than any other range. Our cooking rate is very low and as we are all living in the Electrical Age, why not accustom yourself to modern conveniences.

We have ranges at any price from $30.00 to $100.00 and our terms are suitable to meet the convenience of anyone.

Remember you are living in the 20th century so call at one of our stores or telephone and we will see that you are supplied with complete information.

THE PROGRESS CO.

Electric Light & Power.

Phones: Murray 105; Midvale 8; Magna 20-w.

Heat vinegar, dissolve mustard in a little cold water, add to mustard the
sugar, salt flour and cream; pour into hot vinegar and stir until thick;
when cold thin with sweet or sour cream.—Mrs. O. W. Kumrow.

Mayonnaise.

1 whole egg or two egg yolks
1½ cups cottonseed or olive oil
4 tablespoons lemon juice
Paprika
Ten grains of Cayenne

1 tablespoon Eddy's Prepared Salad
    mustard, or 1 teaspoon dry
    mustard
2 teaspoons powdered sugar

Beat egg thoroughly with Dover egg beater, in small bowl; add oil gradually, as mixture thickens alternate oil and lemon juice; add seasoning
when half finished.—Mrs. R. E. Robson.

Tomato Jelly Salad.

1 quart of tomatoes
Two-thirds box gelatine
½ cup chopped celery
½ cup shredded shrimps
¼ cup chopped olives
¼ cup chopped sweet pickles

1 teaspoon Worcestershire sauce
1 teaspoon salt
1 teaspoon powdered sugar
Paprika
Cayenne

To one quart of stewed and strained tomatoes add two-thirds box gelatine
which has soaked fifteen minutes in one-half cup cold water; add seasoning.
When mixture is partly cooled add celery, shrimps, olives, and sweet pickle.
Pour into individual moulds and chill. Serve on a bed of lettuce and garnish
top with mayonnaise.—Mrs. R. E. Robson.

Prize Salad

½ box gelatine
½ cup cold water
½ cup vinegar
1 pint boiling water
1 teaspoon salt

1 cup finely shredded cabbage
Juice of one lemon
½ cup sugar
2 cups celery cut in small pieces
¼ can pimentoes, finely cut

Soak gelatine in cold water five minutes; add vinegar, lemon juice, boiling water, sugar and salt; strain and when beginning to set add ingredients; pour in mold and chill. Serve on lettuce leaves with mayonnaise
dressing.—Mrs. E. E. Nelson.

Pineapple and Cheese Salad

1 cake Neufchatel cheese
½ cup shelled pecans

1 teaspoon butter
6 slices canned pineapple

Cream cheese, nuts and butter, roll in small balls and place in center of
pineapple. Serve with mayonnaise on lettuce.—Mrs. O. W. Kumrow.

Cabbage Salad.

2 eggs
¼ teaspoon salt
¼ teaspoon black pepper
¼ teaspoon red pepper

½ teaspoon mustard
2 tablespoons sugar
2 tablespoons vinegar
1 tablespoon flour
Butter size of walnut

Cook until thick, add a little cream when cold, shred small cabbage, salt to
taste and mix with dressing.—Mrs. O. W. Kumrow.

Stuffed Tomato Salad.

6 tomatoes
1 can crab or shrimp

½ cup chopped celery
1 pint mayonnaise

Peel tomatoes and remove part of pulp, mix crab or shrimp with celery and mayonnaise; fill tomatoes and serve on lettuce with a teaspoonful of the dressing on top of each tomato.—Mrs. R. H. Hawley.

Fruit Salad.

2 oranges	1 box Angelus marshmallows
1 small can sliced pineapple	1 cup nuts
2 bananas	

Cut in small pieces; serve on crisp lettuce with whipped cream or boiled salad dressing.—Mrs. F. G. Janney, Jr.

German Potato Salad.

6 medium sized potatoes	2 teaspoons salt
¼ pound bacon	¼ teaspoon black pepper
1 onion	½ cup hot vinegar
2 tablespoons olive oil	¼ cup hot water

Boil potatoes, drain and set on back of stove to dry; peel and slice while warm and cover at once with dressing made as follows: Cut bacon in small dice, put in pan over slow fire, slice onion in large bowl, add salt, pepper and hot liquid; when the bacon is well crisped and a light brown add olive oil and pour into vinegar and onion, stirring slowly. Serve at once on crisp lettuce leaves garnished with pickled beets.—Mrs. O. W. Kumrow.

California Fruit Salad.

2 slices pineapple	½ cup Maraschnos cherries
4 oranges	2 cups green grapes
2 bananas	3 apples
½ pound English walnuts	

Dressing.

1 cup sugar	Yolks 3 eggs
3 tablespoons flour	½ pint whipped cream
1 cup scalded milk	Juice of 1 orange
1 tablespoon butter	1 lemon; 2 teaspoons sherry or pineapple juice

Mix flour with little cold water, pour on scalded milk and cook until flour is done; add yolks of eggs and sugar, which have been beaten until creamy, add butter; cook in double boiler until eggs thicken, remove from stove and add juices of fruit. Before serving add whipped cream.—Mrs. Cambria A. Wilson.

Fruit Salad.

6 large oranges	2 small cans pineapple
6 bananas	½ pound of dates
4 large apples	½ pound of English walnuts
Add juice of one-half	½ pound of grapes
lemon	2 small cans marshmellows

Dressing.

Melt half pound of butter, add four tablespoonsful flour, one large can of cream, one cup water, one scant cup of sugar; when thick add the juice of half a lemon, this will serve twenty people.—Mrs. Lillie M. Healey.

Pineapple Salad Dressing.

Part I.

Juice of 1 can pineapple   1 teaspoon flour
1 cup sugar   Pinch of salt.

Part II.

Beat one egg, add one tablespoon water, add to part one and let come to a boil, add juice of one lemon.   This is delicious on fruit salad.—Mrs. Mary Gauthrie.

Sweet Salad Dressing.

½ cup pineapple juice   ¼ cup lemon juice
Rind of one lemon   2 eggs well beaten
Pinch of salt   Sugar to taste

Cook until thick; add one-half pint whipped cream.—Mrs. R. W. Ashworth.

Salamagundi Salad.

In the bottom of small moulds or one large mould place a layer of bottled pearl onions. Line the sides of the moulds with alternate strips of red and green sweet peppers or pimentoes and green string beans. Over the pearl onions place a layer of sliced tomatoes, then string beans, then a few cooked peas with sliced tomatoes on top; soak two tablespoons granulated gelatine in one-fourth cup cold water, dissolve in one and one-quarter cup boiling water, add six tablespoons lemon juice and one-half cup sugar. Mix all well together and pour over salad until it comes to the top of the moulds. Set away in cold place until well set; chill, then turn out of moulds and serve. Asparagus may be used instead of the beans and other substitutes may be made if desired.—Mrs. Alfred K. Fail.

Banana Salad.

Cut bananas in half, dip in sweetened mayonnaise, sprinkle with chopped nuts, a little whipped cream and a strawberry on top.—Mrs. De Camp.

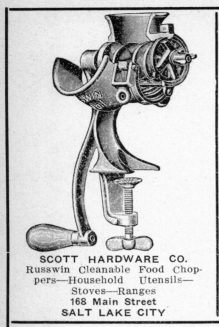

BREADS

Compiled by Mrs. A. C. Ensign.

"God is Great and God is good,
And we thank him for his food,
By his hand are all things fed,
Give us Lord, our daily bread."

WHITE BREAD.

2¾ quarts flour	1 tablespoon lard
½ cup sugar	1 cake Magic yeast
1 tablespoon salt	

Make a sponge with three-quarter quart flour and one pint potato water, add yeast cake which has been soaked in a little warm water and one tablespoon sugar, beat well, cover and let stand over night in a warm place. In the morning put the sponge into the rest of the flour to which has been added the sugar, salt and lard and enough warm water to make a stiff dough; knead 15 minutes.—Mrs. J. M. McLachlan.

Parker House Rolls.

2 cups scalded milk	1 teaspoon salt
3 tablespoons butter	1 yeast cake, dissolved in ¼ cup
2 tablespoons sugar	luke warm water

Add butter, sugar and salt to milk when luke warm, add dissolved yeast cake and three cups flour. Beat thoroughly, cover and let raise until light. Cut down and add enough flour to knead (about two and one-quarter cups) let raise again, knead and roll out to one-third inch in thickness, cut with biscuit cutter and brush with melted butter, fold over and press edges together, place in greased pan one inch apart, cover, let raise and bake in hot oven 12 to 15 minutes.—Mrs. A. C. Ensign.

French Rolls.

4 cups flour	1 tablespoon home-made yeast or
½ cup cornstarch	¼ yeast cake dissolved in luke
¾ teaspoons salt	warm water
1 egg	2½ cups new milk
2 tablespoons butter	

Scald milk, add butter and cool till luke warm, add the yeast and well beaten egg. Sift dry ingredients and add to the liquid, beat well but do not knead, when risen form into rolls with as little handling as possible and bake at once.—Mrs. Minna Mitchell.

English Tea Rolls.

1 pint milk	½ cup butter
½ cup yeast	1 teaspoon salt
1 tablespoon sugar	2 egg whites

Scald milk, adding to it when cool sugar, yeast and flour enough to make stiff batter, let rise over night, in the morning add butter, salt and beaten whites of eggs, mix, knead well and let rise, then knead again and roll out until three-fourths inch thick, cut with biscuit cutter, spread butter on one-half and roll the other half over, let rise until very light and bake.—Mrs. Minna Mitchell.

Hot Cross Buns.

1 cup scalded milk
¼ cup sugar
2 tablespoons butter
½ teaspoon salt
½ yeast cake dissolved in ¼
cup luke warm water

¾ teaspoon cinnamon
3 cups flour
1 egg
¼ cup raisins stoned and quartered
or ¼ cup currants

Add butter, sugar and salt to milk, when luke warm, add dissolved yeast cake, cinnamon, flour and egg, when thoroughly mixed add raisins, cover and let rise over night, in morning shape in form of large biscuit, place in pan one inch apart, let rise, brush over with butter, egg and bake twenty minutes. Cool and with ornamental frosting make a cross on top of each bun. If preferred the buns may be scored with a knife in the shape of a cross just before baking.—Mrs. E. E. Nelson.

Company Rolls.

1 Flieshman's yeast cake
1 pint of milk
4 cupfuls flour
2 tablespoons butter

2 tablespoons sugar
1 teaspoon salt
3 eggs

Scald milk, add butter, sugar and salt; when luke warm add the yeast cake which has been previously soaked in one-quarter cup warm water and enough flour to make a fairly stiff batter, when risen to double its size add the three eggs, one at a time and beat well, then add the rest of the flour and knead lightly.—Mrs. J. McLachlan.

German Coffee Cake.

1 cake yeast
2 tablespoons sugar
1 egg
1 tablespoon butter
½ teaspoon salt

1 cup sugar
1 tablespoon lard
1 teaspoon nutmeg
Flour

Dissolve yeast cake in one pint luke warm water and two tablespoons sugar, add enough flour to make a sponge and let rise; when light and foamy add sugar, egg, well beaten, butter, lard, nutmeg, and salt and beat well; gradually add more flour to make a soft dough, beating while you add; let rise about one hour and then roll and spread one-half inch thick in flat pan; spread with milk, cinnamon and sugar and when risen again bake forty minutes in oven.—Mrs. Murray Howard.

Graham Bread.

2 cup graham flour
1 cup white flour
½ cup sugar
One-third cup molasses

1 teaspoon soda
1 teaspoon baking powder
2 cups sour milk

Sift soda and baking powder in white flour and mix in order given; bake in moderate oven one hour.—Mrs. Harry Bible.

Boston Brown Bread.

1 cup graham flour
1 cup cornmeal
1 cup rye flour
¾ tablespoon soda

2 cups sour milk
¾ cup molasses and sugar
1 teaspoonful salt
1 cup raisins

Mix in order given and steam in buttered mould three hours.—Evelyn M. Paddock.

Apple Cake.

2 cups flour	1/8 pound butter
2 tablespoons sugar	1 eggs
1/4 teaspoon salt	1 cup milk
1 teaspoon baking powder	

Sift dry ingredients together, add butter melted, beaten egg, and milk; pour with buttered pan, cover with sliced apples, one-eighth pound melted with sugar and cinnamon.—Mrs. D. D. Puncheon.

Nut Bread.

1/4 cup sugar	2 cups flour
1 egg	1 1/2 teaspoons baking powder
1 cup milk	1/2 cup walnuts
Pinch of salt	

Mix together in above order and let raise thirty minutes; bake thirty minutes.—Mrs. W. E. Beane.

Nut Bread.

3 cups flour	1 cup raisins
1 1/2 cups milk	1 teaspoon baking powder to
1/2 cup brown sugar	each cup flour
or mollasses	Salt
1 cup chopped nuts	

Bake in moderately hot oven about forty-five minutes.—Mrs. S. K. Smith.

Tea Biscuits.

1 pint flour	1 egg
Pinch salt	2 1/2 tablespoonsful melted lard
1 1/2 tablespoonsful of sugar	1 1/4 cups milk
1 1/2 teaspoonsful of baking powder	

Sift flour, salt, sugar and baking powder together, add beaten egg, then the milk, then lard; mix all together with a spoon, turn out on a well floured board; knead lightly with the hands, roll out and cut, then bake in a quick oven. This makes eighteen biscuits.—Mrs. R. M. Leasy.

Muffins.

Mix one pint sifted flour	1/4 cup butter
2 1/2 teaspoons baking powder	1 large cup milk
1/4 teaspoon salt	2 eggs, beaten light
1/4 cup sugar	

Bake in gun pans.—Mrs. Collinwood.

WALNUT MUFFINS.

2 cups flour	1 tablespoon butter
1/2 teaspoon salt	1 cup chopped walnuts
1 heaping teaspoon baking powder	2 tablespoons sugar

Sift the flour, salt and baking powder, add the butter, walnuts and sugar. Mix to a soft dough with milk. Mold out with the hands and bake.—Mrs. Wm. Le Cheminant.

Best Receipe for every Housewife. Ride in the **DAISY**. It never fails. Watch, for the Big Red Cars.

Salt Lake and Garfield Time Card.

DAISY AUTO STAGE

Howard-Hout, Mrgs.

LEAVE SALT LAKE.

6:00 a. m.	Shift-Men	3:30 p. m.	Passenger
7:00 a. m.	Passenger	4:00 p. m.	Passenger
8:00 a. m.	Passenger	5:00 p. m.	Passenger
9:00 a. m.	Passenger	6:00 p. m.	Passenger
10:00 a. m.	Passenger	7:00 p. m.	Passenger
11:00 a. m.	Passenger	8:15 p. m.	Passenger
12:00 Noon	Passenger	9:30 p. m.	Passenger
1:00 p. m.	Passenger	10:30 p. m.	Passenger
2:00 p. m.	Passenger	11:45 p. m.	Passenger
3:00 p. m.	Passenger		

LEAVE GARFIELD.

7:45 a. m.	Passenger	4:50 p. m.	Shift-Men
8:45 a. m.	Passenger	5:45 p. m.	Passenger
9:45 a. m.	Passenger	6:45 p. m.	Passenger
10:45 a. m.	Passenger	7:30 p. m.	Passenger
11:45 a. m.	Passenger	8:30 p. m.	Passenger
12:45 p. m.	Passenger	9:45 p. m.	Passenger
1:45 p. m.	Passenger	11:00 p. m.	Passenger
2:45 p. m.	Passenger	12:00 Midnight	Passenger
3:45 p. m.	Passenger	1:15 a. m.	Passenger
4:45 p. m.	Passenger		

LEAVE PLEASANT GREEN.

8:10 a. m.	Passenger	5:15 p. m.	Shift-Men
9:10 a. m.	Passenger	6:00 p m.	Passenger
10:10 a. m.	Passenger	7:10 p. m.	Passenger
11:10 a. m.	Passenger	7:50 p. m.	Passenger
12:10 p. m.	Passenger	8:50 p. m.	Passenger
1:10 p. m.	Passenger	10:00 p. m.	Passenger
2:10 p. m.	Passenger	11:15 p. m.	Passenger
3:10 p. m.	Passenger	12:15 a. m.	Passenger
4:10 p. m.	Passenger	1:30 a. m.	Passenger
5:10 p. m.	Passenger		

Waffles.

1¾ cups flour
3 teaspoons baking powder
½ teaspoon salt
1 tablespoon melted butter

1 cup milk
Yolks 2 eggs
Whites 2 eggs

Mix and sift dry ingredients; add milk gradually, yolks of eggs well beaten, butter and whites of eggs beaten stiff; cook in a greased hot waffle iron. Serve with maple syrup.—Mrs. R. E. Robson.

Bread Crumb Griddle Cakes.

Add one and one-half cups scalded milk and two tablespoons butter to one and one-half cups stale bread crumbs, soak until crumbs are soft, add two eggs well beaten and one-half cup flour, one-half teaspoon salt and four teaspoons baking powder sifted together; bake on hot griddle. Sour milk, soda and very little baking powder may be used. When baking cakes use a bag of salt to rub off griddle and cakes will not stick.—Mrs. Alfred K. Fail.

English. Sweet Buns.

2 cups bread sponge
3 eggs
½ cup sugar
½ cup melted butter

½ cup seedless raisins
1 teaspoon lemon extract
¼ teaspoon nutmeg

When making bread take two cups sponge, add other ingredients and flour to thicken; let raise once, roll and cut with biscuit cutter, place in pans and let raise until light and bake in quick oven about fifteen minutes.—Mrs. Gilbert Palmer.

CAKES

Compiled by By Mrs. R. B. Tempest.

"Wouldst thou both eat thy cake and have it?"

Devil's Food Cake.
Prize Cake Country Fair.

1½ cups sugar
1½ cups milk
½ cake chocolate
2 teaspoons vanilla extract
2 eggs
2 cups flour

½ cup Crisco
1 teaspoon soda
3 tablespoons boiling water
½ teaspoon salt
(Nuts if wanted)

Put one-half cup sugar into saucepan, add chocolate and one cup milk. Put on stove and stir till it boils five minutes stirring now and then; remove from fire, add vanilla and set aside to cool.

Beat Crisco and remainder of sugar to light cream then add eggs, well
beaten, and beat two minutes, now add remainder of milk, soda dissolved
in boiling water, flour, salt and chocolate mixture; divide into two large
greased and floured layer tins; bake in moderate oven twenty-five minutes.

Frosting.

2 tablespoons Crisco	6 tablespoons coffee
2 squares melted chocolate	½ teaspoon salt
2 cups powdered sugar	½ teaspoon vanilla extract
	(Nuts if wanted)

Knead Crisco into sugar, melt chocolate add coffee, sugar, salt and Crisco,
stir until thick then add vanilla. This receipe can be used right away
or kept two or three days in cool place.—Mrs. G. S. Piatt.

Burnt Sugar Cake.

Prize Cake Country Fair.

2 cups sugar	4 yolks of eggs
1 scant cup butter	2 heaping teaspoonfuls baking
2 cups water	powder, a few drops of vanilla
5 cups flour	Burnt sugar

Cream, butter and sugar together, to this add lightly beaten egg yolks,
mix well, stir in water, sift baking powder in flour and beat in a little
at a time till all has been used, then add just a few drops of vanilla, not
enough to flavor and lastly add burnt sugar till batter is a rich brown, or
to suit taste. To burn the sugar putany amount of sugar on the stove in
a saucepan and stir constantly. The sugar crystalizes and then melts,
when sugar is melted add hot water, for every cup of sugar add one cup
of water; let mixture boil a few minutes and put in a jar then syrup is
ready for use at any time.

Filling.

2 cups sugar	Two-thirds water
Burnt sugar to taste	

Cook till the syrup hangs in drops on the spoon, then beat into whites of
four eggs that have been lightly whiped, and beat till icing is thick enough
to stand up on the cake, add burnt sugar to taste.—Mrs. H. F. Synder.

White Cake.

Prize Cake Country Fair.

1½ cups sugar	Pinch of salt
One-third cup butter or Crisco	2 scant teaspoons baking powder
1 cup sweet milk	3 scant cups flour
1 teaspoonful lemon extract	Whites of 4 eggs

Cream thoroughly, sugar and butter add milk and flavoring, then sift in
flour and baking powder, add whites of eggs last.—Mrs. W. B. Boucher.

Devil's Food.

Prize Cake Country Fair.

Cream until white, one and one-half cups sugar, two tablespoons cottolene,
one-quarter of a pound butter, then add four eggs (leaving out the whites
of two for the frosting), two teaspoons baking powder mixed with flour,
add flour and one and one-half cups milk, alternately to make lighter,
teaspoon vanilla, pinch of salt, flour enough for right consistency, then add
two full squares of Baker's chocolate, melted, one pound English walnuts.

Bake slowly. Either chocolate or white frosting to suit the taste.—Mrs. A. C. French.

Sponge Cake.

6 eggs
½ lemon

1 cup sugar
1 cup flour

Separate yolks from whites, mix sugar and yolks well, add lemon juice, mix thoroughly, beat whites stiff and fold into yolks, sugar and lemon juice, slowly, add flour; bake in buttered pan from forty-five to sixty minutes. Best to use wooden spoon for mixing.—Mrs. Axelrad.

Fudge Cake.

1 cup sugar
1 cup milk
Two-thirds cup butter
or lard
2½ cups flour

3 eggs beaten separately
½ cup chopped walnuts
½ cup melted chocolate
1 teaspoon baking powder

Mix in regular way, bake as loaf cake.—Mrs. W. C. Barton.

Eggless Raisin Cake.

1 quart of flour
1 package raisins, cooked
in one pint of water
1 cup of butter or Crisco
1 cup sugar creamed with
butter

1 teaspoonful of soda
1 teaspoonful of salt
¼ teaspoonful of cloves
1 teaspoonful of cinnamon
1 teaspoonful of nutmeg

—Maggie E. Larson.

Pork Cake.

1 pound ground fat pork
(raw)
1 pound ground raisins
1 pound ground citron
1 pound ground green
apples
1 pint boiling water
1 quart molasses

1 tablespoon cloves
1 tablespoon cinnamon
1 tablespoon allspice
1 tablespoon nutmeg
1 tablespoon soda
½ cup nut meats
Flour enough to make stiff batter
½ pound sugar

Mix in order given, bake in loaf in slow oven.—Mrs. John Buckley.

Sponge Cake.

1½ cup sugar
3 eggs
1¾ cups flour

1 cup boiling water
1 teaspoon baking powder
Vanilla

Beat eggs and sugar together ten minutes, add hot water, flour and baking powder, beat well, bake in slow oven forty minutes. Use orange icing.—Mrs. O. M. Evans.

Nut Cake

1 small cup sugar
One-third cup butter
2 eggs

2½ cups flour
2 teaspoons baking powder
1 pound ground walnuts

Beat sugar, butter and eggs to a very soft cream, add milk and flour a little at a time, sift flour and baking powder last, flour some of the nuts and mix in last, make a boiled icing, spread between layers and sprinkle with remaining nuts.—Mrs. L. P. Madsen.

Apple Sauce Cake.

1 cup sugar
One-third cup butter
2 cups flour
1 cup unsweetened apple
sauce
1 cup raisins

1 teaspoon soda
1 teaspoon cinnamon
½ teaspoon cloves
½ teaspoon nutmeg
½ teaspoon allspice
1 cup chopped nuts

Cream, butter and sugar together, add ingredients in order given, sifting spices and soda with flour, flour raisins and nuts before adding; bake in a deep pan for forty minutes.—Mrs. E. E. Nelson.

Spice Cake.

1 cup sour cream
2 small cups brown sugar
1 level teaspoon soda
3 eggs, white and yolks
beaten separately

2 teaspoons cinnamon
½ teaspoon cloves
½ teaspoon nutmeg
1 teaspoon allspice
1 teaspoon ginger

Flour to make a batter not too stiff, stir cream and brown sugar until all lumps are dissolved, then add soda and other ingredients.—Maggie E. Larson.

COFFEE CAKE

1 cup butter
1 cup sugar
3 eggs beaten separately
1 teaspoon cinnamon
1 teaspoon allspice

1 pound raisins chopped, mixed
in flour
1 cup strong coffee
1 teaspoonful soda mixed in coffee
½ teaspoon cloves
Vanilla to taste

Cream, butter and sugar, add ingredients in order given; bake one hour in slow oven.—Mrs. K. Mander.

Marble Cake.
White Part.

1½ cups sugar
½ cup butter creamed with
sugar
1 cup milk

Whites of 3 eggs, beaten stiff
1 teaspoon lemon extract
2 teaspoons baking powder
3 cups flour

Mix in order given.

Dark Part.

½ cup butter
1 cup brown sugar
1 cup molasses
1½ cups sour milk
1 teaspoon soda mixed with
milk

½ teaspoonful clover
½ teaspoonful cinnamon
½ teaspoonful nutmeg
½ teaspoonful allspice
Yolks of three eggs
Flour for stiff batter

Drop white and dark parts alternately into greased pan and bake in slow oven.—Mrs. G. A. Bernard.

Ginger Cake.

Cream 1 cup butter with
½ cup brown sugar
1½ cup molasses
1 cup sour milk
1 tablespoon ginger

1 teaspoon cinnamon
3 well beaten eggs
1 teaspoon soda dissolved in water
Flour for stiff batter

Mix in order given and bake fifty minutes in a slow oven. Serve with whipped cream or white icing.—Mrs. Ted Peterson.

Orange Cake.

1 cup sugar	1 cup orange juice
3 eggs	2½ cups flour
½ cup melted butter	2 teaspoons baking powder

Mix sugar, eggs, melted butter together, beat thoroughly, add orange juice, then flour and baking powder. Bake in layers.—Mrs. H. M. Heuson.

Filling.

1 cup sugar	1 tablespoon grated orange peel
½ cup orange juice	1 teaspoon butter
1 tablespoon lemon juice	1 egg
2 tablespoons flour	

Mix in order given and cook in double boiler ten minutes; spread when cool.

Egyptian Cake.

½ tablespoon butter	1 cup milk
½ tablespoon lard	4 tablespoons ground chocolate
1½ cup sugar	5 tablespoons hot water
2 egg yolks	1½ teaspoons baking powder
3 eggs, whites	1 teaspoon vanilla

Cream, butter, lard and sugar, add egg yolks, chocolate dissolved in water and other ingredients, add lastly the egg whites, beaten stiff.

Nouget Filling.

2 cups powdered sugar	3 tablespoons milk
1 egg yolk	1 cup nut meats
	Vanilla flavoring

Mix in order given.—Mrs. H. E. Atchison.

Almond Nut Squares.

6 eggs	1 cup flour
1 cup sugar	1 teaspoon baking powder

Beat yolks of eggs till light, add sugar and half of sifted flour, egg white s beaten stiff and remainder of flour,beat well and add one teaspoon vanilla.

Icing.

2 cups powdered sugar	1 egg white, beaten stiff
¼ pound butter	Almond or banana flavoring

Cut cake in squares, ice and roll in chopped nuts; bake five minutes.—Mrs. R. Alexander.

Raisin Filling.

1 cup sugar	Whites of 2 eggs
½ cup boiling water	One-third package raisins

Boil sugar and water until it threads, add two egg whites, beaten stiff; wash and grind raisins, add to filling.—Mrs. O. M. Evans.

Sea Foam Icing.

2 cups brown sugar   Whites of 2 eggs
½ cup granulated sugar

Cover sugar with water, boil until it threads, pour slowly into well beaten whites, beat until quite stiff, add a little powdered sugar to harden, nuts and vanilla.—Mrs. Ralph Saum.

Chocolate Filling.

10 tablespoons chocolate   10 tablespoons milk or cream
10 tablespoons sugar

Cook until thick and smooth, spread between layers and on top.—Mrs. L. P. Madsen.

Angel Food.

1½ cups egg whites   1½ cups granulated sugar
1 teaspoon cream of tartar   1 cup flour
½ teaspoon almond extract

Have egg whites very cold, beat in two portions on large platters until so stiff as to be easily cut with a knife. Sift sugar and cream of tartar four times, place all the whites in large mixing bowl and, with a big spoon, fold in the sugar, dusting on a little at a time until all is used; have flour sifted four times and fold into mixture in same way, being careful not to beat it as that makes the mixture fall into a batter, when instead it should look like a great heap of frosting, when folding in flour add extract. Pour into ungreased pan, bake forty-five minutes in moderate oven. When done, take out, turn pan up side down and allow it to rest on cups until cold, then shake out of pan. Frost with soft boiled icing.—Mrs. T. F. Maher.

Date Cake.

1½ cups brown sugar   2 cups flour
½ cups butter   1 tablespoon cinnamon
1 cup sour milk   1 cup chopped dates
1 egg   1 cup walnuts
1 small teaspoon soda

—Mrs. Dwight Meteer.

Spice Jam Cake.

1 cup sugar   ½ teaspoonful of cloves
½ cup butter   1 teaspoonful of soda
4 eggs   2 tablespoonsful of any jam
1 teaspoonful each of   1 cup sour milk
   allspice and cinnamon

Flour to make the right consistency.—Maybel DeBusk.

Cream Cakes.

½ cup butter   4 eggs
1 cup boiling water   1 cup flour

Heat butter and water to boiling point, add flour all at once, and stir vigorously, remove from fire as soon as mixed, and add unbeaten eggs one at a time, beating until thoroughly mixed, between the addition of eggs, drop by spoonfuls on a buttered sheet, one and one-half inches apart, shaping with handle of spoon as nearly circular as possible, having mixture slightly piled in center, bake thirty minutes in a moderate oven; with a sharp knife make a cut in each, large enough to admit of cream filling. This recipe makes eighteen small cream cakes. Precaution: Do not remove cream cakes from oven before thoroughly cooked, they will fall. Test by removing one.

Cream Filling.

⅞ cup sugar
One-third cup flour
⅛ teaspoon salt

2 eggs
2 cups scalded milk
1 teaspoon vanilla or ½ teaspoon lemon extract

Mix dry ingredients, add eggs slightly beaten and pour on gradually scalded milk; cook fifteen minutes in double boiler, stirring constantly until thickened, afterwards occasionally cool and flavor.—Mrs. R. E. Robson.

Eclairs.

Shape cream cake mixture four and one-half inches long by one inch wide, by forcing through a pastry bag and tube; bake twenty-five minutes in a moderate oven; split and fill with vanilla, coffee or chocolate filling, frost with confectioner's frosting to which is added one-third cup melted fondant, dipping top of eclairs in frosting while it is hot.—Mrs. R. E. Robson.

Delicious Graham Layer Cake.

20 graham crackers rolled fine
½ cup sugar
2 tablespoons butter

3 eggs
½ cup milk
1½ teaspoons baking powder

Cream, butter and sugar, add beaten yolks of eggs, milk and rolled crackers sifted with baking powder, lastly add well beaten whites of eggs, bake in two layers.

Filling for Center.

One-third cup butter
1½ cups confectioner's sugar

1 tablespoon boiling water
½ teaspoon vanilla

Add boiling water to butter, cream with sugar, add vanilla and spread between layers. Cover with boiled White Mountain Frosting.—Mrs. R. E. Robson.

Fruit Cake.

3 tablespoon lard and butter mixed
2 cups strong coffee, hot
2 cups brown sugar
½ cup molasses
3 cups flour
3 eggs
1 teaspoon salt
1 teaspoon soda

2 teaspoons cloves
2 teaspoons cinnamon
2 teaspoons nutmeg
1 teaspoons ginger
1 pound raisins
1 pound almonds
1 pound currants
1 pound figs
½ pounds citron

—Mrs. M. J. Butler.

Spice Cake.

½ cup butter
1 cup sugar
2 cups sifted flour
2 level teaspoons baking powder

½ teaspoon cinnamon
½ teaspoon nutmeg
½ teaspoon salt
¾ cup water
2 eggs

Cream, butter and sugar, add eggs, sift together three times the dry ingredients and add alternately with water; bake in moderate oven.—Mrs. T. H. Morgan.

COOKIES and DOUGHNUTS

Compiled by Mrs. E. E. Nelson.

"A home without a cookie jar,
Is not the home for me,
A home without a cookie jar,
I hope to never see."

Vanilla Strips.

1 pound almonds
Whites 4 eggs
1 pound powdered sugar

1 tablespoon vanilla or
1 vanilla bean

Beat whites of eggs, add sugar gradually; put half of this aside for icing, to remainder add ground almonds (do not blanch) and vanilla, roll in thin strips, spread with icing and bake.—Mrs. H. P. Allen.

Ginger Snaps.

1 cup molasses
½ cup butter and lard
     mixed
2½ cups flour

1 tablespoon ginger
1 tablespoon soda
2 tablespoons warm milk
Two-thirds teaspoon salt

Heat molasses to boiling point, add shortening, soda and ginger, dissolved in milk, salt and flavor; chill thoroughly, roll as thin as possible, place near together and bake in moderate oven. During rolling keep remaining mixture in cool place or it will be necessary to add more flour which makes cookies hard, rather than crisp.—Mrs. T. W. Bird.

Chocolate Nut and Fruit Cookies.

One-third cottolene
1 cup sugar
¼ cup grated chocolate
1 cup chopped nuts
1 cup raisins seeded and
     chopped

2¼ cups flour
2 tablespoons boiling water
2 tablespoons sugar
2 eggs well beaten
3 tablespoons baking powder
¼ teaspoon salt

Cream cottolene, add sugar, chocolate melted over boiling water and beaten eggs, mix flour (reserve one-fourth cup), baking powder and salt, add fruit and nuts dredged with flour (one-fourth cup), chill mixture, drop from spoon on well greased baking pans, one and one-half inches apart; press a raisin or half nut meat in center of each and bake in a moderate oven.— Mrs. T. W. Bird.

Chocolate Brownies.

2 eggs
1 cup sugar
½ cup butter
2 squares chocolate

½ cup flour
1 teaspoon vanilla
1 cup chopped nuts

Melt butter and chocolate together, add sugar, eggs, unbeaten, and other ingredients; pour into a buttered pan about one-fourth inch thick and bake; cut into squares and remove from pan.—Mrs. E. E. Nelson.

Oat Meal .Cookies.

1½ cups sugar
1 cup butter
½ cup sour milk

2 cups of oatmeal
4 cups white flour
1 cup raisins and currants

1 teaspoon soda dissolved   3 eggs
   in milk   1 cup chopped nuts

Drop these by spoonfuls in pans.—Mrs. A. G. Grosnick.

Spriets.

1 pound butter   Pinch of baking powder
1 cup sugar   Almond flavoring
1 egg   Flour

Cream, butter, add sugar and beaten egg, sift baking powder with flour and stir in as much as possible then knead on a board until stiff; shape by running through spriet machine, if too much flour is added cakes will fall apart when put through machine and if not enough the little points will not stay in shape.—Mrs. D. D. Puncheon.

Honey Cookies.

1 cup of lard   1 teaspoonful of cloves
1 cup of sour cream   1 teaspoonful of allspice
1 cup of honey   1 teaspoonful of cinnamon
1 cup of sugar   1 teaspoonful nutmeg
1 egg   2 tablespoonsful of melted
2 teaspoonsful of soda   chocolate
   Pinch of salt

Flour to make a soft dough; do not bake too long, roll them quite thick. —Maggie E. Larson.

Lemon Queens.

½ cup butter   ¼ teaspoon soda
1 cup sugar   4 eggs
1 lemon (rind and juice)   1¼ cups flour
¼ teaspoon salt

Cream the butter and sugar, add yolks of eggs, well beaten, lemon juice and grated rind, add flour with salt and soda and beaten whites last. They may be baked as cup cakes or as thin wafers.—Mrs. A. E. MacArthur.

Drop Ginger Cookies.

1 cup molasses   4½ cups flour
1 cup sugar   ½ teaspoon ginger
1 cup melted butter   ½ teaspoon cloves
1 cup hot water   ½ teaspoon nutmeg
2 eggs   ½ teaspoon allspice
1 teaspoon cinnamon   1 teaspoon soda

Mix ingredients in order given, sifting flour, spices and soda together, drop on buttered pans, place a raisin in center of each cookie and bake.— Mrs. D. L. Barnard.

Pfefferunesle.

1 pound sugar   1 teaspoon nutmeg
½ pound almonds   1 teaspoon cinnamon
½ pound citron   1 teaspoon cloves
½ pound candied lemon peels   ½ teaspoon baking powder
4 eggs   Flour

Grind ingredients and mix by kneading, adding enough flour to make stiff enough to drop on buttered pans; let them stand over night then bake; put in a covered jar to soften for one month.—Mrs. R. F. Barker.

Filled Cookies.

1 cup sugar	3½ cups flour
½ cup butter	2 teaspoons cream of tartar
1 egg	1 teaspoon soda
½ cup sweet milk	1 teaspoon vanilla

Mix ingredients in order given, roll them and cut out; press two cookies together with a teaspoonful of filling between.

Filling.

1 cup chopped raisins	1 teaspoon flour
½ cup sugar	½ cup water
	1 tablespoon lemon juice

Cook raisins, sugar, flour and water until thick, cool and add lemon juice.
—Mrs. H. J. Butcher.

Wandering Jews.

1½ cups sugar	Flour enough to roll
1 cup butter	1 teaspoon soda
3 eggs	¼ teaspoon cloves
1 cup chopped nuts	¼ teaspoon nutmeg
1 cup fruit (figs, raisins	½ teaspoon cinnamon
and citron)	

Cream, butter and sugar, add eggs well beaten, spices and fruit well flavored, flour and soda dissolved in a little hot water.—Mrs. H. P. Allen.

Sour Cream Cookies.

1½ cups sugar	1 teaspoon soda
1 cup butter	1 teaspoon lemon extract or ½
2 eggs	grated nutmeg
1 cup sour cream	

Cream, sugar and butter, add eggs well beaten, then flavor, cream and soda, enough flour to make dough soft as can be rolled, dip in chopped walnuts mixed with sugar, bake quickly.—Mrs. H. C. Christie.

Peanut Wafers.

1 tablespoon butter	½ cup flour
2 tablespoons sugar	½ teaspoon baking powder
2 tablespoons milk	½ teaspoon salt
1 egg, well beaten	½ cup peanuts finely chopped

Cream, butter and sugar, add milk and egg, sift together flour, baking powder and salt, add to mixture, then add peanuts, drop by teaspoonsful on an unbuttered tin one-half inch apart, place one-half peanut on each and bake slowly.—Mrs. Gilbert Palmer.

Doughnuts.

1 cup sugar	2 teaspoons cream of tartar
2 eggs, beaten light	2 teaspoons soda
1 tablespoon melted lard	½ teaspoon nutmeg
1 cup milk	

Flour to knead as soft as possible; fry in hot lard.—Mrs. A. E. Hardesty.

38

Castle Gate and Clear Creek Coals make Baking Days Easier

For over a quarter of a century these two famous Utah Coals have been Used

REG. UNITED STATES PATENT OFFICE

by thousands of western housewives, because they are Clean Free-Burning and Dependable. Ask Your Dealer

Mined Only By

Utah Fuel Company

The Business of

HOUSEKEEPING

IS A BIG ONE—Whether one considers the capital invested or The Health and Efficiency of the family. The matter of securing suitable food for the family at low cost is certainly a very important problem and the saving of a dollar or two is welcomed by everyone when made without a sacrifice of quality. Foods of questionable quality never find shelf room at the UNITED while our tremendous quantity buying enables us to quote lowest prices always.

UNITED GROCERY COMPANY

Phone Main 600.

Prompt Service, Salt Lake City.

DESSERTS

Compiled by Mrs. J. W. Brewer.

"What moistens the lips and brightens the eye?
What calls back the past like a rich, juicy pie?"

Carrot Pudding.

1 cup grated raw carrot	1 cup raisins
1 cup grated raw potatoes	1 teaspoon soda
1 cup sugar	½ teaspoon cloves
1 cup flour	¼ teaspoon cinnamon
½ cup butter	¼ teaspoon nutmeg

Add soda to potatoes, flour, fruit and mix other ingredients in order given, pour into a buttered mould and steam three hours. Serve with either hot or hard sauce.—Mrs. J. W. Brewer.

Pineapple Bavarian Cream.

1 can pineapple	½ package gelatine
2 tablespoons sugar	½ cup water
	½ pint cream

Drain juice from medium sized can of pineapple, add sugar and beat, soak gelatine in cold water and add to the hot juice, when cool add the sliced pineapple and cream, whipped stiff.—Mrs. O. R. Hagen.

Chocolate Tart.

One-third cup chocolate (grated)	¾ cup nuts, chopped
	1 teaspoon baking powder
1 cup cracker meal (grind soda crackers)	1 cup milk
	1 teaspoon vanilla
1 cup sugar	Whites of 3 eggs

Mix ingredients in order given, beating whites of eggs stiff and folding in lightly; bake forty minutes in a round baking pan, when cold whip one-half pint of cream, flavor with vanilla and spread on top.—Mrs. O. R. Hagen.

Orange Cream Pie.

3 eggs	Butter size of walnut
3 tablespoons flour	1½ cups sugar
1 pint milk	Pinch salt
Grated rind of an orange	1 cup orange juice

Mixed together yolks of eggs, sugar, flour, salt, grated rind, milk and orange juice, boil until thick, beat with egg beater; take from fire and add butter, fill pastry shells and cover with whites of eggs or whipped cream. —Mrs. A. P. Kimball.

Cocoanut Pie.

3 cups milk	1½ cups sugar
½ cup cocoanut	2 eggs
4 tablespoons flour	Butter size of walnut

Beat yolks, add dry ingredients, then milk, gradually stirring until smooth, then cook, fill pie shells soon as taken from oven, whip whites for meringue, return to oven to brown. This makes two pies.—Mrs. R. C. McLeese.

Hot Water Pie Crust.

1 cup lard
½ cup boiling water
3 cups flour
1 teaspoon salt
½ teaspoon baking powder

Mix lard with boiling water and stir until lard is melted, sift dry ingredients and add while the mixture is still hot. This quantity makes two pies.—Mrs. W. C. Barton.

Date Pudding.

1 cup walnuts
1 cup dates
3 eggs
9 crackers rolled
1 heaping teaspoon baking powder

Chop walnuts and dates, add beaten eggs, crackers and baking powder, bake and serve cold with whipped cream in tall sherbet glasses.—Mrs. Cambria A. Wilson.

Butter Pie.

3 eggs
¼ pound butter
3 tablespoons flour or cornstarch
4 teacups water
1½ teacups sugar
Vanilla

Bake crust as for lemon pie, mix well together sugar, flour and butter, add water and yolks of eggs, well beaten, cook in double boiler, put in crust, cover with whites of eggs, well beaten, sweetened and flavored, brown in oven.—Mrs. F. Riley.

Walnut Pie.

2 eggs
2 tablespoons lemon juice
1 tablespoon cornstarch
1 cup finely chopped
English walnuts
½ cup sugar
2 oranges (juice)

Mix as for lemon pie; bake in shell, using whites for meringue.—Mrs. Alfred K. Fail.

Strawberries—French Fashion.

Stem and cut the strawberries into slices, put them into punch or lemonade glasses, fill each glass two-thirds full with orange juice, add one tablespoon of powdered sugar, one tablespoon of chipped ice.—Mrs. B. Calk

Food for the Gods

1 pound walnuts
1 pound dates
4 tablespoons grated bread crumbs
1 teaspoon baking powder
½ pound powdered sugar
6 eggs

Mix yolks of eggs with bread crumbs, add the beaten whites last, bake 20 minutes. Serve cold with whipped cream.—Mrs. A. W. Ashworth.

Date Pudding

¾ cup soft bread crumbs
½ cup nuts, chopped
½ teaspoon baking powder
½ cup sugar
½ cup milk
½ cup dates, chopped
1 egg
1 tablespoon butter

Mix dry ingredients, add butter melted, then milk and egg (beaten). Pour into greased gem pans, bake until well browned. Serve with cream or brandy sauce.—Mrs. Garr.

Pineapple Dainty

1 envelope gelatine
1 pint can shredded pine-
apple
1 cup sugar
¾ cup cold water
1 pint boiling water

Dissolve gelatine in cold water, add boiling water and sugar; when this boils add pineapple, pour into moulds and serve cold with whipped cream and chopped walnuts.—Mrs. Dwight Meteer.

Fig Pudding.

¼ pound beef suet
1 large apple
2 cups bread crumbs
2 eggs
½ pound figs
¾ cup brown sugar
¼ cup milk
12 tablespoons flour

Grind suet, figs and apple, cream, suet, add figs, apple and sugar. Pour milk over bread crumbs and add yolks of eggs well beaten, combine mixtures, add flour and whites of eggs well beaten. Steam four hours in buttered pan. Serve with lemon sauce.

Lemon Sauce.

One-third cup butter
Yolks 3 eggs
3 tablespoons lemon juice
1 cup sugar
One-third cup boiling water

Cream butter, add sugar, yolks of eggs well beaten and water. Cook in double boiler, add lemon juice.—Mrs. O. M. Evans.

Pumpkin Pie.

1 pint boiled dry pumpkin
1 cup brown sugar
3 eggs
2 tablespoons molasses
1 pint milk
1 tablespoon melted butter
1 tablespoon ginger
1 teaspoon cinnamon
Pinch salt

Put good layer of flour, patted down on bottom of crust to keep filling from being absorbed. Bake in moderately slow oven. This makes two pies. May use canned pumpkin if desired.—Mrs. A. M. Henderson.

Stewed Pumpkin for Pies.

Deep colored pumpkins are best. Cut pumpkin in half, remove seeds, pare and cut in small pieces. Put in sauce pan with a very little water and cook slowly until tender. Now set on back of stove and cook slowly for half a day. Stir often to keep from burning. When cool, press through a colander.—Mrs. A. M. Henderson.

Graham Pudding.

1½ cups graham flour
1 cup chopped suet
½ cup milk
½ cup raisins
½ cup currants
½ cup walnuts
½ cup molasses
¼ cup butter
1 egg, well beaten
1 level teaspoon soda

A little salt, one-fourth teaspoon each of mace and cinnamon. Mix all together thoroughly. Steam two and one-half hours, add flour last, the butter may be omitted.—Mrs. Hodge Marshall.

Delicious Pudding.

1 pint fine bread crumbs
1 quart milk
5 yolks of eggs
½ pint sugar
5 tablespoons powdered
sugar
5 whites of eggs
1 tablespoon melted butter
Little grated rind lemon
2 tablespoons lemon juice
1 teaspoon vanilla
½ pint cocoanut

Soak crumbs in milk fifteen minutes. Beat yolks and sugar light, stir in butter, add rind and juice lemon and vanilla, add these to bread and mix in cocoanut. Bake until custard is set in middle. Beat whites with sugar and when pudding is done cover with cocoanut and meringue. Brown and serve cold.—Mrs. Cambria Wilson.

Lemon Pies (Superior).

2 lemons
1¼ cups sugar
2 heaping tablespoons cornstarch

3 eggs
1½ cups boiling water
1 tablespoon butter

To the grated rind and juice of the lemon add the sugar and cornstarch then add the water and butter, cook in double boiler until it drops from the spoon like honey. When cool pour into deep crusts, which have previously been baked. Beat the whites of the eggs, add three teaspoons of sugar, spread on top and brown in a hot over.—Mrs. Katherine Manders.

Raisin Pie.

1 pound raisins
1 cup water
1 cup sugar

Juice of ½ lemon
2 tablespoons flour

Boil raisins and water until soft, add flour mixed with sugar and lemon juice. Bake in a rich pie crust.—Mrs. Wm. Cavanaugh.

Pineapple Cream.

1 can grated pineapple
1 cup sugar
½ package gelatine
3 cups whipped cream

½ lemon
1 teaspoon vanilla
1 cup walnuts

Cook pineapple and sugar ten minutes, add gelatine softened in cold water, add juice of lemon, vanilla and walnuts. When cold fold in cream, will serve twelve.—Mrs. W. M. Rees.

Hamburg Sponge.

2 lemons
1 cup sugar

8 eggs
½ package gelatine
Whipped cream

Heat juice of lemons, and one-half cup sugar, add beaten yolks of eggs and one-half cup sugar. Beat all together, cook in double boiler until thick, add gelatine softened in cold water. When cold fold in beaten whites of eggs. Mould and serve with whipped cream.—Mrs. W. M. Rees.

Mince Meat.

5 cups chopped cooked meat
2½ cups chopped suet
7½ cups chopped apples
3 cups cider
½ cup vinegar
5 cups sugar
¾ pound citron
2½ cups chopped raisins
1 cup brandy

1 tablespoon mace
3 tablespoons cinnamon
2 tablespoons cloves
2 tablespoons allspice
2 tablespoons nutmeg
2 tablespoons lemon extract
1 tablespoon almond extract
Juice of 2 lemons
Juice of 1 orange

Mix above ingredients, reduce liquor in which meat was cooked to three cups full, add to mixture. Season with salt. Bring to boiling point and let simmer one and one-half hours, seal and it will keep for years.—Mrs. T. F. Maher.

Mince Meat.

2 pounds boiled lean beef chopped fine
1 pound suet minced to powder
5 pounds apples chopped
2 pounds raisins
2 pounds Sultana raisins
2 pounds currants
¾ pound citron, cut fine

2 tablespoons cinnamon
1 tablespoon nutmeg
2 tablespoons mace
1 tablespoon cloves
1 tablespoon allspice
1 tablespoon fine salt
2½ pounds of brown sugar
1 quart sherry
1 pint of brandy

Do not cook. Mix thoroughly and cover closely.—Mrs. Gilbert Palmer.

Chocolate Pie.

2 cups milk
Yolks 2 eggs
Two-thirds cup sugar

2 tablespoons cornstarch mixed in a little milk
2 tablespoons grated chocolate

Heat the milk and sugar together, when hot add rest and boil until thick. Put in a baked crust.—Mrs. H. H. Murphy.

Buttermilk Pie.

1 cup sugar
1 tablespoon flour
1 tablespoon butter

1 pint buttermilk
2 eggs
Lemon extract

Cream, sugar, butter and flour together, then add two eggs well beaten and one pint of fresh buttermilk. Lemon flavor to taste, put in pie tins and bake.—Mrs. H. H. Murphy.

French Macaroon Cream.

1 tablespoon gelatine
2 cups milk
2 teaspoons cocoa
1 teaspoon vanilla

3 eggs
½ cup sugar
Two-thirds cups crushed macaroons Or ground nuts

Soak gelatine in three tablespoonsful cold water, place milk in double boiler with cocoa, heat until scalded, beat yolks of eggs, add sugar, add to milk and stir until it thickens, remove from fire, when cool add whites of eggs beaten stiff, add pinch of salt. Last stir in the macaroons and flavor with vanilla. Serve with whipped cream.—Mrs. R. H. Hawley.

Angel Ginger Bread.

1 egg
½ cup sugar
¼ cup molasses
½ cup hot water

¼ cup melted butter
1 heaping cup flour
1 teaspoon soda
½ teaspoon salt
½ teaspoon ginger

Dissolve soda in hot water, mix ingredients in order given and bake in moderate oven. Serve hot with whipped cream.—Mrs. A. E. Wells.

Lemon Pie.

4 eggs
½ cup sugar
1 lemon

4 tablespoons water
1 tablespoon butter

Separate yolks from whites, beat the yolks to a thick cream, add sugar, the grated rind and juice of the lemon, water and butter, cook in double boiler till a thick custard is formed, then fold in the stiffly beaten whites of two eggs. Turn into a baked shell, bake and add two whites as meringue.—Mrs. Gilbert Palmer.

FROZEN DESSERTS

Compiled by Mrs. Hodge Marshall.

"And each one asks, 'What can this be?'
'Tis frozen dainties, that I see."

Frozen Eggnog.

4 eggs	½ cup sugar or more to taste
1 pint milk	½ cup whiskey
1 pint cream	Little nutmeg

Beat yolks of eggs and sugar to cream, add milk, beat whites of eggs stiffly and fold in, whip cream and fold in, add nutmeg, freeze, add whiskey and freeze more and let stand an hour before serving.—Mrs. W. D. Leonard.

Peach Ice.

1 can, or 12 large peaches	1 pint water
2 coffee cups sugar	3 eggs, whites only

Break peaches rather fine, beat eggs to stiff froth, stir all ingredients together and freeze.—Mrs. C. W. Evers.

Grape Juice Sherbet.

6 cups grape juice   1½ cups sugar   4 juicy lemons

Dissolve sugar into grape juice, add juice of lemons strained, free, serve with Maraschino cherry on each dish.—Mrs. C. F. Anderson.

Southern Sherbet.

1 can grated pineapple	1 pint sugar
1 tablespoon gelatine	1 egg whites
	Juice of 1 lemon

Strain pineapple, dissolve gelatine in a little hot water, beat egg white to froth, and mix, freeze.—Mrs. MacArthur.

Maraschino Ice.

4 cups water	2 cups Maraschino cherries
2 cups sugar	¼ cup lemon juice
Grated rind of 2 oranges	

Make syrup, boiling water and sugar twenty minutes, add lemon juice, cool and strain, add Maraschino and freeze.—Mrs. D. L. Barnard.

Berry Sherbet.

1 quart berries	1 quart water
1 pound sugar	2 lemons

Boil sugar and water five minutes, for syrup crush berries in lemon juice, pour cold syrup on berries and strain. When nearly frozen add white of one egg well beaten.—Mrs. D. L. Barnard.

Chocolate Ice Cream.

1 pint milk	2 squares chocolate
2 level tablespoons flour	2 teaspoons vanilla
1 cup sugar	1 quart thin cream

Bring milk to boiling point, add sugar and flour thoroughly mixed, cook in double boiler twenty minutes stirring constantly. Melt chocolate by placing in sauce pan and pouring in one cup boiling water, stir until perfectly smooth, add boiling milk. When cool add cream and vanilla.—Mrs. Harry Bible.

Lemon Milk Sherbet.

1 quart milk	2 cups sugar
3 lemons, juice	½ cup pineapple

Dissolve sugar in milk, add lemon juice which will curdle it, add pineapple, then freeze.—Mrs. R. F. Barker.

Grape Sherbet.

¾ quart water	2 lemons' juice
¾ quart sugar	2 oranges' juice
10c box marshmellows	1 pint bottle grape juice

Boil water and sugar five minutes, to make syrup dissolve marshmellows in hot syrup, add juice of lemons and oranges, last add grape juice and freeze.—Mrs. Claude Anderson.

Pineapple Cream.

½ can grated pineapple	½ lemon juice
3 tablespoons sugar	2 tablespoons gelatine
1 pint whipped cream	

Mix pineapple, sugar and lemon juice together, dissolve gelatine in one-third cup cold water, let stand fifteen minutes before adding to pineapple, place mixture in pan of cold water, stir until it strings, then add whipped cream. Mould and serve very cold, with strawberry syrup.—Mrs. A. C. French.

Frozen Pineapple Custard.

1 can grated pineapple	1 cupful sweet cream
1 two-thirds cups of sugar	2 eggs
1 pint milk	

Beat yolks of eggs with two-thirds of a cup of sugar, add one pint of milk, heat to near boiling point, stirring constantly, when cold add the cream and the beaten whites of the eggs, place in freezer and turn until nearly solid, then stir in the pineapple which should stand one hour with a cupful of sugar over it, freeze.—Mrs. H. C. Christie.

Strawberry Sherbet.

2 boxes berries, crushed	Whites of 3 eggs
3 cups sugar	Water to make 2 quarts of Sherbet

Make a syrup of the sugar and water, add the crushed berries and freeze. When nearly frozen add the well beaten whites of eggs and freeze till done. —Mrs. Harold Blatch.

Orange Ice.

1 cup sugar	Juice of 1 lemon
1 pint water	Juice of 1 orange
1 egg, white	

Make syrup of water and sugar, add juice of fruit, pour over beaten white of egg, beat five minutes and cool. Freeze rapidly, drain and pack.—Mrs. Thos. Alexander.

Maple Sugar Ice Cream.

1 cup maple syrup	1 pint cream	4 eggs

Heat syrup to boiling point, beat yolks and stir very slowly into heated syrup, beat cream and add, freeze, when freezing has begun put in beaten whites. This amount will serve six people.—Mrs. H. C. Christie.

Macaroon Mousse.

1 quart chilled double cream	2 tablespoons cold water
2 small cups crushed macaroons	3 tablespoons hot water
	1¼ tablespoons granulated gelatine
1 small cup sugar	½ cup of maraschino cordial

Soak gelatine in cold water and dissolve in hot water, cool and add to sweetened cream set in pan of ice water and whip steadily until it will hold its shape, then mix in macaroon crumbs and add cordial. Pour into round moulds with watertight cover and bury in ice and rock salt for four or five hours. To serve unmould and serve on paper doiley on dessert plates.—Mrs. J. McLachlan.

LUNCHEON and SUPPER DISHES

Compiled by Mrs. Harry Bible.

"The smile of the hostess is the cream of the feast."

Chili Con Carnie.

1½ to 2 pounds beef, off the round is best	2 large onions
	2 sauce peppers
2 cups Mexican beans	Salt and pepper to taste
1 can tomatoes	

Cut beef in small pieces, brown in butter, then cover with water and stew until very tender, then add beans, which have been boiled till tender, onions cut in slices, tomatoes and seasoning, simmer till thick, add olives just before serving. Some prefer the small brown kidney bean as the Mexican beans are bitter. Also they prefer three or four chili pepper cut up fine, or chili powder. If the latter chili powder is used then add red instead of black pepper.—Mrs. Goodman.

Croquettes With Peas.

2 cups cold roast lamb, chopped fine	2 cups cold mashed potatoes
	1 egg well beaten with ½ cup milk
1 medium size onion, chopped fine	Salt and pepper to taste

Mix well, shape and roll in bread crumbs, and fry in deep fat, (for peas.) 1 can peas thickened with milk and flour seasoned with salt, pepper and a small piece of butter, arrange croquettes on platter and pour the peas over them. Left over salmon can be used in place of lamb.—Mrs. Garr.

Salmon Croquettes.

1 can salmon	1 tablespoon celery, chopped fine
2 eggs	A scant ½ cup white sauce
1 tablespoon onion, chopped fine	Cracker crumbs
	Salt and pepper

Remove bones and skin from the salmon, drain off the liquor and mince salmon fine with fork, add the liquor which has been previously mixed with an equal amount of white sauce, add one well beaten egg and salt and pepper to taste. Mix well together, then add enough fine cracker or bread crumbs to make stiff enough to handle. Form in small cakes, dip in

beaten egg, roll in cracker crumbs and fry in deep, hot fat. The celery may be omitted or celery salt substituted. Serve with or without tomato sauce. —Mrs. Goodman.

Spanish Rice.

1 cup uncooked rice	1 green pepper
1 onion	1 bay leaf
1 can tomatoes	Salt and black pepper

Brown rice in a little bacon dripping, chop onion fine and brown with rice, pour on this tomatoes with green pepper and season. I sometimes add one can of crab or shrimp. Cook slowly on back of stove from three to four hours.—Mrs. W. D. Leonard.

Jellied Veal.

1 veal shank	2 pounds lean beef
1 pork shank	1 onion, salt and pepper

Cook all meat together with onion until very tender, remove bones and put meat through chopper, when broth is cold remove all fat from top. There should be about three cups broth. Return chopped meat to broth, season and cook a few minutes. Turn into individual moulds or large one and let stand over night.—Mrs. Harry Bible.

Salmon Balls.

1 cup canned or fresh salmon	1 tablespoon cream
½ cup canned or fresh peas	Cracker crumbs
4½ tablespoons butter	Salt, pepper and lemon juice for
½ teaspoon sugar	seasoning
3 tablespoons flour	½ cup milk, hot

Make white sauce by melting two tablespoons butter and stirring into it two and one-half tablespoons flour, add one-half cup milk and cook till usual thickness. Mix with salmon, seasoned with salt, a pinch of cayenne pepper, a little lemon juice and spread on a plate to cook. Then prepare peas, first heat them then add two and one-half tablespoons butter, one-half teaspoon sugar, one teaspoon flour, one tablespoon cream. Cook a minute or more. Shape a small portion of the salmon mixture into flat round cakes. Put a spoonful of peas in center. Press salmon up over. Roll in cracker dust and fry in deep, hot fat. To be extra nice dip in beaten egg after rolling in crackers, then roll in crackers again. Let stand several hours before frying.—Mrs. Goodman.

Sausage and Spaghetti in Tomato Sauce.

1 pound link sausage	½ package spaghetti
1 can tomato soup	½ cup hot water

Prick sausages and place in frying pan, cover with boiling water and simmer till thoroughly done, about one hour. Cook spaghetti in boiling water till tender, drain, rinse in cold water and drain again, combine with sausage, add soup diluted with one-half cup hot water and heat thoroughly.— Mrs. MacArthur.

Scalloped Cheese.

1 cup bread crumbs	1 tablespoon melted butter
2 cups milk	½ pound grated cheese
3 eggs	

Soak bread crumbs in milk, beat in three eggs, add melted butter and cheese, sprinkle top with fine bread crumbs and bake one-half hour in hot oven.—Mrs. Marshall.

Tomato Rarebit.

1 tablespoon chopped onion	2 cups finely cut cheese
3 tablespoons butter	½ teaspoon mustard
1 cup tomatoes	½ teaspoon salt
2 tablespoons flour	Paprika
¾ cup thin cream	2 eggs

Cook onion in one tablespoon of butter five minutes, add one cup tomatoes and cook two minutes and strain, in a sauce pan melt two tablespoons butter, add two tablespoons flour, rub together and add three-forths cup thin cream. Cook till thick and add two cups finely chopped cheese, the tomatoes and one-half teaspoon each mustard, salt and a little paprika. Stir till cheese is thoroughly blended and add two lightly beaten eggs. Cook one minute and serve on toast.—Mrs. Harry Bible.

Salmon Loaf.

1 can salmon picked fine with a fork	4 teaspoons butter
4 eggs	¾ cup bread crumbs
	Salt and pepper to taste

Combine ingredients and steam one hour in a quart bowl. Serve with white sauce or egg sauce.

Ham Canape.

Small loaf bread	1 tablespoon melted butter
½ pound boiled ham	1 cup grated cheese
2 tablespoons milk	White pepper
3 hard boiled eggs	

Cut bread into slices one-half inch thich. Shape with biscuit cutter. Brown on both sides in melted butter. Grind ham, season with pepper and moisten with milk and place on browned bread. Sprinkle with cheese, place in oven until cheese is melted, garnish with slices of eggs and serve hot.—Mrs. Cambria A. Wilson.

Deviled Crab.

1 tablespoon butter	½ teaspoon paprika
1 tablespoon flour	1 teaspoon lemon juice
1 cup milk	½ cup sherry wine
1 teaspoon salt	1 cup crab meat
	¼ cup mushrooms cut in quarters

Melt butter, add flour and when blended milk, then other ingredients. Serve on toast or in ramequins. I used in ramequins buttered crumbs, should be sprinkled over top and browned in oven.—Mrs. E. E. Nelson.

Shrimp Wiggle.

½ teaspoon Armours' beef extract	2 tablespoons flour
½ teaspoon salt	⅛ teaspoon paprika
4 tablespoons butter	1 cup shrimp
1½ cups milk	1 cup canned peas

Melt butter and add flour with salt and paprika, stir constantly. Pour on milk gradually, when thick add beef extract and shrimps broken pieces and peas drained of liquor.—Mrs. A. Gallacher.

Lobster a la Newberg.

2 small lobsters	2 tablespoons brandy and sherry
1 cup cream	Yolks of 4 eggs
4 tablespoons butter	1 teaspoon salt
Few grains of mace	Few grains cayenne

Cut lobster into small pieces, cook slowly in butter for five minutes, add seasonings, brandy and sherry and simmer five minutes longer. Combine the cream with the beaten eggs and pour slowly into the cooking mixture. Stir constantly for one and one-half minutes. Serve at once on toast. —Mrs. O. W. Kumrow.

Fluffy Omelet.

1 egg
Salt
1 teaspoon butter

Beat yolks till very light. Beat white until stiff. Pour yolk over white and gently fold in. Pour into hot pan with butter and cook slowly ten minutes. Put in oven to dry top. Season well and fold one-half over other. Before folding chopped ham, jelly or cheese may be put on.—Mrs. Chas. Reese.

Stuffed Peppers.

Chopped meat (any kind)   Moisten with white sauce
Add onion, salt and pepper

Remove end and seeds from large green peppers. Fill with mixture and bake one-half hour.

White Sauce.

1 cup milk
2 tablespoons flour
1 tablespoon butter
Salt and pepper to taste
—Mrs. Chas. Reese.

Croquettes.

3 cups meat (veal, lamb
1 cup white sauce
and chicken) chopped

Season with salt, pepper, onion, parsley. Mix thoroughly and allow to set one hour. Shape in croquettes, roll in cracker crumbs, dip in egg, roll again in cracker crumbs, fry in hot fat.—Mrs. Chas. Reese.

Rice Croquettes.

2 cups steamed rice
Salt to taste, add egg to rice
1 egg (well beaten)
and mix thoroughly

Spread thin layer on plate and shape by spoonful, dip in egg and cracker crumbs and fry in hot fat. Serve with cheese sauce.

Cheese Sauce.

1/2 to 1 cup cheese (grated)   Paprika
2 cups white sauce
—Mrs. Chas. Rees.

Cheese Souffle.

1 tablespoon flour
4 tablespoons bread crumbs
1/2 cup cold milk
1/2 pound cheese (grated)
1 cup hot milk
1/2 teaspoon salt
Stir until smooth and
Pepper
thick

Stir until cheese is melted, add two eggs, one whites beaten separately. Bake until brown, fifteen minutes. Serve at once.—Mrs. R. W. Ashworth.

Veal Birds.

Round veal stake cut in pieces four inches by three inches.

Dressing.

One small loaf bread crumbled and seasoned with salt, pepper. Chopped celery, parsley, one egg, one tablespoon butter, mix well. Put dressing on each piece of veal, roll and fasten with toothpick. Dip in egg and cracker crumbs, fry brown on all sides. Pack in pan, cover with water. Bake in covered dish one hour.—Mrs. Harry R. Allen.

Creamed Ham.

Chopped ham.
1 cup white sauce

3 eggs (hard boiled and chopped)
Serve on toast.

White Sauce.

1 tablespoon butter
1 tablespoon flour

1 cup of milk

Cook to proper consistency in double boiler.—Mrs. L. P. Madsen.

Pressed Chicken.

One chicken cooked until it drops from bone. Remove from broth. Season broth with onion, salt, celery, pepper and boiled down to make one cup. Chop chicken fine, moisten with strained broth, pour into mould, cover and put on weight. Stand over night.—Mrs. L. W. Wardleigh.

Oyster Cocktail.

1 pint Olympia oysters
4 tablespoons vinegar
4 tablespoons grated
  horseradish

4 tablespoons tomato catsup
8 tablespoons lemon juice
Dash of tabasco

Have oysters very cold and serve in glasses.—Mrs. O. W. Kumrow.

Chicken Souffle.

2 cups cold chicken chopped
2 cups scalded milk
2 tablespoons butter
2 tablespoons flour
1 teaspoon chopped parsley

½ cup bread crumbs
1 teaspoon salt
Few grains of cayenne
4 eggs

Melt butter, add flour and seasonings, cook, add gradually the milk and cook until smooth, add chicken, bread crumbs and parsley, combine with beaten yolks, then fold in the whites beaten stiff. Turn into buttered baking dish and bake thirty-five minutes.—Mrs. O. W. Kumrow.

Veal Loaf.

3 pounds veal, chopped
¾ pounds salt pork or ham
1 dozen crackers, rolled

Onion, pepper and salt
2 eggs, well beaten

Mix and cover with one-half of cracker crumbs. Bake one and one-half hours. Serve hot or cold.—Mrs. Christy.

Chili Stew

2 pounds beef, sliced
2 tablespoons lard
1 chopped onion
  Cook 30 min. and add

1 quart water
½ pint tomatoes
4 diced potatoes
1 tablespoon chili powder

Cook slowly until done.—Mrs. W. E. Kelley.

Nut Loaf.

1 pound English walnuts, chopped	1 large chopped onion
2 cups cracker crumbs	2 tablespoons butter
1 cup chopped celery	3 eggs, well beaten
	Cayenne pepper and salt

Mix nuts and cracker crumbs with butter, add seasoning and last eggs. Bake forty minutes in hot oven. Baste with melted butter and hot water. —Mrs. Christy.

Cheese and Chili.

1/2 pound cheese finely cut	1 egg, salt
1 tablespoon butter	1 teaspoon chili powder
4 tablespoons milk	teaspoon mustard

Mix butter and mustard, add chili powder, stir until thoroughly mixed, add salt and cheese, then milk, stirring constantly when smooth, add egg when it begins to thicken. Serve on crackers.—Mrs. W. E. Kelley.

Moulded Chicken Jellied.

Wipe veal knckle, cover with cold water and bring to boiling point, then add foul, six pounds, and cook until meat is tender, adding the last hour of cooking one teaspoon salt. Remove foul and let cool. Force lean meat from veal through meat chopper. There should be one and one-half cups. Let stock simmer until reduced to two cups, then add one-fourth teaspoon salt, one-eighth teaspoon pepper, a few drops onion juice; cool and clean. Add to veal one cup stock and season to taste with salt, paprika, onion and lemon juice. When well mixed add one cup celery cut in small pieces. Place in bread pan in ice water, pour in stock one-eighth inch deep. When firm decorate with two whites and yolks of hard boiled eggs, canned pimentos cut in fancy shapes and fresh mint leaves. Add remaining stock, a spoonful at a time, that decorations may not be disarranged. When firm add alternate layers of veal, sliced chicken, until all is used. Cover top with buttered paper, on this place pan and weight. Let stand in ice box several hours, remove from pan to serving dish and garnish with cress. In very hot weather add one teaspoon gelatine to stock.—Mrs. French.

Hudson Sandwiches.

2 tablespoons butter	2 hard boiled eggs
1/2 pound ham	Salt and pepper
6 ground olives	12 picked shrimps
1 teaspoon capers	Parsley

Put all ingredients through meat chopper and yolks of eggs, add butter and seasoning. Spread on slices of buttered brown bread, cut round and sprinkle surfaces with chopped whites of eggs. Place sandwiches around sides of a circular dish with lettuce and shrimps in the center. Decorate with few sprigs of parsley.—Mrs. J.MacLachan.

Oxeyes.

Mould one tablespoon of mashed potatoes into the shape of a ramekin. Break an egg into the center of the potato, dust on a little salt and pepper and add a bit of butter, bake in the oven until the egg is done. Slip on to a warmed plate and serve immediately.—Mrs. Corrigan.

Potatoes German.

Rub lightly with dry mustard and sugar the amount of ham required for a meal. Place this in the bottom of a baking dish and cover with diced raw

Garfield Trading Company

Headquarters for

Drugs, Jewelry, Furniture, Hardware, Meats, Groceries, Dry Goods—We Sell Anything and Everything. Prompt Service and All Goods Guaranteed.

We are the sole Representatives of the Salt Lake Glass and Paint Co. of Salt Lake City in Garfield. When wishing any paint, wall decorating, glass or anything in this line. let us figure with you. We handle the celebrated Muresco wall coloring.

HAVE YOU A SICK WATCH?

We Have the Doctor—His Work Guaranteed.

All Kinds of Jewelry, Clocks, Watches, Etc., Repaired at Reasonable Prices

Give Us a Trial

Garfield Trading Company

WILLIAM GORDON

Watchmaker

potatoes, add barely enough milk to cover and place in oven. Cook until potatoes are done. The flavoring of both ham and potatoes is very delicate and appetizing.—Mrs. C. J. Ridd.

AFTERNOON TEA DAINTIES

Compiled by Mrs. R. F. Barker.

"Polly put the kettle on, we'll all have tea."

Chocolate Macaroons.

4 eggs, whites only	8 large tablespoons cocoa
1 pound pulverized sugar	1/4 teaspoon cinnamon
	1 teaspoon vanilla

Gradually add the sugar to the stiffly beaten whites of eggs, beating well, add other ingredients and drop by teaspoonsful on well greased and floured pans. Bake in slow oven for twenty-five minutes.—Mrs. H. P. Allen.

Puffs.

8 tablespoons flour, level	Filling
4 eggs, beaten	1 cup pulverized sugar
Pinch of salt	3 tablespoons butter, melted
1 pint milk	1 teaspoon vanilla

Mix ingredients in order given, bake in greased muffin tins for twenty minutes in a moderate oven. Fill and serve warm.—Mrs. L. N. Foster.

Scottish Fancies.

1 egg	1/4 teaspoon vanilla
1/2 cup sugar	Two-thirds cup wheat flakes
Two-thirds tablespoon melted butter	One-third shredded cocoanut
	One-third teaspoon salt

Mix ingredients in order given. Drop on buttered pans and bake in a moderate oven. Let cool in pans before removing.—Mrs. E. E. Nelson.

Sweet Meringues.

Whites 4 eggs, beaten stiff	1/4 teaspoon baking powder
2 cups granulated sugar, sifted	1/2 pound chopped dates
1 teaspoon vanilla	1 cup chopped almonds (unblanched)

Mix ingredients in order given. Drop by teaspoonful on well greased and floured pans and bake in moderate oven.—Mrs. R. H. Hawley.

Cheese and Nut Wafers.

Beat white of egg stiff, add grated yolk of hard boiled egg with equal parts of grated cheese and chopped nuts. Drop small spoonful on salted crackers and place in hot oven to brown.—Mrs. W. W. Watters.

Ripe Olive Sandwiches.

Ripe olives, hard boiled eggs, and nuts chopped fine. Mix with mayonnaise until a butter. Spread on thin slices of white or brown bread.—Mrs. W. W. Watters.

Mosaic Sandwiches.

Cut the bread, brown and white in slices about one inch thick, spread with butter or a cheese filling and put four slices together alternating the colors. After pressing firmly, cut in slices from the end.—Hrs. E. E. Nelson.

Apple and Nut Sandwiches.

½ cup ground peanuts and 2 large apples ground
walnuts

Salad dressing to form paste. Spread on thin slices of bread and butter.
—Mrs. H. Marshall.

Pimentos and Cheese Sandwiches.

½ cup milk	¼ teaspoon mustard
1 tablespoon butter	Pepper to taste
2 jars McLaren's cheese	1 egg beaten and added last
¼ teaspoon salt	Pimento cut fine

Mix in order given and cook until cheese is melted, remove from stove, add egg and pimento. Spread on bread while warm.—Mrs. Guy Piatt.

Candied Orange Peel.

Boil orange peel for twenty minutes. Drain water off and scrape the white pulp away with a spoon being careful not to break outer skin. Cut in narrow strips, boil again in a heavy syrup for twenty minutes and sprinkle with granulated sugar. Allow to dry thoroughly before serving.—Mrs. R. F. Barker.

Orange Sticks.

Cut rich pie paste into strips four inches long, two inches wide. Fold lengthwise and bake. Spread open and cover with orange marmalade then cover the top with orange icing. Sprinkle candied orange peel.—Mrs. Gilbert Palmer.

Secuskl Sandwiches.

Remove bones and tails from a can of imported sardines, mash with silver fork into a smooth paste, add a piece of butter size of a walnut, lemon juice, paprika, and a little Worchestershire sauce. Mix well and spread on very thin slices of buttered rye bread. Do not remove crusts.
—Mrs. H. E. Blatch.

Walnut Wafers.

1 cup light brown sugar	½ cup flour
2 eggs	¼ teaspoon baking powder
1½ cups chopped English walnuts	½ teaspoon vanilla

Mix yolks and sugar together, add nuts, flour and baking powder. Whip whites or eggs stiff, add last. Drop one-half teaspoon of batter on greased tins. Bake in moderate oven.—Mrs. J. Horn.

Marshmallow Dainty.

Place a marshmallow with a nut meat on a small sweet wafer. Toast in a quick oven.—Mrs. R. B. Tempest.

Brandy Syrup.

Equal parts brandy and water, sugar to make a good syrup. Serve with either hot or cold tea.—Mrs. W. W. Watters.

Pimento Cheese Toasties.

Spread pimento cheese on small circles of buttered toast. Sprinkle with paprika. Place in oven to melt the cheese and place on top of the other with cheese between.—Mrs. J. C. Hardy.

Orange Marmalade Toast.

Trim crust from bread and butter. ᴗpread thin layer of marmalade on one and place a slice of buttered bread on top. Toast in quick oven. Cinnamon toast is made in the same way, instead of marmalade use cinnamon. Serve hot.—Mrs. Gilbert Palmer.

Marguerites.

1 cup sugar	Whites 2 eggs
½ cup water	2 teaspoons cocoanut
5 marshmallows	¼ teaspoon vanilla
	1 cup walnut meats

Boil sugar and water until it threads, place on back of stove and add marshmallows, cut fine. Pour on stiffly beaten whites of eggs, add cocoanut and nut meats, and spread on salted wafers. Toast in oven till light brown.—Mrs. Tom Bird.

English Rolled Wafers.

½ cup molasses	Two-thirds cup sugar
½ cup butter	1 tablespoon ginger
1 cup flour, scant	

Heat molasses to the boiling point, add butter then slowly add flour, mixed and sifted with ginger and sugar, stirring constantly. Drop small portions from tip of spoon on buttered tins two inches apart. Bake in slow oven. When slightly cooled remove and roll over handle of a wooden spoon.—Mrs. Fred Hanson.

Rolled Vanilla Wafers.

¼ cup butter	⅞ cup flour
½ cup powdered sugar	½ teaspoon vanilla
¼ cup milk	

Cream, butter, add sugar gradually and cream well, add milk, drop by drop and last flour and flavoring. Spread very thin with broad beaded knife on bottom of a square or oblong tin. Bake till light brown. Cut in squares and roll, up beginning at one corner. If squares become brittle place in oven again to soften.—Mrs. R. H. Saum.

Waltham Sandwiches.

Put between small round unsweetened wafer crackers, a thin slice of cream cheese and one-half a marshmallow. Arrange on thin sheet and bake until cheese begins to melt.—Mrs. R. E. Robson.

THE large number of our customers who bring their friends here to buy is a significant endorsement that is worthy of comment.

We are winning a new customer every day simply by pleasing our old ones.

Every article we sell is carefully fashioned of the best material. We invite the patronage of all, one visit to our store will make you a steady customer.

Our prices are reasonable, our goods are right and our fitting service perfect.

CANDIES

Compiled by Mrs. H. White.

"Little Tommy had some candy, on a painted stick,
Little Tommy ate that candy and it made him sick."

Marshmallows.

1 envelope gelatine   10 tablespoons cold water

Soak for ten minutes. Boil one and one-half cups of sugar and one-half cup of water until it hairs. Add the soaked gelatine to the syrup, while still hot beat until white, cut and fold into whites of two eggs beaten dry. Turn on to platter and when stiff cut into squares and roll in chopped nuts or toasted cocoanut.—Mrs. R. J. Caffall.

Fudge.

3 cups sugar   2 squares chocolate
1 cup cream   Butter size of egg
                       1 teaspoon vanilla

Mix sugar and cream together well, then add butter and chocolate, let th is boil hard until it forms a soft ball in water. Pour into buttered platter and let cool. Beat this until it is hard enough to mould with the hands, into any shape desired.—Mrs. A. White.

Peanut Brittle.

Put four cups of white sugar in a pan and melt over a hot fire, stirring constantly so as not to burn. When melted pour into a buttered dripping pan, already covered with a layer of peanuts. Set away to harden.—Mrs. R. C. Hatton.

Stuffed Figs.

Steam figs until soft, when cool cut : ngthwise and insert one-half of a marshmallow and a walnut meat.—Mrs. De Camp.

Peppermint Drops.

Beat the whites of two eggs to a stiff froth, add enough powdered sugar to stiffen and one drop oil of peppermint. Drop in wax paper and set aside to cool.—Evelyn M. Paddock.

Olympian Creams.

2 cups sugar   1 cup thin cream
One-third cup corn syrup   ½ cup walnuts

Cook until it forms a soft ball in water, when cool beat till creamy, then add nuts and mould.—Mrs. R. P. Culivan.

Patience.

1 cup cocoanut or peacon   2½ cups sugar
   nuts   1 cup milk

Carmalize one-half cup sugar, then add milk and remaining sugar and cook until it forms a soft ball in water, cool and beat until creamy then add cocoanut or pecan meats and drop from spoon on butter plates.—Mrs. T. W. Bird.

Butter Taffy.

2 cups brown sugar   6 tablespoons water
2 tablespoons butter   Grated cocoanut or chopped nuts

Cook sugar and water together, let syrup come to boiling point then add butter and cook to a soft ball stage, then add cocoanut or nut meats, let cool and pull.—Mrs. T. W. Bird.

Karo Fondant.

½ cup Karo   ¼ teaspoon cream of tartar
1½ cups sugar   One-third cup hot water

Boil without stirring until it threads. When partially cool beat until creamy. Keep cool and dry till needed.—Mrs. F. Hagen.

Butter Scotch.

Put one pound lump sugar with one cupful milk into a sauce pan, stir in pinch of cream of tartar and one-half pound of butter, a small piece at a t'me. Boil until it thickens and a little dropped in cold water forms a moderately hard ball, then add one teaspoon orange juice. Pour into a buttered tin and when half cold mask in squares, when quite cold break in pieces and wrap in wax paper.—Mrs. F. Hagen.

Pinoche.

1 cup white sugar   1 teaspoon butter
½ cup brown sugar   ¼ cup nut meats
½ cup milk   Few drops of vanilla

Boil the sugar, milk and butter until a soft ball can be formed in cold water. Remove from fire, cool and beat until creamy, add nut meats and flavoring, spread on platter, cut in squares.—Mrs. H. White.

Chocolate Taffy.

4 cups sugar   3 tablespoons cocoa
1 cup molasses   1 cup water
Large piece of butter   Vanilla to taste

Mix sugar and three tablespoons cocoa (or more if desired) together then add molasses, water and butter and cook until it hardens in water, then pull.—Mrs. T. W. Bird.

Maple Fudge.

3 cups sugar   2 teaspoonsful extract
1 cup milk   ¼ teaspoonful butter
1 cup cocoanut   1 cup chopped nuts

Put sugar and milk in a pan and bring to a boil, then cook about eight minutes, add butter, maple extract, and cocoanut, beat until mixture is quite stiff, place in pans to cool, add nuts if desired.
—Mrs. O. E. Lindley.

Divinity.

2 cups sugar   Two-third cup corn syrup
¼ cup boiling water   1 cup nuts
Whites of 2 eggs

Put sugar in pan, put syrup over it, then add the boiling water, mix well and set on stove. Do not touch the pan until done. Do not stir. When it makes a firm ball in water, pour over the whites which have been well beaten. Beat and add nuts.—Mrs. G. S. Piatt.

BEVERAGES

Compiled by **Mrs. A. M. Henderson.**

"Here's to your good health, drink."

Unfermented Grape Juice.

Wash thoroughly fresh ripe grapes, boil in a little water till tender, strain through cheese cloth but do not squeeze. Hang up to drip several hours. Measure the juice, boil up and add half as much sugar as juice. Boil till sugar dissolves. Seal while hot.—Mrs. De Camp.

Ginger and Grape Beverage.

Use equal parts ginger ale and grape juice. Serve ice cold in cocktail glasses with a maraschino cherry and cracked ice.—Mrs. De Camp.

Fruit Punch.

1½ dozen lemons
1 dozen oranges
1 dozen bananas
10 quarts water

8 cups sugar
1 pint canned raspberry juice
Strawberries or cherries

Roll lemons and oranges to loosen juice, slice bananas, add the other ingredients and ice and serve from punch bowl.—Mrs. De Camp.

Currant Punch.

1 cup cracked ice
½ cup sugar

l cup currant juice
1 tablespoon lemon juice
10 sprays fresh mint

Shake ice and sugar till sugar is dissolved, then add mint pouring over it the lemon juice, add currant juice and enough water to make one quart of this liquid, if too strong add more water.—Mrs. De Camp.

Ginger Ale Punch.

1 cup mint leaves crushed
2 lemons

1 cup sugar
2 bottles ginger ale

Add the lemon juice and sugar to the crushed mint leaves and allow the mixture to stand for several hours. Just before serving, strain and add the ginger ale.—Mrs. E. E. Nelson.

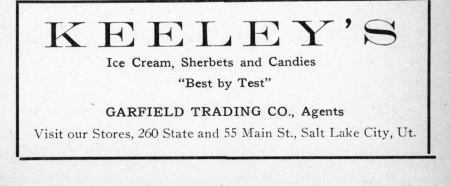

LUNCH BOX SUGGESTIONS

Compiled by Mrs. A. E. MacArthur.

Sardine Loaf.

1 can sardines
2 tablespoons melted
  butter
Salt to taste

2 eggs
2 cups bread crumbs
Pinch cayenne pepper

Mix, turn into mould, cover and steam one hour. When cold cut in thin slices for sandwiches.—Mrs. H. E. Atchison.

Cheese Filling for Sandwiches.

3 level tablespoons butter
4 level tablespoons flour
¾ cup grated cream cheese
¼ cup shredded pimentoes

¼ cup chopped olives
1 cup milk
Salt to taste

To the white sauce add cheese just before taking from the fire, other ingredients when partially cooled.—Mrs. A. K. Fail.

Sandwich Filling.

3 slices boiled ham
½ small onion

3 sweet pickles
Salad dressing

Put through meat grinder and moisten with salad dressing, may use fried ham if preferred. This will make about ten sandwiches.—Mrs. R. C. Henderson.

Stuffed Baked Apples.

Core apples, stuff with nuts, raisins and stoned dates. Bake in ramekins. Sugar to taste.—Evelyn M. Paddock.

The small oiled paper bags which hold Jello powder will keep sardines, onions, etc., from flavoring the entire lunch.—Mrs. A. E. MacArthur.

Deviled eggs taste different when flavored with chopped onion.—Mrs. D. Barnard.

Sandwich Combinations.

Crisp bacon and currant jelly.—Mrs. W. D. Leonard.

Ground steak ends and Worchestersnire sauce.—Mrs. A. C. Cole.

Ground fried ham and catsup.—Mrs. R. S. Hales.

Baked beans and lettuce.—Mrs. A. C. French.

Tomato jelly and mayonnaise. Chopped chicken and celery. French toast and sugar. Lamb or mutton and mint or catsup. Roast beef ground with onion, seasoned with salt and pepper. Spread on brown bread.—Mrs. A. E. MacArthur.

Egg with yolk broken, fried on top of a thin slice of ham.—Mrs. A. C. Cole.

PICKLES, JAMS, MARMALADES, Etc.

Compiled by Mrs. A. M. Henderson.

"The jelly, the jam and the marmalade,
And the cherry and quince, 'preserves' she made!
And the sweet, sour pickles of peach and pear,
With cinnamon in 'em, and all things rare!
And the more we ate was the more to spare."

Apricot Jam.

1 peck apricots	6 small oranges

Pare the apricots but not the oranges. Slice the oranges very thin and quarter the slices. Weigh apricots and oranges together, add equal weight of sugar. Crack the stones, put the kernels in cold water and boil five minutes. Skin kernels and add to the mixture. Boil one and one-half hours, stirring often.—Mrs. A. E. MacArthur.

Orange Marmalade.

1 orange	1 grape fruit
1 lemon	

Pick out hard centers, run through chopper, cover with eight cups cold water. Let stand twenty-four hours, boil twenty minutes. Let stand twenty-four hours, boil twenty minutes. Weigh and use equal parts sugar. Boil till it jellies.—Mrs. A. E. MacArthur.

Orange Marmalade.

2 dozen oranges	4 lemons
4 grape fruit	Cane sugar

Shred fine, thin outside peeling of four oranges and two lemons. Cook in little water till tender. Squeeze juice from fruit. Boil twenty minutes, add cooked peeling and equal measure of sugar. Boil and skim, cooking slowly until jellied.—Mrs. Thos. Alexander.

Cabbage Relish.

2 heads cabbage	¼ pound mustard
6 green peppers	½ ounce tumeric
1 red pepper	½ ounce celery seed
5 onions	½ cup flour
2 cups sugar	1 tablespoon white mustard seed
2 quarts vinegar	

Chop vegetables and place in jar over night with a sprinkle of salt between each layer. Next morning squeeze dry and mix with dressing.

Dressing.

Mix mustard, tumeric, celery seed, flour and sugar in a little cold vinegar and beat until smooth, then add the two quarts boiling vinegar and boil five minutes.—Mrs. J. W. Brewer.

Green Tomato Chow Chow.

½ bushel green tomatoes	1 tablespoon cloves
1 dozen onions	1 tablespoon pepper
½ dozen peppers	½ cup ground mustard
2 pounds sugar	1 pint horseradish
2 tablespoons cinnamon	Vinegar enough to mix
1 tablespoon allspice	

Chop tomatoes, onions and peppers fine and mix with one pint salt. Let stand over night then drain off brine. Cover with good vinegar and cook slowly one hour, then drain and pack in jars. Have second mixture boiling hot and pour over first in jars and seal.—Mrs. G. H. Paddock.

Mustard Pickle.

2 dozen green tomatoes	2 tablespoons mustard
1 dozen good sized onions	1 tablespoon tumeric
1 head cauliflower	4 cups vinegar
2 heaping tablespoons flour	2 small cups sugar

Cut tomatoes, onions and cauliflower in small pieces and soak over night in salt water. In morning boil in same water until clear. Rinse twice in cold water. Mix other ingredients to a smooth paste in water or vinegar and add to vegetables and cook until flour is done. Bottle and seal.—Mrs. L. P. Madsen.

Mustard Pickles.

5 quarts small cucumbers	6 red peppers (ground fine)
6 cauliflowers (separated)	3 cups salt
4 quarts onions	10 large green peppers

Mix thoroughly and let stand over night. Drain and wash in fresh water, add green peppers, ground fine, but no more salt.

Gravy for Pickles.

½ pound mustard	3 tablespoons tumeric
3 cups flour	1 gallon vinegar
1 cup white sugar	

Mix with enough water to form thin gravy. Into this mixture pour the boiling vinegar and stir well. Pour this gravy over pickles and let heat through thoroughly and seal.—Mrs. A. L. Hewett.

Chili Sauce.

8 quarts tomatoes	3 teaspoons cloves
3 cups peppers	3 teaspoons cinnamon
2 cups onions	2 teaspoons ginger
3 cups sugar	2 teaspoons nutmeg
1 cup salt	½ teaspoon celery seed
1½ quart vinegar	

Chop tomatoes, peppers and onions very fine. Mix with other ingredients. Boil three hours. Bottle and seal.—Mrs. Ted Peterson.

70

Cold Chili Sauce.

1 package firm ripe tomatoes	18 small chili peppers
6 large onions	5 cups vinegar
6 green peppers	2 pounds light brown sugar
6 red peppers	1 cup salt
	2 ounces white mustard seed

Chop tomatoes, onions and peppers, add salt and drain over night, add vinegar, sugar and mustard seed. Mix thoroughly and put in bottles or glasses. Will keep all winter without sealing.—Mrs. A. C. Cole.

Green Tomato Pickle.

½ package green tomatoes	1 teaspoon pepper
1 cup salt	1 teaspoon cloves
1 quart cold water	1 teaspoon celery seed
1 pound sugar	1 tablespoon allspice
1 quart vinegar	1 tablespoon mustard
	1 tablespoon cinnamon

Dissolve salt in cold water and pour over tomatoes cut up. After standing two hours drain through colander until dry, add other ingredients. Let boil half hour and simmer two hours.—Mrs. Murray Howard.

Sweet Cucumber Pickle.

1 peck pickling onions	1½ gallons vinegar
100 small cucumbers, cut in small pieces	2 teaspoonsful extract
5 heads cauliflower	1 tablespoon each of whole cloves
1½ quarts sugar	Allspice and celery seed
	Piece of alum size of walnut

Put onions, cucumbers and cauliflower in salt water and let stand thirty-six hours. Have vinegar and sugar boiling and add vegetables. Boil slowly until you can pierce with broom straw, add spices, and bottle.—Mrs. George Pugsley.

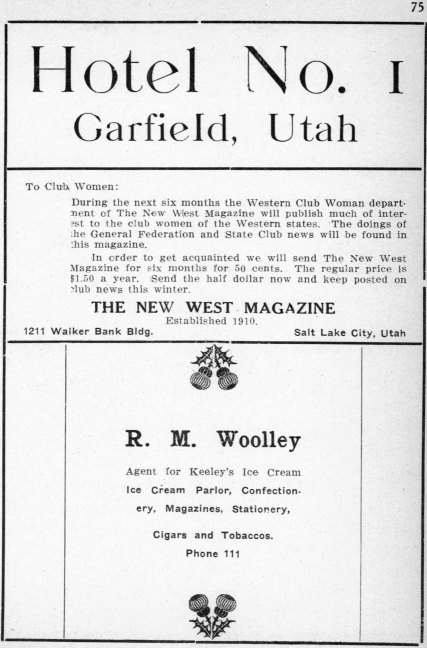

Professional Cards

Miss Evelyn Paddock

Instructor

PIANO and VIOLIN

Studio 62 W. 16 Ave.   Garfield   Phone 103-W.

Dr. A. A. Bird   Dr. L. P. Musser

Physicians and Surgeons

Office Phone Gar. 161

Res. Phone 34   Res. Phone 81

Magna, Utah

Dr. Wallace Mace

Dentist

Phone—Garfield 14   Cooper Bank Bldg.

Magna, Utah

Geo. E. McBride, M. D.

Calls Answered Day or Night

Phone 72-J   Magna, Utah

Dr. C. F. Westphal

Dentist

Office Hours—9 to 12; 1 to 5.   Magna, Utah

Wendell B. Hammond

Lawyer

Cooper Building   Magna, Utah

77

78

CONTENTS

	Page
Soups	9
Meats	11
Vegetables	14
Salads and Salad Dressings	17
Breads	23
Cakes	27
Cookies and Doughnuts	35
Desserts	39
Frozen Desserts	45
Luncheon and Supper Dishes	47
Afternoon Tea Dainties	57
Candies	61
Beverages	63
Lunch Box Suggestions	65
Pickles, Jams, Marmalades, Etc.	67

CHOCTAW INDIAN DISHES

Compiled by

AMANDA AND PETER J. HUDSON

Tuskahoma, Oklahoma

1955

Publisher's Note: The following article was reprinted from an original manuscript compiled by Amanda and Peter J. Hudson, members of the Choctaw tribe. Mrs. Hudson explained the recipes to her husband who typed them, adding his own comments.

The process of preparing corn for Tash-lubona and Ta-fula is about the same.

For Tash-lubona, soak the corn for a short time or until hull is loosened, and then beat it in a mortar until the hull has slipped off leaving the grain of corn as whole as possible. Then take the corn out and fan it in a basket (ufko) to separate the hulls from the grain of corn. This basket or ufko is made of stripped cane. It is about three feet long and 18 inches wide. One half of this basket is flat, having no sides, but starting from the center of the length, sides gradually rise from a fraction of an inch to five inches, one end being five inches in height. The corn is fanned and the grains all go to the end with the sides while the hulls are blown off the flat end. After the hulls are all disposed of, put the corn in a kettle with lots of water, salt and pieces of fresh pork and boil it down until it is thick. When it is done you have Tash-lubona, which is very rich. Don't eat too much Tash-lubona as it will make you sick.

With Ta-fula, the same process is followed as with Tash-lubona, only the corn is beat until the grains of corn are broken into three or four pieces, then take it out into the basket and separate the hulls from the grains. It can then be cooked with beans, with wood ashes or in any other way you wish. Meat is not cooked with Ta-fula. Use plenty of water and boil it down until there is a lot of juice. You can eat all the Ta-fula you want as it contains no grease.

For Bread or Banaha or, in English, Shuck Bread, soak the corn a long time, maybe all night, then beat it in a mortar until the hulls are off and then put in the basket and separate the hulls from the grains, after which put it back in the mortar and beat it into meal. Then sift it. That meal is as fine as wheat flour. Of course there will be some grits left that cannot go through the sieve.

In making Sour Bread, the grits are mixed with the dough. The dough is made the night before and allowed to sour and then it is cooked.

In making Banaha the meal is made into dough and then rolled out into lengths of Hot Tamales, but about four or five times bigger around than Hot Tamales, and each one covered with corn shucks and tied in the middle with a corn shuck string. The middle is smaller than the ends when tied up. It is then boiled in water until done and the shucks taken off when ready to eat. When Banaha is to be carried on a trip the shucks should be left on.

Another bread is made with this meal by wrapping the dough

3

in green fodder and boiling It is very fine. Sometimes the hulls of peas are burned and the ashes put in this dough which makes it a brownish color.

Holhponi is old Choctaw word for Ta-fula and the Choctaw Indians in Mississippi call this dish Holhponi to this day.

In Byington's dictionary, Tash-lubona is spelled Tanlubona or Talubo. Tanlubona came from two words, Tanchi which means corn, a noun, and luboni, verb, meaning to boil. In Choctaw language, when you unite two words, a vowel and sometimes a syllable of the preceding word is dropped. So in this case "Chi" is dropped, leaving Tanluboni. Luboni, to boil, then becomes a past participle and then it is spelled lubona. The "N" in Tan is there because of the fact of the nasal sound. Old missionaries adopted a short line drawn under a vowel to give it a nasal sound, so I prefer using a short line drawn under the vowel to denote a nasal sound rather than the use of N. Therefore, I would spell the word Talubona. In a few cases the "Ch" is changed to "sh," so in this case "ch" is changed to "sh" and the word becomes Tash. The Choctow people will recognize the word as it is used interchangeably.

Ta-fula, came from two words, Tanchi, a noun meaning corn, and fuli, a verb, which means "to stir." Then when they are joined together "chi" is dropped, leaving Ta-fula. The "i" is changed to "a" because it is a past participle, and in Choctaw when two consonants come together it calls for a vowel.

Walakshi is another Choctaw dish made on special occasions. Wild grapes are gathered in the Fall and put away on stem to dry to be used when wanted. To cook, the grapes are boiled and then strained through a sack, only the juice being used. Then dumplings are made of the corn flour described above and dropped in the grape juice and cooked until done. Of course more or less grape juice is absorbed by the dumpling and the remainder of the juice is thickened. Walakshi was always furnished by the bride's relatives at weddings, while the bridegroom's relatives furnished the venison.

Bota-Kapvssa is a cold meal made of parched corn. The grains of corn are poured into a kettle; a fire is built under it and hot ashes are poured in the kettle with the corn. The corn is stirred continually until it is parched brown and then it is taken out and put in the basket described above to be fanned, the ashes being separated from the corn. Then the parched corn is put into the mortar and the hulls loosened from the grain of corn and then put back in the basket again to be fanned, separating the hulls from the grain of corn. Then it is again put in the mortar and pounded until it becomes a fine meal. This is Bota-Kapvssa and is very nourishing. The Indian hunters and warriors used to take a small sack of it on their journeys and when they became hungry or thirsty, a small amount was put in a cup of water and upon drinking it, the thirst as well as the hunger was satisfied.

At roasting ear time, roasting ears were gathered, a fire in a long string was built and a pole laid over the fire, then the roasting ears were laid against the pole in front of the fire and the ears turned every few minutes so that they will cook evenly and also to keep them from burning. When they are all cooked, the corn is shelled from the ear and dried in the sun, and then sacked and put away for winter use. It is cooked in water and because it swells a great deal, a little corn will make a big meal. It is good for invalids.

In making Choctaw dishes, flint corn is preferable but if flint corn cannot be obtained any corn can be used. Horses will not eat flint corn. Flint corn is called by the Choctaws Tanchi Hlimimpa. It is the only kind of corn the Choctaw Indians in Mississippi had when the white people found them.

In making Hickory Ta-fula, the hickory nuts are gathered and put in a sack over the fire place to dry for a month at least. Then when ready to make Hickory Ta-fula, the nuts are cracked real fine, shells and kernels together, then put in a sack and hot water poured over the nuts to drain. After this water is drained, it looks like milk. This hickory nut water is then poured into the Ta-fula and cooked. This makes a very rich dish.

When pumpkins are gathered in the fall, they are peeled and cut into narrow strips and dried for winter use.

INDIAN COOK BOOK

By

The Indian Women's Club

Of

Tulsa, Oklahoma

INDIAN COOK BOOK

By

The Indian Women's Club

Of

Tulsa, Oklahoma

CLUB OFFICERS 1932-1933

President	Mrs. Lilah Denton Lindsey
Vice-President	Mrs. Lena F. Barnard
Second Vice-President	Mrs. Norma S. Bryant
Third Vice-President	Mrs. Roberta C. Lawson
Recording Secretary	Mrs. Edna Audrian Wilson
Corresponding Secretary	Beulah Wadley Abbot
Treasurer	Mrs. Mary Jackson Smith
Parliamentarian	Mrs. Lulu J. Harvey
Historian	Mrs. Margaret J. Farris
Past President	Mrs. Ida Mae Goodale

FOREWORD

We are sending forth this little pamphlet to you and the public as a souvenir of other days among the early Indian home-keepers, hoping it will prove to be not only a useful, but one of your cherished possessions.

Sincerely,

Lilah D. Lindsey, *President*

Creek and Cherokee

SOCIAL ECONOMY AMONG THE AMERICAN INDIANS

Since the days of Adam and Eve in the Garden of Eden human interest in things good to eat has never languished, for man must eat to live and thrive age after age; else, how survive? The food problem, always of primary importance to the human race, has become increasingly significant in modern times when the welfare of individual and the progress of the nation have become so vitally involved in the problem of nutrition, physical fitness and mental power being no longer regarded as gifts of chance, but the result of generations of right living in accordance with the natural laws of diet and fresh air.

For illustration, take the American Indian, whose primitive regime, in the opinion of some scientists, left little to be improved. Note his fine physique, compared to the ancient Roman for symmetry of form and grace of action; his tireless vitality; his quick understanding and his broad intelligence.

The Indian's astonishing knowledge of native foods and their specific values in relation to his welfare, together with the life he lived in complete harmony with his environment, produced a people singularly free from noisome diseases and exceptional for longevity. There were men and women "in those days" whose span of life went far beyond the century mark, according to history and tradition. But where are the Tamenunds and the Nancy Wards of by-gone centuries? An alien culture does not foster such types among Indians today.

What, then, did the Indians eat, and how did they live, to have attained such physical perfection and such length of days in the past before their hunting grounds were circumscribed and then preempted, their industries superceded and their manner of living completely revolutionized?

At the time of its discovery America was furnishing its inhabitants an abundant and varied supply of food, rich in all the life-giving vitamins, produced as it was, in nature's own way. There were meat and eggs; vegetables and cereals; wild fruits, luscious with refreshing juices; oil, both animal and vegetable, roots and herbs for healing; and there was the precious tobacco for rituals and for soothing, peace-promoting meditations. But there was no "Fire Water," nor fermented liquors.

Meat, that formed so large a part in primitive provisioning, was brought home by the men of the village. Twice annually they organized the great buffalo hunts at the time of the "Hunting Moon." But they never hunted for sport, for the sheer love of slaughtering wild life. Sufficient to supply their needs as carefully estimated on the basis of population and former experience was all they sought, and when that had been secured it was enough. They had a trenchant saying among themselves: "Enough is sufficient; more is the wolf's pack bait."

The mothers of the tribe kept the lodge fires burning; tended the maize fields; cared for the children; made clothing and bedding and pottery and baskets. Enough, but not too much; and they directed many of the activities pertaining to community life. With infinite tact and skill women chosen for ability in leadership apportioned tasks with discretion and fairness and from their decisions were no appeals.

At the feet of these women the hunters laid the fruit of the chase when they arrived. Deft and willing hands sorted and bore it away to be prepared for the hunting feast or to be cured and stored for future use.

Everybody was given some useful task suited to his capacity; even the children had their little duties which they discharged with swift accuracy watching with eager eyes their elders and learning from them things never written in books nor needing any words to tell. Only the weary hunters relaxed in idleness and silence.

For every great hunt there was a hunter's feast, for which preparations had been made beforehand. Great earthen pots of meat were put on to boil and kept at the right temperature by means of hot stones dropped in at exactly the right intervals. Sometimes corn and beans were added producing a rich, savory stew, whose fragrance filled the clear air, giving zest to appetites already as keen as scalping knives. Other hands prepared the barbecue by cutting long strips of flesh, piercing each strip with a long sharp stick and laying these sticks across a pit filled with red hot coals for a process of slow roasting.

Not all cooks were women. Among the Osages, according to a noted traveler and artist who visited them a century ago, there were expert men cooks who took great pride in their meat dishes. Some travelers of a still earlier day have said that Indian women were the best cooks in the world. While they knew how to prepare meat to a chief's taste, they took pride also in the bread they made. In its preparation they exercised their supreme culinary skill, for was not bread an important item of every meal and second only to meat at the Hunting Feast?

The staple bread-stuffs were corn meal, pounded in a mortar, beans, peas, and a variety of starchy tubers, now almost if not quite extinct. From the pulp of ripe persimmons delicious little cakes were concocted and dried in the sun, then put away carefully as a choice morsel for a feast or to be offered some honored guest upon his arrival.

Many vegetable indigenous to America are regarded as staple groceries today. Beans some varieties of peas, corn, pumpkin and squash are a few taken at random from a long list for purposes of illustration. A dish much relished by primitive Americans was wild onions, gathered in spring while they were yet tender. Boiled in clear water, drained and dipped in oil they were regarded with high favor. Scrambled with eggs they are served as choice tid bits even yet by a very few who are fortunate enough to be able to get them.

Greens of many varieties were tested out by our ancestors centuries ago when in search of things safe to eat and at the same time palatable and nourishing. Among them poke boiled with bear's bacon, was found to be both nourishing and medicinal, especially when their shoots were young and tender. Hog jowl may be substituted for bear's bacon with satisfactory results it is said by no less an authority than a prominent state official who gives it a place on his own table when poke is in season.

A people of out-door life require a certain amount of oil in their diet. Animal fat, such as bear's grease and buffalo tallow rendered with sassafras and slippery elm bark, had its place at almost every meal. Nut oil was also a staple product to be found in many larders of the forest regions. Great quantities of nuts were gathered while they were just right, crushed and placed in pots of hot water until the oil rose to the top, when it was skimmed off. After proper treatment the oil was stored in cool underground storehouses and portioned out thriftily as needed Nut oil served the forest tribes for butter long after they were raising herds of cattle to sell to Europeans. The vegetable oils in modern markets therefore are by no means a new discovery.

The customs of hospitality prevalent among American Indians in keeping with their mode of life, were simple and gracious. Food was always set before a guest upon arrival, came he as friend or foe. Who could know? Perchance the path had been long and dangerous and there was sore need of refreshment. Therefore the pot must be always on, the coals alive.

For the old fire to die before the new had been kindled presaged misfortune. So Fire Keepers were appointed to watch and feed the flames from time to time, with fresh fuel, lest light and warmth not fail the clans in time of need.

Desiring to preserve some embers of old tribal fires, some traditions and customs of their ancestors, the members of the Indian Women's Club constituting themselves Fire Keepers, have assembled the contents of this little volume, which in all reverence, they dedicate to those tribesmen, who, having kept the faith, passed on to join the Immortals in that Darkening Lang beyond the setting sun.
in that Darkening Land beyond the setting sun.

DR. RACHAEL CAROLINE EATON (Cherokee)

BREADS

→→ ← ←←

INDIAN CORN BREAD

1 quart of meal; add boiling water. Roll into a loaf and bake slow for 1 hour.

MARY JACKSON SMITH (Cherokee)

→→ ← ←←

BEAN BREAD

Cook colored beans until done. Sift quart of meal. Use one pint of the beans and enough of its liquor (boiling hot) on meal, enough to make soft-stiff dough. Use hands and make into pone (about two), and bake brown in hot oven.

BESS SCHRIMSHER LEWIS (Cherokee)

→→ ← ←←

CORN-DODGER CRACKLING BREAD

Sift corn meal, add pinch of salt, pour in boiling water and make stiff. By using hands make into a ball and mash flat. Bake in real hot oven. Crackling Bread is made by adding cracklings to suit taste.

MRS. S. R. LEWIS (Cherokee)

→→ ← ←←

SWEET POTATO BREAD

This bread is made by boiling sweet potatoes, then mixing with corn meal, seasoned with salt, and baking powder, if desired, and baked in a hot oven.

MRS. MINNIE McKEE CROWDER (Cherokee)

→→ ← ←←

BEAN BREAD

1 cup of pinto or chilli beans; cook until tender, with 1 teaspoon of salt and seasoning. Take the soup and scald 3 cups of meal; have the dough stiff enough to make into pones with your hands, place in a dutch oven with hot coals on the lid, serve hot with plenty o fbutter.

MRS. ANNA BALLARD CONNER (Cherokee)

→→ ← ←←

PECAN CORN BREAD

Make corn bread in usual manner and stir in 1 cup of pecan meats. Pour into hot greased pan and bake 30 minutes.

MRS. VICTORIA MARTIN ROGERS (Cherokee)

FRIED CORN BREAD WITH CREAM SAUCE

Slice cold corn bread 1 inch thick and brown in hot grease, place on a dish.

SAUCE—Take equal parts of meat fryings and butter, add 1 table spoon of flour and brown; pour in 1 pint of sweet milk; boil until thick cream, salt and pepper to taste. Pour over corn bread and serve hot.

MRS. VICTORIA MARTIN ROGERS (Cherokee)

BEAN BREAD

Take about 1 quart of corn meal which has been pounded in an old fashioned Indian mortar, or better, when the corn is nearly hard grated on a large grater. Use corn field beans; boil 1 pint in plenty of water until tender; add teaspoon of salt, then pour over the meal, stirring all the time. Make a stiff dough, mix the beans in and bake in an old oven or skillet. Sweet potato bread is made the same way.

MRS. CARRIE BREEDLOVE (Cherokee)

SQUAW BREAD

2 tablespoons Royal baking powder, 1 quart luke warm water, 1 teaspoon salt, 1 tablespoon compound, flour enough to make about like biscuit dough. Roll and cut any shape desired. Fry in kettle of boiling compound.

NANCY ROGERS WARE (Cherokee)

SYRUP FOR SQUAW BREAD

1 quart white corn syrup, 15c worth of brown sugar. Boil together, using no water. 1 tablespoon of mapleine. Take from fire and beat into above one-half cup bacon fryings.

NANCY ROGERS WARE (Cherokee)

ROASTING EAR BREAD

Grate the corn from the cob on a grater, mix amount needed as making corn bread.

MRS. LILAH D. LINDSEY (Creek)

BEAN BREAD

1 cup of brown beans boiled until tender; drain in collander and cool. 2 cups of white corn meal, 1 teaspoon salt, 1 tablespoon of short-ening, enough boiling water to make stiff dough and beat well, fold in beans carefully; make into pones and bake 30 minutes.

MRS. VICTORIA MARTIN ROGERS (Cherokee)

CRACKLIN BREAD

Fry cracklins to a crisp, grind or mash them, scald a desired amount of meal, add cracklins to this. Salt to taste, bake in a hot oven about 40 minutes.   MRS. NANNIE LOWERY HITCHENS (Cherokee)

SOUR CORN BREAD

Take 1 gallon of sofkey grits, soak over night, next morning drip dry in a riddle or sugar sack, pound or grind into meal, mix as for corn bread with salt, soda, baking powder, and 1 cup of flour, pour in a jar, set in a warm place to ferment for 12 hours, then pour into hot greased iron kettle and bake same as corn bread.

MRS. LILAH D. LINDSEY (Creek)

DOGHEADS

Di-Ga-Nu-Li

Grit roasting ear corn after it gets too hard for roasting ears. Its meal will be as hard as soft mush. Get wide fodder; wash clean and put about two or three large cooking spoons of this into a leaf of fodder. Have dough about five or six inches long and as thick as you can wrap up nicely with one long leaf. By putting it on the widest end, double back over bread five or six inches, then around until it will hold the dough; tie and put into kettle of boiling water. Boil until done. Unwrap and eat for bread while hot.

BESS SCHRIMSHER LEWIS (Cherokee)

BROADSORED

Hull or shell green beans. Boil until done and add to the above dough and cook the same way. This makes another bread.

BESS SCHRIMSHER LEWIS (Cherokee)

MEATS

To use ragged edges of meat, beef or pork, wild meat, etc., cut meat in large squares, seer hastily in hot skillet, then roll in flour and season. Put into saucepan and barely cover with cold water. Let slowly cook until tender.

ROBERTA CAMPBELL LAWSON (Delaware)

SCRAPPLE

Cook a fresh hog head until very tender. When the meat is cool mince very fine and season. Then make a corn mush and as it cools add the meat and then mould. Slice dip in egg and fry when ready to serve.

ELIZABETH WILLIAMS AUDRAIN (Shawnee)

DRIED BEEF HASH

Slice beef steak real thin, place in a kettle, salt freely and stir well —spread out on a clean shed in hot sunshine, cover with a mosquito bar cloth for two days until thoroughly dry, place the amount you want to use in a kettle of warm water to soak until softened. Remove all water by drying with a cloth, either grind or cut fine. Place in a skillet with slices of onion and salt if desired. This is delicious.

LILAH D. LINDSEY (Creek)

ROAST SQUIRREL

Dress squirrel and wash clean, place on fork or stick in front of open fire turning often until thoroughly brown.

NANNIE LOWERY HITCHENS (Cherokee)

FRIED PORK

Cut pork into pieces of two pounds each, drop in a kettle with hot grease (1 gal. or more) the more meat requires same proportions of grease. Let it boil slowly until done, not hard. To keep put meat in large container and cover with grease. When meat is desired remove from lard and melt surplus grease.

LILAH D. LINDSEY (Creek)

DRIED FISH (Kee-qus-no-swa Po-son-gee)

Dig pit in ground, fill with wood fire and let it burn down to red embers, then lay sticks across pit, on which place the dressed fish. Turn frequently until thoroughly done. Remove from fire, take all bones out and lay in the sun until dry. This meat can be kept indefinitely. Our people stored it away in bags made of buck skins. To prepare this meat it should be moistened and heated. It is very fine creamed.

MRS. LENA FINLEY BARNARD (Piankeshaw)

VEGETABLES

BEAN DUMPLINGS

1 quart of meal, 2 cups of brown beans and ½ teaspoon of salt, mix with boiling water, roll into small balls and drop in boiling water. Cook slow until well done.

NANNIE SHELTON PEEBLES (Cherokee)

SHAWNEE RECIPE FOR CORN

To a cob of corn put enough water to steam thoroughly; mix with bacon grease. Fry in skillet. This is especially good served with turkey or wild meats.

ROBERTA CAMPBELL LAWSON (Delaware)

SHAWNEE RECIPE FOR DRYING CORN

Select corn (field corn will do) that is firm but not hard. Scrape off of cob into deep pan. When pan is full set in slow oven and bake until thoroughly heated through—that is an hour or more. Remove from oven and turn pone out to cool. Later crumble on drying board in the sun and when thoroughly dried sack for winter.

ROBERTA CAMPBELL LAWSON (Delaware)

BROAD SOARDS

The same meal and bean mixture as the bean bread is fine wrapped in roasting ear shucks and roasted in hot ashes; fine when camping.

MRS. CARRIE BREEDLOVE (Cherokee)

DOG HEADS

Grate corn before it is too hard and make a soft mixture, pat into cakes and wrap in green corn blades and boil 30 minutes. The Indians used very little salt. It can be added to taste. Serve with bacon fryings or butter.

MRS. NANNIE LOWERY HITCHENS (Cherokee)

WILD GREENS

Such as wild mustard, wild lettuce, polk, thistle, lambsquarter, are cooked the same as spinach. Boil until tender, then pour off the water, salt and season with fryings and serve.

EDNA AUDRAIN WILSON (Cherokee)

INDIAN DISH

1 cup of dried corn, 1 cup of pumpkin (either dried or canned), salt and season with pork or meat fryings and add a little sugar if you like.

ROZELLE (CHOUTEAU) LANE (Osage)

WAH-WE-NO-KONE-MIN-GUY

Gather green corn when too hard for roasting ear stage and grate. (The Indians used the jaw of deer, grating on the teeth). Place the grated corn in the sun to dry, cook and serve like rice or oatmeal or can be used to make bread.

LENA BARNARD (Piankasaw)

RECIPE FOR DRIED CORN

Boil corn on cob in clear water. Cut from cob to drying board; let it remain in the sun until thoroughly dried.

ROBERTA CAMPBELL LAWSON (Delaware)

RECIPE FOR WILD RICE

Sometimes called "Indian Rice," because it is one of the principal food commodities of the Indians in these regions. The Chippewas are particularly noted for their ability to prepare this rice for cooking. Grows in profusion in the Lake region.

8 cups of water to one cup of rice.

Salt to taste.

Cook very slowly. When finished cooking, remove from fire and place in collander; rinse very thoroughly in cold water; return to kettle, keeping it warm until ready to serve.

Left over rice cooked in the above manner is very palatable for breakfast, stirred in with scrambled eggs; or, for dinner this cooked rice, moulded in small croquets or balls, is also very fine with fricassee of chicken. Wild rice is also good with sugar and cream.

ROBERTA CAMPBELL LAWSON (Delaware)

DRIED CORN

Take good roasting ears cut from the cob and spread on a clean sheet in the hot sun 2 or 3 days until thoroughly dry, put in sacks and hang up—is ready the year round and fine in winter. Cook like canned corn.

LILAH D. LINDSEY (Creek)

WILD ONIONS AND EGGS

2 bunches of wild onions, bacon grease, salt and a little water. Cook 10 or 15 minutes then break 6 or 7 eggs and scramble in with the onions and serve hot.

MRS. CHEROKEE ADAIR MOORE (Cherokee)

As this is one of Will Rogers' favorite dishes, Mrs. Rebecca Swain suggests we call it Will Rogers Delight (Cherokee).

REMARKS:

In all instances where lye is mentioned the water dripped from wood ashes is intended. Where the words pound or grind is used the best method is to use the morter and pestle for pounding corn or meat.

This is a short log about 3 feet long, one end of which is cut down 1 foot in a cornicopia shape, the pestle is about 2 inches in size at one end and about 6 inches in diameter at the other end, using the small end to fit into the opening of the log.

LILAH D. LINDSEY (Creek)

INDIAN DUMPLING WITH SEQUOYAH SAUCE

3 cups of meal, teaspoon of salt, ½ cup of ash lye (or 1 teaspoon of soda). Mix well, pour boiling water over mixture to make a stiff dough, make into ball ssize of Indian biscuits and drop into 2 quarts of boiling salted water. Cook 15 minutes.

Take 3 tablespoons of dumpling dough, thin to cream thickness and pour in and cook 5 minutes longer.

MRS. VICTORIA MARTIN ROGERS (Cherokee)

SOUPS

BEEF SOUP

Take sofkey grits hominy and large chunks of beef, about 1 pound each, and boil together.

MRS. LILAH D. LINDSEY (Creek)

GRAPE SOUP

Put desired amount of grapes on stove in a small amount of water, cook until well done, strain off the juice, placing it back on the stove, sweeten to taste and thicken with corn meal.

MRS. NANNIE LOWERY HITCHENS (Cherokee)

HOMINY SOUP

This soup is made from hominy, first by beating into grits, and then boil until tender. It is then ready to serve.

JANE ANN THOMPSON PHILLIPS (Cherokee)

SQUIRREL SOUP

This soup is first made by barbecuing squirrels whole, and then cut into pieces and place in vessel of cold water. Season with salt and pepper. Boil slowly and serve as broth.

MRS. S. R. LEWIS (Cherokee)

BEAN VINE SOUP

This soup is prepared by boiling bean vines, and use drippings of bacon and salt.

MRS. S. R. LEWIS (Cherokee)

VEGETABLE SOUP

This one is called "Canutchee." It is a combination of hickory nuts, hominy, and sometimes sweet potatoes. Prepared by beating hickory nuts, and then with water shape into balls about the size of a baseball. After this has been done, at any time, take one ball or more and put in pan of hot water and strain through sifter to separate the hulls. Then boil with hominy. Add sweet potatoes if desired. It is now ready to serve.

MRS. S. R. LEWIS (Cherokee)

DESERTS

PEACH BREAD

Use soft free-stone, mash together with meal about half and half, add small amount of sugar. If there isn't enough juice in peaches to make soft hard dough add boiling water. Bake in pone.

BESS SCHSIMSHER LEWIS (Cherokee)

CORNMEAL DUMPLINGS

A preparation made from corn meal as in making biscuits and drop into hot water and cook slowly until done. Brown or pinto beans may be added. Serve hot.

MRS. S. R. LEWIS (Cherokee)

HUCKLEBERRY DUMPLINGS

Boil huckleberries. Take berries out, leaving soup. Then use corn meal and flour as in making bread. Use baking powders to make rise. Roll flat, then drop into the huckleberry soup and cook until dumplings are done.

MRS. S. R. LEWIS (Cherokee)

SWEET POTATO PIE

Prepared the same as any other fruit pies.

MRS. S. R. LEWIS (Cherokee)

INDIAN PUDDING

3 cups of sweet milk, meal to make it thick like mush. 1 cup Crisco 1 cup sugar, 1 cup raisins, 1 teaspoon salt, 1 teaspoon vanilla. Let the milk come to a boil and add the meal, then rest and bake in a slow oven for 45 minutes.

MRS. MARGARET JONES FARRIS (Cherokee)

GRAPE DUMPLINGS

Take nice ripe grapes, wash and cook until nice and tender. Run through a colander, then place on the stove to cook 30 minutes. Make dumplings as for chicken roll and drop in the juice and cook.

MRS. LILAH D. LINDSEY (Creek)

BLUE DUMPLINGS

Scald whole white corn in lye water, drain until dry, pound into meal. Burn pea hulls (black eyed or cow pea, or any kind) and pound to a powder, sift and add to your corn meal; using hot water, knead into balls size of baseball, drop into boiling water and cook one-half hour. To one part of meal use one-half part pea meal.

MRS. LILAH D. LINDSEY (Creek)

DRINKS

OSAFKEE

5 gallons of water, 3 quarts of hominy grits (either ground or pounded) 1 pint of Ash lye and cook 3 hours. Hickory nut kernels may be added which makes a delicious flavor; if used the lye should be omitted.   LILAH D. LINDSEY (Creek)

CAW-WHEE-SA-KA

Take flour corn, brown in oven until it will crumble. then pound into a flour, mix with water for a healthful drink.

The old Indians always drank plenty on going on a long journey, hunting or fishing trip.

MRS. CARRIE BREEDLOVE (Cherokee)

TEAS

Spice wood tea made from broken limbs of spice wood.
Sycamore tea from the chips.
Raspberry tea from the vine.
Sassafras tea from the bark of the roots.
Parched corn for coffee.

LENA BARNARD (Piankashaw)

COLD FLOUR (A Drink)

Use roasting ears just before hardening, break a grain to see if the kernel is moist, place the whole grains in a large kettle with wood ashes over a medium heat, stir continually until brown, sift or separate from the ashes, pound or grind into fine meal. Take 2 tablespoons to a glass of water, sweeten to taste and you have a delicious drink.
LILAH D. LINDSEY (Creek)

GANUTCHIE PREPARED TO SERVE

Take one or one and one-half balls and put into a bowl or granite pan. Pour over it hot water—boiling point but not boiling. A little bit at a time, mashing and working the balls to a soft waxy-mush state, rubbing hard with spoon continually; then keep adding the hot water and mashing or rubbing the substance from the nut balls until you get it thin as cream. Strain this through a sieve into about two gallons of Ga-no-he-na. Rinse cream off hulls with a little more hot water, having it about one-half gritts and one-half of its own liquor already cooked done and at boiling heat. When it comes to boiling point remove from fire. Serve as drink in glasses or cups with or without sugar.

BESS SCHRIMSHER LEWIS (Cherokee)

GA-NO-HE-NA

Shell five or six ears of good hickory cane corn. Cover with lye, made from ashes, until the corn turn a golden-yellow and its skin loosens off by pounding in a mortar. It is then pounded and riddled and whole grains put back and pounded until all is cracked. The husks are fanned out and put aside. The gritts are boiled until done, and the husks, which always have lots of fine meal mixed with it from its own pounding. Wash out good and put the water into the gritts for a thickening. This much will make a small wash kettle full—to eat and drink. BESS SCHRIMSHER LEWIS (Cherokee)

MISCELLANEOUS

APPLE BUTTER

3 gallons of cooked apples, 1 quart of cider vinegar, and 5 pounds of brown sugar. Boil down to about 2 gallons very slowly and flavor with cinnamon.

MARY JACKSON SMITH (Cherokee)

BUTTON SNAKE ROOT TEA

This is a wild herb and grows on the prairie, has a tall stem with a pink funny flower. This tea is very good for children in case of dysentary.

EDNA AUDRAIN WILSON (Cherokee)

GA NUTCHI

Gather hickory nuts in fall and hull. Dry sear over slow fire in chimney. Dont get too hot. Put them away to use as needed. When needed crack nuts and discard largest empty hulls. Put small hulls with its meats in mortar. Pound fine until you can make it into balls a little larger than a baseball. It will be gummy and greasy like.

BESS SCHRIMSHER LEWIS (Cherokee)

ASH LYE

Any wood may be used but the black jack wood when burned to ashes makes the strongest lye, the ashes are placed in a vessel with a perforated bottom, pour hot water over and let drain until all strength is exhausted. Makes good seasoning for sofee.

LILAH D LINDSEY (Creek)

MA-CHING-WAH MING-ZAH

Cook burr oak acorns in wood ashes or lye from same until the hulls all come off. Wash in several waters and cook with meat.

LENA BARNARD (Piankashaw)

WATER LILY SEEDS

Gather the seed of large white water lilies crack the hull of each seed then boil in wood ashes or lye made from wood ashes until the hull comes off by washing several times and cook with game.

LENA BARNARD (Piankashaw)

WA-LUX-SIA

Stew peaches, pears or any kind of fruit until tender and juicy; make a batter by beating 1 or 2 eggs until light and fluffy, add 1 pint of sweet milk, 1 teaspoon of salt, 2 tablespoons of flour, 1 tablespoon of butter, 1 cup of sugar, flavor with nutmeg or to suit, nuts can be added if you like.

MRS. CARRIE BREEDLOVE (Cherokee)

PAN-GEE-TAKE MIN-GYP

Parch flour corn, pound, sift hulls, pour syrup or molasses over the fine siftings, form into balls like popcorn balls.

The coarser siftings is cooked with game for soup.

LENA BARNARD (Piankashaw)

COUGH REMEDY

Hickory chips boiled with broom weed tops makes a good enough medicine.

MRS. ROBERTS (Cherokee)

A CHEROKEE RHEUMATISM CURE

Take a piece of "trumpet vine" root 5 or 6 inches long, scrape the bark carefully into a cup of water, have a small thin muslin bag and when you are through pour into bag and you have a poultice, saving the water to moisten the poultice 2 or 3 times if needed. The effect is very peculiar. It stings like prickly heat and will relieve any ordinary rheumatic pain.

EDNA WILSON (Cherokee)

PO-KEK-KOYL-YOKEE

Gather the roots of large white water lily, clean and dice and cook with meat or game, is very much like navy beans.

LENA BARNARD (Piankashaw)

WAH-LOWE-KEE-PANE-KEE (Wild Potatoes)

Wash clean and tie smaller ones together and boil with peeling on. When tender remove peelings and eat as domestic potatoes.

LENA BARNARD (Piankashaw)

KA-WISITA

Parch the corn, grind and sift. Can be used so or with sugar.

MRS. CHERRY ADAIR MOORE (Cherokee)

CURE FOR "SNAKE BITE"

Take the leaves of cockle-burr sufficient for a poultice and simmer in plenty of water until tender then apply to wound and drink half of teacup of the water off the leaves.

This was given by Mrs. Narcisso Owen (who saved her sister, Mrs. Jane Bruton).

EDNA WILSON (Cherokee)

"JACK WAX" AN IROQUOIS CONFECTION

Submitted by HARRIETTE B. JOHNSON WESTBROOK, Mohawk,

Onondaga and Algonquin

Take any desired quantity of maple sap, boil it down to the consistency of thick syrup, skim off the impurities. Have at hand a pan of clean snow. Drop large spoonsful of the hot syrup on the snow and leave until hard as beeswax. It can then be picked up from the snow with the fingers and eaten at once. The syrup is never stirred in this process. Sap from the mountain maple and the sugar maple were both used.

INDEX

	Page
Foreword, by the President	2
Social Life Among the American Indian	3
Breads	6
Meats	9
Vegetables	10
Soups	13
Desserts	14
Drinks	15
Miscellaneous	16

The
JUNIOR LEAGUE *of* DALLAS
(INCORPORATED)
Cook Book

The
JUNIOR LEAGUE *of* DALLAS
(INCORPORATED)

SECOND EDITION
REVISED AND ENLARGED

Compiled and Edited by members of the
DALLAS CHAPTER
of
THE ASSOCIATION OF JUNIOR LEAGUES OF AMERICA
(INCORPORATED)

45 MENUS
250 ADDITIONAL RECIPES

*Proceeds to be used for
financing the Junior League Home
for Convalescent Children.*

Dedicated

To

The many friends whose generous support and hearty co-operation has made our Junior League work possible.

To

The future growth of the Junior League Home for Convalescent Children.

To

A broader understanding of service.

To

Our friends who have contributed recipes.

To

Those through whose efforts the first Edition of the Junior League Cook Book was published.

To

Those who have made possible the second Edition.

Tables of Weights and Measures

FOR the convenience of those who have no scales the following table has been arranged. The measures correspond as nearly as possible with the weight of the different articles specified. These measures will answer for all the plainer cakes, etc., but greater accuracy is necessary for the richer kinds.

Avoirdupois is the weight employed in this table.

Sixteen ounces are..one pound
Eight ounces are..half a pound
Four ounces are..a quarter of a pound

White sugar (pulverized), four gills and a half equal one pound.
Light brown sugar, three half pints equal one pound.
Light brown sugar, nine heaping tablespoonfuls equal one pound.
Wheat flour, one quart and one tablespoonful equal one pound.
Wheat flour, fifteen heaping tablespoonsfuls equal one pound.
Ten eggs, equal one pound.
Fine Indian meal, one quart equals one pound, five ounces.
Coarse Indian meal, one quart equals one pound, nine ounces.
Butter, one common sized teacup holds a quarter of a pound.
Spices (ground), two large tablespoonfuls equal one ounce.
Nutmegs (whole), seven common sized equal one ounce.

Liquid Measure

Two gills are..half a pint
Four gills are..one pint
Two pints are..one quart
Four quarts are..one gallon
Six common tablespoonfuls equal..one gill
One wine glassful equals..half a gill
One common sized tumblerful equals..half a pint

6

Time Tables for Cooking

Boiling

	Hours	Minutes
Mutton leg	2 to 3	
Ham (12 to 14 pounds)	4 to 5	
Corned beef or tongue	3 to 4	
Turkey (9 pounds)	2 to 3	
Chicken (3 pounds)	1 to 1¼	
Cod and haddock (3 to 5 pounds)		20 to 30
Halibut (2 to 3 pounds)		30
Small fish		6 to 10
Asparagus		20 to 30
Peas		20 to 30
String beans	1 to 2½	
Lima or other shell beans	1 to 1¼	
Beets (young)		45
Beets (old)	3 to 4	
Cabbage		35 to 60
Onions		45 to 60
Parsnip		30 to 45
Spinach		25 to 30
Green corn		12 to 20
Macaroni		25 to 30

Baking

	Hours	Minutes
Bread (white loaf)		45 to 60
Bread (graham loaf)		35 to 45
Biscuits or rolls (baking powder)		12 to 15
Gems		25 to 30
Muffins (baking powder)		20 to 25
Gingerbread		20 to 30
Cookies		6 to 10
Baked batter pudding		35 to 45
Plum pudding	2 to 3	
Pies		30 to 50
Scalloped oysters		25 to 30
Scalloped dishes of cooked mixtures		12 to 15
Baked beans	6 to 8	
Braised beef	3½ to 4½	
Mutton (saddle)	1¼ to 1½	
Lamb (leg)	1¼ to 1½	
Veal (leg)	3½ to 4	
Pork	3 to 3½	
Chicken (3 to 4 pounds)	1 to 1½	
Turkey (9 pounds)	2½ to 3	
Goose (9 pounds)	2	
Duck (domestic)	1 to 1¼	
Duck (wild)		20 to 30
Fish (small, 3 to 5 pounds)		20 to 30

What Is the Junior League?

THE JUNIOR LEAGUE is a National Organization with over 15,000 members and branches in 92 cities.

The Junior League was founded in New York City in 1901, by a group of debutantes, headed by Mary Harriman, who wished to undertake some constructive charity, which would be separate and distinct from their mothers' charities.

The object of the Junior League is to foster among its members, interest in social, economic and educational conditions, and to increase the value of volunteer service.

Every Junior League member is required to do an average of three hour's work a week, or its equivalent, from the middle of October to the middle of May each year.

The Junior League of Dallas maintains a Home for Convalescent Children at 2530 Ross Avenue, where without cost to their families, under-nourished and convalescent children are cared for, clothed, fed and given medical treatment as long as is deemed necessary by attending physicians. The Home is financed entirely through the League's efforts, and with the exception of a staff of two attendants and a cook, the Home is operated by committees of Junior League members. A House Committee, a School Committee, a Recreational Committee, a Sewing Committee and an Entertainment, or Finance Committee, give voluntary service, and funds raised through the sale of the Junior League Cook Book will be used to help carry on the work of the Home.

CONTENTS

	PAGE
Menus	11
Hors d'Oeuvres and Cocktails	25
Soups	31
Fish and Oysters	40
Poultry and Game	53
Meat and Meat Accompaniments	66
Vegetables	78
Breads and Muffins	91
Cakes and Icings	108
Salads	144
Pastry	167
Puddings and Desserts	176
Eggs and Omelets	201
Ices and Ice Creams	204
Beverages	213
Candies	216
Luncheon Dishes and Sandwiches	223
Preserves and Pickles	247

{ *Complete Index
in back of book* }

Menus

Luncheon

HORS D'OEUVRES
TOAST MELBA
CHICKEN A LA KING
HOT BISCUITS
DRESSED LETTUCE WITH CREAM CHEESE BALLS AND
BAR-LE-DUC JELLY
DATE ROLLS
COFFEE

Mrs. Tom Camp.

Luncheon

CREAMED SNAPPER THROATS IN PATTY SHELLS
COLD CUTS, DRESSED LETTUCE
SPINACH SOUFFLE
HOT ROLLS
ORANGE ICE
YELLOW ANGEL FOOD CAKE
COFFEE

Mrs. Tom Camp.

Luncheon

AVOCADO COCKTAILS   CHEESE STRAWS
NOODLE RING WITH CREAMED WHITE MEAT OF CHICKEN
AND
FRESH MUSHROOMS IN CENTER
GARNISHED WITH GLACE FRUIT
FRESH PEAS   HOT ROLLS
RELISHES, JELLY AND SALTED PECANS
ORANGE BOMBE
ANGEL FOOD CAKE
COFFEE

Informal Luncheon

FRUIT COCKTAIL

CHEESE SOUFFLE   TOMATO SAUCE

GREEN ASPARAGUS   DRAWN BUTTER

BISCUITS AND PRESERVES

HOT TEA CAKES AND COFFEE

Luncheon

INDIVIDUAL RING MOULDED CLEAR TOMATO ASPIC

CENTER FILLED WITH HEART OF

PALM—MAYONNAISE

HOLDER'S CHEESE STICKS

CREAMED SWEETBREADS AND FRESH MUSHROOMS

SERVED IN PATTY SHELL, SIZE OF CHOP DISH

GARNISH DISH WITH BROILED HAM

GREEN ASPARAGUS   DRAWN BUTTER

ROLLED BISCUITS

PICKLED PEACHES   SALTED NUTS

CREAM SHERBERT   ALMOND STICKS

Luncheon

MINT ICE AND GRAPEFRUIT COCKTAIL

TOASTED TRISCUITS

HOT CHICKEN MOUSSE, CENTER FILLED WITH

FRESH PEAS SEASONED WITH WORCESTERSHIRE

NEW POTATOES WITH PARSLEY AND DRAWN BUTTER

POP OVERS

ASSORTED CHEESE, BAR LE DUC JELLY

AND CRACKERS

COFFEE

Informal Luncheon

MOULDED HOT TAMALI LOAF WITH BORDER
ALTERNATING INDIVIDUAL STEAMED SPINACH MOULDS
(Grated egg yolk on top of each)
AND CREAMED BEETS
GARNISHED WITH LETTUCE OR PARSLEY
RELISHES: DIFFERENT KINDS OF SPICED
CUCUMBERS AND ONION PICKLE
BOSTON BROWN BREAD OR CRISP ROLLS
FROZEN FRUIT SALAD *(Mrs. Sabin's)*
SWEDISH WAFERS   COFFEE

Mrs. Frank Cullinan.

Luncheon

EGGS A LA BENEDICT
BAKED POTATOES   ORANGE ROLLS
HOT TEA

Mrs. Frank Austin.

Luncheon

GRAPEFRUIT COCKTAIL
STUFFED CABBAGE AND TOMATO ASPIC
BEATEN BISCUITS
COFFEE

Mrs. Frank Austin.

Luncheon

JELLIED CONSOMME
SALMON WITH GREEN MAYONNAISE
CARROTS AND PEAS MIXED WITH PLAIN MAYONNAISE
ROLLS
FROZEN FRUIT SALAD
ICE TEA

Mrs. S. W. King, Jr.

Spring Luncheon

ARTICHOKE HEARTS SURROUNDED BY GRAPEFRUIT

HOT CHEESE BALLS   TOASTED BUTTERED SWEDISH WAFERS

SQUAB—PLATTER GARNISHED WITH SLICES OF ORANGE

ON WHICH IS GRAPE OR PLUM JELLY

NEW POTATOES WITH BUTTER AND PARSLEY SAUCE

ASPARAGUS SOUFFLE

ROLLS

MANHATTAN PUDDING

(This is a moulded dessert with orange sherbert at the top and parfait at bottom)

COFFEE

Makes a beautiful table when orchid sweet peas and a very few jonquils
are used with yellow candles and the dessert (which is white with layer
of yellow at top) surrounded by candied rose petals made in orchid
and yellow.

Mrs. Wm. J. Lewis.

Luncheon

ALLIGATOR PEAR AND GRAPEFRUIT SALAD

FRENCH DRESSING

TOASTED SWEDISH WAFERS

BROILED CHICKEN ON TOAST   MUSHROOM SAUCE

JELLY   SWEET PEACH PICKLES

ENGLISH PEAS   IRISH POTATOES

HOT ROLLS

ORANGE MOUSSE

ANGEL FOOD CAKE

COFFEE

NUTS   CANDY

Mrs. W. D. Felder.

14

Luncheon

CREAM OF OYSTER SOUP   CRACKERS
STUFFED CREAMED LOBSTER   HOT ROLLS
MUSHROOMS ON TOAST UNDER GLASS
LETTUCE, BAR-LE-DUC AND CREAM CHEESE DRESSING
TUTTI-FRUTTI ICE CREAM

CAKE   COFFEE
Mrs. J. T. Trezevant.

Luncheon

CREAMED SHRIMP IN PATTIES
SPINACH RING WITH CHOPPED BEETS IN CENTER
INDIVIDUAL MOULDS OF WILD RICE WITH BUTTER SAUCE
HOT ROLLS   PICKLED PEACHES
PEARS STUFFED WITH SEASONED NEUFCHATEL CHEESE
MAYONNAISE
STRAWBERRY SHORT CAKE
COFFEE
Mrs. Holmes Green.

Luncheon

TOMATO WITH CAVIARE (*Mrs. Puterbaugh's*)
CHICKEN AND BRAINS IN RAMEKINS
CAULIFLOWER WITH HOLLANDAISE
FRESH PEAS   POTATO CHIPS
HOT ROLLS   BRANDIED FIGS
KISSES SHELLS WITH RASPBERRY ICE CREAM
SALTED NUTS
COFFEE
Mrs. Ballard Burgher.

Dinner

FRESH MUSHROOM COCKTAILS   CONSOMME WITH PATE AU CHOU
BREADED SHAD ROE, SAUCE TARTARE
SLICED TOMATOES WITH HORSERADISH MAYONNAISE
PAPRIKA CHICKEN EN CASSEROLE
POTATO CROUQUETTES—ATLANTA FASHION
CRESS AND ORANGE SALAD
FIG ICE CREAM   ANGEL FOOD CAKE
COFFEE

Miss Ada Walne.

Dinner

STUFFED ARTICHOKES
BROILED CHICKEN   HOT ROLLS
CAULIFLOWER WITH HOLLANDAISE SAUCE
NEW PEAS
ENDIVE SALAD   BEATEN BISCUITS
CREAM PUFFS FILLED WITH ICE CREAM
COFFEE

Mrs. Tom Camp.

Dinner

CAVIARE   TOAST MELBA
BOUILLON   CHEESE STRAWS
CROWN ROAST OF LAMB
NEW POTATOES WITH PARSLEY AND
DRAWN BUTTER
GREEN CORN
FRESH ASPARAGUS   HOME MADE BREAD
BAKED ALASKA
COFFEE

Mrs. Tom Camp.

Valentine Dinner

FRESH STRAWBERRIES ON STEM WITH POWDERED SUGAR

CROWN OF LAMB, CENTER FILLED WITH CREAMED

POTATOES, SURROUNDED BY BAKED WHOLE

TOMATOES STUFFED WITH DEVILED HAM FILLING

ROLLS   SWEET PICKLED PEACHES

SALAD

(Cut lettuce heads across in slices, stuff a green gage plum
with cheese and nuts and surround with grapefruit.)

FRENCH DRESSING   BUTTERED TOASTED SWEDISH WAFERS

CHARLOTTE RUSSE—SURROUNDED WITH LADY-FINGERS AND

GARNISHED WITH WHIPPED CREAM TOPPED WITH ONE

GLACE CHERRY

COFFEE

This makes a very beautiful table, quite in keeping with the season
when served on a pale green dinner cloth and tulips. American Beauty
candles and candies are used.

Mrs. Wm. J. Lewis.

Dinner

SAUTED OYSTERS AND MUSHROOMS ON TOAST

BROILED STEAK AND BAKED BANANAS

RICE   MUSTARD GREENS   CORN

CORN DODGERS

GELATINE BESSIE

COFFEE

Mrs. Frank Austin.

17

Dinner

JELLIED ARTICHOKE   FRENCH DRESSING
PLATTER OF SQUAB ON TOAST WITH PATE DE FOI GRAS
RED APPLES JELLIED AND MARRONS
DUTCHESS POTATOES   OYSTER PLANT AND BUTTER SAUCE
SPINACH, BEET BALLS
HOT ROLLS
VICTORIA PUDDING
ANGEL FOOD CAKE
COFFEE

Mrs. Frank Austin.

Dinner

THICK SLICE OF LETTUCE, GARNISHED WITH ANCHOVIES AND
HARD BOILED EGGS
FRENCH DRESSING   TOASTED WAFERS
ROAST LEG OF LAMB, BROILED CARROTS AND
BAKED ONIONS AROUND LAMB
WILD RICE   ROLLS   JELLY
ALBERT L. RICH'S SHERRY WINE JELLY, SERVED IN CAKE SHELLS
MADE FROM VERY LIGHT MUFFIN CAKES—WHIPPED CREAM
COFFEE

Mrs. Eugene Duggan.

Dinner

CRAB FLAKES, CREAMED IN INDIVIDUAL CHAFING DISHES
MELBA TOAST
GUINEA BREAST   FRENCH BEANS CREAMED WITH ALMONDS
WILD RICE   HOT ROLLS
CONDIMENTS
GRAPEFRUIT AND AVOCADO SALAD
FRENCH DRESSING   CRACKERS
MARRON MOUSSE   ANGEL FOOD CAKE
COFFEE

Mrs. Jack Beall.

Dinner

ARTICHOKE WITH HOLLANDAISE SAUCE
FRIED TURKEY BREAST
SPINACH CREAMED WITH MUSHROOMS IN CARROT CUPS
SWEET POTATO APPLES   ROLLS
RELISHES
NESSELRODE PUDDING
COFFEE

Mrs. Jack Beall.

Dinner

HORS D'OEUVRES
CREAM OF FRESH MUSHROOM SOUP   TOASTED CRACKERS
BREAST OF GUINEA HEN, GARNISHED WITH BAKED ORANGES
NEW POTATOES
BAKED TOMATOES STUFFED WITH FRESH CORN
ORANGE AND AVOCADO SALAD, FRENCH DRESSING

WAFERS

STRAWBERRY MERINGUE SHORTCAKE

COFFEE

Dinner

GRAPEFRUIT SALAD   TOASTED CRACKERS
CREOLE STEAK
STUFFED OR RICED IRISH POTATOES
GREEN ASPARAGUS WITH DRAWN BUTTER SAUCE
DAINTY CORNBREAD PONES
CELERY, OLIVES, SPICED CUCUMBER PICKLES
RED CHERRY TART
COFFEE

Mrs. Frank Cullinan.

Dinner

TOMATOES STUFFED WITH CREAM CHEESE AND CAVIARE
TOASTED BEATEN BISCUITS
CHOICE OF FOWL OR MEAT
SCOLLOPED GREEN BEANS AND ALMONDS
PARISIAN POTATOES
KENTUCKY SPOON BREAD
HEATED BRANDIED RED CHERRIES
RELISHES
GREEN GAGE ICE CREAM   COCOANUT BALLS

Mrs. Frank Cullinan.

Dinner

JELLIED TOMATO BOUILLON WITH A THIN SLICE OF LEMON
AND A TEASPOON OF CAVIARE IN CENTER OF CUP
CHEESE STRAWS
BREAST OF GUINEA ON TOAST
GARNISH PLATTER WITH PICKLED PEACHES
SQUASH SOUFFLE   FRESH CORN IN GREEN PEPPER CUPS
ROLLS
BALLS OF ORANGE ICE ROLLED IN FRESH COCOANUT
KISSES   COFFEE

Mrs. Lang Wharton.

Dinner

CREAM CORN SOUP   CRACKERS
CELERY   OLIVES   NUTS
BROILED LOBSTER WITH DRAWN BUTTER SAUCE
DRY TOAST
ROAST TURKEY   GRAVY   DRESSING
CRANBERRY JELLY
STRING BEANS   CANDIED SWEET POTATOES
ARTICHOKES AND HOLLANDAISE SAUCE
ENDIVE AND SLICED BEET SALAD WITH FRENCH DRESSING
WAFERS   CHEESE   CRACKERS
RASPBERRY BAVARIAN CREAM   RASPBERRY SAUCE
CAKE   COFFEE

Mrs. W. D. Felder.

20

Dinner

CREAMED TOMATO SOUP   CRACKERS
CROWN ROAST OF LAMB
GREEN PEPPERS, STUFFED WITH FRESH CORN
FRENCH GREEN BEANS
POTATO CROQUETTES
HOT ROLLS   MINT JELLY
LETTUCE WITH ROQUEFORT CHEESE DRESSING
SWEDISH WAFERS
CARAMEL NUT ICE CREAM
SPONGE CAKE
COFFEE

Mrs. Ballard Burgher.

Buffet Supper

COLD CHICKEN MOUSSE GARNISHED WITH
SLICED TOMATOES AND CELERY HEARTS
COLD CUTS
HOT ROLLS   SPICED CRAB APPLES
SANDWICHES
WATERCRESS AND CHEESE BALLS SALAD
FRENCH DRESSING, SEASONED WITH WORCESTERSHIRE, TOMATO
CATSUP AND A LITTLE INDIAN RELISH
FROZEN STRAWBERRIES
DEVIL'S FOOD CAKE
COFFEE

Mrs. H. R. Aldredge.

Buffet Supper

BAKED HAM
RING MOULD OF TOMATO ASPIC WITH ASPARAGUS
TIPS IN ASPIC, FILL CENTER WITH CHICKEN SALAD
GARNISH WITH LETTUCE AND SERVE WITH MAYONNAISE
FRESH CORN AND BUTTER BEANS
ROLLS   PICKLED PEACHES
OLIVES   PICKLES
ALMOND ICE   CAKE
COFFEE

Buffet Supper

BROILED CHICKEN   EGGS AND MUSHROOMS
POTATO CHIPS   ROLLS
CUCUMBER AND PINEAPPLE SALAD, MAYONNAISE
RELISHES   SALTED KASHIR NUTS
MARRON MOUSSE   COCOANUT CAKE
COFFEE

Buffet Supper

BAKED HAM WITH HAM SAUCE
ESCALLOPED OYSTERS AND MUSHROOMS
BEATEN BISCUIT
VEGETABLE STUFFED TOMATO SALAD
MAYONNAISE
WATER MELON PICKLE   RIPE AND GREEN OLIVES
SHERRY ICE CREAM
PECAN KISSES   CHOCOLATE DROP CAKE
COFFEE
Mrs. H. R. Aldredge.

Buffet Supper

BAKED HAM   STUFFED CRABS
SPAGHETTI SALAD
THIN SLICED RYE AND LIGHT BREAD, BUTTERED
SWISS CHEESE
OLIVES   JUMBO PEANUTS
BOSTON CREAM PIE
COFFEE
Mrs. Lewis Spence.

Sunday Night Supper

INDIVIDUAL OYSTER LOAVES
BAKED TOMATOES STUFFED WITH FRESH MUSHROOMS
POTATO SALAD   CHEESE BISCUIT
CUCUMBER RINGS   SPICED GRAPES
SALTED AND SUGARED NUTS
PEACH MERINGUE SHORT CAKE
COFFEE
Mrs. H. R. Aldredge.

Terrace Supper

BARBECUE CHICKEN OR MEATS   POTATO CHIPS
GOLDEN BANTAM CORN ON COB
SPLIT TOASTED BUNS
COLE SLAW
RELISHES   DILL PICKLES, SLICED BERMUDA ONIONS
BUDWEISER   ICED TEA
ICED WATERMELON

Mrs. Collett Munger.

Supper

CREAMED CHICKEN WITH FRESH MUSHROOMS
BAKED HAM   OLIVES, SALTED NUTS
POTATO CHIPS   BUTTERED HOT ROLLS
FRENCH GREEN BEAN SALAD
VANILLA ICE CREAM, STRAWBERRY SAUCE
CAKE AND COFFEE

Mrs. Lewis Spence.

Summer Buffet Supper

SALTED ALMONDS
CUCUMBER RINGS   PICKLED ONIONS
FRIED CHICKEN AND BAKED VIRGINIA HAM
DEVILED EGGS
FRESH PEAS OR CORN   HOT ROLLS
STUFFED TOMATOES, MAYONNAISE
RASPBERRY ICE
ANGEL FOOD CAKE

Mrs. Collett Munger.

Chili Supper

CHILI   SCRAMBLED EGGS   LITTLE PIG SAUSAGES
PICKLED PEACHES   WATERCRESS
PICKLES   BUTTERED TOASTED ROLLS
CAKE AND COFFEE

Mrs. Lewis Spence.

23

Supper

FRIED CHICKEN   STUFFED DEVILED CRABS, TARTARE SAUCE
STUFFED POTATOES   ROQUEFORT SLAW
ROLLED BISCUITS
BUTTERED NUT AND RASIN BREAD
CONDIMENTS
BRAMA CREAM PIE
COFFEE

Sunday Night Supper

FISH ASPIC   COLD SLICED VIRGINIA HAM
COLD SLICED TURKEY OR WILD DUCK
WITH JELLY
CRISP HEAD LETTUCE AND GRAPEFRUIT SALAD, FRENCH DRESSING
ONE HOT FRESH GREEN VEGETABLE
HOT BISCUITS
CHARLOTTE ROUSSE WITH MADEIRA SAUCE
COFFEE

Mrs. Karl Hoblitzelle.

Sunday Night Supper

ICED CRABS OR SHRIMP, MAYONNAISE
COLD SLICED LAMB (MINT SAUCE)
VEGETABLE SALAD
HOT BREAD
CHEESE AND CRACKERS
JELLY   COFFEE

Mrs. Karl Hoblitzelle.

Sunday Night Supper

BAKED TURKEY   CRANBERRY SAUCE
GREEN ASPARAGUS ON TOAST
SOUTHERN SWEET POTATOES
HOT ROLLS
ALMONDS, PICKLES AND OLIVES
JELLIED CUCUMBERS AND CHEESE SALAD
MAYONNAISE DRESSING
ICE CREAM AND CAKE
COFFEE

Mrs. Collett Munger.

Barbecue Supper

CHICKEN BARBECUE   POTATO SALAD
APPLES IN CRANBERRY
ROLLS   COFFEE

Mrs. S. W. King, Jr.

Hors d'Oeuvres & Cocktails

Pastry Canape

Make short puff paste, roll and cut with biscuit cutter small rounds. Take small sardines, place on one side of round, folding over the other side and pressing edges together with a fork. Bake in oven and serve. Use small pieces of little pig sausage in place of sardines if desired. Use caviar seasoned with lemon juice.

Sardines and Bacon

Mash sardines well, season with mayonnaise, little mustard, onion juice. Spread on slices of bacon and roll, sticking with toothpick, broil and serve.

Cheese Crackers

Spread Educator crackers with a well blended mixture of anchovy paste and Neufchatel cheese. Serve. Spread others with a mixture of Anchor brand cheese and very finely chopped garlic. Season to taste. Serve.

Tuna Fish Canape

Mix can of white tuna fish with Durkee's salad dressing. Spread on rounds of toast and put in oven to brown.

Make very small rounds of toast. Place on toast a round slice of hard boiled egg, top with mayonnaise with an anchovy placed on top.

Make rounds of toast and place on toast a very thin slice of onion, spread onion with caviar and place small amount of mayonnaise on top. Alternate caviar on top of onion and onion on top of caviar.

Eggs Stuffed with Pate de Fois Gras

Hard boiled eggs. Cut lengthwise into halves. Remove yellow and stuff whites with pate de fois gras.

Potato Chips and Cheese

Make a mixture of Anchor brand cheese and finely chopped garlic, thinned to right consistency with cream. Season and spread on large crisp potato chips. Serve immediately.

Ham, Cheese and Chutney

Grind boiled ham, mix with small amount of Major Grey's chutney, season with chili sauce, red pepper. Spread on rounds of toast and sprinkle with cheese. Slip in oven to brown. Serve.

Cheese and Bacon

1 package Snappy cheese   paprika
1 egg beaten   mustard

Mix and spread on bread, lay two strips of bacon on each slice, and broil quickly.

Stuffed Artichoke Hearts

Fill the centers of half the desired number of artichoke hearts with caviar. Put a little grated white of hard-boiled egg around edge and a little grated yolk in center. Fill the other artichokes centers with pate de fois gras. Put a little mayonnaise on top. Serve one of each on lettuce leaf. First course.

Eggs Stuffed With Caviar

Hard boil eggs. Cut in halves lengthwise. Remove yellow. Stuff whites with well seasoned caviar.

26

Tomato With Sauce

Scoop out desired number of tomatoes, chop the pulp with 2 hard boiled eggs, 1 box caviar. Season to taste and fill tomatoes. Serve on lettuce with following sauce: Boiled mayonnaise, two teaspoons Worcestershire sauce, ½ cup chili sauce, 2 tablespoons pearl onion and paprika.

Deviled Almonds

Mix in frying pan two tablespoons of chopped olives, two tablespoons chopped gherkins, one tablespoon chili sauce, 1 teaspoon French mustard and 1 teaspoon Worcestershire sauce. Cook 1 cup shredded almonds in butter until brown, sprinkle with salt and paprika and add above mixture. Put on toast, spread with cream cheese.

Eggs Stuffed With Sardines

Boil the required number of eggs until hard. Cut lengthwise and remove the yolk. Fill the center of whites with mashed sardines that have been very well seasoned with lemon juice, mayonnaise, red pepper, so forth. Make a border around rim of egg with grated yolk and serve.

Shrimp

Cut thick slices of peeled tomato, marinate in olive oil and garlic for a long time. Place them on rounds of buttered toast, put three cooked shrimp on tomato, sprinkle with minced green pepper and top with mayonnaise.

Philadelphia Scrapple Canape

Remove skins from tomatoes, cut in thick slices and place a slice (same size as tomato) of Philadelphia Scrapple on top of tomato. Place on crisp lettuce leaves and serve with highly seasoned French dressing.

Mrs. Lang Wharton.

Pickled Oysters

Wash some oysters and serve them in a hors d'oeuvre dish with the following sauce: Mix some finely chopped shallots with vinegar, oil, pepper, sweet herbs, yolk of hard-boiled eggs and the whites finely chopped.

Mrs. S. W. King, Jr.

Tuna Fish Canape

Mix tuna fish with tart French dressing, a little onion and grated cheese. Put on round of toast and run under flame until brown.

Mrs. Peter O'Donnell.

Hors d'Oeuvre

fresh tomatoes	egg
sardines	lemon
salt	potato chips
anchovy paste	olives

Slice tomato ½-inch thick after removing skin. Squeeze lemon juice over top and sprinkle salt. Grate the egg that has been hard boiled, making a layer on top of tomato. Place 2 small sardines across this with an olive with red center placed between them. Mix a little anchovy paste with lemon juice and spread thin layer over the potato chips, about 6 or 8, enough to form a circle around the tomato. A spoonful of French dressing poured over the tomato helps it. Serve with cheese straws for first course.

Mrs. John O. McReynolds.

28

Alligator Pear Cocktail

3 alligator pears   juice of 2 lemons
1 cup chopped celery   salt and pepper to taste
3 tbsp. tomato catsup

Cut the pulp of pears in dice, chop celery and add sauce made of catsup, lemon juice and salt and pepper. Stand on ice for 2 hours before serving.

Mrs. H. R. Aldredge.

Shrimp Cocktail

3 cups well seasoned mayonnaise, add one cup stiffly beaten cream.

1 cup India relish   ½ cup chili sauce
2 cups celery cut in small pieces.

Mix all together, then add chilled shrimp cut in halves. Let stand after mixing for half an hour before serving.

Mrs. Frank Callier.

Avacado Cocktail

1 medium avacado   ½ tsp. Worcestershire
1 cup tomato catsup   sauce
1 tsp. onion juice   juice of ½ lemon

Peel and dice avacado, mix tomato catsup, onion juice, lemon juice and Worcestershire sauce. Mix with diced avacado, chill thoroughly and serve in cocktail cups. Serves 6 people.

Mrs. T. W. Griffiths, Jr.

Tomato and Egg Hors d'Oeuvre

thick slices of tomato	poached eggs
thin slices of cucumbers	bacon
(marinate in French dressing several hours)	mayonnaise

Poach eggs quite firm, plunge in cold water to harden and set. Drain well. Put cucumbers on tomato slices. Then put eggs on cucumbers, next mayonnaise, and then small pieces of crisp bacon.

Oyster Hors d'Oeuvre

Dip oysters in seasoned beaten egg and cracker crumbs. Wrap oysters in small pieces of bacon and stick with toothpick to hold. Put in very hot fat. Fry quickly and serve immediately.

Chutney and Bacon

Major Grey's chutney mixed with finely chopped crisp bacon, serve on rounds of toast.

Mrs. Huey Hughes.

Jellied Artichokes

1 qt. chicken broth	1 envelope gelatine.
celery	onions
4 artichokes	

Boil broth with celery and onions and season. Strain. Soften gelatine in ¼ cup cold water and dissolve in hot broth. Have the artichokes boiled and the tender part scraped off the leaves, chop the hearts and add both to the broth mixture. Mould in individual moulds and serve on lettuce with either French dressing or mayonnaise.

Mrs. Frank Austin.

30

Soups

Okra Gumbo

Made same way as any gumbo only fry sliced okra, one small can tomatoes with onions and flour, and meat. Do not use file with okra.

Mrs. Franklin Pugh.

Mushroom Soup

1 lb. fresh mushrooms	2 tbsp. flour
3 pts. milk	salt and pepper

Chop six mushrooms and cook in butter, add flour and milk, salt and pepper to taste. Cook remainder of mushrooms in water to cover well. Strain through sieve and add this water to chopped mushroom mixture.

Mrs. Knight Zoller.

Almond Soup

½ lb. almonds	1 cup cream
6 bitter almonds	3 tbsp. cornstarch
1 small onion	3 pts. chicken or veal
3 tbsp. butter	(stock)
paprika	salt

Wash almonds well and put through food chopper and grind until like coarse meal. Melt butter, add cornstarch, add one cup stock and make very smooth sauce. Add almonds to remaining stock and cook for a few minutes, add salt, paprika and cream. Blend together both mixtures. Serve with whipped cream.

The Commission Shop of Minneapolis.

Tomato Bisque

1 small can tomatoes	1 heaping tbsp. flour
1½ pts. milk	salt to taste
1 heaping tbsp. butter	pepper to taste
1/3 tbsp. soda	whipped cream

Stew tomatoes 15 to 20 minutes; cream butter and flour together and stir into milk as it begins to heat, stirring continuously until flour is thoroughly cooked and milk becomes the consistency of thick cream, but do not let boil; season to taste with salt and tabasco sauce. When ready to serve, stir into the tomatoes the soda, while effervescing pour tomatoes into the milk—mix, strain and serve immediately with a spoonful of whipped cream on top of each cup.

Mrs. Lewis S. Smith.

Gumbo

1 chicken (fried)	¾ lb. okra
½ large onion (fried)	1 clove garlic
½ large onion raw	1 can tomatoes
pepper	salt

Cut okra in small pieces, flour and fry it. Add one half onion fried and one half onion raw, add garlic, tomatoes, salt and pepper. Put fried chicken in pot, cover with above mixture, cook slowly until chicken falls to pieces.

Mrs. Turner Pittman.

Cream of Mushroom Soup

1 large can mushrooms	2 tbsp. butter
2 qts. well seasoned chicken broth	1 tbsp. flour
	1 cup whipped cream
1 pt. cream	salt and pepper

Put chicken broth in a double boiler to heat. In another pan, put mushrooms that have been drained, rinsed in cold water and chopped fine, butter and scraping of onion (onion may be omitted). Let this simmer for fifteen minutes, adding the flour. Mix thoroughly. Add two cups of the chicken broth, stirring slowly until smooth. Add this to the broth in the double boiler. Just before serving, add cream and re-heat. Take off the fire, add salt and pepper and whipped cream. Serve at once.

Mrs. H. Ostrand.

Oyster Soup

1 qt. milk	1 tsp. pepper
1 tbsp. butter	1 tbsp. flour
1 tsp. salt	1 qt. oysters

Put milk in a sauce pan, add butter, salt, pepper and flour. Stir constantly until it comes to a boil. Add oysters and allow to boil until edges curl. Serve at once.

Mrs. W. R. Willing.

Italian Stew

1 2-lb. can tomatoes	1 tbsp. olive oil
1 can mushrooms	1 small onion
1 cup chopped cold meat	salt and pepper
garlic, if desired	

Stew tomatoes, mushrooms and meat together in olive oil. Add salt and pepper.

Mrs. John F. Williams.

Fresh Mushroom Soup

1 lb. fresh mushrooms	butter
milk	

Peel and chop mushrooms, saute in butter until light brown. Make a milk soup, season to taste and add mushrooms. Serves 10.

Mrs. Seth Miller.

Mulled Wine for Twelve

3 pts. claret	cloves
sugar	cinnamon bark
½ cup pearl tapioca	allspice

Serve in cups in place of cold bouillon. Sweeten claret to taste. Tie spices in lawn sack and boil in wine. When wine comes to a boil, plunge a red hot poker into it. Do this twice, re-heating the poker. Set away to chill. Soak and boil tapioca and put some into each serving of wine.

Mrs. J. B. Oldham.

Bouillon

4 lbs. round steak	1 stalk celery
2 turnips	3 bay leaves
2 carrots	salt
2 onions	

Cover round steak with cold water. Cook slowly one and one half hours. Add turnips, carrots, celery, bay leaves, chopped, and salt to taste. Cook seven or eight hours. Next morning take off fat, strain, salt and serve.

Mrs. Geo. N. Aldredge.

Pot au Feu

3 lbs. round beef	1 large marrow bone
6 carrots	3 turnips
1 or 2 leeks	1 bunch parsley
bay leaf	2 or 3 cloves
1 lump sugar	salt

An earthernware pan with lid must be used in making Pot au Feu. Put the beef into the pan and cover with as many quarts of water as there are pounds of meat. Add a little salt. Let is come to boil, then skim very carefully and add a little cold water. Let it boil again, then skim again. Add vegetables and cover with lid, allowing a little air in. Cook on good fire constantly on boiling point for several hours. Chicken may be cooked in Pot au Feu. When finished, the meat is taken out and the bouillon is skimmed. Add small slices of bread. The meat which has been cooked in the Pot au Feu may be served with thick tomato sauce.

Mrs. S. W. King, Jr.

Bouillabaisse

4½ lbs. fish
2 cloves
2 bay leaves
2 small pieces of garlic
2 carrots
salt
1 small chili

1 tsp. powdered saffron
1 lb. sliced onion
1 small bunch parsley
1 spray of thyme
2 shallots
4 tbsp. olive oil
pepper corns
2 qts. water

Cut fish, (lobster may be added) into three-inch squares and put into a large sauce pan or earthen pan. Add onions, cloves, parsley, bay leaves, thyme, garlic, shallots, carrots, olive oil, salt and pepper corns, chili and water. Cover pan and let mixture cook for twenty-five minutes. If whiting is used, it must be put in later. When the fish is cooked strain it off carefully, pass the liquor through a colander and stir in the saffron. Serve with small squares of slightly toasted bread.

Mrs. S. W. King, Jr.

Gumbo File

1 onion	1 cup flour
½ lb. cut veal	½ lb. cut raw ham
2 lbs. raw shrimp	2 qts. water
parsley	green onion
piece of garlic	1 bay leaf
pinch of thyme	pinch cloves

heaping tsp. powdered creole file

Brown finely cut onion in flour, fry cut veal and cut raw ham. Scald raw shrimp in 2 qts. water and remove shells. Add same water to fried meat and onions. Add also finely chopped parsley, green onions, piece garlic, bay leaf, thyme and pinch of cloves. Let boil slowly for half an hour. Add peeled shrimp and continue boiling slowly another half hour. Just before serving add file. Serve with rice. Crabs or oysters may be used instead of shrimp. Or all three used are good. Chicken with oysters makes a good gumbo without the veal.

Mrs. Franklin Pugh.

Creamed Onion Soup au Gratin

6 medium sized onions	2 qts. milk
(cooked in beef	1 pt. cream
stock until tender)	½ lb. butter

Make a rue of celery, carrots, turnips and butter. Add milk and cream. Cook slowly for two hours. Strain through a sieve, add onions and season to taste with salt, pepper and paprika. Put finely grated cheese on bread and toast. Serve one piece in each bowl of soup.

The Commission Shop of Minneapolis.

Shrimp or Crawfish Bisque

1 lb. shrimp or crawfish 1 onion
  garlic parsley
1 green onion ½ green pepper
    stale bread

Scald shrimp or crawfish in 1 qt. water. Peel and chop fine. Add one onion, parsley, garlic, one green onion, green pepper and stale bread. Add this to browned flour and onions and shrimp water in which fish were scalded. Cook half hour slowly and serve with little squares toast as a soup. Serves six. *Mrs. Franklin Pugh.*

Cream of Corn Soup

1 can corn 3 cups milk
½ cup cream 2 tbsp. flour
1 small onion 1 egg
1 red pepper or salt to taste
1 canned pimento pepper to taste

Put milk and corn in double boiler. Mince the onions and let simmer in butter without browning, for five minutes. Add flour. Turn into milk. Cook 20 minutes, strain and just before serving, add egg well beaten and mix with cream. Re-heat and serve with chopped pepper if fresh peppers are used.

Mrs. Frank Cullinan.

Grape Juice Bouillon

1 pt. grape juice allspice, cloves and
  juice 1 or 2 lemons cinnamon (whole
1 cup water spices)

Boil all together, putting spices in thin gauze bag. Serve hot with or without whipped cream on top.

Miss Ada Walne.

37

New Orleans Gumbo

1 chicken cut in bits from bone	3 onions
½ lb. ham chopped	3 doz. oysters
6 crabs cut in small bits	1 qt. okra
1 lb. peeled shrimp	1 red pepper
1 green pepper	2 spoons lard
2 spoons flour	4 cloves
1 pinch nutmeg	1 bay leaf
1 sprig thyme	½ cup chopped celery
	½ cup chopped parsley

Mix flour and lard, fry seasoning in this. Tear up chickern, cut fine, use broth you boiled chicken in, after grease is removed from top, to pour over fried or boiled chicken. Add enough water to cover well and steam three hours. Serve with rice steamed dry. Fry the ham. If the gumbo is greasy on top it is not good. Do not put in ham fat.

Mrs. A. T. Lloyd.

Bortsch

4 beet roots	2½ lb. meat (including cuttings and bone of ham)
¼ lb. bacon	
1 onion	
2 bay leaves	pepper
1 lb. tomatoes	2 lbs. cabbage
3 tbsp. water	2 apples
6 sliced cooked potatoes	¼ glass of white beans
	1 tbsp. flour
	½ glass milk

The day before the bortsch is to be served, a beet root stock should be prepared by peeling 4 beet roots, cooking them in water until soft, then put in cool place. Next day make a stock of ham, bacon and add to beet root stock before putting in the water. Boil this mixture several times, removing the scum each time. Then add onion, pepper, bay leaves and cabbage and cook this mixture again. Cut up tomatoes and apples and put in separate sauce pan with 3 tbsp. water and cook until soft. This should then be rubbed through a sieve and added to the bortsch. Add beans, (cooked separately) a little before serving. Fifteen minutes before serving, add potatoes and 2 beet roots cooked the day before. A tbsp. of flour diluted with a little stock and milk are added last and stirred in well. The whole mixture should be brought to a boil.

Mrs. S. W. King, Jr.

Creme Cressonniere

fresh watercress	several diced potatoes
lump butter	1 cup cream

Stew watercress in butter, then cover with water and add diced potatoes. When these are thoroughly cooked, pass soup through a fine sieve and add cream. Cress leaves should be added as a garnish.

Mrs. S. W. King, Jr.

Oyster Soup

1 qt. milk	salt and pepper to
1 qt. oysters	taste
1 large potato	½ onion
1 tbsp. butter	4 pieces celery

Cook potato, onion and celery until done sufficiently to mash through very fine strainer. Put milk in pan, add salt, pepper and butter, and puree of vegetables. Stir until comes to boil. Add oysters and cook until the edges curl.

Mrs. Peter O'Donnell.

Fish and Oysters

Oysters Rockefellow I

1 bunch shallots	1 bunch parsley
stale bread	salt to taste
pepper to taste	dash of tabasco sauce

Grind together in meat grinder. Cover oysters on half of shell with sauce and place in hot oven for thirty minutes. Place oysters in flat pan lined in ice cream salt.

Mrs. George F. Howard.

Oysters a la Rockefellow II

1 lb. spinach	2 tbsp. cream
piece of garlic	1 onion
salt to taste	1 tbsp. of Worcester-
pepper to taste	shire sauce
tabasco sauce to taste	

Boil spinach with onions and garlic. Pass it through a fine seive. Add cream, tabasco sauce, salt and pepper. Broil oysters in butter. Serve on toast or in shell with above sauce.

Mrs. Franklin Pugh.

Keebobbed Oysters

oysters	cracker crumbs
1 egg	chopped celery
bacon	butter

Clean oysters of sand and bits of shell. Season well, dip in beaten egg, then cracker crumbs and place in pan. Dot generously with butter, sprinkle with chopped celery, and add another layer of oysters, dipped in egg and cracker crumbs. Place bits of butter and bacon over the top and cook in hot oven about ten minutes. Do not have more than two layers.

Mrs. William J. Moroney.

Broiled Fish

4 or 5 fish	4 or 5 large lumps
juice 1 lemon	butter
3 tbsp. Worcestershire	1/3 cup spiced vinegar
sauce	pepper

Salt fish well several hours before cooking. Put fish in a broiler pan with a large lump of butter on each. Pour over them lemon juice, vinegar, Worcestershire sauce and pepper. Broil under fire very slowly for 30 or 40 minutes. Do not turn fish, but baste with the sauce every 5 minutes. If the fish are large, slice in half to cook.

Mrs. T. H. Obenchain.

Cocktail Sauce for Shrimp

2 cups stiff mayonnaise	2 tsp. onion juice or
3 tbsp. chili sauce	finely chopped
2 tbsp. catsup	onion
2 tbsp. very finely chop-	red pepper
ped celery	tabasco to taste
	2 tsp. anchovy paste

Mix all ingredients except celery, stirring until thoroughly blended. Season with red pepper and tabasco to taste. Add finely chopped celery just before serving.

Mrs. Peter O'Donnell.

Manhattan Shrimp

1 tbsp. butter	1 cup finely cut cheese
½ cup thin cream	1/3 cup stewed and
1 egg	strained tomatoes
1½ cups shrimp	mustard to taste
cayenne to taste	salt
1 tbsp. flour	pepper to taste

Melt butter and add flour. Stir until blended. Add gradually while stirring, constantly, cream and tomatoes. Bring to a boil and add cheese, egg slightly beaten, and shrimp cut in small pieces. Season to taste with salt, pepper, mustard and cayenne. Serve as soon as cheese is melted.

Mrs. Allen Charlton.

Broiled Oyster

Oysters   Worcestershire sauce—generous amount of butter
Salt, pepper and red pepper to taste

Make sauce of Worcestershire sauce, salt, pepper, butter and red pepper. Place oysters, which have been drained, in pan and pour sauce over them. Run under flame until browned. Serve immediately on hot toast.

Mrs. Peter O'Donnell.

Oysters and Noodles

Butter baking dish, lining with the home made noodles. Drain oysters, dip in beaten eggs and cracker crumbs. Put layer of these, and alternate oysters and noodles until dish is filled. Put generous amount of butter in and fill dish with very thick cream. Bake slowly about 45 minutes.

Mrs. Peter O'Donnell.

Fish With Marguery Sauce

Broil any small fish with few bones. Make white sauce of cream, butter and yolks of two eggs. Season well and add one cup fresh mushrooms, one cup fresh shrimp (cooked) and one dozen mussels. Canned ones will do. Pour over boiled fish. Put in oven for few minutes until sauce sets.

Mrs. Frank Callier.

Deviled Shrimp

1 tbsp. butter	1 tbsp. flour
1 onion (minced fine)	3 tbsp. vinegar
1 sprig parsley	about 1½ cups water
1 bay leaf (minced)	salt, pepper, cayenne
½ clove garlic	½ tsp. mustard

Melt butter, add onion, parsley, bay leaf, and garlic. Let simmer gently without browning and then add flour. Mix thoroughly and add 3 tbsp. vinegar. Stir well and add water. Season well with salt and pepper to taste and cayenne. Add 1 tsp. prepared mustard. Simmer about 5 minutes and pour over hot cooked shrimp on pieces of toast.

Edna Ball.

Baked Fish

1 nice fish	1 garlic button
1 can tomato paste	1 cup water
1 bay leaf	salt, pepper and lots
½ to 1 lemon	of butter

Dry fish well, put salt and pepper on and spread with tomato paste (thickly). Add lemon and butter. Cut garlic very fine, put in bay leaf and water and cook in moderate oven for about 25 or 30 minutes. From time to time, baste fish.

Mrs. S. I. Munger, Jr.

Fish In Aspic

1 pt. vinegar	36 allspice
1 pt. water	10 bay leaves
40 pepper corns	8 slices lemon
8 slices onions	

Boil vinegar and water ½ hour with salt, pepper, allspice, bay leaves and 8 slices of onions. Add lemon slices, cook 5 minutes then remove them. Simmer the fish in this liquor until you can pull out a fin. Cook only a few small fish or slices of fish at one time. Pack fish as cooked into stone crock with one or more raw sliced onions between layers. Pour over the hot liquid with seasonings. Cover and keep in a cool place. This liquid is enough for ½ gallon of fish and will keep several weeks. Serve crackers with this and mayonnaise dressing. Make two or three days before needed as it requires that time to become firm.

Mrs. Karl Hoblitzelle.

Baked Halibut Steak

1½ lbs. halibut steak	salt, pepper, ta-
1 tsp. Worcestershire	basco
sauce	½ cup butter
1 tbsp. lemon juice	

Take halibut steak 1¼ inches thick, wash and wipe dry, sprinkle with salt and pepper, spread both sides with soft butter, dust lightly with flour. Butter a shallow baking pan, put in steak, place under a broiler and let it brown on top, taking care not to brown too quickly. Melt butter and mix with lemon juice and Worcestershire sauce and a few drops of tabasco. Pour this over fish and place in a moderately hot oven for thirty minutes. Baste often. Serve carefully without breaking on a hot dish. Pour in sauce left in pan, garnish with lemon and parsley.

Mrs. H. Ostrand.

Salmon Loaf

1 lb. can salmon	1 tsp. dry mustard
½ tsp. salt	cayenne pepper
1 tbsp. sugar	2 eggs
1 tbsp. flour	1½ tsp. butter
2/3 cup milk	½ cup vinegar
1 tbsp. water	1 can mushrooms
½ bottle capers	1 envelope gelatine

Mix dry ingredients, add beaten eggs, butter, milk and vinegar. Cook in double boiler until mixture thickens. Add gelatine which has been dissolved in a little cold water. Beat until thoroughly dissolved in hot mixture and add salmon, mushrooms, capers. Set away to mould. Slice on lettuce with mayonnaise.

Mrs. J. B. Adoue, Jr.

Sauce Victoria

1 cup whipped cream	2 tbsp. Heinz tomato
1 pimento	catsup
½ tsp. lemon juice	salt and pepper to taste

To whipped cream, add lemon juice, salt and pepper, chopped pimento and Heinz tomato catsup. Mix well. Excellent for shrimp or lobster.

Mrs. J. B. Oldham.

Cocktail Sauce

3 tbsp. tomato catsup	1 tbsp. Worcestershire
1 tsp. horseradish	sauce
1 tsp. salt	½ lemon juice

tabasco to taste

Mix all well, and put on ice. Serves four people.

Mrs. A. B. Webster.

Little Pigs

1 can sardines   Bacon

Use sardines that have been put up in mustard. Mash them to a pulp, spread on strip of bacon, roll and pin with a toothpick. Broil, in oven and serve hot.

Mrs. J. B. Shelmire.

Oysters au Gratin (6 people)

18 oysters   2 tbsp. butter
18 mushrooms   ½ tsp. salt
1/8 tsp. cayenne   1 cup white sauce

Cook mushrooms in hot butter for a few minutes. Place 3 oysters in an oyster shell, then the mushrooms, some white sauce and seasoning. Sprinkle with cracker crumbs and grated cheese and bake until brown.

The Commission Shop of Minneapolis.

Sauted Shrimp

Melt butter in pan, dredge with flour, add 1 can of chopped mushrooms and the liquor. Then add shrimp and sherry wine, season highly and add ½ cup sour cream.

Oysters en Brochette

Drain the oysters, slice breakfast bacon very thin and cut into pieces the length of an oyster. Take metal or wooden skewers such as used in pinning roasts together and string them with a piece of bacon and then an oyster, alternating till skewer is filled. Bacon must be last. Lay on a broiler in a hot oven and cook until edges curl. When ready to serve, place on long narrow strips of buttered toast and pour over a little melted butter. A skewer should be served to each person.   *Mrs. Lewis S. Smith.*

Moulded Fish With Mushrooms and Lobster Sauce

3 lbs. white fish   salt and pepper

Boil fish well done. Flake fish, add enough cream sauce to hold mixture together. Turn into a buttered dish mould and put mould into boiling water and cook until fish is firm.

Sauce:

3 tbsp. butter   3 tbsp. flour
1½ cups heavy cream   2 egg yolks
1 can lobster   1 can mushrooms
      salt, lemon juice and paprika to taste

Melt butter, add flour. Mix well, add cream and eggs well beaten. Cut lobster and mushrooms in cubes and add to sauce. Serve 10 or 12 people.

Mrs. J. C. Duke.

Fried Lobster

1 large lobster   3 oz. butter
      salt, pepper, flour, lemon juice

Cut lobster in slices, season with salt, pepper and lemon juice. Dip the slices in flour, then in beaten eggs and last in bread crumbs or cracker meal. Lay slices in the hot butter and fry until golden brown. Turn several times. Serve with tartar sauce.

Mrs. M. G. Mathews.

White Sauce

1 tbsp. butter   salt, pepper, paprica to
1 cup cream   taste
1 tsp. flour

Heat butter in sauce pan, add flour and stir until smooth. Then add gradually cold cream. Let boil up once. Season to taste and serve.

Mrs. Helen L. Ardrey.

Fricasse of Oysters

50 oysters	1 pt. milk
2 tbsp. butter	2 egg yolks
2 tbsp. flour	4 tbsp. cream
salt, pepper, cayenne to taste	

Drain and wash oysters. Cook until quills curl, drain again, saving the liquor and add to it enough milk to make a pint. Put flour, and butter into a sauce pan, mix, add liquor and milk and stir until boiling. Add salt, pepper and cayenne and oysters. Heat over hot water; beat egg yolks with the cream, stir quickly in the oysters. Serve on toast, sprinkle with parsley and garnish with lemon rings.

Mrs. Fred Fleming.

Salmon Loaf

1 lb. can salmon	1 tsp. cream
1 tbsp. butter	juice of 1 lemon
3 eggs	½ cup crackers

Mash salmon, removing bones, add butter, eggs well beaten, cream, lemon juice and cracker crumbs. Bake half an hour.

Mrs. A. B. Griffiths.

Salmon Souffle

1 qt. milk	1 cup flour
2 onions	1 cup salmon
parsley	1 cup cheese
1 cup cracker crumbs	

Boil milk, add flour, onions (medium sized) and parsley chopped fine. To this add salmon and cheese which has been grated and cracker crumbs. Mix well, season with butter, salt, pepper. Serve hot.

Mrs. J. L. Dreibelbis.

Baked Shrimp

5 lbs. shrimp	1 kitchen spoon butter
4 cloves chopped garlic	2 tbsp. grated buttered bread crumbs
1 tbsp. chopped parsley	1 cup water

Boil shrimp in brine highly seasoned with red pepper. Brown garlic and parsley in butter, add cooked shrimp, heat thoroughly, then put in baking dish. In same skillet put small amount extra butter and add bread crumbs soaked in water. Cook until thick and pour over shrimp. Dot with butter and bake.

Mrs. J. B. Adoue, Jr.

Shrimp Cutlets

1 small can shrimp	½ tsp. salt
1 cup white sauce	¼ tsp. red pepper
1 tbsp. crumbs	1 egg

Soak crumbs in cream. Mix all ingredients well. Shape as a chop or cutlet. Dip in sifted cracker crumbs, then in an egg beaten up with a tablespoon of water, again in crumbs and fry in deep fat. Put a chop stick in the end in which is placed a frill of paper. Serve a rich white sauce or tomato sauce.

Mrs. Helen L. Ardrey.

Shrimp Creole

½ green pepper	1 can tomatoes
1 tbsp. butter	shrimp
¼ onion (chopped)	rice

Sprinkle onion with flour and fry brown. Strain a can of tomatoes, boil and mash and add fried pepper and onion. Then add shrimp. Place boiled rice in center of platter and pour the shrimp around it and serve.

Mrs. W. O. Connor.

Cream Fish

tenderloin of trout	1 pt. sweet cream
salt to taste	pepper to taste

Grind fish through meat grinder, season with salt and pepper. To this add cream. Beat all together like a cake. Put in a round pan covered tightly, set in a pot of boiling water and cook one half hour. When fish is done, turn out like a cake and slice.

Sauce for Fish

1 large spoon butter	1 can mushrooms
1 heaping tsp. flour	½ lemon (juice)
1 cup cream	salt and pepper

Melt butter, add flour, mushrooms, (cut in quarters), salt, pepper, lemon juice and cream. Let this come to a boil, stirring constantly.

Mrs. Max Ortlieb.

Moulded Salmon

1 can salmon	½ tbsp. flour
1 tbsp. sugar	red pepper
1 tsp. mustard	1½ tbsp. butter
2 egg yolks	¼ cup vinegar
¾ cup milk	¾ tbsp. gelatine

½ tsp. salt

Mix dry ingredients. Melt butter, add eggs, butter, milk and vinegar to dry ingredients. Cook over boiling water until it thickens.

Add gelatine which has been soaked in cold water. Then add flaked salmon. Mould and serve with mayonnaise dressing.

Mrs. A. A. Green.

Lemon Sauce For Fish

Boil fish in water with a little vinegar, butter, salt and pepper until done. Beat yolks of two eggs with a little sugar and mix in the juice of a lemon. Take fish out of gravy and stir in a little butter to thicken. Then pour gravy into eggs, mixing well and pour over fish. Dress fish with slices of lemon, grated hard boiled eggs and almonds cut fine. Serve hot or cold.

Mrs. Max Ortlieb.

Deviled Oysters

1 stalk celery (chopped)	3 hard boiled eggs (chopped)
½ cup pecans (chopped)	1 qt. oysters
parsley	3 raw eggs
½ cup thick cream	large piece butter
	cracker crumbs

Mix all, using only enough crumbs to hold together. Put in ramekins, sprinkle with crumbs and dot with butter. Bake. *Miss Elizabeth Dumas.*

Shrimp Curry With Rice

Have rice cooked and moulded in an oval ring, brush with butter and put in oven until hot. Have shrimp cooked in brine and red pepper. Remove shells and cut them in pieces. Put them in sauce as follows: ½ onion fried in 2 tablespoons butter (garlic may be used), remove onion, add 1 teaspoon curry dissolved in ½ cup white stock, ½ teaspoon salt, ¼ teaspoon paprika, ½ cup cream and 2 tablespoons fresh grated cocoanut or blanched chopped almonds. When boiling, pour over rice.

Mrs. Paul Platter.

Oyster a la Italienne

50 oysters	8 tbsp. Snyder's tomato
1 tbsp. flour	catsup
8 tbsp. Snyder's oyster	4 drops tabasco sauce
cocktail dressing	1 tbsp. butter

Cream butter and flour well. Mix all the sauces and seasoning. Add to the flour and butter and beat twenty minutes before serving. Put in oysters last and serve on buttered toast. *Mrs. R. C. Burke.*

Oyster a la St. Anthony

Use very huge oysters. Springle the open oyster on the shell with celery, green peppers chopped fine. Cover them with a thin layer of bread crumbs fried until brown and mixed with paprika and pepper. Cover all with a thinly sliced strip of bacon and bake in a quick oven until the oysters are well cooked and bacon crisp. Serve in a soup plate filled with parsley. Place in the center of the plate a fancy lemon cup or green pepper cup filled with chow-chow.

Mrs. H. D. Ardrey.

Baked Shrimp

3 lbs. shrimp	1 tsp. brown sugar
1 small bottle dark	1 heaping tbsp. butter
mustard	salt and pepper
1 tbsp. Worcestershire	cayenne to taste
sauce	

Parboil shrimp with dash of cayenne in water. Drain, peel and cut into 1 inch bits. Place in baking dish and cover with following sauce: Mix mustard, brown sugar, Worcestershire sauce, butter, dash of tabasco, salt and cayenne pepper, cover with bread crumbs and lots of butter. Cook in oven fifteen or twenty minutes. Serve at once.

Mrs. H. R. Aldredge.

Poultry and Game

Roast Turkey

Thoroughly wash inside with soda water, then rinse in clear water; wipe dry, then rub inside and outside with salt. Stuff with dressing. Rub over with butter and dredge with flour; sprinkle with pepper and put into a roaster. Pour in a pint of boiling water. Baste frequently. From two to two and one-half hours required for a 12 to 14 pound turkey. Test with fork, if juice runs out perfectly clear, fowl is done.

Gravy: When you remove fowl, remove surplus grease, add a little flour to thicken, and boiling water. Let boil up good, then add liver and gizzard boiled and cut fine. Garnish with parsley, water cress, and fried oysters.

Mrs. John F. Williams.

Dressing For Fowls

There are many kinds of dressings. A good every day one if made of half and half meal, egg bread and stale light bread, chopped onion, parsley, celery, butter, salt and pepper, moistened with cream or hot water. Sage can be used instead of onions. If the dressing is to be used for turkey, 2 eggs and one-half teaspoon baking powder added just before stuffing fowl. If for chicken, 1 egg, less baking powder.

Mrs. John F. Williams.

Oyster Dressing

3 pints oysters	salt
½ pt. butter	pepper
3 stalks celery	
1 loaf stale bread soaked in tepid water	

Moisten with liquid from oysters and add a little cream.

Mrs. John F. Williams.

53

Chicken Croquettes

1 chicken	2 green peppers
4 stalks celery	1 tbsp. flour
1 tbsp. butter	1 cup milk

Boil hen until tender, remove meat and run through food chopper with the celery and green pepper. Make a cream sauce of the butter, melted and smooth with flour and the milk. Moisten the chicken mixture and shape into croquettes. Set on ice for at least two hours. Dip in egg and bread crumbs and fry in deep hot fat. Serve with spoonful of rich cream sauce.

Mrs. A. B. Webster.

Fricassee Chicken

Cut up hen as for fried chicken and roll into seasoned flour. Fry to a golden brown, take out chicken and brown one small onion, one tablespoon celery, one tablespoon parsley and one garlic button. Strain out above and make a thick brown gravy with milk and seasoning. Put chicken into a covered roasting pan and pour gravy over the chicken. Squeeze one orange and add two bay leaves. Put on back of stove and let simmer until tender.

Mrs. S. A. Leake.

Hot Jellied Chicken

Cook till tender a large hen. Cut in pieces as for salad and to each cup of diced chicken add one whole egg and one cup of thick cream dressing. Season with salt and pepper. Mix well, put in moulds or a large baking dish and bake till set. Take two cupfuls of the stock in which chicken was cooked, thicken with one heaping tablespoon of flour, add one can peas, one can of mushrooms and serve as a sauce over the chicken. A four pound hen serves about eight people.

Mrs. R. C. Munger, Birmingham.

Ducks a la Carte

1 duck   2 cups water
2 tumblers claret   1 glass red jelly

Prepare duck, place in roaster, slightly sprinkle with flour, put water in pan and cook two hours. Pour in claret and jelly and baste for an hour. When ready to serve, fill duck with red jelly. Use dressing if preferred.

Mrs. Edward B. Williams.

Pressed Chicken

1 chicken   1 bottle stuffed olives
1 slice onion   pecan meats
  parsley   celery hearts

Cook fowl in salted water with onion until meat falls from bones. Remove and reduce stock to one cupful. Cool and strain off excess grease. Separate chicken from bone, skin and gristle and cut fine. Line mould with sliced stuffed olives, celery cut in rings, and nuts. Season chicken to taste and line mould. Pour reduced stock over it, place weight on it and let stand until firm. Slice and serve with mayonnaise. *Mrs. A. Folsom.*

Terrapin Chicken

1 large old hen boiled tender in salt water
6 hard boiled eggs   2 large tbsp. butter
1 nutmeg   1 tumbler sherry wine
1 tumbler stock   1 can mushrooms
1 pt. cream   (chopped fine)

Cut hen in pieces. Rub hard boiled yolks to a cream with butter, add nutmeg, sherry, stock, mushrooms, then add chicken and let cook until it begins to thicken. Add cream and let cook until thick enough to serve on toast or in ramekin.

Mrs. R. C. Burke.

Chafing Dish Birds

birds	1 pt. sweet cream
1 tsp. butter for each bird	1 tumbler stock
	1 can mushrooms
3 tbsp. Worcestershire sauce	3 red peppers
	salt
1 lemon (rind and 1 slice)	pepper
	1 tumbler sherry wine

Split birds down back. Salt and pepper well, put in long pan and put butter on each bird. Add rest of ingredients except cream. Cook until tender, basting often. Pour cream over birds when you turn the breast up. Baste well. Serve on buttered toast.

Mrs. R. C. Burke.

Chicken a la King

1 boiled hen	1 cup cream
2 tbsp. butter	1 cup milk
4 tbsp. flour	2 cups stock
2 egg yolks	2 cans mushrooms
4 green peppers	2 large tbsp. sherry wine
Worcestershire sauce	salt
tabasco	paprika

Make a cream sauce with milk, cream butter and flour add stock, then well beaten egg yolks. Cook until creamy, stirring constantly. Add mushrooms, chicken, peppers, salt, tabasco, Worcestershire sauce and enough paprika to make mixture a good salmon color. Just before serving, stir in sherry.

Camilla Padgitt.

Broiled Quail on Toast

Cut the quail open through the back bone, sprinkle with salt and pepper and rub in bacon grease. Have iron skillet hot, put into it a tablespoon of butter to keep bird from sticking, place bird on skillet, cover and weight down, place on back part of stove, allow to cook slowly to a light brown, which takes about 40 minutes. When done serve on buttered toast, pouring over the quail hot butter which has been salted and peppered. Garnish dish with crisp white lettuce leaves.

Mrs. John F. Williams.

Cold Chicken Mousse

1½ cups white meat
    (chicken cooked
    and ground very
    fine)
½ cup chicken stock
3 egg yolks
¼ cup cold water

1 scant pt. cream
    (whipped)
1½ cups sweet milk
    tbsp. Knox gelatine
¼ tsp. salt
    few grains paprika

Beat yolks, add milk and cook in a double boiler until a light custard. Soak gelatine in cold water, add hot chicken broth, stir until dissolved, then add to custard. Add minced chicken (be sure chicken is minced very fine). Season to taste and when cool, add whipped cream. Let stand in ice box several hours or over night. Place on large platter, garnish with lettuce and sliced tomatoes and fill center of mould with salad dressing.

The Commission Shop of Minneapolis.

Hot Chicken Mousse

1 chicken breast (raw)	½ cup milk
1 cup soft bread crumbs	5 egg whites
½ cup cream	salt and pepper

Put bread crumbs, cream and milk on stove and boil. Put raw chicken through grinder and add seasoning. Boil two minutes. Remove from stove, add whites of eggs stiffly beaten. Butter cups or ring moulds and sprinkle with dry crumbs. Fill two-thirds full with mixture; bake twenty minutes in pan of hot water. Turn out, serve with creamed mushrooms. Halibut may be used in place of chicken and served with hard boiled egg sauce. Serves 8 people.

The Commission Shop of Minneapolis.

Chicken Creole

2 chickens	2 tbsp. butter
2 tbsp. flour	6 large tomatoes
6 green peppers	2 cloves of garlic
3 large onions	3 sprigs thyme
3 sprigs parsley	2 bay leaves
salt to taste	pepper to taste
1 pt. consomme or boiling water	

Cut chickens at the joints. Season well with salt and pepper. Put butter into a stew pan and when it melts, add chickens. Let this brown slowly for five minutes. Add onions to chickens and let them brown. They must be well browned, but care must be taken not to burn. Add flour. Let brown. Then add sliced tomatoes and let these brown. Cook very slowly, allowing the mixture to simmer. Add chopped parsley, thyme, bay leaf, cloves and garlic finely minced. Let all brown. Cover and let it smother over a slow fire. Add peppers, removing seed first, and slice finely. Stir well. Let smother for 20 minutes, keeping covered. Stir occasionally. Then add 1 cup consomme. Cook again for an hour very, very slowly. Season again to taste and cook ten minutes more. Serve hot.

Mrs. S. W. King, Jr.

Jellied Chicken

4 lbs. chicken   2 slices onion   ½ tsp. salt

Put chicken and onion on to boil, covering chicken with boiling water. When half done, add salt and continue boiling until meat falls from bones. Remove chicken and reduce stock to ¾ cup. Strain and skim off fat. Decorate bottom of ring mould with parsley and hard boiled eggs. Pack in meat, freed from skin and bones. Sprinkle with salt and pepper. Pour on stock and put a heavy weight on mould. In summer, add one tsp. dissolved gelatine to stock. Serve on large round platter garnished with lettuce and sliced tomatoes. Fill center of mould with mayonnaise.

Mrs. John L. Puterbaugh.

Fricasee Chicken

young hen   onion
1 cup flour   2 cups water
1 cup tomatoes   1 piece garlic
parsley   green onions
½ green pepper

Cut up hen and fry in fat until tender. Remove chicken and fry flour and onions in same grease until brown. Add water for gravy, tomatoes, garlic, parsley, green onions and green pepper, all cut fine. Let smother slowly half an hour, until gravy thickens and chicken is tender. Serve with rice.

Mrs. Franklin Pugh.

Barbecued Chicken I

5 chickens
½ bottle Worcester-
    shire sauce
½ lb. butter
    salt to taste
    pepper to taste

½ bottle tomato catsup
    as much vinegar as
    Worcestershire and
    catsup combined
1 chopped onion
    dash of tabasco sauce

Baste chickens often with sauce.

Mrs. George F. Howard.

Pigeon Pie

4 pigeons
    salt
2 hard cooked eggs
2 doz. mushrooms
    black pepper
1 egg

½ tsp. celery salt
¼ tsp. paprika
1 cup thin cream
2 tsp. butter
2 tbsp. flour
    rich biscuit dough

Clean and split pigeons, simmer until tender in water, season when nearly done with celery salt, paprika. Remove larger bones and arrange in a buttered baking dish together with the livers and hearts, the hard cooked eggs quartered lengthwise and the mushrooms (if fresh ones are used they should be washed, skinned, sliced. If dried ones are used, they should be soaked for an hour in warm water). Use the broth reduced to one pint to make a highly seasoned gravy, thickening it well with butter and flour blended together and adding more seasoning if needed. Pour this over the birds and cover with a rich biscuit dough, not too thick, cutting a cross in the center and turning back the corners. Bake one-half hour in a 400° F. oven then pour in the cream, baste over the crust with beaten egg and bake fifteen minutes longer. *Mrs. Karl Hoblitzelle.*

Sauce Cumberland

2 shallots (young green onions)

6 tbsp. red currant jelly

pinch cayenne

juice 1 lemon

rind of 1 orange

rind of 1 lemon

pinch ginger

juice of 1 orange

Chop shallots as finely as possible. Put them into a sauce pan with the rind of orange and lemon cut into small thin strips. Add a little water. Boil for twenty minutes and strain off the water. The rinds and the shallots are then put into a bowl with the jelly, ginger, cayenne, juice of lemon and orange. This sauce is served cold with cold game.

Mrs. S. W. King, Jr.

Chicken Curry

Cook hen tender, cut white meat in large cubes, make sauce of 2 cups stock, one cup of cream and season with salt, pepper, paprika and a little garlic or onion. Thicken slightly with flour. Add 1 tsp. curry powder and mix with chicken. Boil rice very dry. Pour sauce over and serve with Major Grey's chutney.

Mrs. Frank Callier.

Creamed Chicken

To one large chicken which has been boiled and cut as for salad, add sauce made of 1 tbsp. melted butter, 3 tbsp. flour, work into a paste, then 3 cups stock, left from chicken. Add one small onion, finely chopped. Add can mushrooms, finely chopped. 1 tsp. Worcestershire sauce. Season with pepper and salt. Cook all for about ten minutes, then add green pepper finely chopped. Cook a few moments and serve hot. *Mrs. M. H. Thomas.*

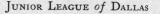

Chicken in Creole Sauce

2 chickens	1 finely chopped onion
1 can corn	1 can tomatoes
lump butter	red pepper to taste
tabasco to taste	steamed rice

Cut chickens in small pieces for frying. Put in pan with hot grease and cook quickly until very brown. On another pan simmer in butter finely chopped onion until onion is tender, then add corn and tomatoes. Put browned chicken into this, cover pan and cook slowly for 1½ hours, adding seasoning, such as red pepper and tabasco to taste. Serve with steaming rice. Green peppers cut finely may also be added to this. Shrimp may also be cooked this way.

Mrs. Peter O'Donnell.

Chicken Pie

1 hen cooked	1 cup peas
2 slices salt pork	2 Irish potatoes
3 hard boiled eggs	

Make rich pie crust and line baking dish, add cut meat from hen, which has been cooked tender. Peas and salt pork cut in small pieces and potatoes cut in cubes and eggs sliced. Season chicken stock well with onion, salt and pepper and pour over other ingredients. Cover with pastry and cook in a medium oven. *Mrs. Frank Callier.*

Paprika Chicken en Casserole

Dress, singe and clean 2 chickens, cut up for serving, brush over with melted butter, sprinkle with salt and pepper. Cook 1/3 cup butter with 1 finely chopped white onion 10 minutes, stirring constantly (do not allow onion to brown). Add chicken (except backs, use these for making stock, cooked with pinions and giblets) and dredge with 1/3 cup flour mixed and sifted with 1 tsp. paprika and ½ tbsp. salt. Pour 2 cups chicken stock (prepared as above), cover closely. Heat to boiling point, let simmer ½ hour, add more stock if necessary. Remove to hot casserole, arranging in this order: Legs and wings bottom, second joints over these and breasts on top. Cover and cook until chicken is tender. Use stock for making Bechamel sauce. Serve in sauce boat.

Miss Ada Walne.

Bechamel Sauce

Melt ¼ cup butter in sauce pan, add ¼ cup of flour, stir until smooth. Add gradually 1½ cups hot cream and beat until smooth and glossy. Season with salt, pepper and nutmeg. If a yellow sauce is desired, remove sauce from range and add the beaten yolks of 2 eggs diluted with ¼ cup warm cream. Do not allow sauce to boil after adding egg yolks.

Miss Ada Walne.

Barbecue Chicken II

1 lb. butter	6 broilers
1 cup chili sauce	tabasco
3 lemons (juice)	red peppers
rind of one lemon	1 cup catsup
2 cups Worcestershire sauce	2 tsp. paprika
2 cups vinegar	1 tbsp. salt

Mix ingredients and cook for 10 minutes. This amount will be sufficient for six chickens. They should be cooked very slowly and basted constantly with this mixture.

Melinda Simms.

63

Chicken Scotti

Make rich sauce of chicken stock and cream and season well with butter, red pepper and onion or garlic. Add diced white meat of cooked chicken. Boil spaghetti and make thick tomato sauce. Strain. Add one cup fresh mushrooms, six pieces breakfast bacon fried crisp and cut up. Put chicken mixed with white sauce, in center of shallow baking dish, cover with spaghetti mixed with tomato sauce. Save enough white sauce to pour over all and sprinkle Parmesan cheese over top. Leave in hot oven till cheese melts. Serve in same dish.   *Mrs. Frank Callier.*

Chicken Spaghetti

1 3 to 4 lb. hen   1 box spaghetti
1 large can tomatoes   ½ lb. American cheese
1 large onion

Simmer chicken gently in sufficient water to half cover, till meat begins to fall off bones. Season with salt, pepper and bay leaf. Allow chicken to cool and then pull apart in small pieces. In the meantime cook tomatoes and finely chopped onion together until tomatoes are pulpy and onion tender. Take about one quart of stock, or more if necessary, bring to a boil and allow spaghetti to cook 12 or 15 minutes. To this spaghetti, add the chicken and tomato mixture and cook until well blended. Just before serving, add the grated cheese and 1 tsp. Worcestershire sauce. Pass grated Parmesan cheese.

Mrs. Philip Miller.

Chicken a la King

Make a rich white sauce by using 5 tbsp. of butter or chicken fat with 6 tbsp. flour, 1½ tsp. salt, ½ tsp. paprika and 2 cups of milk. Cook until thick, remove from fire and when partially cooled, stir in the well beaten yolks of two eggs. Take 2 tbsp. of chopped green pepper, simmer gently in a little water for 5 minutes with 4 tbsp. of pimento. To the sauce add 1½ cups of cold diced chicken, ½ tsp. of salt, 1/3 cup of mushrooms cut in quarters and the pimento and green pepper and 2 hard boiled eggs, cut up. This amount serves 8.

Mrs. M. W. Carroll, Jr.

Meats and Meat Accompaniments

Recipe For Cooking Hams—Virginia Style

The ham in question weighed 18 pounds. Some people soak them in cold water over night. I do or do not soak them in cold water over night as I happen to have time. If the ham is not soaked in cold water over night it should be thoroughly washed and put on the stove in a kettle of cold water, and then let it boil from 9 o'clock A. M. until 2:30 P. M. (Some cooks say that 20 minutes should be allowed to each pound of ham). Then take it out of the water, take off the skin and remove the bones. Then put it in a baking pan, putting sugar and pepper on top, and also bread crumbs mixed with the sugar and pepper. Then put it in the oven and bake moderately for about 30 minutes. Keep the ham well covered with water while it is boiling, pouring in boiling water as it boils away.　*Mrs. R. M. Balthis*

Spaghetti

1 pkg. spaghetti
½ cup broken pecans
1 onion grated or finely chopped
4 tbsp. olive oil
2 tbsp. of Worcestershire sauce

½ can of sweet red pepper or pimento cut small
4 tbsp. of tomato catsup
dash of red pepper
1 tsp. salt

Cook spaghetti until tender then put in all ingredients, place in the stove to get thoroughly hot and slightly browned. Use casserole.　*Mrs. Charles W. Flynn.*

Sauce For Baked Ham

2 tbsp. tomato catsup   2 tbsp. butter
2 tbsp. sherry   1 tbsp. Worcestershire
1 tbsp. Tarragon vinegar   sauce
                1 tsp. dry mustard

Mix vinegar and mustard, then other ingredients.   Heat and serve with ham.

Mrs. Murrell Buckner.

Ham and Noodles

   noodles   2 slices raw or boiled
1 onion   ham
          sweet milk

Boil noodles twenty minutes, fry the ham, remove and brown onion in grease. Drain noodles and add to onion. To mix—put ham in casserole, then noodles and onions. Cover with sweet milk and bake twenty minutes.

Mrs. Chas. L. Dexter.

Noodles

1 egg yolk   1 tsp. salt
2 tbsp. water   2 cups flour

Beat egg and water together. Work in salt and flour sifted together. Roll very thin. Lay in cloth to dry. Roll as for jelly roll and shred very fine.

Mrs. Chas. L. Dexter.

Veal Loaf

2 lbs. veal	1 lb. ham
2 cups bread crumbs	2 eggs
ground cloves	onion juice

salt to taste

Grind veal and ham and add bread crumbs, eggs well beaten, cloves, onion juice, and salt to taste. Mix, shape into loaf. Put in baking pan with water and bake two hours.

Meat Loaf

2 lbs. ground round steak	1 medium white onion, chopped
¾ cup white rolled oats	2 cups canned tomatoes
1 doz. ripe olives, chopped	1 tsp. salt
	dash white pepper

Mix well in order given and bake in bread pan for one hour. This loaf is better if served cold.

Mrs. Allen Charlton.

Steak Creole

large sirloin steak 1½ in. thick	slices of onion
large size bottle Heinz catsup	slices of lemon

Have pan with heated butter. Sear steak on both sides to keep juice in steak. Place steak in Dutch oven or any large baking pan. Cover with whole thin slices of onions. Slice a lemon and place slices on onions, then take large size bottle of Heinz catsup, pour all over top of onions, steak, etc. Place several bits of butter on top. Place in oven. Cook very slowly about 1 hour. Sauce should be a nice creamy mixture. Don't let cook dry.

Mrs. Frank Cullinan.

Baked Ham

1 cup vinegar   1 cup black strap molasses
cracker crumbs   brown sugar
whole cloves

Soak ham over night. Drain. Put on in water to which has been added vinegar and molasses. Simmer slowly for 2 hours. Remove from fire and skin. Mix cracker crumbs and brown sugar. Rub all over ham and stick ham with whole cloves. Put in very slow oven and bake slowly until ham is very brown.

Mrs. Peter O'Donnell.

Sauce For Baked Ham

1 jar jelly   ½ jar mustard

Dissolve grape or currant jelly in double boiler. When thoroughly dissolved add French's mustard. Leave in double boiler until ready to serve.

Brain Entree

2 sets brains   2 tbsp. Worcestershire
1 can tomatoes   1 tbsp. tomato catsup
1 can small peas
1 tbsp. butter

Cook brains tender, leave whole, drain water. Let tomatoes come to a boil and season to taste. Heat peas and season to taste. Mix these and add butter, Worcestershire sauce and catsup. Thicken with a little milk and flour and pour over brains. Serve on toast.

Mrs. Devereux Dunlap.

Tomato Stuffed With Rice

Take large firm tomatoes, remove inside and mix with boiled rice one cup of ground ham, season with onion juice, red pepper and 2 tbsp. melted butter. Mix together well. Fill the tomato shells. Bake in a slow oven.

Mrs. Frank Callier.

French Griande

Take 2 young veal rounds, cut in small pieces, salt and pepper and flour well, then sear in hot grease. Cover thoroughly with boiling water, add celery, green pepper, parsley and onion all cut fine. Add can of tomato pulp, let all simmer slowly for 1½ to 2 hours until meat is tender enough to be cut with a fork. Serve on platter surrounded by dry rice.

Mrs. Ruth B. Lindsley.

Spiced Tongue

1 medium tongue	2 tbsp. sour wine or
2 tbsp. flour	1 tbsp. lemon and slice
4 tbsp. butter	of lemon
1 tbsp. capers	1 onion
	bay leaf

1 tbsp. seedless raisins

Boil tongue in salt water with bay leaf 2½ hours. Skin tongue and make a sauce. Put butter in pan, add flour and brown. When brown put in water in which tongue has been cooked and add onions chopped fine and let simmer 30 minutes. Then put in wine or lemon juice and lemon, capers and raisins. Slice tongue and put into sauce and simmer 10 minutes.

Mrs. Curt Beck.

Apples Stuffed With Sausage

Core apples, taking as much inside out as possible. Mix inside with seasoned sausage, stuff apples with mixture and bake slowly until done. Serve with meats or poultry as garnish around platter.

Mrs. Frank Callier.

Yorkshire Pudding—Serve With Roast Beef

½ pt. flour   pinch salt
1 pt. milk   1 tbsp. lard

2 eggs

Put milk with salt in bowl. Break into this without beating, 2 eggs. Dust flour into this. Beat vigorously with egg beater until all lumps are out. Have ready pan with lard very hot. Pour batter in until it is at least one inch thick. Bake about 20 minutes. Cut in squares and put on platter with roast beef. This is to be served with roast beef only.

Mrs. W. J. Moroney.

Steak and Spaghetti

1 big onion (cut fine) salt
1 clove garlic (cut fine) red pepper
2 cans tomato pulp paprika
1 tbsp. chili powder 1 box of spaghetti
1 thick round steak Parmesian cheese

1 can tomatoes

Fry round steak brown—put through meat grinder. Fry onion and garlic in bacon grease, add tomato, chili powder, salt, red pepper, paprika. Cook a few minutes, add ground steak, cook. Pour all over cooked spaghetti, sprinkle with cheese and serve.

Mrs. Frank Callier.

Roast Beef

Salt and pepper both sides of roast, put into the dripping pan, cover it well with flour and pieces of suet, put sufficient water around roast to keep it from sticking; put into a hot oven (it is very essential to have oven hot before putting meat in), baste often; an hour's roasting sufficient for seven pounds of roast. Be guided by preference for rare or well-done meat. Make a gravy of drippings by adding flour and a little water. Mutton, lamb or pork roasted the same way. Irish potatoes are very good roasted, around beef or lamb, sweet potatoes around pork.

Mrs. John F. Williams.

Tomato Sauce For Meats

½ can tomatoes	3 tbsp. butter
1 small onion	2½ tbsp. flour
1½ tsp. salt	cayenne pepper
soda	1 cup cream or milk

Cook onion and tomato together 15 minutes. Strain and place on stove again and add butter, salt and pepper. Stir in soda, and add flour rubbed smooth in milk. Let come to boil and serve at once.

Mrs. Elliott Rickenbaker,
Summerville, S. C.

Breaded Veal Cutlets

Leave cutlets whole, or cut into pieces of uniform shape and size, salt and pepper, dip in beaten egg and bread crumbs, fry in plenty of hot fat and serve with tomato or cream sauce.

Mrs. Elliott Rickenbaker,
Summerville, S. C.

Lamb or Vension Sauce

3 eggs	1 cup vinegar
2 cups sugar	½ cup mustard (pre-
1 cup butter	pared as for table
1 glass currant jelly	use)

Cook in double boiler, stir until it thickens.

Mrs. J. Robert Carter.

Brains

1 set brains	2 slices lemon
1 qt. water	4 cloves
4 allspice	

Boil brains until tender and serve sliced on toast, or in ramekins with sauce made as follows:

1½ tbsp. butter	1 tbsp. celery, chopped
1 onion, chopped fine	fine
1 small can tomato	1 tbsp. parsley
pulp	1 can mushrooms
salt	cayenne

Rub stew pan with garlic, stew all ingredients except mushrooms until tender, add mushrooms, boil 15 minutes.

Mrs. Julia N. Burke.

Lamb Noisettes

1 pt. mashed potatoes	1 tbsp. butter
½ tsp. salt	3 eggs
lamb chops	cauliflower

To hot mashed potatoes, add butter, salt and the beaten yolks of eggs. Form in flat rosettes. Brown in quick oven and arrange on platter. Above each rosette place a broiled lamb chop that has been boned and rolled. Garnish with flowerettes of cauliflower. *Mrs. J. H. Miller.*

Ham Sauce

1 small glass jelly, 3 tbsp. French's mustard beaten together until jelly is melted and all well blended.

Mrs. Ralph Bulkley.

Leg of Lamb Roast

1 leg of lamb   salt, pepper, flour
dressing   sliced bacon

Remove bone from lamb, fill opening with dressing, sew up opening and rub side with salt, pepper and flour. Place in roaster with strip of bacon across roast, cook slowly 1½ hours.

Bread Dressing:

1½ cups dry grated   onion juice
   bread crumbs   celery extract
1/3 cup melted butter   ½ tsp. salt
1 tbsp. finely chopped   ½ tsp. paprika
   parsley

Mrs. William Anderson.

Braised Brains

2 sets calves brains, washed,
   parboiled and skinned
salt   ½ cup melted butter
flour   1 tsp. Worcestershire
1 tsp. lemon juice   sauce
pepper   ½ cup cream

Place brains in shallow baking dish. Sprinkle with salt, pepper and flour. Pour over the butter, lemon juice and Worcestershire sauce, broil under flame for thirty minutes. When done pour cream over it and heat thoroughly in moderate oven.   *Mrs. H. Ostrand.*

Kentucky Ham

2 lb. cut of ham   2 tbsp. dry mustard
1 pt. sweet milk

Place ham in heavy iron skillet, cover with milk to which mustard has been added. Cook over slow fire, covered. Baste frequently and stir milk. Cook one hour or longer until perfectly tender. Serve hot or cold.

Mrs. H. R. Aldredge.

Barbecue Sauce

½ lb. butter   4 tbsp. Worcestershire
2 lemons (juice)   sauce
1 cup hot water   salt and pepper

Melt butter, add other ingredients. Use to baste chicken while barbecueing, or as follows: Fry four large fryers, as usual. Place them in a roasting pan, pour sauce over them and allow to roast until very tender, basting often.

Miss Olive Shelmire.

Baked Ham

1 ham   1 doz. bay leaves
1 cup chopped celery   sherry wine
cloves

Remove skin from ham, stick thickly with whole cloves, and let soak in sweetened water over night. Next morning, add celery, bay leaves and sweetened water and boil 30 minutes. Remove from water, cover with sugar, pour sherry wine over ham, put in oven in covered pan and baste frequently until ham is done and top is golden brown. Let cool in juices.   *Mrs. Mike T. Lively.*

Spaghetti

About 7 young veal round steaks

5 cans of tomatoes	4 green peppers
2 cans tomato soup	a bunch of parsley
2 cans tomato pulp	4 to 5 pods of garlic
1½ lbs. salt pork	1 doz. bay leaves
5 onions	2 cans of mushrooms

TO PREPARE: Cut steaks into pieces about the size of palm of hand and sprinkle with salt and paprika, then grind green peppers, parsley, onions, garlic, etc. in meat grinder and spread on the meat. Roll these and tie with string. Cut salt pork into small pieces and render fat from it. Remove the hard pieces of the meat of salt pork and fry the meat balls in the hot grease (fry in iron pot, more satisfactory), then into this mixture put whatever is left of the chopped onions, garlic, peppers, etc., then pour in the tomato soup and tomato pulp, and cans of tomatoes. Cook about an hour and a half to two hours over a slow fire with bay leaves, 2 tablespoonfuls of sugar, salt, pepper, paprika, cloves, allspice to taste, and mushrooms. When finished remove meat balls from juice and remove strings, placing in a separate pan with a little of the juice over to keep from drying out. Just before serving heat two to three cans of small peas, pour some of the juice over them and serve them garnished, with meat balls.

About half an hour before ready to serve, place 4 pounds of spaghetti (without holes), small size, into a pan of boiling water and drain off in colander and wash once with cold water before serving. Serve on hot plates, pouring the juice over each portion at serving. Grate 1 to 1½ lbs. of Italian cheese to be served on dish if desired.

This dish should be served with rye bread, dill pickles, Budweiser or coffee, and if another course is needed, suggest grapefruit salad with plain French dressing.

Mrs. Eugene Duggan.

Veal Loaf

2 lbs. veal	2 cups bread crumbs
1 lb. ham	3 eggs well beaten
ground cloves	salt to taste
onion juice	

Mix, shape into loaf, put into baking pan with water and bake 2 hours. *Mrs. Julian Smith.*

Meat Sauce

2 cans tomatoes	½ cup vinegar
1 large green pepper	½ cup sugar
1 large onion	1 tsp. allspice
1 tsp. salt	

Let cook down.

Mrs. Owen Carter.

Tamale Loaf

1 lb. chopped meat	1 onion
3 crackers rolled	6 olives, chopped red
1½ cups rice	pepper, salt

Boil rice, fill buttered pan with rice, pour in other ingredients, which have been mixed. Cover with rice and steam one hour. Turn on platter and serve with tomato gravy.
Mrs. J. T. Elliott, Jr.

Tomato Gravy

1 can tomatoes, strained	1 tbsp. butter
1 small onion, chopped fine	1 tsp. flour
	salt
red pepper	

Mix flour with little water, and mix all together. Cook until thickened. *Mrs. J. T. Elliott, Jr.*

Vegetables

Baked Onions

12 onions	1 tbsp. butter
1 tsp. salt	1/8 tsp. paprika
2 tsp. honey or brown	parsley
sugar	toast chips

Peel onions, cut in halves cross-wise and place in buttered casserole or baking dish. Add seasoning (no water) and bake 1½ hours in moderate oven at 400° F. Serve with strips of hot buttered toast to absorb any gravy and garnish with parsley dipped in lemon juice. Serves four.

Mrs. Karl Hoblitzelle.

Spinach Timbales

1 cup cooked spinach	2/3 tsp. pepper
1 cup milk	2 tbsp. melted butter
1 tsp. onion juice	2 tsp. vinegar
2 eggs, or 2 yolks and 1 egg	

Beat eggs, add milk and other ingredients. 2 lbs. spinach to make enough. Place in pan of water and bake until firm.

Mrs. Helen Ardrey.

Cabbage au Gratin

½ large cooked cabbage	1 pt. white sauce
¾ cup grated cheese	salt
paprika	½ cup toasted crumbs
3 tbsp. melted butter	½ tsp. soda

Drop cabbage in boiling water, add salt and soda. Cook hard until tender only. Put a layer of cabbage, coarse chopped, into a buttered baking dish, sprinkle with grated cheese, paprika and salt as needed, and cover with a layer of rich white sauce. Repeat the layers until all the ingredients have been used, having the last layer of sauce. Cover with toasted crumbs mixed with the butter. Let stay in the oven only long enough to make very hot and brown the crumbs.

Mrs. Karl Hoblitzelle.

Potatoes With Savory Sauce

12 small potatoes	juice of ½ lemon
1 tsp. chopped parsley	1 tsp. salt
2 tbsp. grated cheese	1 tbsp. chopped red or
¼ tsp. pepper	green sweet pepper
4 tbsp. butter	

1 tsp. chopped onions or chives

Wash potatoes and boil in their jackets. Remove skins. Melt the butter, add parsley, chives, pepper, lemon juice. Season with salt and pepper, add cheese last. Stir until cheese is melted. Pour sauce over the potatoes.

Mrs. Karl Hoblitzelle.

Egg Plant

egg plant	butter
salt	cream

Peel and then cut into small squares, soak in cold water for some time. Have water boiling and cook until tender, about 25 minutes. Add salt just before taking off. Drain in colander and put back in pan. Add butter and a small amount of cream and serve.

Mrs. Seth Miller.

Baked Egg Plant

2 large egg plants
juice of 1 lemon
pepper
butter

3 lb. can tomatoes
salt
chopped parsley
celery

Peel and slice egg plant in thin slices, salt each piece and put them under a heavy weight for 2 hours. Make a sauce of the tomatoes, lemon juice, salt, pepper, chopped parsley and boil for 15 minutes and strain. Place the slices of egg plant in a pan and pour the sauce over them. Put a small lump of butter and cut up celery on each slice. Bake in oven for 30 minutes.

Mrs. T. H. Obenchain.

Carrot Pudding

2 cups raw carrots (grated)
3 eggs (beaten separately)
1 cup sweet milk

1 tsp. salt
1 tbsp. sugar
1 tbsp. butter

whipped cream

Beat egg yolks in bowl. Add grated carrots, milk, salt, sugar and butter and place in baking dish, mixing in the stiffly beaten whites and bake for 20 or 25 minutes in a moderate oven.   *Mrs. O. T. Poyntz.*

Celery au Gratin

Cut celery in small pieces. Stew until tender. Make rich cream sauce to which add grated cheese. Butter baking dish, put layer of celery and layer of cheese sauce, until dish is filled. Put little butter on top and run into oven until brown.

Mrs. Peter O'Donnell.

Egg Plant

1 egg plant	1 slice bacon
1 egg	onion to taste
salt and pepper	

Cook egg plant until tender. Beat egg and add to egg plant. Fry bacon and onion together then add to egg plant. Salt and pepper to taste. Put in casserole, add bread crumbs to top, cook in oven till bread crumbs are browned.

Mrs. S. I. Munger, Jr.

Stuffed Egg Plant a la Creole

1 egg plant	2 slices toast
½ onion	parsley
½ lb. shrimp	1 egg
garlic	celery
green pepper	

Boil egg plant and scoop out inside. Soak toast. Add to egg plant, also onion, parsley, green pepper, celery, garlic, shrimp finely chopped. Fry all together. Add one egg. Stuff egg plant shells and sprinkle with toasted cracker and bread crumbs.

Mrs. Franklin Pugh.

Okra Patties

2 cups cooked okra, liquid included	little pepper
little salt	corn meal
	1 egg

Cut cooked okra in small pieces, add egg well beaten, a little salt, pepper and enough corn meal to make a drop batter. Drop by spoonfuls in well greased skillet and brown on both sides.

Mrs. Huey Hughes.

Braised Celery

8 stalks celery	1 tsp. salt
1 qt. soup stock	1 tsp. sugar
1 tbsp. butter	2 tbsp. marrow

1 tbsp. sherry

Cook 8 stalks celery in 1 qt. of soup stock until tender (about 30 minutes). Drain on platter and dredge with flour. Put a tbsp. of butter, 1 tsp. of salt, 1 tsp. sugar in skillet, saute celery until brown (not too dark) on both sides. Have ready about 2 tbsp. of marrow which has been chopped fine and browned in oven. Sprinkle over celery, pour remaining stock over celery and let simmer very slowly for about 15 minutes. Just before serving, add one tbsp. of sherry. *Mrs. Carl Langenberg,*
St. Louis, Mo.

Stuffed Artichokes (6)

Boil 8 artichokes. Scoop out chokes and center leaves of 6. Scrape leaves and cut hearts of extra 2. Cream brains or sweet breads and add artichoke meat. Add 1 can of cut mushrooms, little chopped celery, small piece pimento and salt to taste. Dash Worcestershire sauce, add little sherry or sherry jell, before stuffing artichokes. Dash paprika on top of each. *Mrs. Franklin Pugh.*

Fried Parsley

8 or 10 sprigs parsley	1 tbsp. lard

Pick off the delicate leaves and branches of very young parsley, wash well, drain. Have lard rather hot, fry parsley slowly, drain and use as a garnish.

Stuffed Squash

6 small white squash (individual size)	½ tsp. salt
1 cup milk	1 hard boiled egg
5 tbsp. melted butter	½ cup blanched almonds
1½ heaping tbsp. flour	

Scoop out center of squash and cook until thoroughly done. Drain well in colander. Make thick cream sauce of milk, flour, butter, pepper and salt. Take off stove and add finely chopped, hard boiled egg and almonds which have been run through meat chopper. To this, add squash. Boil hulls until tender with little salt in water. Stuff with above mixture and sprinkle with toasted bread crumbs and butter. Run in oven to brown. *Mrs. Robert S. Yancey.*

Okra and Tomatoes

1 lb. okra	1 can tomatoes
1 onion cut fine	1 big tbsp. butter
salt	cayenne

Fry onion in butter until brown. Then add sliced okra, fry together for about five minutes, add tomatoes, season with salt and cayenne and let simmer slowly until okra is quite tender and all is thick. Green pepper may be added to the recipe and a clove of garlic may be used.

Mrs. Chas. Dexter, Jr.

Fried Celery

1 cup flour	½ cup milk
2 eggs	salt
½ tsp. baking powder	pepper

Make batter of above ingredients, beat well. Cut celery in three-inch pieces, dip in batter and fry in lard. Serve around fried chicken or roasted meats.

Sweet Potato Balls

Six sweet potatoes boiled dry, ½ cup of sugar, one table-spoon of butter, salt to taste, cinnamon to taste, cream well, add a few chopped pecans, form into medium size balls, placing a small marshmallow in center of each. Put on ice, chill thoroughly, roll very lightly in flour, dip in beaten eggs, then in finely rolled cracker crumbs. Fry in deep fat and serve *immediately*.

Mrs. Collett Munger.

Baked Potatoes

Core potato from end to end. Put into the hole a well fried Jones sausage. Bake.

Spinach Souffle

1 lb. spinach	3 eggs (beaten separately)
1 onion	
3 tbsp. butter	¼ tsp. salt
3 tbsp. flour	¼ tsp. pepper
½ cup Parmesian cheese	nutmeg
1 cup thin cream or full milk	crumbs

Prepare spinach in usual way, adding onion to water while cooking. Remove onion and drain spinach very dry. Put through a puree strainer; there should be 1 cup. Melt butter, add flour, salt, pepper and nutmeg (if desired). Add gradually cream or milk, spinach pulp and yolks of 3 eggs beaten until thick and lemon tinted, fold in freshly grated cheese and stiffly beaten whites. Turn into a buttered baking dish, sprinkle with buttered, seasoned crumbs. Set in pan of hot water and bake 25 minutes. Serve with Hollandaise or mushroom sauce.

The Commission Shop of Minneapolis.

Spinach Mousse

1 cup spinach (cooked and cut fine)
4 eggs (beaten together)   1 tbsp. butter
1 cup whipping cream (fold in)
1 tsp. sugar   salt and pepper

Steam in ring mould for one hour and serve with mushroom sauce.

The Commission Shop of Minneapolis.

Asparagus Loaf

3 bunches fresh asparagus   2 tbsp. butter
4 or 5 eggs beaten separately   2 tbsp. flour
2 cups milk   salt and pepper

Cut asparagus (all but few stalks) in small pieces and cook 25 or 30 minutes or until soft. Drain, mix cut asparagus, 2 cups white sauce (made with milk, butter and flour). Fold in beaten whites. Bake in angel food cake tin. Set in hot water in moderate oven for about 30 minutes. When done, turn out on platter and serve, garnished with whole asparagus. Pour melted butter over all.

The Commission Shop of Minneapolis.

Simple Hollandaise Sauce

1 tbsp. flour   1 glass boiling water
2 tbsp. butter   1 lemon (juice)
2 eggs (yolks only)   salt and cayenne

Blend flour and butter well together, add glass of boiling water, cook in double boiler. When thick, add juice of 1 lemon, remove from fire and pour over well-beaten egg yolks. Season with salt and cayenne.

Mrs. J. B. Adoue, Jr.

Spinach Ring

3 lbs. spinach	2 eggs well beaten
2 tbsp. butter	2 hard boiled eggs
salt and pepper to taste	

Boil spinach until tender, drain well, season with salt and pepper. Add butter and two well beaten eggs. Pack in ring mould, steam 45 minutes. Turn on platter, garnish with the grated hard boiled eggs. Fill center of ring with broiled fresh mushrooms or mushroom sauce or diced buttered beets.   *Mrs. J. B. Adoue, Jr.*

Hot Slaw

3 cups cabbage shredded	1 tbsp. vinegar
1 green pepper cut in strips	salt to taste
1 cup celery cut small	½ pt. sour cream
onion to taste	2 hard boiled eggs
cayenne pepper	

Mix cabbage, celery, pepper and onion and sprinkle with salt to taste and a little sugar. When ready to serve, pour over a dressing made as follows: Pour hot vinegar in sour cream heated very hot and pour into well mashed hard boiled eggs. Add cayenne pepper.

Mrs. W. E. Crowe.

Caramel Sweet Potatoes

4 large potatoes	½ cup butter
1½ cups sugar	1 tsp. vanilla
salt to taste	

Peel and quarter potatoes, boil in clear water until tender. Pour off water, leaving just enough to cover potatoes. Pour in other ingredients and cook down until syrup is very thick.

Mrs. D. G. Dunlap.

Asparagus Pudding

4 eggs	2 bunches asparagus
1 tsp. butter	(tender tops only
3 tbsp. flour	or 1 can of aspara-
1 scant cup milk	gus)

Beat eggs well, add butter and salt to taste, then flour and milk and asparagus last (if fresh asparagus is used, boil it tender first). Put in well greased mould with a top. Cook in pot of boiling water two hours. Turn out, pour over it a cup of drawn butter. Garnish with a tomato cut in petals from center and curled over.

Mrs. Huey Hughes.

Squash Souffle

2 lbs. squash (cooked and rubbed through colander)	
2 egg yolks	½ tsp. onion juice
1 tbsp. flour	½ tsp. Worcestershire sauce
salt and pepper to taste	

Mix these together. Two egg whites beaten stiff. Fold into whites the squash mixture. Bake in moderate oven 30 to 40 minutes. Serve with rich cream, mushroom dressing.

Mrs. Jno. W. Wright.

Sweet Potato With Sherry

6 large potatoes	butter
cream	pepper
sherry	salt

Bake potatoes, cut lengthwise in halves, remove inside and mash, adding seasoning, butter and cream to suit and a few tablespoons sherry. Stuff and bake.

Mrs. J. L. Gilbert.

Sweet Potatoes With Pineapple

6 medium size potatoes   large lumps of butter
1 small can sliced pineapple   about 1 doz. marshmallows
                    salt to taste

Parboil sweet potatoes until done, drain, mash, season with salt, butter, add pineapple juice, (a little sugar if needed) cream well, then add pineapple, sliced very finely. Put in baking dish, cover with marshmallows, bake slowly, until steaming hot, and browned on top. *Mrs. T. L. Lauve.*

Stuffed Tomatoes

8 large ripe tomatoes   1 cup thick cream sauce
1 tbsp. butter   1 onion (chopped)
1 cup boiled ham   1 small can mushrooms
  (ground)   1 cup bread crumbs
            1 cup grated cheese

Cut off stem of tomatoes, scoop out pulp. Mash fine, add onion and mushrooms. Cut fine and fry together in butter, add ham, then bread crumbs. Remove from fire, add cream sauce. Season well. Refill tomatoes, sprinkle cheese over top. Set in pan with a little hot water and bake in moderate oven. Baste with butter melted in little hot water.
Mrs. A. B. Webster.

Potatoes au Gratin

1 pt. cold diced potatoes   2 level tbsp. flour
2 level tbsp. butter   1 cup milk
½ tsp. salt   pepper
        ¾ cup yellow cheese, grated

Make a sauce of all ingredients except potatoes, cooking in double boiler until cheese is dissolved. Put alternate layers of potatoes and sauce in baking dish until all are used. Cover top with buttered bread crumbs and brown in quick oven. *Mrs. G. L. Crofford.*

Pea Roast

¾ cup bread crumbs	1 tbsp. sugar
½ cup canned pea pulp	¼ tbsp. English wal-
1 egg	nuts (chopped)
¼ cup butter	¾ tsp. salt
¾ cup milk	⅛ tsp. pepper

Use sifted bread crumbs. Mix all ingredients, put in small bread pan lined with paraffin paper. Let stand 15 minutes. Cover and bake in slow oven 40 minutes. Remove hot serving dish and garnish with carrot timbales.

Mrs. Hugh Prather.

Stuffed Cabbage

1 small cabbage	2 eggs
2 tbsp. butter	8 crackers, rolled
	black pepper

Remove four or five nice outside leaves, placing to one side. Cut rest of cabbage fine as for slaw. Boil in salted water until tender, drain, add butter, salt, pepper, cracker crumbs. If dry, add little milk. Arrange outside leaves on thin cloth, mould mixture with hands and place in leaves. Tie cloth around and boil 20 to 30 minutes in salted water. Carefully lift on dish, pull back outside leaves and serve with drawn butter.

Mrs. John Phelan.

Baked Stuffed Potatoes

6 good sized potatoes	½ cup cream
2 tbsp. butter	½ small onion grated
6 pieces celery (grated)	½ cup grated yellow
	cheese

Bake potatoes until soft, scoop out, add other ingredients, re-fill shells and bake 15 minutes in moderate oven.

Mrs. Will Lawther.

French Fried Onions

Peel onions, cut in ¼-inch slices. Separate into rings. Dip in milk, drain, dip in flour and fry in deep hot fat, drain on brown paper and sprinkle with salt. Serve around broiled steak.

Sweet Potato Croquettes

4 large sweet potatoes	½ cup sweet milk
2 tbsp. butter	cracker meal

Boil potatoes until done, peel and cream while hot; add butter and milk. Mould in desired shape. Roll in cracker meal and put on ice to get firm. Fry in hot lard and serve at once.   *Mrs. C. W. Lamberth.*

Egg Plant Fritters

1 large egg plant	1 tsp. salt
1 large kitchen spoon flour	1 tsp. white pepper
½ cup milk	3 eggs (well beaten)

Boil egg plant whole until very soft. Remove pulp, take off skin, mash pulp fine and allow to get cold. Mix flour and eggs, then milk and salt and pepper, lastly egg plant. Drop batter like fritters into deep smoking hot fat and brown.   *Mrs. John Phelan.*

Sweet Potato Pone

3 or 4 medium sweet potatoes (grated)	2 cups sweet milk
2 eggs	½ cup molasses
½ cup sugar	lump butter
	spices to taste

Bake very slowly in deep greased pan one and one-half hours.   *Mrs. John Phelan.*

Breads and Muffins

Beauregard Biscuit

3 eggs	1 cup water
1 cup sweet milk	1 cup sugar
1 tbsp. lard	1 tsp. salt

1 yeast cake

Put milk and sugar on the fire until they come to a boil, set aside to cool. Put yeast cake in a cup of water until dissolved; when dissolved, add to milk and sugar, then stir in the well beaten eggs, salt, lard, and enough flour to make a stiff batter; let rise over night. Next morning work in enough flour to roll, cut with small cutter and set aside until light. *Mrs. B. H. Gardner.*

Scotch Short Bread

¾ lb. flour	½ lb. butter
¼ lb. rice flour	¼ lb. sugar

Cream butter and sugar until very smooth, work in flour and rice flour. Roll one-half inch thick. Cook in slow oven until light brown through and through.

Mrs. Lewis Smith.

Cheese Straws

2 cups of grated cheese	1 tsp. ground mustard
2 cups sifted flour	1 tsp. baking powder
cayenne pepper	2 tsp. butter

salt

Sift all dry ingredients together, then add cheese, butter and enough ice water to thin. *Mrs. J. L. Dreibelbis.*

Corn Bread

1 cup cornmeal   1 tsp. salt
1 cup boiling water   1 tbsp. sugar
            shortening

Mix this 12 or 15 hours before using. Stir in: 1 tbsp. flour, mixed with 1 tsp. baking powder. Add 3 eggs beaten separately. Serve in baking dish in which it was baked.

Mrs. Warren Jones.

Cincinnati Coffee Bread

1/3 cup sugar   1/3 cup butter
½ tsp. salt   1 cup milk, scalded
1 yeast cake   ¼ cup water
2 eggs   flour

Put sugar, butter and salt in a bowl and pour over it the scalded milk. When lukewarm, add yeast which has been dissolved in ¼ cup lukewarm water. Add eggs which have been slightly beaten and enough flour to make a stiff batter. Cover and let rise until it has doubled its bulk. Cut down, beat thoroughly and spread evenly in two buttered round layer cake tins. Sprinkle with nut mixture, let rise and bake in a hot oven 40 minutes.

Mrs. Hugh Prather.

Nut Mixture

Mix two tablespoons of sugar and ¾ teaspoon cinnamon and add ¾ cup soft stale bread crumbs, two tablespoons melted butter and 3 tablespoons chopped blanched almonds.

Mrs. Hugh Prather.

Light Bread

1 cup mashed potatoes	3 cups potato water
¼ yeast cake	1 cup water
½ cup sugar	flour

1 large spoon lard

Dissolve yeast in water. Mix with mashed potatoes, potato water, sugar and enough flour to make a stiff batter. Set aside to rise over night. In the morning add lard, work out and let rise. When double its size, work into loaves, let rise to top of pan and bake one hour in moderate oven. Will make four loaves. *Mrs. C. W. Lamberth.*

Drop Biscuits

1½ cups Swansdown cake flour	2 rounded tsp. baking powder
1 rounded tbsp. Crisco	½ tsp. salt
	1 cup sweet milk

Mix baking powder and salt in flour and shortening. Add milk. Drop with spoon on well greased pan and bake.

Mrs. Warren Jones.

Salad Rolls

2 cups milk (lukewarm)	1 cake yeast
1 tsp. salt	3 tbsp. sugar
2 tbsp. butter (melted)	5 cups flour

Pour milk in mixing bowl, dissolve yeast in milk. Add salt, sugar, butter and flour. Mix smoothly, put in warm place and allow to rise double the quantity. Then knead and allow to rise 30 minutes. Then roll out, cut and fold into rolls about ½ inch thick. Place on buttered pan 1 inch apart, brush with melted butter and let rise for one hour. Bake 12 to 15 minutes. When baked, brush with melted butter. *Mrs. Warren Johns.*

Orange Bread

1 cup sugar	1 tsp. baking powder
1 egg, thoroughly beaten	1 cup sweet milk
3 cups flour, well sifted	1 cup chopped,
1 cup nut meats	candied orange peel

Mrs. Manning Shannon.

Salt-Rising Bread

1 cup milk scalded and thickened with meal at noon. Two pints milk, two pints boiling water, flour to make stiff batter, add scalded meal and let rise until morning. Two pints milk, two pints warm water, one tablespoon sugar, one teaspoon salt, a little lard, add sponge, let rise and make into loaves. When light, bake one hour.

May Burgoyne.

Cinnamon Rolls

1 pt. milk	1 cup sugar
1 large kitchen spoon shortening	1 tsp. salt (scant)
	flour (about 2 qts.)
1 cup water	enough flour to make
2 eggs	moderately stiff batter

1 yeast cake,
dissolved in warm water

Scald milk with shortening. Cool, add water. Beat eggs with sugar until very light and add above mixture. Add salt, flour and dissolved yeast cake. Let rise until twice its size. Roll out, cover with butter, sugar and cinnamon. Roll as for jelly roll, cut, place in pans, and again put melted butter, sugar and cinnamon on top. Allow to rise twice its size again and bake in warm oven.

Mrs. Manning Shannon.

Nut Biscuits

2 cups flour
2 tbsp. butter
1 tsp. salt

1 cup chopped pecans
4 tsp. baking powder
milk

Mix as usual, using enough sweet milk to make a sticky dough. Drop from spoon on pan and bake in hot oven.

Mrs. R. C. Munger, Birmingham.

Nut Bread

2 cups graham flour
4 tsp. baking powder
1 egg
1 cup nut meats

2 cups white flour
2 cups sweet milk
1 cup sugar
1 tsp. salt

Do not sift graham flour. Mix all ingredients well, let stand twenty minutes, then cook in slow oven forty-five minutes.

Mrs. Chas. L. Bolanz.

Brown Bread

1 cup buttermilk
1 cup molasses
2 cups graham flour

1 tsp. soda
1 cup corn starch
1 cup nuts or raisins

Steam in cans 2/3 full for two hours and bake twenty minutes.

Mary Manion Smith.

Sally Lunn

3 eggs
1 cup sweet milk
1 tsp. salt

2 tsp. baking powder
½ cup sugar
½ cup butter

4 cups flour

Beat eggs well, beat sugar and butter together, add milk, salt, and baking powder and flour.

Mrs. Arthur Boice.

Brown Bread

2 cups white flour
1 egg
1 cup raisins
2 tsp. baking powder

2 cups graham flour
1 cup sugar
1 cup nuts
1 tsp. salt

Mix all ingredients well. Fill baking powder cans about 2/3 full and bake in slow oven about one hour.

Mrs. Geo. W. Truett.

Virginia Corn Bread

2 cups scalded meal
pinch of salt
soda

1 egg
2 tbsp. grease

Scald meal, add salt and soda and enough buttermilk to make a soft batter, and egg well beaten. Put grease in skillet and heat and pour in corn bread. Cook a few minutes on top of stove, then in oven till brown.

Mrs. Milton Ragsdale.

Potato Rolls—Plain

1 cup flour
1 cup milk
1 cup potatoes
1 tsp. salt
2 cups lukewarm water

¾ cup lard
½ cup sugar (scant)
2 eggs
1 yeast cake

Mix thoroughly the lard, potatoes (which have been put through a potato ricer), sugar, salt, and the eggs which have been well beaten. Then add the milk and yeast which has been dissolved in the lukewarm water. Set aside to rise for two hours. Make into a soft dough by adding about a quart of flour and set to rise again. Make into rolls or loaf, butter the top and set to rise. Bake in a quick oven.

Mrs. W. C. Martin.

Kentucky Spoon Bread

2 cups corn meal	2 tsp. salt
2 eggs	1½ cups buttermilk
1 tsp. soda	1½ tbsp. butter or
1 tbsp. sugar	shortening

Scald corn meal with enough hot water to make consistency of mush. Add sugar, salt and butter and let cool. Then beat in eggs, whipped light, dissolve soda in buttermilk, beat into the mixture and bake in rather deep pan in quick oven, 30 to 40 minutes.

May Burgoyne.

Sweet Potato Biscuits

Take a pint of boiled and mashed sweet potatoes, one tablespoon of butter, 1 pint of sour milk, 2 eggs, 1 level teaspoon soda and flour to make a very soft dough. Roll out and bake in a moderate oven.

Mrs. Raymond Lawther.

Light Bread

1 yeast cake	3 qts. flour
1 gallon warm water	3 tbsp. sugar
1 tbsp. salt	lard size of an egg

At noon put yeast cake in cup of water and let stand until evening. Take a dishpan and sift into it the flour, make a hole in the center and put in the lukewarm water (potato water is good). Add yeast, sugar, salt, and lard. Work all this, then flour until it gets pretty stiff. Then put on bread board and work until it blisters and is worked smooth. Set away in a warm place until morning and it will be ready to make out into loaves. Let stand until light and then bake for one hour. This makes 8 or 9 loaves and a pan of rolls.

May Burgoyne.

97

Orange Biscuits

When regular baking powder biscuits are ready to be cooked, take a square lump of sugar and dip it in orange juice, allowing sugar to absorb just enough juice without dissolving sugar. With the thumb make a hole in the center of each biscuit and place in it the orange soaked lump of sugar. Cook the same as ordinary biscuits.

Mrs. James B. Walker.

Sally Lunn

2 eggs

1 cup milk (scant)

½ cup butter

2 cups flour

2 tsp. baking powder

Stir all into a smooth batter, but do not beat. Bake slowly 30 minutes. *Mrs. Julian Smith.*

Beaten Biscuits

1 qt. flour

1 cup sweet milk

¾ cup lard

1 pinch salt

Mix ingredients well, roll and beat until dough pops. Cut into small biscuits and bake in moderate oven.

Mrs. Seth Miller.

Light Baking Powder and Soda Biscuits

1 qt. flour

1 tsp. salt

1 tbsp. lard (heaping)

1 tsp. baking powder

1 scant tsp. soda

1 pt. buttermilk

Mix ingredients, work five minutes, cut and bake quickly.

Mrs. W. C. Martin.

Flop Crumbles

1 lb. flour

¾ lb. butter

10 tbsp. rich cream

Mix thoroughly. Roll like biscuits, cut in rings and bake; when brown dip in melted butter, roll in sugar and cinnamon mixed. *Mrs. Arthur Boice.*

Baking Powder Biscuits

1 qt. flour	1 tbsp. lard
½ tsp. salt	2 tsp. baking powder

Mix flour, lard, salt and baking powder. Add half milk and half water to make a soft dough. Handle very little. Roll and cut out and bake in quick oven.

Mrs. W. C. Martin.

Muffins

1 cup sugar	½ cup Cottolene
3 eggs	½ cup sweet milk
1 tsp. vanilla	2 cups flour
2 tsp. baking powder	

Cream sugar and Cottolene, add eggs one at a time and beat each well before adding next. Then add milk, vanilla, and flour which has been sifted twice before measuring, and then again with the baking powder in it. Beat until light and smooth. *Mrs. Milton Ragsdale.*

Brioche Cake (Crescent Rolls)

½ cup sugar	1 tsp. salt
2/3 yeast cake	2 cups milk (scalded)
4 eggs	6 cups flour
½ cup butter (melted)	

Add sugar to scalded milk when lukewarm, add yeast which has been dissolved in a little warm water, add three cups of flour, mix well and let rise. When bubbly (1½ or 2 hours) add whole eggs well beaten, melted butter, salt, and 3 cups of flour. Let rise till light (1½ hours) and mould into horseshoe shape. Let rise ¾ to 1 hour and bake. To make into horseshoe or crescent shape, roll out ½ inch thick and cut in triangles; start rolling from the base of triangle and let the little point come on top, then pull both ends down, making a horseshoe.

Camilla Padgitt.

Pocket Book Rolls

1 yeast cake	2 cups water (warm)
2 eggs	½ cup sugar
1 cup warm milk	1 tsp. salt
1 tbsp. lard	flour

Dissolve yeast in warm water. Put in enough flour to make a medium stiff batter. Let stand till it looks bubbly. Beat eggs, dissolve sugar in warm milk. Let cool, add eggs, salt, and lard. Put all this in the batter. Work in enough flour to make smooth dough. Let rise two hours. Roll out into pocketbook rolls, let rise again and bake.

Mrs. Julian Smith.

One Egg Muffins

2 cups flour	½ cup sugar
1 tsp. salt	2 tsp. baking powder
¼ cup melted lard or butter	1 egg
	1 cup milk or water

Sift dry ingredients together three times. Stir to a smooth batter with other ingredients. Bake slowly until raised, then increase heat to brown quickly.

May Burgoyne.

Waffles

2 cups flour sifted	1 tbsp. bacon grease
lump of butter, size walnut	

Mix above ingredients well together, add pinch of salt, 1 cup sweet milk, or a little more if needed to make a good batter. Add two eggs beaten separately, heaping teaspoon baking powder added the last thing before cooking.

Mrs. Mike T. Lively.

Muffins

¼ cup sugar
2 eggs
little salt

¼ cup butter
¾ cup sweet milk
2 cups flour sifted

2 tsp. baking powder

Cream butter and sugar, add eggs well beaten, then milk, salt, flour which has been sifted, and last before baking, add baking powder.

Mrs. Mike T. Lively.

English Muffins

2½ cups flour
2 tsp. baking powder
1 tbsp. melted butter

2 eggs slightly beaten
1½ tea cups milk
salt

Beat salt into the eggs and gradually add milk, then flour in which baking powder has been sifted, and lastly, the melted butter. Bake in buttered muffin rings on buttered griddle. When brown on one side, turn and brown on other. Split and butter before serving.

Mrs. S. J. Houghton.

Nut Bread

4 cups sifted flour
8 level tsp. baking
  powder

1 level tsp. salt
1 cup chopped nuts

Beat 2 eggs and ½ cup sugar, 2 cups milk. Put in with dry ingredients and beat well. Put in greased and floured bread pan and let stand 20 minutes. Then bake 30 to 35 minutes. Makes two loaves.

Mrs. S. J. Houghton.

Cheese Muffins

2 cups flour
4 level tsp. baking
powder
1 cup grated cheese

2 tbsp. butter (not
melted)
1 tsp. salt
1 cup milk

Mix like baking powder biscuits and bake in greased muffin tins.

The Commission Shop of Minneapolis.

Waffles

1½ cups flour
1 tsp. salt
1 tbsp. melted lard
2 cups milk

2 tbsp. cornmeal
3 tsp. baking powder
1 egg

Sift flour, sugar, salt, and baking powder together, add milk and stirring, beat in yolk of egg and fold in well beaten white.

Mrs. A. G. Joyce.

Cream Fruit Rolls

2 cups pastry flour
½ tsp. salt
4 tsp. baking powder

1 tbsp. butter
¾ cup cream
dates

Sift flour, salt and baking powder, together. Rub in butter with finger tips, and mix to a soft dough with cream. Toss lightly on a floured board and roll ½ inch thick. Cut with biscuit cutter and place a half of a date on one-half of each biscuit. Brush edges with cream, fold over (as Parker House rolls) and bake in hot oven 12 or 15 minutes. Serve with salad or tea.

Mrs. H. R. Aldredge.

Date Loaf

1 lb. dates	1 lb. English walnuts
1 cup flour	4 eggs
2 tsp. baking powder	1 cup sugar

pinch of salt

Mix sugar and yolks, beat until light, pour in the dates and nuts after cutting each in halves, then add cup of flour with baking powder. Beat whites stiff and mix, add salt. Put in biscuit pan and bake like sponge cake.

Mrs. Raymond Lawther.

Batter Bread

1½ cups meal	3 eggs well beaten
1 tbsp. lard	1 tsp. soda (dissolved in
1 tbsp. salt	milk)

3 cups buttermilk

Melt lard in pan in which bread is to be baked. Cook in a moderate oven until set. Serve in baking dish bread was baked in.

Mrs. John Phelan.

Orange Nut Bread

2 cups bread flour	½ cup candied orange
2 cups graham flour	peel
4 tsp. baking powder	2 cups milk
2 tsp. salt	1 egg
½ cup sugar	½ cup pecan meat

Mix dry ingredients thoroughly and sprinkle 2 tbsp. flour over nuts and orange peel. Beat egg until light and add to milk. Then pour over dry ingredients stirring and beating the mixture smooth. Last add the floured nuts and orange peel. Pour into 2 oiled bread tins and bake 45 minutes.

Mrs. Frank Callier.

Louisiana Calar

½ cup rice	3 cups hot water
3 eggs	½ cup sugar
½ cake yeast	½ tsp. nutmeg
½ tsp. powdered sugar	½ tsp. boiling lard
	3 tbsp. flour

Put 3 cups of water in granite pot and allow to boil. Add rice and cool until soft and mushy. Remove and cool, mash well and mix in yeast cake. Let rise over night. Next morning beat eggs well and then add the sugar and flour to hold it together. Beat this batter until creamy and set to rise 15 minutes. Last add grated nutmeg and fry in deep fat. Dust with powdered sugar. This is not a doughnut, but a rice cake which used to be sold with early coffee at sunrise in the streets of New Orleans.

Mrs. A. T. Lloyd.

Potato Flour Muffins

4 eggs	2 tbsp. ice water
½ cup white potato flour	pinch salt
½ tsp. baking powder	1 tbsp. sugar

Beat whites of eggs dry. Add salt and sugar to beaten yolks and fold into whites. Sift flour and baking powder twice and thoroughly beat into egg mixture. Add ice water last. Bake in moderate oven 15 to 20 minutes.

Mrs. Jack Beall.

"Pain Perdu" or Lost Bread

stale bread	3 eggs
½ cup sugar	2 cups milk

Slice bread one inch thick. Mix eggs, sugar and milk. Dip bread in this batter and fry in hot grease. Serve hot.

Mrs. Franklin Pugh.

Cheese Puff

½ lb. New York cheese (grated)
2 whites of eggs
paprika
2 tbsp. melted butter
salt
rounds of bread

Toast rounds of bread on one side. Mix grated cheese, beaten whites of eggs, melted butter, salt and paprika. Spread on other side of bread and toast in oven.

Mrs. Jack Beall.

Spoon Bread

1 cup corn meal
2 cups buttermilk
1 tbsp. lard
1 cup boiling water
pinch salt
2 eggs
1 level tsp. soda

Scald meal with boiling water, add lard and stir until smooth, then add the soda, salt, buttermilk and well beaten eggs. Beat well and pour in a greased pan. Bake about 40 minutes.

Mrs. W. G. Sterett.

Blueberry Muffin

2 cups sifted flour
2 tsp. baking powder
½ cup sugar
1 cup milk
1 pinch salt
¼ cup butter
2 eggs
1 heaping cup blueberries

Mix berries in a little flour. Sift flour, salt and baking powder together. Cream butter and add sugar, then egg yolks beaten. Add milk, fold in whites. Bake in gem pans.

The Commission Shop of Minneapolis.

Rice Muffins

1 cup cooked rice	1 tsp. salt
1 tsp. melted butter	1 tsp. sugar
2 eggs well beaten	1 cup flour

Rub rice with a fork until well separated. Add salt, butter, sugar. Beat this mixture to a cream and add eggs, and flour, beat thoroughly. Bake quickly in hot greased muffin pans.   *Mrs. A. T. Lloyd.*

Bran and Fig Muffin

2 tbsp. shortening	¼ tsp. salt
½ tsp. soda	1 tsp. baking powder
¼ cup sugar	1 cup bran
1 egg	1 cup flour
1 cup sour milk	2 cups chopped figs.

Mrs. Frank E. Austin.

Refrigerator Rolls

1 cup cold Irish potatoes freshly cooked	
2 tsp. salt	1 cup sugar
1 yeast cake	2 tsp. (heaping)
1 scant tsp. soda	baking powder
1 cup shortening	1 qt. sweet milk,
	scalded and cooled

Add enough flour to make a batter. Let rise 1½ hours, then make into a stiff dough. Place in refrigerator and when ready to use, roll out to desired amount. Cut with biscuit cutter and place on greased baking sheet. Let rise 1½ hours and then bake. Part of the dough may be made into cinnamon rolls or orange rolls. For latter, after pocketbook rolls have been baked, place a section of orange between each roll as it is opened, cover top with icing made of powdered sugar and orange juice well beaten. Then place rolls back in oven and re-heat.   *Mrs. Allen Charlton.*

Waffles

2 2/3 cups flour
2 heaping tsp. bak-
    ing powder
1 pt. milk

2 eggs
1 tbsp. Crisco
1 tsp. salt

Sift flour, salt, baking powder. Add Crisco, then milk. Beat until smooth. Beat eggs separately. Fold in whites last.   *Mrs. Frank Cullinan.*

Pop Overs

1 cup flour
½ tsp. salt

1 cup sugar
1 cup milk

3 eggs

Sift sugar, salt and flour into bowl, break in eggs unbeaten and add milk and beat all well and hard. Put a little lard or Crisco in muffin pans. Melt before putting in batter. Makes about 10 pop overs.   *Mrs. Lang Wharton.*

Cheese Biscuits

2 cups grated cheese
1 heaping cup flour
1 lump lard size of
    small egg

pinch of salt
dash of cayenne

Mix to a thick dough using water as needed. Roll to 1/3 of an inch thick, cut into biscuits or sticks. Bake to a nice light brown.   *Effie Arnwine.*

Potato Flour Muffin

4 eggs
  pinch salt
½ cup potato flour

1 tsp. baking powder
2 tbsp. sugar
1 tbsp. ice water

Beat egg yolks, add salt and sugar and fold in the stiffly beaten whites. Sift flour and baking powder twice. Thoroughly beat in egg mixture. Add ice water last. Bake in muffin pans in a moderate oven for 20 minutes.

        Mrs. O. T. Poyntz.

Cakes and Icings

Fruit Cake

8 eggs
1 lb. flour
1 lb. raisins
1 lb. currants
1 lb. citron
2 lbs. nuts; pecans
½ lb. brown sugar
1 lb. butter

1 level tsp. baking powder
1 cup molasses
1 cup whiskey
2 tsp. cinnamon
1 tsp. cloves
1 tsp. allspice
¼ tsp. soda stirred in molasses

Before mixing the cake, take enough flour out of the pound and dredge the nuts and fruits so they will be separated.

Cream butter and sugar until light. Add the well beaten eggs, flour, molasses, spices, fruit and nuts, and last the whiskey. This makes about nine pounds. Bake your cake in a very slow oven three and one half hours.

Mrs. W. G. Sterett.

White Fruit Cake

1 lb. flour
3 lbs. citron
1 doz. eggs
1 cocoanut grated
1 dessert spoon mace
1 lemon juice

1 lb. butter
1 lb. sugar
1½ lbs. blanched almonds
1 wine glass sherry

Icing:—Pulverized sugar, 2 lemons and 4 egg whites.

Mrs. C. W. Lamberth.

Meringue Strawberry Shortcake

6 egg whites, stiffly
   beaten
1 tsp. vanilla

1 pt. cream
1 tsp. vinegar
2 cups granulated sugar

berries

Add vanilla and vinegar to stiffly beaten whites, then add the sugar. Bake in round tins, that have been greased, for forty minutes. Have oven well heated before putting this is and then turn gas as low as for angel cake. Put whole berries between and on top of layers and cover with whipped cream. Serve with sauce of crushed sweetened berries. Sliced peaches and vanilla ice cream may be substituted for strawberries and cream. Elaborate. Serve at once.

Mrs. J. B. Oldham.

Chocolate Cake

1 tbsp. butter
1 cup sugar
¾ cups milk
2 eggs well beaten

1½ cups flour
1 heaping tsp. baking
   powder
½ cup chopped nuts

2 squares chocolate (melted)
vanilla

Bake in square cake, cover with chocolate icing and decorate with pecan halves. Cut in squares.

Mrs. Harold D. Parmelee.

Fruit Cookies

2 cups sugar
1 cup butter
4 large tbsp. milk
1 tsp. cinnamon

2 eggs
1 tsp. soda
1 cup raisins chopped
½ tsp. cloves

Flour enough to roll smoothly. Drop on greased pan and bake in hot oven.

Mrs. A. G. Joyce.

Marshmallow Meringue Cake

5 egg whites	¾ cup sugar
½ tsp. cream tartar	½ cup flour

¼ tsp. almond extract

Beat egg whites very stiff, add cream tartar and beat again. Add gradually sugar and other ingredients and bake in layers twenty minutes in moderate oven.

Filling:

1 cup sugar	4 tbsp. water
2 egg whites	20 melted marshmallows

Boil sugar and water together for six minutes. Pour over beaten whites, add marshmallows and beat until very stiff.

Mrs. Wm. Anderson.

White Cake With Chocolate Filling

1 cup milk	3 cups flour (sift 3
10 whites	times)
2 cups sugar	2 heaping tsp. baking
½ lb. butter	powder

2 tsp. vanilla

Cream butter and sugar, add milk, then flour which has had baking powder sifted with it. Add well beaten whites and bake in moderate oven twenty minutes.

Filling:—Two oz. of Baker's chocolate, 2 cups sugar, 2/3 cup cream, 1 heaping teaspoon butter. Cook all until a soft ball will form in cold water, remove from fire. Set in cold water ten minutes, then add 2 teaspoons vanilla. Whip until creamy, place between layers.

Icing:—Whites of 2 eggs, 1 oz. chocolate, 1 teaspoon vanilla, 1 cup sugar, 1/3 cup water. Boil sugar and water until it forms a thick syrup. Beat whites lightly, pour syrup over them, add vanilla and melted chocolate. When right consistency, spread on top and sides of cake.

Mrs. W. J. Lawther.

Short Cake

2½ cups flour	¼ cup shortening
2 level tsp. baking powder	½ tsp. salt
	2 tsp. sugar
1¾ cups sweet milk	

Sift flour and measure, add baking powder, sugar, salt and sift three times. Put in shortening and milk. Put in three well greased pans and bake 20 minutes in moderate oven, increasing heat last five minutes.

Mrs. D. W. Sanders.

Dainty Yellow Cake

3 eggs	1/3 cup melted butter
1 cup sugar	¾ cup flour
flavoring	½ tsp. baking powder

Break eggs in mixing bowl, add sugar and place bowl in boiling water and beat for fifteen minutes. Add butter, flavoring, flour sifted with baking powder. Beat quickly and bake in layers in moderate oven twenty minutes. Can be baked in loaf also.

Mrs. Wm. Anderson.

Chocolate Roll

5 eggs, beaten separately	2 tbsp. cocoa
½ cup sugar	½ pt. cream

Beat egg yolks, sugar and cocoa until very light. Add stiffly beaten whites and bake in a long shallow pan, well greased. Turn in paper sprinkled with sugar; when cold, spread with whipped cream and roll as for jelly roll. Serve with sauce as follows: 1 cup sugar, ¼ cake chocolate, 1 cup milk, 2 tablespoons cornstarch, butter size of walnut, cook until thick. Bake slowly.

Mrs. Louise Higgins.

Irish Potato Cake

1 cup butter	1 cup boiled mashed
2 cups sugar	potatoes
½ cup grated chocolate	4 eggs
½ cup sweet milk	2 cups flour
1 tsp. cinnamon	1 tsp. cloves
1 large cup pecans	1 tsp. allspice

1 tsp. baking powder

Cream butter and sugar, add well beaten eggs, chocolate, spices, potatoes and milk. Mix well, then add flour, baking powder and pecans.

Mrs. Owen Carter.

Date Loaf

4 eggs, beaten separately	½ tsp. salt
1 package dates	1 tsp. vanilla
2 tsp. baking powder	1 cup sugar
1 lb. nuts	1 cup flour

Beat sugar and yolks well, add flour and baking powder, then beaten whites. Add seeded dates and nuts. Bake in moderate oven.

Mrs. B. H. Gardner.

Angel Food Cake

11 whites	1½ cups sugar (sifted)
1 tsp. cream tartar	1 cup flour

vanilla

Beat eggs lightly, add cream tartar and beat to stiff froth, add sugar gradually. Fold in flour sifted five times, add vanilla and bake 45 minutes in unbuttered pan.

Mrs. Virginia Bower.

Sponge or Muffin Cake

1 cup sugar
½ cup sweet milk
2 cups flour
½ cup butter

3 eggs, beaten separately
2 heaping tsp. baking powder
vanilla

Bake in loaf or muffin rings.

Mrs. Mike Lively.

Hermits

1½ cups sugar
3 eggs
1 tsp. cinnamon
1 tsp. ginger
1½ cups raisins
3 cups flour

1 cup butter
1 tsp. cloves
½ tsp. soda dissolved in warm water
1½ cups nuts
vanilla

Cream butter and sugar, add well beaten eggs and soda water, raisins, nuts, and flour. Drop from spoon on buttered pans. If too thin, add flour.

Mrs. A. G. Joyce.

Prune Cake

2 eggs, beaten separately
1 level tsp. salt
1 level tsp. cinnamon
1 cup stewed mashed prunes

1½ cups sifted flour
1 level tsp. soda
1 tbsp. melted butter
1 cup sugar
½ cup prune juice

Bake in two layers in a very slow oven.

Filling:—Cream ½ cup butter, add 2¼ cups powdered sugar, 2 tablespoons cream, 2¼ tablespoons cocoa, 1 teaspoon vanilla.

Mrs. Helen Ardrey.

Sour Cream Cake

1 egg	1½ cups flour
½ tsp. soda	1 cup sugar
½ tsp. nutmeg	½ tsp. cinnamon
½ tsp. allspice	1 tsp. baking powder
vanilla	chopped nuts

sour cream

Beat eggs in cup, fill cup with sour cream, add soda, sift flour and baking powder, sugar and spices together, mix all and add vanilla and nuts last. Bake either in layers or loaf.

Mrs. A. E. Hutchinson.

Coffee Cake

½ cup sugar	4 tbsp. melted butter
½ cup milk	1 tsp. cinnamon
1 egg well beaten	3 level tsp. baking
¼ tsp. salt	powder
1 cup flour	

Mix well flour, cinnamon, sugar, salt and baking powder, then add butter, milk, egg. Cook in hot oven.

Mrs. Owen Carter.

Preserve Cake

1 cup butter	4 eggs, beaten separately
2 cups sugar	ately
3 cups flour	1 cup buttermilk
1 tsp. cinnamon	1 tsp. soda
1 cup peaches, preserved	½ tsp. cloves
or evaporated	1 cup nuts

Mix as usual, dissolving soda in buttermilk and chopping fruit and nuts together.

Mrs. A. G. Joyce.

Jelly Roll

4 eggs, beaten separately	1 cup sugar
½ tsp. soda	1 cup flour
	1 tsp. cream tartar

Add soda mixed in flour and put cream of tartar in whites when half beaten. Bake quickly. Spread with jelly and roll while hot.

Mrs. Raymond Lawther.

Superior Soft Ginger Bread

1 cup sugar	1 cup dark molasses
1 cup butter	4 cups sifted flour
1 cup sour milk	4 eggs, beaten separately
1 heaping tbsp. ginger	2 tsp. soda dissolved in little warm water
1 lemon (grated rind only)	

Bake in slow oven.

Mrs. Wm. Doran.

Jelly Roll

2 eggs	1 cup flour
1 cup sugar	1/3 tsp. salt
2 level tsp. baking powder	1 lemon (juice and rind)
1/3 cup hot sweet milk	

Beat eggs, add sugar, milk, then flour, salt, and baking powder, sifted together three times; add lemon and bake in long greased and floured pans. Have batter quite thin in pan; bake in moderate oven. Turn out on tea towel, cut off crusts and spread with jelly and powdered sugar, and roll. Leave rolled in towel until jelly roll is set.

Mrs. A. B. Webster.

Oatmeal Cookies

½ cup butter	1 cup sugar
¼ cup lard	3 eggs (beaten separately)
2 cups uncooked oatmeal	
¼ tsp. soda (sifted in flour)	2 scant cups flour
	½ tsp. cinnamon
	1 cup chopped raisins

Mix soft, drop from spoon.

Mrs. Dero E. Seay.

Rocks

1½ cups sugar	1 tsp. salt
1 cup butter	1 tsp. cinnamon
3 eggs, well beaten	1 tsp. soda
4 tbsp. hot water	1 cup chopped raisins
1 cup chopped nuts	3 cups flour

Cream butter and sugar, add eggs, then soda dissolved in hot water, flour, spice, raisins and nuts. Drop from spoon on well floured pan. Bake in moderate oven.

Mrs. Arthur A. Everts.

Almond Cake

½ cup butter	½ lb. almonds
1 cup fine granulated sugar	1 tsp. vanilla
	½ cup whipped cream

Use thin layer angel or plain white cake. Cut in strips one inch wide and two inches long. Make a butter filling by creaming together butter and sugar until very, very light. Add all other ingredients except almonds. Spread cakes with filling and roll in almonds that have been blanched, toasted very dry and chopped fine.

Mrs. H. Ostrand.

Mock Angel Cake

1 cup sweet milk	1 cup sugar
1 cup flour	3 level tsp. baking powder
2 egg whites	pinch of salt

Put milk in pan of water and let heat to boiling point. Sift flour, sugar, baking powder and salt together four times, add boiling milk, stir until smooth and add beaten whites. Recipe better doubled.

Mrs. J. L. Dreibelbis.

Burnt Sugar Cake

¼ cup butter	1 cup water
1½ cups sugar	2 eggs (beaten separately)
3 tsp. burnt sugar	1 tsp. vanilla
2½ cups flour	2 tsp. baking powder

Beat butter to a cream, add sugar gradually, water, egg yolks; cream all well. Then add two cups flour and beat continuously for five minutes. Then add burnt sugar, vanilla and remaining one-half cup flour. Beat thoroughly again. Next, add baking powder and beaten whites.

To burn sugar:—½ cup granulated sugar in granite pan, stir constantly until it melts and throws off intense smoke. It really must burn. Have ready one-half cup boiling water, pour over sugar, and return to fire and let boil until it is thick like molasses.

Filling:—One-half cup sugar, one-half cup boiling water. Stir until sugar is dissolved, let cook quietly without stirring until it spins. Pour 1 teaspoon over frothy (not stiff) beaten whites of two eggs, beat stiff, then add remaining syrup, and 1 teaspoon vanilla and two of burnt sugar syrup.

Mrs. J. C. Duke.

Date Cookies

1 cup butter	1½ cups sugar
3 eggs	3 cups flour
1 scant tsp. soda	¾ cup luke warm water
1 tsp. allspice	1 tsp. cinnamon
1 tsp. nutmeg	1 lb. dates (cup up)

1 lb. pecans

Cream butter and sugar. Mix soda in water, proceed as usual. Drop from spoon on pan. Bake.

Mrs. A. B. Webster.

Chocolate Nut Cake

½ cup butter	4 eggs (beaten separately)
2 cups sugar	
¾ cup broken walnuts	1 cup milk
4 level tsp. baking powder	2½ cups flour
	2 squares chocolate
	½ tsp. vanilla

Frosting:—2 cups sugar, one-half cup water. Cook until threads, pour over beaten whites of two eggs. Add ¼ teaspoon cream of tartar, and 9 marshmallows.

Mrs. E. M. Reardon, Jr.

Ginger-Bread

2 eggs	1 cup molasses
½ tsp. salt	1 cup sugar
1/3 cup Crisco (melted)	3 cups flour
1 cup sour milk	1 tbsp. ginger
2 tsp. soda (dissolved)	1 tsp. cinnamon

Beat eggs light, add molasses, sugar and Crisco. Mix dry ingredients and mix alternately with milk, add dissolved soda last. Bake twenty-five minutes in shallow pan.

Mrs. J. S. Lamberth.

Doughnuts

2 eggs
1 cup sugar
1 tsp. soda

½ cup butter
¼ cup lard
flavoring

Cook in boiling lard.

Mrs. Milton Ragsdale.

Doughnuts

1 cup shortening
1½ cups sugar
4 cups flour

2 eggs
1 cup milk
2 tsp. baking powder

Mix shortening, sugar, and eggs together, add flour and baking powder, then milk. Turn on well floured board and roll one-half inch thick, cut and fry in deep fat. Sprinkle with powdered sugar.

Mrs. Arthur A. Everts.

Apple Cake

½ cup butter (or scant
    ½ cup Crisco)
2 cups flour
2 tbsp. grated choco-
    late
1 cup raisins
1 cup nuts
1 cup sugar

1½ cups apples (peel
    and put through
    coarse food chop-
    per)
2 level tsp. soda
1 tsp. cinnamon
1 tsp. allspice
1 tsp. nutmeg
1 tsp. vanilla

Cream butter and sugar, add spices and chocolate, then raisins, apples, nuts and flour, in which soda has been sifted. Flavor, bake forty minutes in moderate oven.

Icing:—One-half cup melted butter, thickened with powdered sugar. Flavor with juice one and one-half oranges. *Mrs. L. S. Sabin.*

Cookies

2 cups sugar   ½ cup butter
3 eggs   ½ cup lard
¼ cup sweet milk   2 tsp. baking powder
                flour

Cream butter, lard and sugar, add eggs and milk and baking powder; sift in enough flour to make soft dough. Roll and cut; sprinkle cinnamon and sugar on top of each cookie and put three halves of pecans on each cookie.

Mrs. J. C. Duke.

Eggless Ginger-Bread

2½ cups flour   ½ cup brown sugar
1 cup apple jelly   ½ cup butter
1 tsp. soda   1 tsp. ginger and spices
            1/3 cup buttermilk

Dissolve soda in milk, melt butter, sugar and jelly together. Bake forty minutes in slow oven.

Mrs. A. A. Green.

Westinghouse Cookies

1 lb. butter   3 eggs, beaten separately
1½ cups brown sugar   2 cups chopped nuts
1½ cups white sugar   2 tsp. cinnamon
½ lemon (juice)   1 tsp. soda
        6 cups flour (not pastry flour)

Mix as usual, creaming butter and sugar first; add flour, one cup at a time; after three cups are added, put mixture on board and knead remaining flour into it. Mould in pan lined with waxed paper. Put in ice-box over night. Slice off as needed and cook fifteen minutes in moderate oven. Add more flour if needed. Will keep in ice-box for months.

Donated: Electric Range Shop, Dallas.

Small White Cake

2 egg whites	sweet milk
1½ cups flour	1 rounded tsp. baking
1 cup sugar	powder
flavoring	creamed butter

Put eggs in cup, fill cup one-half full with creamed butter, then finish filling cup with milk. Mix flour, sugar and baking powder, add first mixture, flavoring, and beat five minutes. Bake slowly in small pan.

Mrs. Milton Ragsdale.

Fudge Icing

2 tbsp. butter	¼ cup milk
1 cup sugar	1 sq. chocolate
½ tsp. vanilla	

Melt butter, add sugar and milk. Boil ten minutes. Add chocolate and boil five minutes, stirring. Remove from stove, add vanilla and beat until ready to spread.

The Commission Shop of Minneapolis.

Lady Baltimore Filling

2 whites	2 cups sugar
½ cup boiling water	1 cup chopped seeded
1 cup chopped blanched	raisins
almonds	½ cup chopped candied
1 cup (¼ lb.) chopped	cherries
walnuts	1 tsp. vanilla

Make boiled frosting of sugar, water, and whites as usual. Before it thickens, add other ingredients and beat all together and spread on cake.

The Commission Shop of Minneapolis.

Kisses

6 egg whites
12 rounding tbsp. sugar
1 cup nuts
1 tsp. vanilla

Add sugar to stiffly beaten egg whites, slowly, then other ingredients. Drop from spoon on brown paper and cook in slow oven one and one-half hours.

Mrs. Geo. Dexter.

Angel Food Cake

1¼ glass sugar (sifted 5 times)
1 glass flour (sifted 5 times)
1 tsp. vanilla
12 egg whites
1 tsp. cream tartar

Beat eggs to stiff froth, add sugar gradually, cream tartar, vanilla, and lastly flour. Pour into dry pan, put in cold oven, then turn on gas very low for fifteen minutes; then turn gas a little higher and bake forty minutes.

Mrs. Chas. L. Dexter.

Chocolate Angel Food Cake

1½ cups sugar
1¼ cups egg whites
2/3 cup Swansdown Flour
vanilla
1/3 cup cocoa
1 level tsp. cream tartar
¼ tsp. salt

Sift flour five times, then measure 2/3 cup. Add cocoa and sift several times until well blended. Beat eggs partly, add cream tartar and salt, then beat stiff, but not dry. Add sugar slowly, then flour mixture, lastly vanilla. Bake in slow oven from forty-five minutes to one hour.

The Commission Shop of Minneapolis.

Devil Food Cake

2½ cups flour	1½ cups buttermilk
2 cups sugar	1 tsp. soda
¾ cup Crisco	1 tsp. vanilla
½ cup chopped nuts	4 tsp. cocoa.
2 eggs	½ tsp. salt.

Cream Crisco and sugar. Sweeten milk with soda and add to mixture. Then other ingredients. Bake in two layers in moderate oven. Put together with white icing.

Mrs. A. A. Green, Jr.

White Cake

1 cup butter	1 cup milk
2 cups sugar	3 level tsp. baking powder
3 cups flour	der
8 egg whites	1 tsp. vanilla

Cream butter, add sugar, cream well together. Mix baking powder with flour and add to first mixture alternately with milk. Add flavoring, and lastly well beaten whites. Bake in three layers in quick oven.

Mrs. Ed. T. Staten.

Caramel Icing

2 small cans Pet milk	4 cups sugar
or 1½ cups cream	1 cup butter

Put two cups sugar, one-half cup butter and all milk in double boiler and let get hot. Put remaining two cups sugar and one-half cup butter in skillet over fire and turn until it is caramelized and light brown. Then pour this in double boiler and stir until dissolved. Then put entire mixture over fire and cook about ten minutes, or until done. Beat and spread.

Mrs. Edgar Padgitt.

Chocolate Fudge Cake

1 cup sugar
½ cup butter
2 eggs

¾ cup flour
4 sq. chocolate
1 tsp. vanilla

1 cup nuts

Bake in shallow pans which have been well greased. Bake slowly and when cold, cut in squares. Should be about one inch thick.

Mrs. L. S. Sabin.

White Icing

2 cups sugar
1 level tsp. cream tartar

12 marshmallows
whites of 3 eggs

¾ cup water

Cook the sugar and water with a cover over it until it boils, then drop in cream of tartar and let boil to 240 degrees, or until it spins a good thread. Then slowly pour over the well beaten eggs, adding the marshmallows while the syrup is hot and beat constantly at least five or six minutes.

Mrs. Ed. T. Staten.

Date Sticks

1 cup sugar
1 cup chopped dates
¾ cup flour

1 cup chopped nuts
2 eggs (well beaten)
pinch of soda

Mix all together, put in square cake pan, greased and floured. Bake in moderate oven for twenty minutes or longer. Cut in sticks desired size and roll in powdered sugar.

Mrs. Chas. L. Dexter, Jr.

Lemon Jelly Filling

Yolks of 4 or 5 eggs   1 cup sugar
Juice of 2 lemons

Beat until well mixed; then cook in double boiler until real thick.

Mrs. Ed. T. Staten.

Pecan Macaroons

3 egg whites (unbeaten)   3 cups pecans (chopping
2 scant cups light brown   before measuring)
   sugar

Gradually mix sugar in whites and add nuts. Drop from spoon and cook in slow oven forty-five minutes.

Mrs. W. E. Crow.

Cocoanut Fillings (very moist)

¾ cup sour cream   1 medium size cocoanut
1 egg white (well   (grated)
   beaten)   sugar to taste
½ tsp. vanilla

Stir cream into beaten egg (which has been sweetened with one-half cup sugar.) Add cocoanut and vanilla.

Mrs. Warren Jones.

Oatmeal Cookies

1 egg   1 tbsp. melted butter
1 cup sugar   ¼ tsp. salt
1 tsp. vanilla

Beat all well together, add one cup rolled oats. Mix well, then drop in a well buttered pan.

Mrs. Huey Hughes.

Chocolate Cakes

2/3 cups butter	4 eggs
1½ cups sugar	1 heaping cup flour
½ cake of bitter choco- late	1 heaping tsp. baking powder
2 cups nuts	½ tsp. vanilla

Cook, cut in squares. Needs no icing.

Mrs. Owen Carter.

Strawberry Short Cake

1 qt. flour	4 large tbsp. gran.
3 oval tsp. baking powder	sugar
	4 tbsp. butter

Make a soft dough with sweet milk, divide and roll into three cakes about ½ inch thick. Bake in rather hot oven. Have ready one quart mashed strawberries, sweetened to taste. When cakes are done, butter top of each separately. Split the middle cake and stack with berries and a generous allowance of whipped cream, sweetened, between each layer and over the top. Delicious if eaten at once, and not allowed to stand.

Mrs. Barry Miller, Millermore.

Short Cake

1 cup flour	1 egg
2 tbsp. butter	1 tsp. sugar
1 rounding tsp. baking powder	1 tbsp. milk

Divide dough in two parts, roll thin, spread one lightly with butter, place other on top and bake. Split. Put fruit or berries between and on top with whip cream.

Mrs. George Dexter.

Fruit Cake

1 lb. butter	1 tbsp. cloves
3 cups sugar	1 qt. flour
10 eggs	1 cup syrup
1 glass black berry jelly	1 cup coffee
2 small cans fig preserves	2 cups wine
2 boxes dates	2 boxes raisins
1/4 lb. pineapple	1/4 lb. cherries
1/3 lb. orange peel	1/3 lb. citron
1 lb. pecans	1/3 lb. lemon peel
1/2 lb. brazil nuts	1/2 lb. walnuts
	1 tbsp. allspice
	1 tbsp. cinnamon

Mix as usual, line pans with greased paper, bake slowly.

Mrs. Owen Carter.

Cream Almond Filling

1 1/2 cups sweet milk	1 tbsp. flour
1 cup sugar	1 tbsp. Knox gelatine
8 egg yolks	1 cup blanched almonds
	1 tsp. vanilla

Dissolve gelatine in one-half cup milk. Put one cup milk in double boiler. Beat eggs until quite light, then add sugar and flour, and when milk reaches boiling point, add, stirring constantly until mixture is quite thick. Remove from fire, add dissolved gelatine at once and beat until very smooth and partially cool. Add vanilla and chopped almonds. Pour custard into a pan the same size of the pans in which the cake was baked and put into refrigerator until quite firm and cold. Slip from pan without breaking and place between two layers of angel-food cake.

Mrs. Thomas W. Vardell.

Angel Food Cake

12 whites of eggs	1 cup cake flour
½ tsp. cream tartar	1¼ cups sugar
¼ tsp. salt	1 tsp. vanilla

Add cream of tartar and salt to whites. Beat until very stiff. Fold in flour and sugar which have been sifted together five times. Add vanilla. Put in ungreased pan in hot oven. Let stay two minutes then turn oven very low. Place pan of water on top rack and let cake cook thirty minutes. When brown around edges, remove water and let top brown. Remove and invert until cold. Doors of oven may be opened as often as wanted.

(*Donated*) *Electric Range Shop, Dallas.*

Swedish Wafers With Nuts

Mix cinnamon and sugar to taste, sprinkle on wafers, chop pecans very fine and put on top of above mixture. Toast in oven.

Mrs. Lang Wharton.

Coffee Cake

1 heaping tbsp. butter	¼ cup milk
½ cup sugar	1 heaping cup flour
1 egg	1 tsp. baking powder
pinch of salt	

Cream butter, sugar and egg, add milk and flour. Mix well. Put in buttered pan. Mix two tablespoons melted butter, ¾ cup flour; stir; add ½ cup sugar and 2 tablespoons ground chocolate, and one teaspoon cinnamon. Put on top of cake and bake in a medium hot oven.

Mrs. Philip Prather.

Meringue Cake

6 egg whites	½ tsp. cream tartar
2 cups sugar	1 tsp. vanilla

Beat eggs and sugar until smooth and stiff, add cream of tartar, beat fifteen minutes. Pour into buttered and floured cake tins and bake one hour in slow oven. To be served with strawberries, peaches, or fruit ice cream.

Mrs. Owen Carter.

Black Fruit Cake

10 eggs	2 lbs. currants
¾ lb. butter	1 lb. citron
1 lb. flour	¼ lb. almonds
2 lbs. raisins	¼ lb. pecans
1 tsp. cinnamon	1 tsp. mace
1 tsp. allspice	4 tsp. nutmeg
1 tsp. cloves	1 tbsp. lemon juice
1 wine glass brandy	1 wine glass sherry
(or good whisky)	1 tsp. yeast powder

1 tbsp. rose extract

Mrs. Julia L. Bedell.

Drop Cake

1 cup sugar	3 eggs (beaten separately)
½ cup butter	
2 cups flour	1 tbsp. soda (dissolved in 4 tbsp. boiling water)
1 tbsp. cinnamon	
1 package dates	

1 cup nuts

Cream butter and sugar, add well beaten yolks, then add nuts and dates which have been chopped. Add flour and water, with soda dissolved in it. Lastly add stiffly beaten whites. Cook in slow oven. *Rhoda Young.*

Icing

1 cup sugar   4 tbsp. boiling water
                1 egg white (unbeaten)

Put all in a double boiler, over boiling water and whip constantly with a dover egg-beater for ten minutes. Remove from fire and flavor, and put on cake when icing is quite thick. Add melted chocolate to taste, if chocolate icing is wanted.   *Mrs. Chas. Dexter, Jr.*

Chocolate Sponge Cake

4 eggs separated   1 tsp. baking powder
2½ cakes Baker's   1 cup milk
    chocolate   vanilla
1 cup flour

Put milk on stove with chocolate, stir until thick, take off, cool. Beat yolks and sugar well, then add chocolate and flour, lastly, the beaten whites.

Edna Ball.

Chocolate Cookies

1 small cup flour   1 egg (unbeaten)
2 tbsp. butter   4 tbsp. hot milk
4 tbsp. sugar   1 cup chopped walnuts
4 tbsp. sweet chocolate   1 tsp. vanilla
    powder   pinch of salt
            1 level tsp. baking powder

Sift flour, baking powder and salt together three times. Cream butter, add sugar, chocolate powder, egg and milk, vanilla, walnuts, and lastly flour mixture. Drop from spoon on buttered baking pans, bake in moderate oven about ten minutes.

Mrs. Philip Prather.

Brownies

1 cup sugar	2 eggs (beaten to-gether)
1/3 cup melted butter	
½ cup flour (sifted)	2 sq. melted chocolate

½ cup chopped nuts

Sprinkle a few nuts on top of cakes and bake in slow oven in shallow pan about twenty minutes. Cut in squares while warm.

Mrs. T. L. Lauve.

Orange Cake Without Butter

1 cup sugar	1 orange (juice and grated rind)
1 cup flour	

6 eggs (beaten separately)

Sift sugar and flour before measuring. Beat the yolks until very, very creamy; add sugar, beat until sugar is dissolved; add orange juice and rind and beat about five minutes. Whip whites to a stiff froth and add to yolk mixture and then add flour, being careful to combine well with as few strokes as possible. Bake in ungreased angel food cake pan for about 1 hour. Can also be baked in layers and put together with orange filling and then iced with orange icing.

Mrs. H. C. Bramley.

Orange Filling

½ cup sugar	½ tbsp. lemon juice
2½ tbsp. flour	grated rind of ½ orange
1 egg	
¼ cup orange juice	1 tsp. butter

Beat egg, mix all and cook in double boiler about ten minutes. Cool and spread.

Mrs. H. C. Bramley.

Orange Icing

1½ cups sugar   3 egg yolks
½ cup orange juice

Cook sugar and orange juice together until it first threads. Have egg yolks beaten and add to them 3 tablespoons of syrup. Beat. Return syrup to fire and cook until it ropes well. Pour over yolks (having beaten them almost continuously) and beat until very creamy and stiff. Requires much beating.   *Mrs. Chas. Dexter, Jr.*

Cocoanut Drops

1 can Eagle brand con-   2 cans dried cocoanut
   densed milk   (Dromedary)
2 cups nuts   1/3 cake Baker's choco-
                                  late

Melt chocolate in milk and set aside to cool (do not let get cold). Add cocoanut and nuts, drop on oiled paper and bake in slow oven twenty minutes.

Mrs. Angus Wynne.

Chocolate Fudge Cake

½ cup butter   1/8 tsp. salt
½ cup sugar   1¾ cups flour
4 eggs   1 tsp. vanilla
¾ cup nuts   4 squares chocolate
5 tsp. hot water   ½ cup milk
2 tsp. baking powder   ½ tsp. cinnamon

Cream the butter, add sugar gradually, and the egg yolks in butter, mix well, add the chocolate, nuts, cinnamon and baking powder and add alternately to the mixture with milk. Add the vanilla and fold in the egg whites, beaten dry. Bake in a moderate oven. Frost with fudge icing or bake in layers and put together with white boiled frosting.

Mrs. S. W. King, Jr.

Fudge Frosting

2 cups sugar
2 squares chocolate
1 tbsp. butter
½ cup milk
⅛ tsp. cream of tarter
2 tsp. vanilla

Boil the ingredients together without stirring until a soft ball can be formed when tried in cold water. Cool until tepid, add vanilla, beat until thick and spread.

Mrs. S. W. King, Jr.

Sour Cream Cake

3 cups sour cream
2 cups sugar
4 eggs
3 cups flour
1/3 cake chocolate dissolved in 1 cup of cream
1 tsp. soda

Sour Cream Filling: Boil ½ cup sugar, ½ cup sour cream together five minutes. Add yolks of two well beaten eggs, ½ cup nut meats. Put in double boiler and boil until thick and creamy.

Edna Ball.

Golden Angel Food

1¼ cups sugar
6 eggs
1 cup cake flour
1 tsp. cream of tartar
1 cup water
1 tsp. vanilla
¼ tsp. salt

Boil sugar and milk together until it threads. Pour over well beaten whites of eggs, beating constantly. Let cool. Beat yolks until foamy, add vanilla and fold into the whites. Sift flour, salt and cream of tartar. Fold into eggs. Grease pan lightly, dredge with flour. Bake one hour at slow constant temperature. Turn pan upside down and let cool before removing from pan.

Mrs. J. C. Cheek.

Fruit Snaps

1 cup butter	1½ cups sugar
1½ cups molasses	3 eggs
1 pkg. raisins	1 cup pecans
1 tsp. soda	3 cups flour
1 tsp. cinnamon	1 tsp. allspice
1 tsp. cloves	1 tsp. ginger

Mix soda with water. Mix all ingredients as with any other cookies.   *Mrs. George F. Howard.*

Cookies

4 eggs beaten light	2 cups sugar
1 tsp. vanilla	flour to thicken
1 or ½ cup butter	1 tsp. baking powder

pinch salt

Mix well then drop in well buttered pan.

Mrs. Frank Cullinan.

Blackberry Cake I

2 cups sugar	1 small cup butter
4 eggs	1 cup buttermilk
1 tsp. soda	1 cup blackberry jam
1 cup chopped nuts	1 tsp. cinnamon
1 tsp. cloves	1 tsp. nutmeg

3 small cups of flour

Mix soda in milk. Bake in four layers. Do not serve for at least twenty-four hours. It is better if it stands two or three days. Use sugar icing.

Mrs. George F. Howard.

Sugar Icing

2 cups sugar   10 tsp. milk

Boil five minutes and stir until cool.

Mrs. George F. Howard.

Nut Loaf

1 cup chopped pecans
1 egg
3 cups flour

1½ cups sweet milk
1 cup powdered sugar
2 tsp. baking powder

1 tsp. salt

Stir all together well and let stand 30 minutes. Bake in slow oven for 45 minutes. Make day before using.

Mrs. George F. Howard.

Mahogany Cake

2 tbsp. grated choco-
late or cocoa
¼ cup butter
½ cup milk
2 tsp. baking powder

2 cups sugar
¼ cup Crisco
4 eggs
2 cups flour
1 tsp. vanilla

5 tbsp. boiling water

Dissolve chocolate in the boiling water and let cool. Cream butter, Crisco and sugar. Add well beaten yolks of eggs. Add chocolate, milk and flour. Mix baking powder and flour together before adding to mixture. Last add the whites of eggs which should be well beaten and flavor with vanilla. Make in 3 layers.   *Mrs. Seth Miller.*

Icing For Mahogany Cake

3 cups powdered sugar
1 yolk of egg
5 tbsp. boiling coffee

½ cup butter
2 tbsp. chocolate or
cocoa

vanilla

Cream sugar with butter, add yolk of egg and chocolate which has been dissolved in boiling coffee. Flavor with vanilla.   *Mrs. Seth Miller.*

Thanksgiving Cake

1 scant lb. butter	1 lb. sugar
6 eggs	1 cup whiskey
1 whole nutmeg grated	1 lb. flour
2 tsp. baking powder	½ lb. raisins

1 qt. shelled pecans (chopped)

Cream buttered and sugar. Bake very slowly.

Mrs. Frank Cullinan.

Devil's Food Cake

1 tsp. soda	5 eggs
3 cups flour	2 cups sugar
1 cup buttermilk	1 cup butter

½ cake Baker's bitter chocolate

1 tsp. mixed spices (cloves, cinnamon and allspice)

Sift flour and sugar four times. Mix butter and sugar and cream well. Add yolks of eggs, buttermilk, 2 cups flour, whites of eggs beaten stiff, then 1 cup flour, with soda. Add chocolate melted in a little hot water. Cook in layers using a chocolate filling.

Mrs. R. R. Penn.

Angel Cake

11 egg whites (beaten stiff)	1 glass flour (scant), sifted five times
1½ glass sugar (scant), sifted five times	pinch salt
	1 tsp. cream tartar

2 tsp. almond extract

Sift sugar into eggs. Mix well. Add salt, then extract and sifted flour (cream of tartar mixed in it). Then fold and pour in pan. Bake in slow oven 45 minutes on bottom rack. Turn upside down one hour before taking out of pan.

Mrs. Turner Pittman.

Jam Cake

½ lb. butter	2 cups sugar
4 yolks of eggs	1 cup jam
1 cup buttermilk	1 tsp. soda
3½ cups flour	1 tsp. baking powder
cloves	allspice
cinnamon	4 whites of eggs

Mrs. W. E. Crow.

Carmel Cookies

1 cup butter	1 scant tsp. soda
4 cups brown sugar	1 tsp. cream of tartar
4 eggs	6½ cups flour

Sift cream of tartar with flour. If needed add more flour. Mix all thoroughly and make into a roll. It may be wrapped in oiled paper and left in ice box until time to bake. Cut in slices and bake slowly. Dough will keep a week.

Mrs. Allen Charlton.

Favorite Layer Cake

7 eggs	2 cups sugar
½ cup butter	1 tbsp. water
2 tsp. baking powder	2 cups flour
(level)	½ tsp. salt

Beat eggs separately. Work sugar and butter to a cream. Mix all ingredients and bake in jelly cake tin.

Use following filling:

1 egg	1 cup sugar
3 apples (grated)	1 lemon

Stir until it thickens in double boiler. Cool. Spread between cake.

Mrs. W. E. Crow.

Kisses Shells

6 egg whites   1 cup chopped nuts
6 tbsp. pulverized sugar, (rounding slightly)

Beat eggs until very stiff, add sugar slowly and beat about ½ hour. Fold nuts in carefully. Do not beat any more. Drop with tablespoon on brown paper. Shape like Mary Ann cake shell. Place in cold oven. Light one burner and turn very low. Cook until kisses are thoroughly died out. About 2 hours. Fill center with ice cream or fruit.

Effie Arnwine.

Chocolate Cake

1 cup butter	2 tsp. baking powder
2 cups sugar	(level)
½ cup sweet milk	2½ cups flour
½ cup boiling water	¼ cake chocolate
1 tsp. vanilla	(Baker's bitter)

4 eggs, leave out 2 yolks for icing

Cut chocolate and pour boiling water over it and set aside. Cream butter and sugar. Add flour, with baking powder sifted with it, and milk. Beat 4 whites and 2 yolks of eggs and add to batter. Then add vanilla.

Mrs. Devereux Dunlap.

Chocolate Filling

2 cups sugar	2 egg yolks
1 cup sweet milk	lump butter

¼ cake chocolate

Cook sugar, milk, butter and chocolate until it thickens as fudge. Beat until it begins to cool and add beaten yolks of 2 eggs and continue to beat.

Mrs. Devereux Dunlap.

Pineapple Up-Side-Down Cake

¼ cup butter
1 cup sugar
2 eggs (beaten sep-
arately)

1½ cups flour
½ cup milk
2 tsp. baking powder
1 tsp. vanilla

Mix as any butter cake, adding beaten whites last. In an iron spider, put 1 cup brown sugar and ½ cup butter. When melted lay in pan, as many slices of canned pineapple as possible, and cook gently, about 10 minutes. Then pour cake mixture over it, cook on top of stove for 1 minute, then put in oven for 40 minutes. Turn on chop plate, so that pineapple is on top, allow to cool and serve with whipped cream. *Mrs. Lewis G. Spence.*

Citron Cake

4 eggs (beaten whole)
1½ cups sugar
½ tsp. salt
1½ cups milk

3 cups flour
½ cup butter
½ cup sliced citron peel
(dusted with flour)

sifted together: 2 tsp. baking powder, ½ tsp. mace

Beat eggs, sugar and salt until light. Add milk and flour, sifted together with baking powder and mace. Add citron dusted with flour. Melt butter in angel food pan, add to cake and mix well. Pour into buttered tin and bake in slow oven for 1 hour.

Frosting

1 cup sugar
1 cup milk

¼ cup butter
2 squares chocolate

1 tsp. vanilla

Boil sugar, milk and butter together for 10 minutes. Add chocolate. Let stand on back of stove until chocolate melts. Add vanilla and beat well. Pour slowly over cake. The center may be filled with stewed fruit or whipped cream.

Mrs. T. W. Griffiths, Jr.

Chocolate Cake

½ cup butter
½ cup bitter chocolate
½ cup milk
4 eggs
1½ cups sugar
vanilla

2 full cups Swans-
down flour
1 rounded tsp. baking
powder
4 tbsp. boiling water

Use measuring cup but silver spoons. Cream butter, sugar and vanilla well. Add boiling water to the chocolate. Let it dissolve over kettle. Add chocolate to cream mixture. Beat well. Add all the flour (which has been sifted once before measuring, twice after and twice more after baking powder is added), and milk, then eggs, whole one at a time, beating well after each. Bake in 2 tins in a moderate oven.

Mrs. Wm. J. Lewis.

Jam Cake

Follow chocolate cake exactly using a little less sugar and substituting ½ cup of blackberry jam for chocolate and boiling water.

Mrs. Wm. J. Lewis.

Fudge Icing

Stir ½ cup of very rich milk and 2 cups of sugar until well mixed. Cook quickly until it boils up high once. Remove from fire, add lump of butter and vanilla. Beat until of right consistency to spread. The secret lies in its boiling up all over at once. If cooked a minute too long it is watery and grainy.

Mrs. Wm. J. Lewis.

Almond Sticks

1 cup butter
¾ cup sugar
2 eggs

2 cups chopped almonds
(don't chop too fine)
2 cups flour

Cream butter and sugar, add eggs and flour last. Cut in strips, after rolling to thickness of pie crust, brush strips with beaten egg yolk, sprinkle thickly with almonds and a little granulated sugar. Bake in medium oven.

Mrs. Earl Hulsey.

Lace Cookies

½ cup butter
½ cup sugar
½ cup molasses

½ cup flour (very generous)
pinch salt

Cream butter and sugar thoroughly, into this slowly work molasses. Sift in flour and salt. Drop from teaspoon onto buttered tins. Bake in medium hot oven until brown and crisp. Watch closely, as they bake quickly.

Mrs. L. S. Sabin.

Rolled Wafers

½ cup powdered sugar
¼ cup butter

¼ cup milk
⅞ cup bread flour

½ tsp. vanilla

Cream the butter, add sugar gradually, and milk drop by drop. Then add flour and flavoring. Spread very thinly with long bladed bread knife on a buttered inverted dripping pan. Crease in three inch squares and bake in a slow oven until delicately browned. Place pan on back of range, cut squares apart with a sharp knife, and roll while warm into tubular or cornucopia shape. Dust with powdered sugar as they are rolled.

Effie Arnwine.

Finland Cookies

Cream 1 lb. butter, 1 lb. brown sugar. Add 2 eggs well beaten, 1 lb. flour, 1 tbsp. baking powder, 1 tbsp. cinnamon and salt to taste. Lastly add 1 lb. shelled almonds whole. Roll out well with rolling pin and mould into roll. Keep mixture in ice box a few days before baking. The longer the better. Slice off with a very sharp knife, so as to cut through the whole almonds, bake in moderate oven.

Compliments World Fellowship Committee,
Y. W. C. A.

Cookies

1 lb. butter
1 qt. flour
3 eggs

2 cups sugar
1 level tsp. baking
    powder

2 tsp. vanilla

Flour and baking powder well sifted together. Add butter and mix well with hands. Beat eggs and sugar together. Add vanilla. Add flour mixture to egg mixture and leave in ice box over night. Roll very thin on board lightly sprinkled with flour. Cut any shape. Sprinkle with little sugar and cinnamon and bake. *Albena Foyt.*

Devil's Food Cake

2 cups sugar
1 cup butter
1 cup sour milk
1 tsp. vanilla
1 tsp. baking powder
½ cake chocolate

2½ cups flour
5 eggs (beaten
    separately)
1 tsp. soda, dissolved
    in 1 tbsp. water

Cream sugar and butter, add beaten yolks, then milk and flour. (Sift baking powder in flour). Add chocolate melted over boiling water, soda and vanilla and lastly the beaten whites. *Edna Ball.*

142

Elephant Ears

8 yolks of eggs
8 tbsp. cream
¼ tsp. salt

enough flour to make
stiff dough

Beat eggs, sugar and cream. Add flour. Roll very thin. Cut in strips. Fold over and fry in deep fat. Sprinkle with powdered sugar. *Mrs. Frank E. Austin.*

Blackberry Jam Cake

1 cup butter
4 cups flour (scant)
1 tsp. each of cloves,
   cinnamon, allspice
   and vanilla
   pinch of black pepper
2 cups sugar

4 eggs (beaten separately)
1 tsp. of soda dissolved
   in 1 cup sour milk
3 tsp. baking powder
1 cup blackberry jam

Cream butter and sugar, add yolks of eggs, then flour sifted with spices and baking powder. Add alternately with the milk. Then add jam and fold in stiffly beaten whites.

Filling:

2 cups sugar   2 cups sour cream

Boil 20 minutes, add lump of butter size of walnut, beat until cool, add one cup each of chopped pecans and raisins and 1 tsp. of vanilla. *Mrs. Philip Miller.*

Salads

Frozen Cheese Salad

1 pt. whipping cream	paprika
3 cakes of Philadelphia cheese	1 medium onion (grated)

1/8 tsp. salt

Whip the cream stiff. Cream cheese and add to cream, add onion and seasoning. Mix well, put into a ring mould and freeze as you do mousse. Unmould on a bed of lettuce; fill center of mould with either grapefruit section or sliced tomatoes and sliced cucumbers. Marinate all with French dressing. Serve with dressing made of equal parts of mayonnaise and whipped cream.

Frozen Salad

2 green peppers	1 pkg. mint gelatin
4 pimentos	1 pt. cream
1 small onion	salt to taste
4 tbsp. Worcestershire sauce	pepper to taste
	tabasco to taste
1 lemon (juice)	1 lb. American cheese

Cut the green peppers fine, pimentos and onion. Grate the cheese into this. Melt the gelatin in small quantity of water and add. Season to taste with salt, pepper, tabasco, lemon juice and Worcestershire sauce. Whip the cream and add. Put in baking powder cans with tops on tight and pack in salt and ice for 2 hours. Slice and serve on lettuce with mayonnaise.

Mrs. Allen D. Sanford, Waco.

Cole Slaw

3 cups of cabbage (shredded)	4 tbsp. sugar
1½ cups chopped crisp celery	cayenne pepper
	1 tsp. mustard
1 small can pineapple (grated)	½ lemon (juice only)
	1 tsp. Taragon vinegar
1 small green pepper (chopped)	salt to taste
	½ tbsp. flour
2 egg yolks	½ cup almonds (blanched)

Shred cabbage, put in ice water and set on ice five or six hours. Drain. Rub bowl with garlic, put in cabbage, celery, almonds, green pepper, and pineapple from which the juice has been drained. Mix well. Make a cooked dressing as follows:

Mix flour, sugar, cayenne pepper and mustard with the pineapple juice, lemon juice and Taragon vinegar and salt. Cook in double boiler until thick. Let cool and when cool add 2½ tablespoons of olive oil. Beat well and add whipped cream. Put enough dressing on slaw to mix well.

Mrs. W. E. Crow.

Avocada Salad

avocadas	2 ounces Brazil nuts
2 green peppers	salt to taste
2 apples	paprika to taste
2 heads lettuce	juice of 1 lemon

Cut avocadas in halves, remove pits, scoop out the flesh and place in bowl. Add peppers and apples peeled and diced, and nuts and lettuce chopped. Season with lemon juice, salt and paprika. Fill the avocada halves and serve with French dressing.

Mrs. R. L. Henry, Waco, Texas.

Cheese Apples

Grate desired amount of yellow cheese, season highly with salt, red pepper, onion juice (if desired), mustard (if desired), blend well together with a little cream. Mixture must remain very stiff. Mould with hands into balls the size of tiny apples. Dent the two opposite sides, shaping as an apple. Stick two tiny leaves in one end and a clove in the other. Tint the side with fruit coloring to look like a crab apple. Serve with salad.

Frozen Tomato Salad

5 medium sized tomatoes
2 stalks celery
1 jar anchovies
1 hard boiled egg
½ bottle capers
Tarragon vinegar

Scoop out tomatoes, cut centers up fine, chop celery, egg and anchovies and mix with tomatoes and capers. Make a French dressing of anchovy oil and Tarragon vinegar. Mix with other ingredients. Stuff tomato shells and put in freezer. Pack in salt and ice and leave 2 hours. Serve on lettuce with mayonnaise.

Mrs. J. B. Shelmire.

Pineapple and Cucumber Salad

3 large cucumbers
1 can sliced pineapple
5 lemons
1 cup sugar
1 package gelatine
pinch of salt

Grate the cucumbers, cut pineapple fine, make a syrup of pineapple juice, lemon juice and sugar boiled together. Add to this the gelatine, softened with a little cold water. Add to cucumbers and pineapple and salt. When cool, pour into mould and set away to harden.

Mrs. Glenway Maxon, Jr.

Cheese Salad

½ lb. American cheese   ½ cup chopped celery
(grated)   3 chopped pimentos
½ cup chopped nuts

Mix with mayonnaise, stuff into green pepper cases, set on ice until ready to serve. Slice and serve on lettuce leaves with mayonnaise.   *Mrs. C. C. Slaughter, Jr.*

Cherry Salad

1 can pitted Queen Anne   1 cup blanched almonds
cherries

Fill centers of cherries with almonds, serve on lettuce with mayonnaise.

Mrs. Guss W. Thompson.

Grapefruit Salad

3 cups grapefruit pulp   1 tbsp. gelatin
½ cup lemon juice   ¾ cup sugar
1 cup water   ½ tsp. salt

Make a syrup of lemon juice, sugar, salt and water; dissolve gelatin with it. Add grapefruit. When cool, put in wet moulds and set away to harden.

Mrs. S. A. Leake.

Russian Salad Dressing

½ cup olive oil   3 dashes of tabasco
¼ cup vinegar   salt to taste
½ cup Worcestershire   pepper to taste
sauce

Mix as in French dressing.

Oscar Rand, Oriental Hotel.

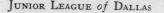

Ginger Ale Salad

1/3 cup Malaga grapes
1/3 cup celery cut in strips
1/3 cup apples cut in strips
2 tbsp. Canton ginger
4 tbsp. diced pine-apple

2 tbsp. gelatine
1/4 cup lemon juice
1 cup imported ginger ale
2 tbsp. sugar
pinch of salt

Skin and halve the grapes. Cut celery, apples and ginger in Julienne strips; dice pineapple. Soak gelatine in 2 tablespoons of cold water, then dissolve in one-third cup boiling water. Add ginger ale, lemon juice, sugar and salt, and let stand until it begins to harden. Then add fruit, and set on ice to mould. Serve with cream dressing.

Mrs. J. B. Oldham.

Argyle Salad

1 can peeled apricots
2 eggs
1 cup nuts
1 cup whipped cream
butter size of a walnut
pepper to taste

1 1/4 tbsp. flour
1 tbsp. vinegar
1 tbsp. mustard
1 tbsp. salt
sugar to taste

For each one to be served, place three apricot halves on lettuce, and pour the following dressing over them: Two eggs well beaten, salt, pepper, mustard, flour and sugar mixed in a small pan, to which add enough vinegar to rub a smooth paste. Add the rest of the vinegar, cook over a slow fire, and stir constantly until it is thick and creamy. When thoroughly cool, add nuts and whipped cream.

Mrs. C. A. Pippin.

Thousand Island Dressing

1 egg yolk
½ pt. olive oil
½ lemon
dash of cayenne

½ cup chili sauce
1 sweet green pepper
1 tsp. tiny pearl onions
salt to taste

Beat egg yolk, and oil drop by drop, beating constantly until thick; add lemon juice gradually. Have this ice cold and just before serving add chili sauce, green pepper chopped fine, and onions.

Mrs. Wesley Norris.

Fruit Salad Dressing

3 eggs
2 level tbsp. flour
1 tbsp. sugar
1 cup sweet milk

2 cups whipped cream
1 level tsp. salt
½ tsp. mustard
dash of cayenne

½ cup vinegar

Beat eggs, add sugar, salt, cayenne and mustard, then the flour blended to a smooth paste with the milk. Heat the vinegar and add when boiling hot. Cook in a double boiler until the consistency of a thick custard. When cold, beat in the whipped cream.

Mrs. G. W. Lamberth.

Salad Dressing

4 tbsp. olive oil
1 tbsp. vinegar
½ tbsp. Worcestershire
sauce

1½ tbsp. tomato catsup
salt to taste
pepper to taste

Mix as in French dressing.

Mrs. P. G. Claiborne.

Cucumber Cheese

1 large cucumber	salt to taste
3 level dessert spoons gelatine	white pepper to taste
	red pepper to taste
juice of 1 lemon	sugar to taste

Wash and grate rind and all of cucumber, season with salt, pepper, lemon juice, red pepper and sugar. Soften gelatine with a little cold water. Then dissolve with two-thirds cup of hot water, stir in the cucumber and strain. Color with Burnett's green color paste. Pour into a wet mould and set away to harden.

Cheese Part:

3 cakes Neufchatel cheese	½ cup broken pecan meats
1 pint cream (whipped)	salt to taste
3 dessert spoons gelatine	red pepper to taste
sugar to taste	

Soften cheese with half of the whipped cream, season with salt, pepper and sugar. Dissolve gelatine (as before), stir into the cheese, add nuts and rest of the whipped cream; melt the top of the gelatine in the mould with a little hot water. Then add cheese mixture and set away to harden. Serve with mayonnaise.

Mrs. Helena Ostrand.

Tomatoes Stuffed With Anchovies

Select firm, ripe tomatoes, remove skin, set on ice. Mix anchovies and chopped hard boiled eggs together with mayonnaise, highly seasoned with onion juice, red pepper and salt. Remove insides of tomatoes, fill with mixture, top with mayonnaise. Put an anchovy on top and serve on lettuce leaves.

Mrs. Frank Callier.

Orange Salad

7 oranges	½ cup chopped almonds
4 lemons	7 tbsp. sugar

1 envelope gelatine

Set gelatine in ½ cup of cold water, then dissolve it in 1/3 cup of hot water. Add sugar to orange and lemon juice, then add gelatine. Stir until all is dissolved, then add almonds and pour into mould. Let set until congealed. Serve on lettuce with mayonnaise.

Mrs. A. A. Green, Jr.

Roquefort Cheese Salad Dressing

1 egg yolk	pinch of mustard
1 cup pure olive oil	1 tbsp. vinegar
1 lemon (juice)	1 tsp. chili sauce
1 tsp. Worcestershire sauce	¼ of white of hard boiled egg (chopped)
1/8 of a green pepper (chopped)	1 tsp. paprika
pinch of salt	

2 oz. Roquefort cheese

Mix egg, oil, salt, pepper, mustard, lemon and vinegar (dissolve mustard and salt in vinegar) as in making mayonnaise. Add other ingredients, having chopped cheese, egg white and green pepper all fine. Blend all well. Serves six people.

Marshmallow Salad

1 box marshmallows	¾ cup whipped cream
1 can pineapple (sliced)	¼ tsp. salt
3 tbsp. lemon juice	½ tsp. paprika

2 tbsp. lemon juice

Cut marshmallows in quarters, add equal measure of diced pineapple. Mix with the whipped cream that has been seasoned with the salt, paprika and lemon juice. Serve on lettuce.

Mrs. J. C. Gilbert.

Old Fashioned Lettuce Salad

1 head lettuce	salt to taste
3 strips bacon	pepper to taste
1 slice ham	1 young onion

3 hard boiled eggs

Fry bacon and ham very hard and chop up. Pour hot grease over lettuce. Mash eggs fine and add a little mustard, vinegar and sugar. Chop lettuce, add egg mixture and ham and bacon. Serve with French dressing.

Mrs. Geo. N. Aldredge.

Tomato With Caviar

Firm, ripe tomatoes skinned and cut in inch thick slices. Make a mixture of caviar, very finely chopped parsley, very finely chopped hard boiled egg, little garlic. Spread mixture on slices of tomato (which must be chilled), top with a little mayonnaise and place one-half of a stuffed olive on the mayonnaise. Have ready rounds of bread (same size as tomato slices) sauted in butter. Place tomato on bread and put all on a lettuce leaf. Serve as a first course.

Mrs. John Puterbaugh.

Kentucky Cheese Salad

2 rolls of Neufchatel cheese	1 small can sliced pineapple
1½ pkgs. Knox gelatine	1 cucumber

1 can white cherries

Thin cheese with highly seasoned mayonnaise to the consistency of cream. Grate cucumber, chop pineapple and cherries. Boil juice from fruits and add to dissolved gelatine. When cold, stir in cheese mixture, fruits and cucumbers. Let stand in very cold place. Serve on lettuce with mayonnaise.

Mrs. Lang Wharton.

Frozen Cheese Salad

1 cup grated cheese	¼ pt. cream (whipped)
½ small bottle stuffed olives (chopped)	1 tsp. salt
	1 tbsp. Knox gelatine
¼ tsp. cayenne	

Make aspic of 1 tbsp. Knox gelatine dissolved in ¼ cup cold water. Add ¼ cup boiling water. Add cheese and whipped cream. Season with salt and pepper, add chopped olives and pack in baking powder tins that have been wet with cold water. Adjust tops and cover with cloth that has been dipped in melted lard. Tie this cloth over top. Bury in salt and ice 3 hours. Turn out, slice and serve on lettuce with mayonnaise.

Mrs. Wirt Leake.

Potato Salad

1 tbsp. onion juice	1 cup whipped cream
4 tbsp. salad oil	2 hard boiled eggs (chopped)
1 bunch celery chopped fine	1 cup finely cut sweet pickles
good boiled mayonnaise	cooled, cooked, diced potatoes
salt and red pepper	

Add onion juice, salad oil and cream to mayonnaise. Mix all ingredients except salt and red pepper. Allow to cool in icebox, stirring occasionally. Before serving, season highly with salt and red pepper, and if salad is dry, add more salad oil.

Mrs. Manning Shannon.

Heart of Palm Salad

Buy canned Heart of Palm. Cut in rounds, marinate in French dressing and serve on crisp lettuce. Slice of orange may be used with Heart of Palm.

Cream French Dressing

4 tbsp. olive oil   ¼ tsp. pepper
2 tbsp. vinegar   ⅛ tsp. paprika
½ tsp. salt   ½ cup heavy cream

Put first five ingredients together in covered bottle and shake thoroughly until emulsified. Beat cream until it begins to thicken. Then add gradually French dressing.

The Commission Shop of Minneapolis.

Tomato Aspic

1 can tomatoes   ¼ gr. pepper
  (mashed fine)   4 tbsp. vinegar
1 cucumber   1 pkg. Knox gelatine
½ bunch celery   2 cups boiling water
1 medium onion   cayenne, salt

Cut cucumber, onion, celery and pepper fine, add to tomatoes; season with 2 tablespoons vinegar, plenty of salt and cayenne. Dissolve gelatine in ¼ cup cold water and add 2 cups boiling water, dissolve thoroughly. Add 2 tablespoons vinegar, salt and pepper to taste. Combine two mixtures, put in mould to harden. Turn out on bed of lettuce, sprinkle with grated yellow cheese and serve with mayonnaise.

Mrs. Chas. Dexter, Jr.

Frozen Fruit Salad

2 oranges   ¼ lb. blanched almonds
1 small can pineapple   (cut in pieces)
1 small can white   1 pt. heavy cream
  cherries   1 small bottle red
2 bananas   cherries

Let fruit stand in French dressing three hours, then drain very dry. Mix fruit with cream which has been whipped stiff. Pack in ice and salt about 4 hours. Serve on lettuce. Serves 12 people.

Mrs. L. S. Sabin.

Avocado Dressing

Two parts French dressing, 1 part mayonnaise, 2 hard boiled eggs, chopped fine, 4 tablespoons chili sauce, chopped chives and three chopped pimentos.

Mrs. Collett Munger.

Delicious Salad

1 qt. of cabbage	1 box marshmallows
1 cup pineapple	1 cup blanched almonds

Shred and chop cabbage fine. Put in cold water one hour and dry in towel. Add 1 cup of pineapple, cut and drained, one cup of blanched almonds, one box of marshmallows. Set aside and make dressing as follows: 2 lemons, 4 tablespoons vinegar, 1 scant tablespoon of flour mixed with a little water, 1/3 cup sugar. Add to whites of 4 eggs beaten stiff. Cook in double boiler until thick. When cool, add one pint of whipped cream and a little salt. Mix and set in refrigerator until cold.

Mrs. J. L. Dreibelbis.

Whipped Cream Salad

½ cup cream (whipped)	dash of tabasco
½ cup water	2 tbsp. gelatine
1 or 2 pimentos (cut fine)	1 cup grated cheese
	½ tsp. salt
	dash of mustard

Soften gelatine in ¼ cup of cold water, add ½ cup of hot water. Stir until cooled. Beat into the whipped cream, add 1 cup of grated cheese, one or two pimentos (cut fine), salt, tabasco and mustard. Turn into moulds, pack in ice for two hours. Serve on lettuce with mayonnaise. For green and white luncheon, pistachio nuts cut fine may be substituted for the pimentos.

Mrs. J. B. Adoue, Jr.

Cucumber and Shrimp Salad

Select cucumbers about 4 inches long, pare nicely and core, leaving a shell. Fill with following: minced shrimp, finely chopped Bermuda onion and the cucumber pulp, salt, paprika and highly seasoned cream mayonnaise. Put on ice to harden and slice in rings. Serve on endive with mayonnaise.

Almond Salad

(Especially good for a buffet luncheon or supper where no dessert will be served, as it is very rich).

1 large can pitted white cherries	1 lb. blanched almonds
1 large can sliced pine-apple	1 envelope of sparkling gelatine dissolved in cold water

½ cup pineapple juice

Allow the pineapple juice to come to boil and add gelatine. When cooling but not quite congealing, add the fruit and almonds. Just when beginning to congeal, add ½ cup boiled salad dressing and afterwards ½ pint of whipped cream.

Boiled salad dressing:—

1 tsp. salt	2 tbsp. flour
1 tsp. sugar	½ cup vinegar, diluted with water to make ¾ cup
dash of cayenne	
melt 2 tbsp. butter	
very scant tsp. mustard	

Cook all together until it thickens. In a separate vessel, let a cup of milk come just to the boiling point, take off and pour over well beaten yolks of 2 eggs. When well mixed, pour all together and cook until thick.

Mrs. Philip Miller.

Tomato Gelatine Cheese Salad

1 large can tomatoes	1 cup water
1 bay leaf	1 onion
1 stalk of celery	1 clove and 1 allspice

Cook ½ hour and strain, salt and sugar to taste. Add ¾ package of gelatine, put in mould. Use more gelatine in hot weather.

Cheese mixture: When tomato jelly is firm, take 1 teaspoon of hot water and pour it on jelly. Take thin knife and run all over, then add cheese mixture:

3 or 4 pkgs. Philadelphia cream cheese	½ pt. whipped cream cup of mayonnaise

Beat mayonnaise with cream, add ½ package of gelatine (whole package if in hurry) then cheese and finely chopped nuts and celery.

Mrs. Edgar Padgitt.

Shrimp Ring

4 lbs. shrimp	1 tsp. mustard sauce
2 cups celery	¾ small (9c) can Italian tomato paste
½ cup green pepper	
small onion or ½ cup chives (chopped)	1½ qts. boiling water
	1¾ pkgs. Knox gelatine
cayenne pepper and salt to taste	juice of ½ lemon
	½ tsp. sugar

Cook shrimp and cut in large pieces. Mix with celery, green pepper, onion and a little parsley. Line a salad ring and pour over this a liquid made as follows: Dissolve gelatine in boiling water, add tomato paste, lemon juice, mustard sauce, cayenne pepper, salt to taste and sugar. Put on ice. Turn out on platter. Serve with center of ring filled with mayonnaise or thousand island dressing. Garnish around ring with asparagus tips and sliced beets.

Mrs. W. E. Crow.

Russian Dressing

1 raw carrot
1 raw beet
1 raw onion

1 cup mayonnaise
1 tsp. mustard
1 tsp. salt

1 tsp. paprika

Grate carrot, beet and onion. Add other ingredients and beat thoroughly until well blended.

Mrs. L. S. Sabin.

Frozen Fruit Salad

1 large can pineapple (chopped)
2 cups almonds, toasted

1 box marshmallows cut in halves
1 pt. cream (whipped)

make a dressing of

4 yolks

4 tbsp. sugar

4 tbsp. vinegar

Mix and cook in double boiler until very thick. Cool, mix with pineapple, nuts and marshmallows. Then add 1 pint of whipped cream. Pack in ice and serve on lettuce.

Mrs. R. C. Munger, Birmingham, Ala.

Cooked Salad Dressing

2 egg yolks
½ cup mild vinegar
¼ cup sugar
¼ cup butter
½ tbsp. flour

¼ tsp. salt
½ tsp. celery seed
½ tsp mixed mustard
¼ tsp. white pepper
dash of cayenne

Put vinegar and all seasoning in cup and mix. Melt butter in stewpan, add flour and stir until smooth, then add vinegar mixture. Put on fire and stir until thick. Pour over well beaten yolks of two eggs. Add desired amount of whipped cream when ready to serve.

Mrs. Seth Miller.

Cherry Salad

1 can white pitted cherries	juice of 1 lemon
1 can sliced pineapple	½ package gelatine

Mrs. Owen Carter.

Frozen Salad Dressing

¼ cup vinegar	¾ cup water
2 yolks eggs	1 tbsp. flour
1 tbsp. sugar	lump butter
raisins	marshmallows
1 pt. whipped cream	salt

Make mayonnaise of vinegar, water, eggs, flour, sugar, salt and butter. Cook until thick. While hot add marshmallows and beat until marshmallows dissolve. Add chopped raisins. When cool, add whipped cream. Serve on frozen fruit salad.

Mrs. Roger Randall.

Fruit Salad

½ can pineapple	½ tbsp. flour
½ cup blanched almonds	pinch salt
½ tbsp. butter	cayenne pepper
1 tsp. sugar (scant)	½ can white seedless
mustard	cherries
1 cup whipped cream	½ tbsp. gelatine

Soak gelatine in a little water. Cut pineapple. Melt butter, add flour, sugar, mustard, salt, cayenne, then add gelatine. Fold this into whipped cream, then add fruits and nuts. Put in moulds. Serve with lettuce and mayonnaise.

Mrs. Jack Beall.

Parsley Ring

4 hard boiled eggs	1 tbsp. gelatine
½ cup thick mayonnaise	season with salt,
½ cup parsley	pepper and
(chopped fine)	paprika

Dissolve gelatine in ¼ cup cold water. Add ½ cup hot water to the gelatine. Put all in a ring mould and when cold fill center with shrimp, crab meat or tomatoes.

Mrs. James B. Walker.

Frozen Cream Mayonnaise

1 cup mayonnaise	1 cup whipped cream

1 tbsp. powdered sugar

Fold into cup of mayonnaise flavored with lemon juice, whipped cream, powdered sugar. Pour into mould. Pack in ice and salt. Let set 1 hour. Serve with any kind of fruit.

Mrs. Jack Beall.

Frozen Tomato

2 cans tomatoes (juice)	1 lemon
4 fresh mushrooms	2 tbsp. Taragon vine-
2 tbsp. tomato catsup	gar
6 green peppers	3 onions
1 fresh tomato	½ box Nelson gelatine
3 cucumbers	mayonnaise

Cut cucumbers and scrape all inside out. Salt and let stand 1 hour. Grind fresh tomato, onion, pepper and mushrooms. Add all to tomato juice and other ingredients. Put in freezer. When well chilled add 2 drops tabasco sauce and lemon juice, 2 cups mayonnaise and ½ box Nelson gelatine dissolved in tomato juice. Serve with mayonnaise.

Mrs. W. E. Crow.

Grapefruit Salad

4 grapefruit   1 cup blanched
2 pound can pineapple   almonds
1½ envelope of gelatine
Mrs. Owen Carter.

Green Mayonnaise

1 cup mayonnaise   handful of spinach
   chopped tarragon   chives
   parsley   1 shallot

Boil spinach and squeeze the juice from the leaves
through a fine cloth into a bowl. Add this green water to
mayonnaise. Add chopped tarragon, chives, parsley and
shallot. Serve with cold boiled salmon.
Mrs. S. W. King, Jr.

Cheese Mould Salad Ring

2 cakes Philadelphia   1 cup whipped cream
   cheese   paprika
1 tbsp. gelatine   ¾ tsp. salt
¼ cup yellow cheese   few grains cayenne
   (grated)

   chopped parsley, green peppers or pimentos to taste
Soak gelatine in ¼ cup cold water, then fill rest of cup
with scalded sweet milk. Work cheese smooth. Add gelatine, seasonings and whipped cream. Wet ring mould and
pour in mixture and place in ice box. When cold fill center
with any salad preferred — shrimp, lettuce hearts, or crab
meat. Serves 10.
Mrs. James B. Walker.

Frozen Vegetable Salad

9 large tomatoes	1 tbsp. Worcestershire
1 stalk celery	½ tsp. grated horse-
2 cucumbers	radish
1 green pepper	1 cup cooked dressing
1 tbsp. grated onion	1 cup whipped cream

Peel and cut tomatoes in small pieces. Put in colander to drain. Peel cucumbers, cut in thick slices, making slices into quarters. Mix with tomatoes, diced celery and pepper, chopped fine. Make a sauce of onion, horseradish and Worcestershire and pinch of salt. Add to vegetables. Have the cooked dressing prepared and cold, to add to vegetables when ready to put in mould. Put layer of salad mixture first, then layer of whipped cream and alternate until mould is filled. Pack in ice and salt for 3½ hours. When ready to serve, place on lettuce leaves and garnish with pepper rings and mayonnaise dressing.

Mrs. H. R. Aldredge.

Spaghetti Salad

1 box imported spagh- etti	1 large onion (chopped fine)
1 stalk celery (chopped fine)	3 pimentos (chopped fine)
1 can green peas	3 green peppers (chopped fine)

Cook spaghetti in salted boiling water until tender. Put in colander and immediately pour ice water over it. Make very thick mayonnaise and season highly. Mix ingredients with mayonnaise.

Mrs. Peter O'Donnell.

Congealed Asparagus Salad

2 tbsp. butter
2 tbsp. flour
4 eggs
1 can asparagus

salt, paprika and pepper to taste
1 tbsp. gelatine (heaping)
1 pt. whipped cream
juice of 1 lemon

Heat butter in double boiler, sift in flour, add 4 or 5 tablespoons water from asparagus. Put on fire and stir constantly. To this add eggs, beaten well, and cook until thick. Add gelatine which has been dissolved in a little water, seasoning and lemon. Let custard cool and add over half of whipped cream. Keep remaining cream for mayonnaise dressing. Cut asparagus in small pieces and mould in layers with custard.

Mrs. Devereux Dunlap.

Bean Salad

String and break in halves, snap beans, boil in water until tender, drain off the water, season with salt, pepper and a little sliced onions. Pour vinegar over them an hour or two before serving. Drain and serve with French dressing or mayonnaise.

Effie Arnwine.

Italian Salad

2 pkgs. spaghetti
1 gr. pepper
2 medium onions

4 stalks celery
1 can pimentoes
1 can peas

Boil spaghetti ½ hour. Drain and rinse in cold water. Cut vegetables in small pieces and mix with spaghetti. Fluff this with mayonnaise and serve. Two well beaten whites of eggs may be put in mayonnaise.

Mrs. Lewis G. Spence.

Frozen Tomatoes

Drain the juice from a can of tomatoes and press the pulp through a fine sieve. Season with salt, cayenne or paprika, a few drops of onion juice and a dash of lemon juice. Freeze as you would ice cream, serve with a slice of pineapple and mayonnaise dressing.

Miss Paulula Dunn.

Cheese Fruit Salad Baskets

American cheese
Swiss or Kraft cheese
1 tbsp. gelatine
olives with pimento
nuts
cloves

cream cheese
eggs, hard boiled
mayonnaise
paprika
salt

mustard

Mould a tomato aspic in individual moulds and scoop out the center, placing a teaspoon of mayonnaise in it. Take small portion of American cheese, mix with a little mayonnaise and shape into small oranges. Take cream cheese in small portions, mix with mayonnaise and chopped nuts and mould into a pear, sticking a clove in the top. Take the yolk of the egg, mix with mayonnaise and shape into small lemons. Take Kraft or Swiss cheese, mix with mayonnaise and a tiny bit of mustard and shape into apples, place a clove in the top and sprinkle paprika on one side to look like apple turning red. Place one each of these fruits and an olive in the cavity and serve on lettuce leaf. Make cheese straws, cut in small strips, twist them and bake in horseshoe shape the size to fit across the aspic mould. Just before serving stick cheese straw in aspic to look like the handle of a basket.

Mrs. John O. McReynolds.

Frozen Fruit Salad

1 large can peaches	1 large can apricots
1 large can pineapple	1 qt. mayonnaise

American cheese

Use all the juice of all three cans of fruit. Cut fruit in small pieces, mix fruit, juice, mayonnaise and add enough grated cheese to cut sweet paste (about 1 cup full). Pack in ice and salt for several hours. Serve with mayonnaise to which whipped cream has been added.

Mrs. Lewis G. Spence.

Mixed Salad

On lettuce, place a thick slice of a medium sized tomato, which has been marinated in French dressing. Place on tomato a spoonful of mayonnaise and on top of mayonnaise, add 3 medium sized boneless sardines and a dash of paprika. On one side of tomato place several small artichokes (Curtis brand, in glass) on opposite side, several slices of heart of palm. Garnish plate with two or three slices of hard boiled egg and a few small pickled pearl onions. Serve with a well seasoned French dressing made of olive oil.

Mrs. T. W. Griffiths, Jr.

Rouquefort Slaw (excellent with chili)

1 cup mayonnaise	juice 1 small lemon
½ cake Rouquefort	or same amount
cheese (about 2 oz.)	vinegar
1 button of garlic	½ large head cabbage

salt and paprika to taste

Chop cabbage, place in ice water until crisp. Drain well and toss up with above ingredients, which have first been well blended. The Rouquefort is best rubbed smooth in the lemon juice, or vinegar. This is better if served promptly.

Mrs. Earl Hulsey.

Moquin Salad

Drain a can of sliced pineapple, cut in halves, sprinkle with salt and lemon juice. Let stand half an hour. Cream neufchatel, moistening with cream. Force through potato ricer over pineapple. Arrange on lettuce leaves and serve with the following dressing: Make own recipe French dressing, using vinegar and paprika, add 4 tablespoons of heavy cream, beaten stiff. Pour over salad. A slice of tomato may be added to pineapple, if desired.

Miss Paulula Dunn.

Cheese Ring Salad

1 tbsp. gelatine	¼ cup cold water
2 tbsp. cream cheese	1 tsp. onion juice
½ cup Roquefort	1 cup whipped cream
¼ tsp. salt	¼ tsp. paprika

canned pear halves

Soak gelatine in cold water, dissolve over hot water. Moisten the cheese with a little cream until smooth, then mix with gelatine, add other ingredients, fold in whipped cream, put in mould, serve on lettuce. Fill center of mould with pears (marinate pears in French dressing, several hours). Pour a little French dressing over pears and serve.

Mrs. Huey Hughes.

Asparagus Salad

Thick slice of lettuce, with three or four large peeled asparagus bars laid across it. Roquefort cheese dressing.

Mrs. Ballard Burgher.

Summer Dressing

½ cup brown sugar	1 heaping tsp. salt
½ cup vinegar	1 level tsp. pepper

1 level tsp. ground mustard

Add mustard to sugar, salt and pepper. Dissolve in vinegar. Thoroughly chill and serve on tomatoes or lettuce.

Mrs. O. T. Poyntz.

Pastry

Caramel Custard

4 eggs	2 tbsp. flour
½ cup sugar	1 tsp. vanilla
2 cups sweet milk	butter size of an egg

Mix the sugar, flour, eggs, butter and milk and cook in double boiler. At the same time, burn 1 cup of sugar and melt to a syrup. When custard cools, add caramel syrup and cook until smooth. Bake crusts and pour custard in, using the four whites for a meringue. Brown in hot oven.

Mrs. Ross Bradfield.

Washington Pie

Cake Part:

3 eggs	½ cup cold water
1½ cups sugar	2 cups flour
2 tsp. baking powder	

Beat eggs 1 minute, add sugar and beat 5 minutes. Add 1 cup flour and beat 1 minute, then add ½ cup water and other cup of flour and baking powder and beat 1 minute. Bake in two floured cake tins. When cake is cold, slice through the middle and fill with the following custard about 1 hour before serving:

Filling for Pie:

3 egg yolks	2½ tbsp. sugar
2 cups milk	2½ tsp. flour
vanilla	

Heat milk in a double boiler. Add beaten egg yolks, sugar and flour, and make a stiff custard. When cool, add vanilla; or nuts or sliced bananas may be added if desired. Fill cake and top with whipped cream.

Mrs. D. W. Sanders.

Orange Pie

3 oranges	1½ heaping tbsp. flour
3 eggs	2 tbsp. melted butter
1 1/3 cups sugar	

Stir together the orange juice, flour and sugar; add to this the egg yolks well beaten and the melted butter. Turn this into a pie tin lined with crust and bake in a quick oven until a firm custard. Spread over the top with 3 whites of eggs beaten stiff with 2 tablespoons of sugar, and brown lightly.

Mary M. Smith, Waco.

Cherry Pie

1 can seeded cherries	2 cups sugar
4 eggs	½ cup sweet milk
2 tbsp. butter	1 tbsp. flour
(vanilla to taste)	

Drain half of juice from cherries, add 1½ cups of sugar and cook until well preserved. Make a thick custard in a double boiler of the 4 egg yolks, butter, ½ cup sugar, sweet milk and flour. When cool, add vanilla and the preserved cherries. Pour into cooked crust; whip egg whites with 1 tablespoon of sugar for each egg, and brown meringue in stove.

Mrs. R. B. Dupree, Waco.

Oh! So Good Pie

4 eggs	1 cup raisins
2 cups sugar	3 tsp. vinegar
1 tbsp. melted butter	1 tsp. cinnamon
1 cup cream	1 tsp. cloves

Beat egg yolks, add sugar, then other ingredients; add the beaten whites last. Put in an uncooked pastry and bake ½ hour.

Mrs. A. W. Samuell.

Mince Meat

2 lbs. raisins	2 lemons
1 lb. currants	¾ pt. whiskey
½ lb. citron	1 tsp. cinnamon
2 lbs. apples	1 tsp. allspice
1 lb. sugar	1 tsp. nutmeg

2 oranges

Put the spices to soak in a little of the whiskey; add orange and lemon juice, raisins, currants, citron, cut in strips, then add apples chopped, and rest of whiskey. Seal in fruit jars.

Mrs. C. L. Maillot.

Pumpkin Ice Cream Pie

¾ cup pumpkin	1 tsp. cinnamon
1 cup milk	½ tsp. cloves
1 pt. cream	1 tsp. vanilla
1 cup sugar	4 egg whites

Freeze the grated pumpkin, sugar, spices, milk and cream. Make a rich pie crust and set away to cool. When cream is frozen, fill in the crust with it, add egg whites and ¼ cup of sugar beaten to a stiff meringue, and brown quickly in a very hot oven. Serve at once.

Mrs. E. M. Reardon, Jr.

Cream Pie

2 eggs	1½ tbsp. corn starch
½ cup sugar	1 tbsp. butter
1½ pts. sweet milk	1 tsp. vanilla

Heat milk in a double boiler, add other ingredients and cook until thick, stirring constantly. When cool, fill a pie crust that has been baked. Top with meringue made of the 2 whites; brown quickly and serve.

Mrs. Lloyd Price.

Chocolate Pie

3 eggs
2 heaping tbsp. corn
    starch
4 heaping tbsp. choco-
    late

1 cup water
1 tsp. vanilla
8 heaping tbsp. sugar

Put sugar, corn starch and grated chocolate in a double boiler; mix well; beat the egg yolks and 1 white together until very light and stir them into the mixture in the double boiler. Add the water and cook until the mixture is thick and smooth, stirring constantly. When cool, add vanilla and put into a pie crust that has already been baked. Top it with a meringue made of the two other whites, beaten stiff with 2 teaspoons of sugar and brown in a hot oven.

Mrs. Walter Dealey.

Spice Pie

1 cup sugar
1½ cups cream
3 eggs
3 tbsp flour

½ tsp. cloves
½ tsp. nutmeg
½ tsp. allspice
½ tsp. butter

1 tsp. cinnamon

Make a custard of the egg yolks, cream, flour, butter and spices. When cool, fill a pie crust that has been baked. Add egg whites beaten to a stiff meringue with 1 tablespoon of sugar for each egg. Brown in hot oven and serve.

Mrs. A. B. Griffith.

Hot Water Pastry

½ cup lard
½ cup boiling water

1½ cups flour
¼ tsp. salt

¼ tsp. baking powder

Follow rule for making pastry.

Mrs. Milton Ragsdale.

Butterscotch Pie

4 tbsp. sugar	4 yolks
butter, size of egg	2 whites
1 cup water	¾ cup sugar
2 cups milk	2 level tbsp. flour

Brown 4 tablespoons sugar slightly, add butter and brown together; then add water and dissolve browned sugar and butter. Put milk in double boiler. When hot, add eggs beaten together until light, and mixed with sugar and flour; then add browned mixture and cook until it thickens. Bake crust and pour the custard in; cover with meringue and brown in oven. *Mrs. J Robert Carter.*

Pineapple Pie

1½ pts. sweet milk	1 tbsp. butter
2 eggs	1 small can grated
½ cup sugar	pineapple
1½ tbsp. corn starch	

Heat milk in a double boiler. Add all other ingredients but pineapple and cook until thick. When cool, add pineapple. Fill a crust that has been baked; add a meringue made of egg whites and a little sugar. Brown and serve.

Mrs. Lloyd Price.

Pecan Pie

4 eggs	2 tbsp. flour
1 cup sugar	1 cup cream
1 cup chopped pecans	

Beat egg yolks, add cream, sugar and flour. Cook until thick in a double boiler. When cool, add most of nut meats, fill in a rich pie crust that has been baked. Top with a meringue made of egg whites and sprinkle with rest of pecans. Brown quickly and serve. *Mrs. J. C. Duke.*

Cocoanut Cream Pie

2 eggs
1 fresh cocoanut
 (grated)
1½ pts. sweet milk

4 tbsp. corn starch
½ cup sugar
1 tsp. vanilla

Mix the corn starch, egg yolks, and sugar, then add milk and cook until very thick. When cool, add most of the cocoanut and vanilla. Make a thin but deep crust and bake before adding the custard. Beat the two whites stiff; add 2 tablespoons of sugar and add to pie. Sprinkle with remaining cocoanut and marshmallows cut in thirds. Brown quickly and serve at once. *Mrs. A. A. Green.*

Butterscotch Pie

1 cup sugar
2 eggs
1 cup cold water

2 tbsp. flour
2 heaping tbsp. butter
1 tsp. vanilla

Brown the sugar and mix to a paste with the two egg yolks, and flour. Add gradually the cold water and butter. Cook in a double boiler until thick, stirring constantly. When cool, add vanilla and pour into a pie crust that has been baked. Make meringue of 2 egg whites, beaten stiff with 2 tablespoons sugar. Brown in hot oven.

Mrs. Ross Bradfield.

Amber Pie

½ cup butter
1 cup sugar
3 eggs

½ glass jelly (any
 flavor)
1 cup buttermilk

2 tbsp. flour

Cream butter and sugar thoroughly, add yolks of eggs, flour, jelly, and buttermilk. Beat whites very stiff, add and mix thoroughly. *Mrs. L. S. Sabin.*

Brama Cream Pie
Pastry:

1 cup butter	3 cups flour
½ cup sugar	1 egg

Custard:

10 eggs	2 tsp. vanilla
2 cups milk	½ cup sugar
1 tsp. corn starch	

Make pastry, roll out in a round of desired size. Bake. Make a custard of the above ingredients listed under custard; set aside to cool. Cut up pecans (or walnuts), cherries, and bananas. Place crust on serving platter. Put a layer of custard on top then a layer of chopped fruits and nuts, then custard and so on until all the custard and fruit are used. Serve with whipped cream.

Mrs. Owen Carter.

Butterscotch Pie

1 cup brown sugar	1 cup milk
2 eggs	2 tbsp. flour
1 tsp. vanilla	

Mix sugar, milk and flour with well beaten yolks. Cook in double boiler until very thick, stirring constantly. Bake in a crust, using whites of eggs for meringue. This makes one pie. *Mrs. F. M. Butt.*

Transparent Pies

yolks of 6 eggs	3 tbsp. flour
3 cups sugar	1½ cup citron, cut very
1 cup butter	small
2 tbsp. each cinnamon, nutmeg, cloves	

Recipe calls for whiskey. I now use 1 cup sherry jell. Bake on pastry using individual pans. Make meringue of whites. *Mrs. Ruth B. Lindsley.*

173

Chocolate Pie

1 pt. milk
2 tbsp. flour or corn
   starch

3 egg yolks (beat well)
1 cake chocolate
   (chop fine)

6 tbsp. sugar

Cook, stirring constantly until thick. Pour into pie crust already browned.

Meringue:—One teaspoon sugar to each white of egg.

Mrs. J. H. Miller.

Apple Meringue Pie

3 egg whites
1 lemon (grated, rind
   only)

2 cups stewed apples
   sugar to taste

Beat the whites to a stiff froth, add the grated rind of 1 lemon then add the two cups of stewed apples (worked through a sieve) and mix thoroughly with the egg whites and lemon. Sweeten to taste. Put in pie shells and bake about 10 minutes.

Mrs. L. S. Sabin.

Lemon Pie

Pastry:—
   1 cup flour
1/3 cup butter and lard
    mixed
    (or all butter)
⅛ tsp. salt
   cold water

Filling:—
4 to 6 eggs (beaten
   separately)
1 lemon (juice and
   rind)
½ cup sugar

Make pastry with above ingredients listed under pastry, using enough cold water to hold together, about 1 tablespoon. Roll dough away from you, bake in hot oven about ten minutes.

Filling:—Beat yolks very light, add sugar and beat until

foamy, mix with juice and rind of lemon, beat again, cook in double boiler until quite thick, stirring constantly. Beat whites stiff; add 2 tablespoons sugar; put half the whites with the custard mixture and put with pie crust. Use other half of whites for meringue. Put in oven and brown.

Mrs. Philip Prather.

Date Pie

4 eggs (beaten separately)
2 cups sugar
3 tsp. vinegar
½ tsp. cloves
1 tsp. cinnamon
1 tbsp. butter
1 cup dates
1½ cups pecans

Beat yolks, add sugar, beat until light. Add other ingredients, folding in the stiffly beaten whites last. Put in uncooked pastry shell and cook in slow oven 45 minutes. Serve with whipped cream or with cheese.

Mrs. T. A. Rose.

French Lemon Pie

3 eggs beaten separately. Beat yolks light and add ½ cup sugar, 2 tablespoons cold water, grated rind of 1 lemon and juice of 2 lemons. Cook in double boiler until thick. Beat the whites stiff and gradually add 2 tablespoons sugar, add to above mixture and cook all together until thoroughly hot. Have crust baked and put in lemon filling and brown under flame. *Mrs. L. S. Sabin.*

Molasses Pie

4 eggs (beaten separately, then together)
1 cup sugar
1½ cups dark molasses
1 cup cream
2 tbsp. butter
2 tbsp. flour
1 small nutmeg

Makes 2 small pies. *Mrs. Henry D. Lindsley, Jr.*

Puddings and Desserts

Woodford Pudding

½ cup butter   1 cup sugar

Cream together and add 3 beaten eggs, yolks and all.

1 cup blackberry jam   ½ cup of flour

½ tsp. allspice and nut-   1 tsp. soda dissolved in
meg to taste   2 tsp. buttermilk

Serve hot with hard sauce of butter and sugar.

Mrs. Barny Miller, Millermore, Dallas.

Date Tarts

3 eggs   1 package dates

¾ cup sugar   1 cup nuts

2 tbsp. flour   1 tsp. baking powder

flavor with vanilla or whiskey

Beat yolks with sugar. Put whites well beaten in last. Bake in well greased muffin pans in slow oven 15 or 20 minutes. Serve with whipped cream.

Mrs. J. L. Puterbaugh.

Rice Pudding

1 cup cooked rice   2 eggs

1/3 cup sugar   1 tsp. vanilla

2 cups milk   ½ cup raisins

Stir all together except whites of eggs and steam in top of double boiler until it forms a custard. Take from stove, pour in glass baking dish. Spread beaten whites together with two tablespoons sugar over top and set in oven until slightly brown. Serve warm or cold.

Mrs. Paul Platter.

Chocolate Pudding

1½ cups powdered sugar
½ cup butter
2 eggs, well beaten, separately
½ cup milk

¾ cake sweet chocolate dissolved in two tbsp. hot water
1½ cups flour
1 tsp. baking powder
1 tsp. vanilla

Cream butter and sugar. Add yolks and flour and milk, chocolate, and well beaten whites. Steam three hours.

Sauce:—One cup powdered sugar, ½ cup butter; cream well together. Add yolks of two eggs. Set away to cool. Just before serving add 4 tablespoons whiskey.

Miss Olive Shelmire.

Burnt Almond Charlotte

½ cup sugar (caramel-ized)
¾ cup almonds (blanch-ed and chopped fine)
¾ cup milk
1 tsp. vanilla

sherry
½ box or two tbsp. of granulated gelatine
1/3 cup hot water
lady fingers
½ cup sugar

Whip 3 ounces cream. Caramelize sugar, add almonds, remove from fire and pound fine. Cook this in ¾ cup milk three minutes and add ½ cup sugar. Soak gelatine in hot water three minutes, add to mixture and put on ice until it jells. Add vanilla to the whipped cream, fold this into the jelly. Line a mould with the lady fingers which have been soaked in sherry wine. Fill mould with jelly mixture and put on ice to harden.

Mrs. J. W. Allen.

177

Boston Cream Pie

Cake part:—

1 scant cup sugar	2 whole eggs
1 scant cup flour	1 tsp. baking powder

6 eggs (yolks)

Beat eggs well, add sugar which has been sifted three times. Beat all ten minutes, add flour which has been sifted three times with one teaspoon baking powder in it. Put in angel food cake pan and bake 30 minutes in slow oven.

Custard part:—

½ qt. milk	2 whole eggs
1 cup sugar	1 tbsp. flour

1 tsp. vanilla

Let milk come to a boil, add sugar, then eggs well beaten, then flour and vanilla. Cook in double boiler until quite thick, stirring constantly. Split cake when cake and custard are cold. Use custard for filling. Ice with icing made as follows:

2 cups sugar	3 egg whites
½ cup water	1 tsp. vanilla

Boil sugar and water until it threads. Pour over stiffly beaten egg whites. Beat until stiff enough to spread on cake; when this icing has set, cover with a chocolate icing made as follows:

½ cup sugar	3 tbsp. water

½ cake Baker's chocolate

Melt chocolate in double boiler, add water and sugar and when sugar has dissolved, spread on cake.

Ollie Dorsey.

Ice-Box Chocolate Freeze

2 cakes sweet chocolate   4 eggs (separated)
  (German or ambro-   2 tbsp. powdered sugar
    sia)   1 tsp. vanilla
      3 tbsp. boiling water

Melt the chocolate, add water, sugar in double boiler. Take off stove; add egg yolks one at a time; beat well, then add vanilla and egg whites, beaten stiff. Line a mould with lady fingers, the round sides out, and cover with the chocolate mixture, then lady fingers, then chocolate, till used. Keep in refrigerator over night. Serve with whipped cream.

Mrs. Paul Platter.

Marshmallow Pudding

½ lb. marshmallows   1 pt. cream
¼ lb. candied cherries   1 cup nuts
      sherry wine

Dice cherries and soak 1 hour in sherry to cover. Chop nuts fine, cut marshmallows in small pieces and mix all ingredients. Add whipped cream, place in a mould and set on ice for several hours.   *Mrs. J. B. Shelmire.*

Orange Pudding

2 oranges   9 tbsp. sugar
2 eggs   4 tsp. cornstarch
2 cups milk   1 tbsp. butter
     4 tbsp. water

Cut the orange small and cover with 6 tablespoons sugar and let stand on ice. Beat egg yolks with rest of sugar, cornstarch, butter, water and milk. Cook until stiff, stirring constantly. Let cool, then pour over oranges and mix well. Beat the egg whites and 2 tablespoons of sugar, and place on top. Brown in quick oven.

Mrs. Ross Bradfield.

Simple Dessert

1 pkg. cherry gelatine	1 cup walnuts or pecans
1 pt. boiling water	1 cup chopped pineapple
½ pt. cream	cherries
1 doz. macaroons	1 pt. water

Add 1 pint boiling water to the gelatine, and set aside to cool. When it becomes a little stiff, whip; then add whipped cream, nuts, pineapple, macaroons crumbled fine. Place in ice-box to set. When ready to serve, top with whipped cream, sprinkled with nuts and macaroon crumbs and cherries. *Edalah Connor Glover.*

Delmonico Pudding

¾ box of gelatine	1 glass of rum
8 eggs	10 tbsp. sugar
6 cups milk	1 tbsp. vanilla

Soak gelatine in milk ½ hour. Then heat until it comes to a boil. Cream sugar and egg yolks, pour hot milk over them and cook in double boiler until thick. When nearly cool, add the egg whites beaten stiff. Line a mould with macaroons and crystalized fruits in alternate layers and add filling, flavored with the rum and vanilla. Serve with whipped cream. *Mrs. L. S. Sabin.*

Apple Batter Pudding

1 egg	½ cup sweet milk
8 apples	½ cup sugar
1 cup flour	1 tsp. baking powder

Beat the egg and make into a batter with the sugar, milk, flour, and baking powder. Into a greased pan, slice the apples, pour the batter over it and bake about 20 minutes. Serve with a nut sauce. *Mrs. R. M. Sanders.*

Old English Plum Pudding

8 eggs	1 pt. flour
1 pt. milk	1 loaf stale bread
1 pt. sugar	1 lb. raisins
cinnamon and allspice	1 lb. currants
to taste	1 lb. citron

1 lb. beef suet

Crumble bread fine, and let soak in the milk. Beat eggs and sugar until light, then add flour. Beat well, then add fruit, spices and suet and add all to bread and milk. This will make 1 large or 2 small puddings. Steam large pudding 4½ hours. The puddings should be put in a bucket and sealed tight to steam. *Elizabeth D. Hardie.*

Date Pudding

6 eggs separated	1 cup powdered sugar
1 cup of chopped and	4 tbsp. bread crumbs
seeded dates	1 tsp. baking powder
1 cup of chopped pecans	1 tsp. vanilla

Cream the sugar and egg yolks. Add baking powder, bread crumbs, nuts and dates and vanilla, then the stiffly beaten egg whites. Cook about 15 minutes in a hot oven, but do not bake until hard. Serve with whipped cream. *Mrs. R. B. Dupree, Waco.*

Cocoanut Pudding

1 grated cocoanut	½ cup bread crumbs
½ pt. milk	½ cup sugar
2 eggs	1 tbsp. butter

Soak the bread crumbs in milk, cream the butter and sugar and mix with the eggs beaten together. Mix with the bread crumbs, add cocoanut and set the pan in a pan of hot water and bake in a moderate oven. Let cool and serve with whipped cream. *Mrs. R. B. Dupree, Waco.*

Bancroft Pudding

1 egg	½ cup sweet milk
1 cup sugar	4 tbsp. butter
1½ cups flour	½ tsp. baking powder

1 tsp. vanilla

Cream butter and sugar, add eggs well beaten, then the flour (sifted with baking powder) and milk, alternately; and last, the vanilla. Bake 30 minutes in a moderate oven. Serve with the following sauce:

2 eggs   1 cup sugar   1 cup cream

Beat eggs together, add sugar and cream and beat until the consistency of whipped cream and serve at once.

Mrs. A. B. Webster.

Candy Pudding

4 lbs. sugar	1 tsp. vanilla
¼ lb. raisins	½ lb. grated cocoanut
¼ lb. dates	¼ cup walnuts
¼ lb. figs	¼ cup pecans
¼ lb. citron	¼ cup almonds
¼ lb. candied pineapple	¼ cup Brazil nuts
¼ lb. candied cherries	1 pt. water
	pinch of cream of tartar

Cook sugar and water and cream of tartar, skimming the top before it begins to boil, but do not touch after boiling begins. Let it boil until it forms a soft ball in cold water, then pour in a large platter to cool. When cool, add vanilla and beat with a large silver fork, giving long even strokes. After it creams, knead on a biscuit board with the hands, adding the chopped fruits, cocoanut and nuts. After it is thoroughly kneaded, place in a buttered mould and allow to stand several days.

Mrs. Warren Jones.

Frozen Plum Pudding

2 eggs	½ cup seeded raisins
1 pt. cream	½ cup currants
1 cup sugar	½ cup candied cherries
1 cup water	½ cup almonds
4 tbsp. sherry wine	½ cup English walnuts

Cook the sugar and water until it threads, then pour slowly over beaten egg whites and beat until stiff. When cold, add the cream, whipped, then sherry and fruits and nuts. Pour into a freezer, cover carefully. Pack in ice and salt and leave for three or four hours.

Mrs. Fred Fleming.

Macaroon Pudding

12 macaroons	½ cup cold water
12 candied cherries	½ cup sugar
1 pt. cream	½ cup hot water
1 tsp. gelatine	½ cup pecans

½ tsp. vanilla

Soak gelatine in the cold water, add hot water and sugar. Cut up cherries, crumble macaroons and have cream whipped just as gelatine is ready to congeal. Stir all ingredients into gelatine and set on ice for ½ hour. This will serve eight people.

Mrs. Walter Dealey.

Lemon Pudding

6 eggs	3 lemons
6 tbsp. sugar	1 cup water

½ cup gelatine

Cream the sugar and egg yolks, add lemon juice, then the gelatine, which has been dissolved in water. Beat until very light and fold in the whites which have been beaten stiff.

Mrs. L. S. Sabin.

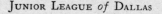

Steam Apple Pudding

3 cups sifted bread crumbs	3 eggs
3 cups chopped apples	1 tbsp. ground cinnamon
1 cup sugar	1 tsp. ground mace
½ cup seeded raisins	½ tsp. ground cloves

Mix the apples, bread crumbs, raisins and spices. Then stir in the beaten egg yolks and fold in the stiffly beaten whites last. Steam in a mould three hours, and serve with a hard butter sauce. *Mrs. H. D. Ardrey.*

Cabinet Pudding

6 eggs	6 tbsp. sugar
½ pkg. gelatine	1 cup sherry
1 doz. macaroons	1 cup nuts
candied cherries	

Beat egg yolks with sugar and sherry and cook until thick in double boiler. Dissolve gelatine in it and let cool. Beat egg whites, add nuts and cherries and mix with custard. Line a bowl with the macaroons and fill with custard. Serve with whipped cream. *Mrs. W. C. Witwer.*

Frozen Pudding

1 cup milk	½ cup raisins
1 cup cream	½ cup currants
2 sqs. chocolate	½ tsp. cinnamon
vanilla or brandy to taste	½ tsp. cloves
	½ cup sugar

Scald the milk, sugar and cream in a double boiler. Add the chocolate, melted over hot water, then the raisins, currants, spices, and when cool, the flavoring. Pack and freeze. Serve with whipped cream flavored with brandy (if possible. *Mrs. C. C. Slaughter, Jr.*

Prune Charlotte

1 lb. large prunes	½ cup sugar
2 eggs	½ cup nuts
½ box gelatine	1 cup prune juice

Stew prunes until very soft in enough water to make 1 cup prune juice. Drain and stone the prunes and run thru a vegetable strainer. Take ½ cup cold prune juice and pour over gelatine; when dissolved, add ½ cup boiling juice. Stir until dissolved. Add to prune pulp with sugar. Stir fast for a few minutes until cold. Then add stiffly beaten egg whites and nuts and place on ice to set. Serve with whipped cream. *Mrs. R. W. Baird.*

Caramel Pudding

4 eggs	1 pt. milk
½ cup sugar (white)	½ cup sugar (burnt)

Beat eggs together, then beat in the white sugar. Let milk come to a boil and add. Burn ½ cup sugar in an iron frying pan and pour into a shallow pudding dish. Then add other ingredients. Set in a pan of hot water and bake twenty minutes. Serve with whipped cream, when cold.

Mrs. Lewis Smith.

Fig Pudding

1 lb. figs	1 cup sugar
½ lb. suet	2 cups milk
1 cup nuts	2 cups bread crumbs
1 tsp. salt	1 tsp. cinnamon
4 eggs (beaten separately)	½ tsp. cloves

Chop figs, nuts and suet. Mix bread crumbs through fig mixture. Add sugar, salt and spices. Add yolks and lastly beaten whites. Steam four hours. Serve with hard sauce. *Mrs. J. L. Dreibelbis.*

Chocolate Souffle

1 tbsp. cornstarch	1 tbsp. sweet chocolate
½ cup cream or milk	3 eggs
2 tbsp. sugar	½ tbsp. vanilla

2 tbsp. butter (warm)

Mix cornstarch with milk or cream to a smooth paste. Add powdered sugar and pour into a sauce pan containing the warm butter. Stir over a fire until it thickens and boils. Pour into a basin. Add powdered sweet chocolate and let cool. Separate eggs, beat separately. Add yolks to cornstarch mixture and add vanilla. Beat well for a few minutes. Add beaten whites and pour into a buttered souffle mould. Bake in quick oven ½ hour and longer if necessary. Serve with whipped cream.

The Commission Shop of Minneapolis.

Refrigerator Cake

½ lb. unsalted butter	1 lemon (juice and rind)
2 cups sugar	(cut in small pieces)
2 eggs	1 orange (juice)
36 lady fingers	1 cup nuts

This must be made in pan, the bottom of which can be removed. Mix all well except lady fingers. Line bottom and sides of pan with lady fingers. Then arrange in alternate layers with the mixture. Let stand 24 hours. Lift out, cover with whipped cream and serve.

Mrs. J. C. Chidsey.

Nut Souffle

3 eggs (beaten separately)   ¾ cup sugar
½ cup grated pecans

Add the sugar to the yolks and cream thoroughly. Then add the stiffly beaten whites and the grated pecan meats. Bake very slowly until set. Serve cold with whipped cream.

Charlotte Russe

3 eggs   ½ pt. cream
1 pt. milk   5 tbsp. sugar
              ½ pkg. gelatine

Heat milk and while hot, put in beaten egg yolks and sugar and cook until thick. Soften gelatine in a little water and dissolve it in custard, while hot. When cool, add the beaten egg whites and whipped cream and beat until thick.

Mrs. A. E. Hutchinson.

Lady Fingers and Fruit Dessert

¼ box gelatine   1/3 cup sugar
¼ cup cold water   1 tsp. vanilla
1 pint cream   ¼ cup boiling water
1 doz. lady fingers   small can of any
                                  fruit

Soak gelatine in cold water until soft. Add boiling water and beat to cream rapidly. Add fruit and whipped cream. Pour into moulds lined with lady fingers.

Miss Olive Shelmire.

Date Pudding

3 egg whites   1 cup nuts (cut in halves)
1 tsp. baking powder   1 cup dates (cut in halves)
1 cup sugar   1 tbsp. flour

Mix baking powder and flour, and mix with dates and nuts, rubbing in well with the hands. Whip whites until stiff; gradually add sugar, and then fold in the floured dates and nuts. Bake in a slow over about 25 minutes. Cut in squares and serve with whipped cream.

Rhoda Young.

Spanish Cream

1/3 box gelatine   1 ½ cups sugar
1 qt. milk   4 eggs

Soak the gelatine in the milk for 1 hour. Beat sugar and egg yolks and add. Cook in double boiler for 20 minutes, stirring often; beat egg whites. Take cream from the fire, stir in whites, flavor with vanilla and beat hard for five minutes. Set in ice-box to chill.

Mrs. A. B. Webster.

Graham Pudding

5 eggs   1 cup ground nuts
1 ½ cups sugar   1 tsp. baking powder
1 ¼ graham crackers

Beat egg yolks and sugar together. Add baking powder to graham cracker crumbs and add nuts. Fold in the stiffly beaten egg whites and bake in a slow oven. Serve with whipped cream.

Mrs. Alf Haynes.

Orange Trifle

½ box or 2 tbsp. of   1 cup sugar
  gelatine   1 cup orange juice
½ cup of cold water   1 tbsp. lemon juice
½ cup of boiling water   whip from 1 qt. cream
  grated rind of one
    orange

Soak gelatine in cold water; add boiling water, sugar; cool and then add orange and lemon juice and grated rind. When the mixture begins to harden, line mould with a layer of jelly, then whipped cream, alternating until all or both are used. Then give all one big slight stir with spoon. Set aside to harden. Serve with whipped cream.

Mrs. J. W. Allen.

Almond Tartlets

Beat to thick froth the yolks of four eggs and 1 cup of powdered sugar. Add the stiffly beaten whites, 2 tablespoons of grated chocolate, one-half cup of blanched almonds and 1 teaspoon baking powder, mixed with very scant cup of cracker dust. Bake in buttered muffin rings. Fill them one-half full and place on a baking sheet covered with buttered paper. When baked and cool, split open and spread whipped cream between and on top.

Edna Ball.

Coffee Chocolate Pudding

1 pt. cream
1 cup very strong coffee, boiling hot
½ cup sugar
4 tbsp. ground chocolate
2 tbsp. ground almonds

Whip cream until stiff, add sugar. Pour boiling coffee over chocolate, add almonds and beat slowly into whipped cream. Mix well, pour into mould and cover lightly. Pack in ice and salt for 4 hours.

Mrs. T. W. Griffiths, Jr.

Cream Puffs

1 cup water
piece of butter size of an egg
3 eggs
pinch salt
flour

Boil water and butter together, stir in flour until smooth. When lukewarm, stir in eggs, one at a time. Cook in muffin pan in slow oven for one hour, or until puffs are dry. This recipe makes six puffs.

Mrs. Tom Camp.

Laurabelle Cake

4 egg yolks	1 cup sugar
3 tbsp. cold water	1½ tbsp. cornstarch
1 tsp. lemon extract	1½ tsp. baking powder
6 whites	flour

Beat eggs and water until very light. Add sugar; beat two minutes. Put 1½ tablespoons cornstarch in cup; fill cup with flour. Sift with 1½ teaspoons baking powder. Combine two mixtures, add flavoring and the stiffly beaten whites of six eggs. Bake in moderate oven 40 minutes. When cold, split crosswise in four layers.

Filling:

1 qt. milk	1 lb. butter (washed or
1/3 cup flour	creamed)
1/3 cup sugar	2 sq. chocolate
1 tbsp. vanilla	

Put milk in double boiler, when scalding hot, add sugar and flour, sifted together. Cook fifteen minutes, stirring constantly. Add creamed butter; stir until melted. To one third of this mixture, add melted chocolate; to remaining two thirds, add vanilla. *Have ready* 1/3 cup chopped fine pecans, ½ cup sugar caramelized together in small frying pan, and put on board to harden. After it hardens, grate to a powder.

Cover first layer of cake with chocolate filling; sprinkle with nut powder; cover second layer with vanilla filling; sprinkle with nut powder; third layer with chocolate; sprinkle top layer and sides with vanilla filling and sprinkle more heavily with nut powder. Filling must be warm to melt nut mixture slightly.

Mrs. Lloyd Leslie, Sherman, Texas.

Ice Box Cake

1½ doz. lady fingers
1 doz. macaroons
¼ lb. butter
1/3 cup sugar
2 eggs unbeaten
½ cup chopped blanched
    almonds
1 tsp. vanilla
½ pt. cream

Use spring mould. Cover bottom with macaroons, line the sides with lady fingers. Cream butter and sugar until very light. Beat in one egg at a time, beating five minutes before adding second egg. Beat again five minutes and add almonds. Crumble remaining macaroons and lady fingers together and add to mixture. Add vanilla. Pack in mould and let set in ice box for 24 hours. To serve, remove sides, pile the center with strawberries or sliced peaches and cover with whipped cream.

Mrs. T. W. Griffiths, Jr.

Almond and Mocha Pudding

2 eggs
2 tbsp. powdered sugar
1 tbsp. butter
¾ cup strong cold coffee
½ pt. cream, whipped
3 doz. lady fingers
½ lb. almonds cut up

Cream sugar and butter, add to eggs, well beaten. Add coffee. Lay one dozen lady fingers in halves on large platter, first placing 2 sheets of wax paper in platter. Spread cake with coffee mixture, sparingly, being careful, however, to moisten all. Sprinkle almonds which have been blanched, cut up, and slightly browned in oven, over moist lady fingers, then spread half the whipped cream. Make three layers thus, leaving the cream off the top layer. Let stand over night (or 5 hours). When ready to serve transfer to serving dish by lifting wax paper and slipping out from under so as not to break the mass of pudding. Cover entirely with half pint of whipped cream and serve whole.

Mrs. Earl Hulsey.

Velvet Pudding

5 eggs, beaten separately   1 cup sugar

1 heaping tbsp. cornstarch dissolved in a little milk and added to yolks of eggs and sugar. Mix well. Boil 3 pts. milk, pour into yolks and sugar. Keep on fire until thick enough to cut with knife. Flavor with vanilla and pour into baking dish. Add ½ cup sugar to whites, spread on pudding, brown and serve very cold. Serves 12.

Mrs. Henry D. Lindsley, Jr.

Pineapple Cake

2 cups flour   1 egg
1¼ cups butter   whipped cream
1 lb. brown sugar   1 can grated pineapple

Sift flour in bowl. Add egg, ½ cup butter and juice from can of pineapple. Put ¾ cup of butter and brown sugar and grated pineapple in frying pan and cook 3 minutes. Then pour this mixture into a deep pan and pour over it the cake mixture. Put in hot oven and bake 30 to 45 minutes. Turn out on big platter and cover with whipped cream and serve while hot. Serves 10.

Mrs. Seth Miller.

Frozen Orange Pudding

5 eggs   1½ pts. cream
8 oranges   3 tbsp. sugar
2 tbsp. flour   1 tsp. vanilla

Cream yolks of eggs with sugar and flour then stir in cream and cook in double boiler, stirring constantly. Let cool then stir in vanilla and orange juice with a little of the grated peel. Let cool and pack in freezer. Use white of eggs as meringue, or serve with whipped cream. This amount serves 8 people.

Mrs. Eugene Duggan.

Brittle Pudding

1 cup chopped pecans   1 tsp. vanilla
½ cup flour   ½ cup sugar
1 tsp. baking powder

Mix all ingredients, put in greased pan and bake quickly until brown. Add powdered sugar slowly just as it comes from oven. When cold, break in pieces and serve with whipped cream.

Mrs. H. R. Aldredge.

Hansel Pudding

Beat the yolks of 6 eggs with 6 tablespoons of sugar. Add one cup of Marchino Cherries with juice, boil, stirring constantly until thick. Dissolve one tablespoon of gelatine in cold water. Stir into mixture and cook again until thick.

Remove from fire and add one cup of chopped pecans and 6 stale macaroons rolled fine. Beat whites stiff and fold in last. Serve cold with whipped cream.

Mrs. Philip Miller.

Raspberry Pudding

1 egg   1 cup flour
butter size of an egg   ½ cup milk
1 tsp. baking powder   ½ cup canned rasp-
½ cup chopped nuts   berries
1 cup sugar

Strain raspberries. Bake mixture until quite crisp and serve with following sauce.

Sauce

1 tbsp. butter   1 tbsp. flour
½ cup sugar   1 cup berry juice

Mrs. Willie Carrow.

Chocolate Sauce

1 cup sugar   ½ cup cream
2 squares chocolate   vanilla
                    butter

Slice chocolate. Mix all ingredients. Boil only 4 minutes. Nice on ice cream or cake. Serve hot or cold.

Mrs. William J. Moroney.

Orange Marmalade Pudding

1 cup bread crumbs   1 tsp. soda
1 cup orange marmalade   1 cup chopped beef suet
1 tbsp. sugar   1 egg
                  1 tbsp. flour

Dry bread crumbs to roll. Dissolve level tsp. of soda in hot water. Steam in closed pan for 2 or more hours and serve with the following sauce.

Sauce

2 tbsp. butter   2 eggs
1 cup sugar   1 tsp. brandy

Beat whites of 2 eggs stiff. Beat butter, sugar and yolks of eggs to a cream. Put all ingredients in a double boiler and beat constantly for 2 minutes. Add brandy.

Mrs. K. N. Hapgood.

Coffee Mousse

1 cup strong coffee   1 cup sugar
yolks 3 eggs   1 tbsp. gelatine
                pt. whipped cream

Beat eggs until light. Add sugar and coffee. Cook until it coats the spoon. Then add gelatine which has been dissolved in a little cold water and when cold add one pint whipped cream. Pack in salt for several hours.

Mrs. J. L. Dreibelbis.

Apple Dumpling

1½ cups flour	½ pt. cream whipped
1 tsp. salt	½ cup Crisco
1 lemon	6 apples
6 tsp. seeded raisins	3 bananas
½ lb. almonds or	nutmeg
pecans	½ lb. butter
1½ cups sugar	½ cup milk
marshmallows	

Sift flour and salt together and add Crisco, mixing very fine with knife or spoon. Add ice water enough to make stiff dough. Roll very thin and cut around a saucer to make six dumplings, or cut in squares. Fill center of each dumpling with an apple that has been sliced thin and about half a banana sliced thin, also add 1 teaspoon raisins, 1 tablespoon chopped nuts, 1 tablespoon melted butter, 1 teaspoon lemon juice and 1 tablespoon sugar. Grate nutmeg over the top, fold pastry over it, and on top place small lump of butter. Put the dumplings in a pan half full of water and pour over all, one cup full of sugar. Set in hot oven and cook until done. Serve with marshmallow sauce made by soaking marshmallows in ½ cup milk or cream until real soft. Whip ½ pint cream sweetened with 2 tablespoons sugar and fold in marshmallows.

Mrs. John O. McReynolds.

Three in One Ice Cream

juice of 3 lemons	3 cups sugar
juice of 3 oranges	3 cups water
3 bananas	½ pt. cream

Mix all in bowl, except the cream, and let stand one hour. Put through a sieve, add cream and freeze. Serves 10.

Mrs. John O. Wharton.

Hot Chocolate Pudding

2 oz. chocolate	1 pt. sweet milk
1½ cups bread crumbs	2 eggs
1/3 nutmeg	1 tsp. salt

1 cup raisins

Grate chocolate. Beat eggs with sugar. Grate nutmeg. Boil chocolate, milk and salt together. Pour this over bread. Let it stand. Do not stir till cold. Beat eggs with butter and sugar. Add fruit and mix with crumbs. Butter mould and steam one hour. Serve with creamy sauce.

Mrs. W. E. Crow.

Date Meringue

3 egg whites beaten light	1 cup dates chopped
1 cup nuts chopped	2 scant cups sugar
1 tsp. baking powder	1 tsp. vanilla

1 tsp. flour

Beat baking powder in whites of eggs. Roll dates and nuts in flour. Add to beaten eggs. Bake about 45 minutes in shallow loaf pan. Cut in squares. Serve with whipped cream.

Mrs. Frank Cullinan.

Carrot Pudding

1 cup raw carrots grated	2 rounding tbsp. butter
1 cup raw potatoes grated	2 cups flour
1 cup brown sugar	1 tsp. salt
1½ cups raisins, chopped	1 tsp. cinnamon
	1 tsp. soda
	1 tsp. cloves

Mix and steam for two hours in baking powder cans. Serve with hard sauce and whipped cream.

Mrs. R. R. Penn.

Pineapple Bavarian Cream

1 pt. canned pineapple	1 small cup sugar
½ cup cold water	½ box gelatine
1 pt. cream	½ cup boiling water

Let gelatine soak in ½ cup cold water for two hours. Chop pineapple. Put on fire with the sugar. Let simmer 20 minutes. Add boiling water to gelatine. Steam it with the cooked pineapple 10 minutes. Let cool and beat in whipped cream. Pack in mould to harden. Serve with whipped cream or custard sauce.

Mrs. W. E. Crow.

Sharky Custard

3 cups sugar	1 cup jam
1 cup buttermilk	½ cup butter
5 eggs	lemon

Cream butter and 1 cup sugar, add jam and buttermilk, then well beaten yolks. Bake on pastry. Make meringue of the 5 whites of eggs. Add 2 cups sugar. Flavor with lemon and brown.

Mrs. W. E. Crow.

Pudding Sauce

½ cup butter	1 cup powdered sugar
1¼ cups cream	4 tbsp. wine or 1 tsp. vanilla

If vanilla is used, add 4 tbsp. more of cream. Beat butter to a cream. Add sugar gradually, beating all the time. When creamy, add wine, then cream. When all is well beaten, cook in double boiler until all is smooth and creamy.

Mrs. W. E. Crow.

Raisin and Nut Pie

2 eggs	½ cup raisins
½ cup butter	1 tbsp. vinegar
2 tbsp. cream	1 tsp. cinnamon

Add a little water to raisins and cook. Melt butter in this mixture. Add other ingredients and the eggs last. Put in uncooked pastry and bake ½ hour. This recipe makes one pie.

Pastry:

1½ cups flour	¼ tsp. baking powder
½ cup Crisco	¼ tsp. salt

4 tbsp. boiling water

Mix above in usual manner.

Mrs. John O. Wharton.

Nesselrode Pudding

1 qt. milk	1 cup sugar
5 eggs	1 cup chopped pecans
1 cup chopped raisins or dates	1½ dozen macaroons vanilla to taste
1 envelope gelatine	3 large spoonfuls brandy or rye

Cream sugar with yolk of eggs. Let milk boil 3 minutes. Dissolve gelatine and add. When cold stir in macaroons, dates and raisins, nuts, vanilla and brandy. This is good frozen, leaving out the gelatine and adding 1 pt. of whipped cream. *Mrs. F. M. Butt.*

Orange Charlotte

One-half envelope Knox gelatine soaked in ¼ cup cold water and dissolved in ½ cup boiling water. To this, add 1 cup sugar and when dissolved, the juice of 1 lemon. Strain and when cool add 1 cup orange juice and pulp. When the jelly begins to form, beat until light, then add the whites of 3 eggs beaten stiff and beat together thoroughly. Turn into a mould lined with lady fingers, and when serving, sprinkle with chopped nuts. A pint of whipped cream may be used instead of the whites of the eggs, or it may be served with the charlotte.

Miss Paulula Dunn.

Charlotte Russe

4 egg yolks	1 pt. milk
2 egg whites	1 pt. cream
4 heaping tsp. sugar	1 pkg. (paper) gelatine

1 tsp. vanilla

Dissolve gelatine in ½ cup cold water for 10 minutes. Fill cup with milk, put pint milk in double boiler and when hot add yolk (beaten with sugar) add gelatine, stirring until it thickens. Remove from fire and pour over whites. Set aside to cool. When it begins to set, add 1 pint whipped cream, flavor, and add more sugar if not sweet enough. Serves 8.

Mrs. L. S. Sabin.

Batter Pudding

8 eggs beaten separately	1 pt. flour
1 qt. sweet milk	¼ tsp. salt

Bake in moderate oven forty minutes. Serve at once with hard sauce. Halve recipe for small pudding.

Hard Sauce:

Cream ½ cup butter, gradually adding 1½ cups sugar. Beat thoroughly, then add unbeaten white of one egg. Beat till smooth. Recipe calls for whiskey or sherry wine for seasoning, but now use ½ cup of sherry jell.

Mrs. Ruth B. Lindsley.

Strawberry Souffle

1 qt. strawberries   3 egg whites, beaten stiff
powdered sugar to taste

Rub strawberries through fine strainer. Add powdered sugar, and mix in the beaten egg whites. Bake in a quick oven between 15 and 20 minutes, and serve immediately. Whipped cream may be added, if preferred.

Mrs. H. R. Aldredge.

Gelatine Bessie

1 pt. grape juice   1 pt. strawberry juice
box gelatine

Soften ½ of the gelatine in a little cold water, then dissolve it in the hot grape juice. Put in ring mould and allow to congeal. When it is ready, repeat the above process, using the strawberry juice which has been sweetened to taste. Allow to cool thoroughly and then pour in on top of congealed grape juice. Garnish with fresh strawberries and serve with whipped cream.

Mrs. Frank Austin.

Eggs and Omelets

Poached Eggs—A La Boeldien

3 eggs   3 bread crusts
2 tomatoes   butter

Poach eggs; scald tomatoes, just enough to peel; drain and cut in slices, then dice. Put the pieces in a pan with oil; cook on a brisk fire until the quantity is reduced, without dissolving. Season highly; bestrew with parsley. With these tomatoes fill the hollowed bread crusts; on each one, place a poached egg. Heat at oven door, basting with melted butter.

Mr. Morrison, Oriental Hotel.

Eggs and Green Peppers

4 eggs   1 tbsp. butter
4 green peppers   1 tbsp. grated cheese
½ cup cream

Beat eggs with the cream, chopped peppers, butter and cheese. Cook all until thick and pour on toast.

Mrs. Walter Lamberth.

Plain Omelet

6 eggs   salt and pepper to taste
3 tbsp. milk   1 tbsp. butter

Beat the eggs separately, stirring the milk into the yolks and melt the butter in a frying pan. Stir the yolks and whites together, season with salt and pepper and turn into hot frying pan. Keep omelet from sticking to pan by slipping knife or cake turner under frequently. When it is set, fold over lightly and brown in a quick oven. Serve at once.

Edalah Connor Glover.

Scrambled Eggs, With Peppers

1 green pepper	butter
1 small onion	4 eggs
2 tbsp. cream	

Beat the eggs and cream together; chop onion and pepper together and fry in butter, mix them with eggs, cook slowly, stirring until done.   *Mrs. M. G. Matthews.*

Cheese Souffle

5 eggs	1 tbsp. flour
1 cup milk	butter size of walnut
1 cup grated cheese	salt, pepper and cayenne

Beat egg yolks, add sweet milk, cheese, flour (mixed to a smooth paste with milk); season with salt, pepper and butter. Fold in the egg whites, beaten stiff. Bake twenty minutes in a slow oven.   *Mrs. Mike Lively.*

Chicken Omelet

½ cup cold chicken	1 tbsp. butter
2 eggs	1 tbsp. milk
salt and pepper to taste	

Beat eggs separately, adding milk to yolks. Melt butter in omelet pan. When hot, stir eggs, chicken and seasoning together. Cook until set, fold over and brown in quick oven. Serve at once.   *Mrs. Walter Lamberth.*

Eggs Poached in Milk

Put milk in shallow sauce pan, bring to boiling point, drop the eggs into milk gently and cook until firm. Serve hot in sauce dish with a little of the milk, butter, salt and pepper. May be served on toast, using the hot milk over the toast, then egg, butter, salt and pepper.

Miss Ada Walne.

Scrambled Eggs Au Parmesian

1 dozen eggs	¼ lb. butter
½ bottle Worcestershire sauce	½ bottle Parmesian cheese
salt to taste	pepper to taste

Beat eggs well then add other ingredients. Stir until done.

Mrs. George F. Howard.

Bread Crumb Omelet

1 scant cup bread crumbs	6 eggs
1 full cup milk	2 tbsp. butter
salt to taste	cayenne pepper to taste

Pick bread apart into small pieces, fill cup lightly, add milk and soak several hours. Seperate eggs, beat yolks well. Add milk and bread mixture, season with salt, pepper and cayenne. Fold in stiffly beaten whites. Heat omelet pan or spider, put in 2 large spoons of butter, pour in mixture and bake in oven until set. This omelet can be varied by serving over it, Spanish sauce, creamed oysters or mushrooms, creamed peas or bacon curls. The following cheese sauce is also very good poured over it.

Cheese Sauce:

4 tbsp. butter	2 tbsp. flour
2 cups milk	2 cups cheese
salt	pepper
cayenne	

Melt butter, add flour, boiling milk, cook ten minutes. Add grated cheese, salt, pepper and cayenne. Do not boil after cheese is added.

Mrs. William J. Moroney.

203

Ices and Ice Creams

Frozen Egg-Nogg

1½ cups of sugar	pinch of salt
1 qt. of sweet milk	1 pt. of cream
3 eggs	8 tbsp. of Virginia Dare
2 level tbsp. of flour	jelly

Put milk in double boiler, and let come to boiling point. Take one cup of sugar and add flour, salt and mix thoroughly; add eggs; beat until creamy. Then add milk. Put back in double boiler, stir and cook until thick; let cool. When ready to freeze, whip cream, add one-half cup of sugar to cream; fold this into custard; last add eight tablespoons of Virginia Dare jelly and freeze. This will serve 10 or 12 people.

Mrs. George Robertson.

Peanut Brittle Ice Cream

1 pt. milk	½ pt. whipped cream
3 eggs	¼ cup sugar
10 cents worth peanut brittle	

Make custard of milk, eggs and sugar; cool; flavor with vanilla; add whipped cream and freeze until a thick mush; then add peanut brittle, which has been pounded to a powder, and finish freezing. Do not get custard too sweet.

Cranberry Ice

6 lemons	3 cups cranberries
3 cups sugar	2 qts. water

Boil cranberries until tender, strain. Boil sugar and water to a thin syrup. When cold, add fruit juices and freeze.

Mrs. Lloyd Price.

Frozen Chocolate Bisque

Beat together yolks of twelve eggs with one breakfast-cup full chocolate, one-fourth pound sugar. Add one quart of milk and cook slowly until thick, stirring and taking care not to let it boil. Remove and strain in bowl. When cold, mix in one quart of whipped cream. Pack two hours in ice. This will serve twelve persons. Serve with whipped cream.

Edna Ball.

Canton Sherbet

2 cups water	2 tbsp. lemon juice
½ cup sugar	4 tbsp. orange juice
⅜ cup preserved and candied ginger	¼ pt. double cream (whipped)
½ cup minced Maraschino cherries	2 tbsp. powdered sugar

Place water, sugar (½ cup) and ginger in sauce pan; boil ten minutes. Cool; add orange and lemon juice; freeze slowly. When mixture begins to freeze, add cherries and whipped cream, which has been sweetened with powdered sugar. Continue to freeze until firm and smooth. This makes small quantity.

Mrs. Paul Platter.

Hot Chocolate Sauce I

1 sq. unsweetened chocolate	1 tbsp. butter
1 cup sugar	1/3 cup boiling water
	½ tsp. vanilla

Melt chocolate, add butter, pour water gradually into it, bring to boiling point, add sugar. Boil five minutes. Cool slightly and add vanilla.

Mrs. Chas. Dexter, Jr.

Good Ice Cream

2 egg whites (well beaten)
2 tbsp. sherry
1 1/3 cups sugar
1¼ pts. cream (whipped)

Mrs. C. C. Slaughter, Jr.

Peppermint Ice Cream

1 lb. peppermint stick candy
1 qt. milk
1 qt. cream

Break candy in pieces, dissolve in milk, add cream and freeze.

Mrs. E. M. Reardon, Jr.

Pineapple Sponge

1/3 box gelatine
¼ cup cold water sugar
1 can grated pineapple
1 cup cream (whipped)
3 egg whites (beaten stiff)
lemon juice

Soak gelatine in cold water. Combine grated pineapple with water to make 2½ cups. Add gelatine and heat until gelatine is dissolved. Set aside to cool. When it begins to thicken, add cream and whites, lemon juice and sugar to taste. ·Mould as desired; serve with whipped cream.

Mrs. R. L. Henry, Waco, Texas.

Cafe Parfait

1½ cups sugar
1 cup liquid coffee
8 egg yolks
1½ qts. whipped cream

Boil sugar and coffee together until thick, pour over the well beaten egg yolks, beating constantly. Add whipped cream and beaten whites, if desired. Pack in ice and salt and let stand 3 hours. Serves twelve people.

Mrs. W. J. Moroney.

Hot Chocolate Sauce II

1 cup sugar
3 cups sweet milk

¼ cake chocolate
   (grated)
2 large tbsp. Karo

½ tbsp. butter

Stir constantly, cover and boil. Try in ice water until gummy. Cook over slow fire, then beat and beat again.

Mrs. Harrell Mason, Ft. Worth.

Grape Ice

2 cups cream
1 cup grape juice

3 tbsp. sugar
1 tsp. vanilla

Mrs. John Phelan.

Maple Mousse

1 cup maple syrup (Log
   Cabin brand)

1 pt. double cream
   (stiffly beaten)

4 eggs (beaten separately)

Put syrup in double boiler, let come to boil, but not boil. Add well beaten yolks, stir constantly until custard is thick and smooth. Take from fire and beat. When cool, add cream and then beaten egg whites. Beat again and put into mould. Pack in salt and ice 3 to 5 hours.

Mrs. Mary H. Sullenberger.

Maple Parfait

4 egg yolks

1 pt. cream

¾ cup maple syrup

Beat eggs very light, add syrup and cook in a double boiler until coating forms on spoon; stir constantly. Remove and beat until cool. Lightly fold in whipped cream. Put in mould and let freeze four or five hours.

Mrs. Wesley Norris.

Loganberry Ice

2 cups cream
1 cup Loganberry juice

3 tbsp. sugar
1 tsp. vanilla

Mrs. Lang Wharton.

Orange Souffle

2 cups sugar
½ box gelatine (dissolved in ½ cup cold water)

5 egg yolks
1 qt. cream
1 pt. orange juice

1 cup hot water

Boil sugar and water to a syrup; beat into beaten eggs and set back on fire to thicken. Pour into gelatine and cool. Stir in orange juice and whipped cream. Mould.

Mrs. J. C. Gilbert.

Frozen Fruit

2 cans peaches
1 can pineapple
8 lemons (juice only)

4 bananas
1 tbsp. gelatine
1½ cups sugar

Put peaches through colander; shred pineapple and slice bananas fine. Dissolve gelatine in one-fourth cup warm water. Mix all thoroughly. Place in secure moulds and pack in ice and salt. Let stand 4 hours. Serve with whipped cream.

Mrs. H. R. Parks.

Cream Sherbet

6 lemons (juice)
4 cups sugar

6 cups double cream
3 cups milk

grated rind of 4 lemons or 1 tsp. full

Mix and freeze.

Miss Ed Dela Wright.

Frozen Pumpkin Pie

1 large can pumpkin	1 pt. cream
2 tsp. cinnamon	1 tsp. nutmeg
2 tsp. cloves	2 eggs (whites)

Mix all and freeze in ice cream freezer. When ready to serve, put into baked pie crust which is cold. Beat the whites of two eggs until very dry; add 2 teaspoons sugar and put on top of pie. Run in very hot oven to brown.

Mrs. E. R. Callier.

Macaroon and Walnut Ice Cream

6 eggs (yolks)	6 egg whites (beaten light)
2 cups sugar	
2 tsp. vanilla	2 glasses of milk
2 doz. macaroons	2 qts. double cream
	2 cups walnuts (cut up)

Cream yolks and sugar together; add milk and fold in the beaten whites. Put in double boiler; stir constantly until very thick. Cool. Add other ingredients and freeze.

Mrs. Theodore Heizmann.

Maple Mousse

3 yolks	1 cup of maple syrup
1 cup of marshmallows	1 cup of nuts
1 tbsp. gelatine	1 tbsp. of cold water
1 pt. of cream (whipped)	½ doz. almond macaroons

Beat yolks and maple syrup together. Put in double boiler and heat until it has thickened. Add soaked gelatine to the maple syrup and eggs; beat until cold. Add all the ingredients to the stiffly beaten cream and put in the mould and pack for three hours.

Rhoda Young.

Green Gage Ice Cream

1 can green gage plums   sugar to taste
1½ cups of cream

Remove skins and seeds from plums. Put pulp through fine strainer. Add juice and sugar to taste. Add 1½ cups of cream to 1 cup plum and sugar mixture and freeze.

Melinda Simms.

Frozen Strawberries

Mash ripe strawberries through sieve, forcing as much of berry pulp through as possible. For each cup of berries take ¾ cup sugar and add enough water to make syrup. Mix together and freeze. Serve with sweetened whipped cream.

Mrs. Peter O'Donnell.

Angel Parfait

2 pts. thick whipping   2/3 pt. wine
cream   2 cups sugar
4 whites of eggs
½ cup cold water

Add wine to cream before whipping. Beat whites of eggs until stiff. Boil sugar and water until it threads. Beat it over the eggs. When cool add whipped cream. Put in ice box.

Mrs. W. E. Crow.

Victoria Pudding

1 pt. orange juice   1 pt. cream (whipped)
sugar

Sweeten orange juice to taste and freeze. Whip cream and sweeten to taste. Put the frozen orange juice and the whipped cream in alternating layers in a mould. Pack in ice and salt for 4 hours.

Mrs. Frank Austin.

Almond Ice

3 pts. water	2 tbsp. almond extract
1½ pts. sugar	1 tbsp. vanilla
juice 5 lemons	level tsp. cornstarch
rind of ½ lemon	dissolved in little
	cold water

Boil for 10 minutes the sugar, water and cornstarch. When cool add juice and extract and freeze. Serve with whipped cream or mould with cream.

Mrs. T. H. Obenchain.

Almond Orange Ice Cream

1½ cups orange juice	¼ cup lemon juice
1 tsp. vanilla	2/3 cup chopped al-
1½ cups sugar	monds

1 pt. cream

Blanch the almonds and brown in oven, then chop finely. Mix the fruit juices and sugar and let the sugar dissolve. Whip the cream, then add the cream, vanilla and almonds and freeze.

Mrs. T. H. Obenchain.

Rasberry or Strawberry Bombe

Fill a melon mould half full of raspberry or strawberry juice, which has been sweetened to taste. (A little lemon juice will bring out the berry flavor). On top of the berry juice, float enough sweetened whipped cream to fill the mould. Pack in ice and salt (2 parts ice to 1 of salt). Let stand 3 hours for 1 pt. mould, or 5 hours for a quart or larger. (Orange, lemon, apricot, peach, pineapple or grape juice may be used in place of the given recipe.)

Mrs. H. R. Aldredge.

Frozen Buttermilk

1 qt. buttermilk	1 cup sugar
1 tsp. vanilla	½ pt. cream

Freeze. Nice for invalids.

Mrs. William J. Moroney.

Frozen Strawberries with Cream

Boil 4 tablespoons of sugar in a quart of water for ½ hour. Drop into the syrup, 2 quarts or more of picked, ripe strawberries and boil for a quarter of an hour longer. When cool turn into freezer and when frozen, mix in a pint of whipped cream and serve immediately.

Miss Paulula Dunn.

Melon Mould Ice Cream

1 qt. cream	1 pt. raspberries, or strawberries
1 tsp. vanilla	

sugar

Whip cream very stiff, sweeten to taste, add the vanilla. Strain the berries and sweeten to taste, then freeze them. Line melon mould with cream, put the frozen berries in the center of cream. Pack in salt and ice for 4 or 5 hours. This serves 12 persons. *Mrs. S. I. Munger, Jr.*

Pear Melba

frozen custard	½ melba pear

Make sauce of marrons, melba sauce and sherry. Pour over all. *Mrs. Turner Pittman.*

Marron Mousse

Whip a quart of cream, flavor with syrup from 1 medium sized bottle of marrons, sweeten to taste, chop marrons finely and add. Pack in salt and ice for 5 hours and serve.

Mrs. Clinton Logan.

Beverages

Twelfth-Night Bowl

Allow one egg and one tumbler sweet hot cider to each person. Beat 6 egg yolks and one cup sugar until thick, add stiffly beaten whites, nutmeg, cinnamon, and cloves to taste. Turn in cider. Beat until frothy. Serve in hot bowl decorated with holly, artificial cherries, grapes and fern.

Mrs. W. C. Martin.

Fruit Punch

2 cups sugar	1 qt. Apollinaris
1 cup water	1 pt. strawberry syrup
1 cup cold tea	5 lemons (juice)
5 oranges (juice)	1 can grated pineapple

½ pt. Maraschino cherries

Make syrup by boiling sugar and water ten minutes; add tea, fruit juices and syrups; let stand ½ hour. Add enough ice water to make 1½ gallons liquid. Turn bowl over a piece of ice; add cherries and Apollinaris. Serves 50 people.

Mrs. Harrell Mason.

Egg-Nogg

3 gills rum	1 qt. cream
1 gill brandy	1 lb. powdered sugar
1 tsp. ground mace	1 nutmeg (grated)

10 eggs (beaten separately)

Beat yolks to a cream, add to them the other ingredients, adding the beaten whites just before the cream. Serve.

Mrs. John F. Williams.

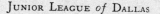

Punch For 75 People

1 gal. wine	1 cup sugar
1 cup brandy	1 cup lemon juice
1 cup Maraschino	2 cups orange juice
cherries	½ gal. Apollinaris
2 cups grated pineapple	

Mrs. C. W. Hobson.

Blackberry Cordial

Boil berries 30 minutes; squeeze out juice; to 1 qt. juice, add ½ lb. sugar, boil and skim well. While boiling, add whole allspice, ginger, cloves and cinnamon, tied in bag. Do not boil long after adding spice. When cool, add 1 pt. best brandy or whiskey to every gallon of cordial.

Mrs. Norman MacDuff, Portland.

Formula For Mixing Tea

4½ oz. Oolong   3 oz. orange Pekoe

½ oz. English breakfast tea

This formula is excellent.

Mrs. Arthur Boice.

Russian Tea

5 oranges	3 lemons
3 grapefruit	12 tsp. tea
12 tsp. allspice	12 tsp. cloves
2 cups sugar	1½ gal. water

fruit peeling of all

Cut peels, steep three minutes in 1½ cups water. Steep spice and cloves three minutes in 1½ cups water. Steep tea three minutes and strain. Mix fruit juice with all ingredients and serve piping hot. This amount will serve 30.

Mrs. S. W. King, Jr.

Pink Milk

Beat 2 eggs to a foam, add sugar and flavoring to taste and stir into a pint of rich milk. Add a few drops of fruit coloring to make it pink. Attractive to children.

Drip Coffee

Have fresh boiling water. One tablespoon ground coffee to each cup water. Pour water over grounds and set back where it will steep and keep hot, but not boil. It is best to serve with hot milk as a substitute for cream. Beat the white of an egg, put to it a small lump of butter and pour coffee into it gradually, stirring so that it will not curdle.

Mrs. John F. Williams.

Old-Fashioned Boiled Coffee

Use 1 tablespoon ground coffee to each cup and one for the pot. Into the grounds stir a little beaten egg, put into pot and add a little cold water so egg will not coagulate when boiling water is added. For each tablespoon coffee, add 1 cup boiling water. As soon as coffee boils up, put aside in a hot place and settle with a little cold water poured through spout.

Mrs. W. C. Martin.

Chocolate

2 oz. chocolate	1 cup boiling water
4 tbsp. sugar	3 cups scalded milk

Break chocolate in pieces and melt over hot water. Add sugar and boiling water. Stir until smooth and glossy. Cook 5 or 6 minutes. Add part of milk and when well mixed, add remainder of milk. Let stand over fire, beating constantly with egg beater to prevent scum forming.

Candies

Fudge

3 cups sugar   2 heaping tbsp. cocoa
1½ cups milk   1 tbsp. of butter

Cook all together until when dropped in cold water will form a soft ball. Remove from fire and pour into three small bowls. Do not touch until almost cold; add drops of vanilla and beat until it begins to cream. Drop from teaspoon on waxed paper.

Miss Marguerite Dale.

Chocolate Creams

3 cups sugar   1 tbsp. of butter
1½ cups milk   pinch of salt

Cook all together until when dropped in cold water will form a soft ball. Remove from fire and pour into a platter. Do not touch until almost cold. Add drops of vanilla and stir with silver knife until mixture crumbles. Mould into balls by rolling between the hands. Melt in double boiler ½ cake of chocolate and one tablespoon of grated paraffin. Dip the cream filling into the chocolate with the icepick. (This tastes better the second day).

Miss Marguerite Dale.

Sugared Nuts

1 cup sugar   lump of butter
1/3 cup water   1 tsp. cinnamon
2 cups pecans

Cook sugar and water until it threads; add pecans, butter and cinnamon; stir until sugared.

Mrs. D. W. Sanders.

Fluffy Ruffle Kisses

4 egg whites   1 tsp. vanilla
½ lb. powdered sugar

Beat whites until frothy; begin adding sugar and beat until it forms a sponge that can be cut with a knife. Dip a teaspoon in cold water and drop the mixture on buttered bread, spoonful at a time. Watch closely, so as not to burn. Put pecans in each kiss before baking if desired.

George Maud Fairey.
Charleston, S. C.

Chocolate Fudge

2 cups sugar
1 very large kitchen
    spoon cocoa
1 cup milk
1 tsp. vanilla

butter size of small
    egg
½ lb. pecan halves
2 rounded tbsp. marsh-
    mallow cream
    (Hipolite)

Mix sugar and cocoa until well blended, add milk and butter. Cook, stirring almost constantly until candy forms soft ball in cold water. Never over-cook as this makes candy grainy. Remove from fire; add Hipolite and vanilla. Beat for a long time until very thick and creamy. Add pecans (not chopped). Pour on greased platter.

Mrs. Chas. Dexter, Jr.

Cocoanut Candy

1 large cocoanut   4 cups sugar

Dissolve sugar in cocoanut milk; cook until it ropes. Remove from fire, beat until cool and add grated cocoanut. Pour on buttered dish and cut when cold.

George Maud Fairey,
Charleston, S. C.

Butterscotch

1½ cups sugar
1 tbsp. water

1 tbsp. vinegar
butter (size of egg)

Melt together sugar, water and vinegar; add butter and boil until it hardens in water. Do not stir. Pour on plates and cut when hard.

Jennie Maud Burgoyne.

Dandy Candy

3 cups sugar
1 cup corn syrup
1 cup milk

½ lb. butter
pinch salt
nuts

1 tsp. vanilla

Put all except nuts and vanilla in pan and stir while cooking. When candy forms a soft ball in cold water, remove and stir until thick. Add nuts and vanilla and pour into buttered dish.

Mrs. Owen Carter.

Patience

2 scant cups fresh sweet
skimmed milk
3 cups coarse granulated
sugar

butter, size walnut
1½ cups shelled pecans
marshmallows

Put milk in pan on back of stove to warm. Brown 1 cup sugar to a syrup; add to the warm sweet milk; stir until syrup dissolves. Add 2 cups sugar and cook until it stands to itself on a plate or until thick as custard. Remove from fire; add butter; beat until it is nearly sugar; add pecans; pour onto a buttered plate lined with marshmallows. Have everything ready before beginning to cook. When cool, cut in squares.

Mrs. Will Lawther.

Patience II

3 cups sugar   1 cup pecans
1 cup milk   marshmallows
⅛ lb. butter

Cook two cups sugar, milk, and butter in stewpan slowly.
Brown 1 cup sugar in skillet, then pour syrup in stewpan
with first mixture. Cook slowly until done. Test in water.
Beat until nearly hard and add pecans. Pour in pan lined
with marshmallows.

Mrs. Turner Pittman.

Candy from Wythville, Va.

2 cups brown sugar   1 cup nuts
1 egg (white only)

Cover sugar with water, boil until syrup will spin a heavy
thread; pour over the beaten egg white; beat thoroughly;
add nuts, pour on a marble slab and cut in squares. Flavor
to suit taste.

Mrs. John F. Williams.

Black Walnut Candy

2½ cups sugar   2 egg whites (very
½ cup Karo corn syrup   fresh)
½ cup water   pinch salt
3 cups black walnuts
1 tsp. vanilla

Mix sugar, Karo and water and let stand ½ hour. Put
eggs in bowl with salt and have walnuts cut up. Put syrup
on to boil and when it sticks in cold water, pour ½ of it over
the stiffly beaten whites; return candy to fire and as soon as it
crystalizes in water, pour into egg mixture, which has been
beaten continuously. Beat all 1 hour or more. Add vanilla and nuts last. Pour into dish to harden.

Mrs. W. E. Crow.

Mints

2 cups sugar	6 drops oil of pepper-
1 cup water	mint

⅛ lb. butter

Mix sugar, water and butter thoroughly. Put on slow fire until thoroughly dissolved. Do not stir. Boil until it forms a hard ball when dropped in cold water. Pour on marble slab. When cool, take up at once and pull until white; add peppermint oil. Cut with scissors into small pieces. Wrap all in piece of old linen and put in covered vessel. This will make it creamy.

Mrs. Eugene Munger, Birmingham.

Date Loaf

2 cups sugar	1 cup nuts (chopped
1 cup sweet milk	fine)
1 package dates	

Put sugar, milk and dates over a slow fire; stir constantly. After the mass has cooked a few minutes, until it will form a ball when dropped in cold water, remove from fire and stir in nuts. Beat until light. Pour on a wet cloth and roll up until cool. Then it is ready to slice. Will keep for several weeks, and is a nourishing and palatable sweet for children's lunches.

Mrs. Warren Jones.

Molasses Candy

1 cup molasses	vanilla
2 cups sugar	small piece butter
1 tsp. vinegar	little water

Boil all for ten minutes, then cool and pull when it can be handled.

Elizabeth Richenbaker,
Summerville, S. C.

Chocolate Caramels

2 cups molasses	½ lb. chocolate
1 cup brown sugar	butter size of egg
1 cup cream or milk	

Mix, beat all together; boil until it thickens in water; turn into large flat tins, well buttered. When nearly cold, cut in small squares.

Jennie Maud Burgoyne.

Pecan Pralines

4 cups granulated sugar	2 tbsp. butter
1 cup thin cream or rich milk	2 or 3 cups pecans

Stir 3 cups of sugar, cream or milk, and butter over fire until the sugar is melted, then cook without stirring to the soft boil stage. At same time stir one cup of sugar over fire until it caramels. Pour first mixture in the caramel and let it boil up once. Take from fire and beat until thick. Add pecans quickly at last moment. Drop in spoonfuls on buttered dish.

Mrs. J. H. McDonough.

Fudge

1 cup milk	1 tbsp. butter
2 cups sugar	1 tsp. vanilla
2 squares Baker's chocolate	

Let milk and chocolate come to a boil and add sugar. Cook until it makes a soft ball in water. Let cool, then add nuts and beat until very thick and creamy. Pour on a greased platter.

Mrs. John O. Wharton.

Turkish Delight

3 cups granulated sugar
1 large orange
powdered sugar
½ cup water

1 large lemon
1 box Knox gelatine
(No. 1)

Soak gelatine in ½ cup water. Let sugar and ½ cup water come to boil and add soaked gelatine. Add juice and rind of orange and lemon and boil 15 minutes. (Orange and lemon juice together must equal ½ cup of juice). Remove from fire and pour into buttered tins. Let stand over night. Cut into squares or long pieces and roll in powdered sugar. *Mrs. L. S. Sabin.*

Peanut Candy

2½ cups sugar
½ cup milk
butter size of an egg

Let this boil. Caramel ½ cup sugar and when brown add to boiling candy and let cook with it until it hardens on sides of boiler, then pour over the beaten whites of 2 eggs, as in icing. Beat, and when ready add 1 cup of pounded peanuts, vanilla to taste and a pinch of salt.
Mrs. F. M. Butt.

Panocha

1 cup light brown sugar
1 cup white sugar
1 tbsp. white Karo

milk
1 tbsp. butter
1 cup nuts

vanilla

Mix 2 kinds of sugar, Karo and milk enough to make a paste (about ½ cup). Cook until it forms a soft ball in water. Remove from fire, add butter. Cool. Add vanilla and beat until very creamy. Add nuts and drop from spoon onto oiled paper. *Mrs. T. A. Rose.*

Luncheon Dishes and Sandwiches

Orange Toast

½ cup grated orange rind (yellow part only)

2 tbsp. juice
1 cup sugar

Mix; spread on toast and return to broiler until it bubbles. Serve hot.

English Cream Entree

1 pt. milk
5 oz. sugar
1 tsp. butter
3 egg yolks

2 tbsp. corn starch
1 tbsp. flour
1 stick cinnamon
½ tsp. vanilla

Heat milk with cinnamon. When it first reaches boiling point, stir in sugar, cornstarch and flour (the two last ingredients having been rubbed smooth with two extra tablespoons milk). Stir over fire three minutes, to cook flour. Remove from fire and add beaten egg yolks; return to fire for two or three minutes, stirring constantly to keep smooth. Remove from fire, take out cinnamon stick; add butter and vanilla; pour in a buttered platter until it is about one inch thick. When cold and firm, cut in strips or shapes; roll first in sifted cracker crumbs, then in eggs beaten with a little sugar in them, then in cracker crumbs again. Dip in boiling lard until a light brown. Remove to a hot oven until a little brown on top. Sprinkle with pulverized sugar and serve at once with hot wafers and strips of delicate pie crust.

Mrs. H. R. Aldredge.

Hot Cheese Sandwiches

Grate cheese and season well with salt, cayenne, mustard, Worcestershire sauce, onion juice and a little mayonnaise or cream. Slice bread about one-half inch thick. Cut in rounds, spread with cheese mixture, making a sandwich. Toast both sides in moderate oven. Serve hot.

Eggs and Mushrooms

8 eggs (hard boiled)	1 can mushrooms
1 gr. pepper	salt
2 onions	black pepper
1 small can tomatoes	cayenne
1 tbsp. AI sauce	2 or 3 cloves, garlic

little sugar

Cut hard boiled eggs in quarters and cover with sauce made as follows: Fry chopped pepper and onion in bacon grease. Add tomatoes, liquor from mushrooms, AI sauce, garlic, sugar to taste, salt, pepper and cayenne. Thicken with a little flour; cook down; add chopped mushrooms and pour over eggs. Serve hot.

Mrs. Ballard Burgher.

Relish

1 cup chopped celery	1 small can of sardines
1 tbsp. French's mustard	1 cup of chopped cucumbers
few drops onion juice	½ tsp. paprika

pinch of salt

One small can of sardines cut in quarters. Soak cucumbers in vinegar and salt for two hours, then drain. Mix thoroughly with other ingredients and fill tomatoes, or mould in small cups, and serve on lettuce, with cold meat.

Mrs. David A. Hughes.

Santa Claus Sandwiches

Place seedless raisins and dates in a pan; cover with warm water and let stand five minutes. Drain well, chop fine and add some chopped nuts. Make a paste with lemon juice or grape juice and spread between thin slices of bread, or butter-thin crackers.

Broiled Pineapple

Stuff the center of pineapple slices with cherries, brush with melted butter and broil slowly. Do not burn. Serve around meat or chicken.

Hominy Souffle

½ cup hominy	1 tbsp. butter
3 cups milk	salt
2 eggs	pepper

Bring milk to boil; add hominy; cook fifteen minutes. Put in butter, beaten yolks and seasoning to taste. Cook ten minutes. Stir in beaten whites and put in buttered baking-dish. Bake one-half hour.

Oranges

Take the required number of oranges and cover well with water. Boil very slowly for one-half hour. Remove and cut in halves. Make a syrup of one cup water to one cup sugar; cook orange halves slowly in syrup for another one-half hour, or until clear and crystalized. Remove from syrup, add one small can sliced pineapple, cut fine, and one small bottle of Maraschino cherries, cut in halves, to syrup and boil slowly until clear. Put a small amount of cherry and pineapple mixture on top of each orange half and serve as a garnishment around broiled chicken or birds.

Mrs. Chas. Dexter, Jr.

Apples and Conserve

Select number of apples needed, peel and core. Cook until tender and red in thin syrup, made of water, sugar and colored very red with fruit coloring. Allow to cool and fill centers with conserve. Serve as an accompaniment with fowl or meats.

Mrs. Chas. Dexter, Jr.

Baked Oranges

Select medium sized oranges, cut off tops and core. Fill each center with granulated sugar and a small piece of butter. Place in a baking pan half full of water and bake slowly (covered) until done (about one hour). Brown slightly. A marshmallow may be placed on top and browned just before serving.

Onion Souffle

1 cup cream sauce
½ cup bread crumbs
1 cup cold boiled
    onions (chopped)
1 egg yolk
1 tsp. chopped parsley
2 whites (beaten)

Mix sauce, bread crumbs, onion, egg yolk and parsley thoroughly. Add whites stiffly beaten. Bake in moderate oven. Serve at once.

Tuna Fish in Ramekins

1 can white tuna fish
1 can mushrooms
2 hard boiled eggs
    cream sauce
butter
crumbs
garlic (onion if preferred)
salt, cayenne, and paprika

Mix all, using enough cream sauce to suit. Season highly. Put into ramekins, sprinkle with crumbs, dot with butter, and brown in oven.

Chicken and Brains in Ramekins

1 hen	1 can mushrooms
2 sets brains	cream sauce
salt, red pepper, pap-	garlic
rika, bread crumbs	butter

Boil hen well; put through food grinder; add brains which have been well cooked. Add cream sauce to make right consistency; garlic-water, (boil chopped garlic) to taste; seasonings to taste and chopped mushrooms. Put into ramekins, sprinkle with bread crumbs and dot with butter. Put in stove to heat thoroughly and brown.

Mrs. Chas. Dexter, Sr.

Chicken Loaf

1 hen (3 lbs.)	1 large green pepper
2 hard boiled eggs,	(chopped fine)
(sliced)	salt
2 chopped pimentos	1 envelope Knox gela-
1 cup cold stock	tine
1 cup boiled stock	red pepper, tabasco
mustard seed	celery salt

Boil hen until meat leaves bones. Remove. Put stock in ice-box; when grease forms on top, remove it all. Cut chicken in pieces two inches long; add eggs, pimentos, salt, green pepper. Soften gelatine in cup of cold stock; dissolve in boiling stock. Stir until clear; season highly with salt, red pepper, mustard seed, tabasco, celery salt. Pour liquid over chicken mixture; mould, and set on ice for two hours or more. Turn out on platter; garnish with parsley; serve with tartare sauce.

Mrs. Perry Baird.

Neufchatel Cheese Sandwiches

2 packages cheese
4 tbsp. milk
1 tsp. salt
red pepper to taste

1 slice onion chopped
fine
1 small green pepper
(chopped fine)
½ cup pecans (chopped
fine)

Mix all, spread bread thinly with butter, then with filling. Put together, cut off crusts and pack as directed. Makes 25 sandwiches.

Mrs. John F. Williams.

Salted Almonds

Blanch the almonds, wipe dry; place in a frying basket; then in Snowflake oil, heated to boiling point. When nicely browned, remove from oil, sprinkle with salt and drain. Cook any other nuts the same way.

Mrs. John F. Williams.

Green Pepper Sandwich

6 green peppers
(ground up)

1 very small onion
(ground)

Mix with mayonnaise and spread thin on bread.

Mrs. Philip Miller.

To Make Sandwiches

Have bread a day old; cut in thin slices and always spread with butter; then spread with sandwich filling to be used; put slices together and cut off crust always. Make an hour or two before serving and cover with wet napkins, rung very dry, and, second, a dry napkin.

Mrs. John F. Williams.

Chicken Sandwiches

Take cold chicken or turkey; chop very fine; mix with melted butter, cream, salt, cayenne, pepper, and celery or mashed celery seed. Spread on sandwiches with lettuce leaf and mayonnaise. Put slices together; cut off crusts.

Mrs. Raymond Lawther.

Philadelphia Scrapple

Cook shoulder of best pork thoroughly; cool and chop fine. Season liquid with salt and black pepper, and stir into it cornmeal until moderately thick. Add meat and cook to thick mush; press into pudding pans, and fry when used. Slice and eat cold.

Mrs. C. W. Lamberth.

Rice Croquettes—Cheese Sauce

½ cup rice
2 tbsp. chopped pi-
   mentos
½ tbsp. boiling water

½ tsp. salt
1 ¼ tsp. milk
¼ tsp. cream

cayenne

Soak rice in water to cover over night, drain and add boiling water; cook in double boiler until water is absorbed; add milk; cook until milk is absorbed. Add cream, pimentos, salt and cayenne. Spread on plate; cool; shape and dip in crumbs, egg, and crumbs again. Fry in deep fat and drain on brown paper. Pile on serving dish; garnish with parsley and pour around it cheese sauce, made as follows: Melt 3 tablespoons butter, 3 tablespoons flour; stir until blended; pour on gradually 1½ cups milk. Bring to boiling point; add ½ teaspoon salt, ⅛ teaspoon pepper, and 1 cup grated mild cheese.

Mrs. Hugh Prather.

Prune and Cheese Balls

Mix Neufchatel cheese with mayonnaise and to each ½ cup add ¼ cup chopped walnut meats. Mould into balls and stuff into prune centers, having cooked the prunes ten minutes in lemon juice. Serve with salad.

Mrs. C. W. Lamberth.

Spanish Stew

3 tbsp. ham drippings	3 cups water
1 tbsp. flour	1 cup cold chopped
1 potato	meat
salt and cayenne to	1 onion
taste	½ can tomatoes
½ button garlic	½ cup macaroni

Brown flour in drippings, add all ingredients except macaroni. When thoroughly boiled, add macaroni and cook ½ hour, stirring often and adding boiling water if necessary.

Mrs. L. Harris.

Chili Loaf

1 lb. round steak	1 2/3 cans pimentos
3 slices bacon	1½ cups strained to-
1 onion	mato juice
bread crumbs	chili powder

Grind steak, bacon, onion, pimentos, season to taste; form into loaf; cover with bread crumbs and chili powder and pour around it tomato juice. Bake in slow oven.

Mrs. Alf Haynes.

Brown Bread Sandwiches

Stone and chop ripe olives, add mayonnaise and chopped walnuts. Spread on one slice of white bread and one slice brown bread, and put together.

Mrs. Warren Jones.

Bird-Nest Toast

For each person, toast 1 slice of bread brown on both sides and spread with butter. Beat white of 1 egg stiff and spread on bread. Make a hole in center and drop in yolks. Sprinkle with salt and pepper and dot with butter. Bake in a hot oven two or three minutes. Serve hot.

Mrs. H. L. Bosworth.

Baked Grits

2 cups milk
1 cup cold grits
1 cup cornmeal
butter size of an egg
½ tsp. baking powder
salt to taste
3 eggs, beaten separately

Mash finely the cold grits; add milk gradually; sift in cornmeal; beat in well beaten yolks; add melted butter, baking powder, salt and lastly the beaten whites. Bake slowly until well browned. Stir while boiling. When brown, stir thoroughly and let bake until brown again. Serve for lunch or breakfast.

Mrs. Helen Ardrey.

Cheese London

1 cup fine bread crumbs
2 cups sweet milk
½ lb. grated cheese
3 eggs whipped light
1 tsp. butter
pepper, salt and pinch soda

Dissolve soda in a little hot water; stir into milk; add butter, eggs, seasoning and last the cheese. Butter a baking dish and pour in the mixture. Put fine bread crumbs over top. Bake in a quick oven. Serve at once.

Mrs. Geo. N. Aldredge.

Baked Brains

1 set brains	1 tbsp. butter (melted)
1 tbsp. lemon juice	1 tbsp. chopped onion
1 tsp. cracker crumbs	2 eggs, beaten separately

Clean brains in boiling salted water. Boil done. Drain dry. Mash and add other ingredients, the well beaten whites of eggs lastly. Pour into well buttered ramekins. Cover with cracker crumbs. Dot with butter and bake quickly. Serve hot. *Mrs. W. R. Dazey.*

Ham and Cheese Souffle

¼ lb. cheese	1 tsp. Worcestershire
¼ lb. cold boiled ham	sauce
6 sq. soda crackers	½ tsp. baking powder
	1 cup milk

3 eggs (beaten separately)

Use finest cutter of meat-chopper. Run cheese through first, then ham and crackers. Add the Worcestershire sauce, milk and salt and red pepper to taste. Mix thoroughly, add yolks of eggs well beaten, then whites, which are stiff and dry. Fold into the batter lightly and sprinkle baking powder lightly over the top. Pour into well buttered baking dish and bake slowly until puffy and brown (about 30 minutes. *The Commission Shop of Minneapolis.*

Chicken Cheese Sandwiches

½ lb. grated Swiss cheese	1 can boneless chicken or white meat of 1 hen (ground)
4 gr. pepper (chopped fine)	

2 cups stiff mayonnaise

Camille Padgitt, Waco, Texas.

Simple Lunch Dish

1 large egg plant	1 tbsp. sugar
3 medium size onions	1 generous slice butter
2 medium size green	1 cup rice
peppers	1 small can tomatoes

Boil rice. Peel and cut egg-plant in squares. Put butter in pan, add egg-plant, let brown about three minutes. Cut onions and peppers up. Add to tomatoes, add sugar, salt and pepper to season. Let cook 15 minutes. Add this to egg-plant. Let simmer until egg-plant is cooked (but not falling to pieces). Serve, placing egg-plant in center of platter with rice around it.   *Mrs. T. W. Griffiths, Jr.*

Cornmeal Souffle

1 pt. sweet milk	1 tsp. salt
¾ cup meal	4 eggs, beaten separately

Let milk come to a boil; stir in meal; cook until like mush; stir in yolks, one at a time, then the salt and whites beaten stiff. Bake 25 minutes. Serve at once.

Mrs. Arthur Boice.

Ham Mousse

½ envelope Knox gela-tine	1 tsp. mustard
½ cup hot stock	½ cup whipping cream
¼ cup cold water	2 cups cold chopped boiled ham
little cayenne	

Soak gelatine in cold water, dissolve in hot stock and add to chopped ham. When cold, add mustard, cayenne, cream beaten stiff. Turn into mould. Serve with Cottage cheese in center.

The Commission Shop of Minneapolis.

Pigs in Blanket

One dozen large oysters; dry well and season with salt, pepper and a little lemon juice. Wrap oysters in small slices of bacon. Stick two orange-wood toothpicks through each to keep the bacon around them. Put them in hot frying pan long enough to brown bacon. Place on pieces of toast and serve hot.   *Edna Ball.*

Chili

1 lb. round steak	1 button garlic
1 lb. beef suet	2 tsp. chili powder
2 lbs. chili beans	1 tbsp. salt

chili pod pepper

Soak beans and pepper over night; boil 3 hours. Place suet in kettle and fry out fat; add ground meat and simmer for 3 minutes; add to beans and other ingredients and cook slowly for 1 hour.   *Mrs. J. W. Lawther.*

Moulded Sweetbreads

1 sweetbread	1 cucumber
1 bay leaf	¼ tbsp. gelatine
1 blade mace	½ tbsp. cold water
1 slice onion	1½ tbsp. boiling water
1½ tbsp. vinegar	½ cup thick cream

Parboil sweetbread with bay leaf, onion, and mace. Cool and cut in small pieces. There should be ¾ cup. Add equal quantity of cucumber cubes. Soak gelatine in cold water, dissolved in hot water; add cream, whipped stiff, vinegar, salt, pepper, sweetbreads and cucumbers. Mould. Arrange on lettuce leaves; serve garnished with asparagus in green pepper rings on thick slices of tomatoes. Serve with French dressing or mayonnaise.

Mrs. John L. Puterbaugh.

Luncheon Dish

3 bay oysters   2 cups macaroni
1 cup grated cheese   bit of butter

Boil macaroni until done; put a layer of oysters, then cheese, then macaroni until casserole is filled. Pour over top 1 tablespoon Worcestershire sauce, salt, black pepper, 1 cup sweet milk thickened with 2 tablespoons butter and 2 tablespoons flour, rubbed together. Cook 20 minutes.

Mary Marrion Smith.

Egg Croquettes

1 dozen eggs   1 pt. cream
½ pt. bread crumbs   1/3 cup butter

Pepper and salt to taste. Boil eggs hard, chop fine. Boil cream and put over bread crumbs; add eggs and seasoning. Form into shape. Roll in beaten whites of eggs and cracker crumbs and fry in hot lard.

The Commission Shop of Minneapolis.

Sauted Sweetbreads

Cook a small amount of butter with a little finely chopped onion; add 1 teaspoon flour and brown slightly. Add eight tablespoons sherry wine, liquor from 1 can mushrooms. Season with Worcestershire sauce and tomato catsup. Add sweetbreads (cleaned and parboiled) and mushrooms. Season to taste and serve on buttered toast.

Cheese Balls

1 cup grated cheese   2 egg whites (beaten
1 heaping tsp. flour   stiff)
pinch of paprika   ¼ tsp. salt

Mix in order given, folding in whites last. Roll into small balls and fry in deep fat.

Mrs. Paul Platter.

Ring Noodles

1 pkg. of noodles   1 pt. of cream   4 eggs

Boil one package of noodles in salt water. Let cool. When cold, add 1 pint of cream, four eggs (well beaten). Bake in well greased ring in medium oven. Put ring in pan of hot water when baking it, and it will not stick. Serve with creamed sweetbreads and mushrooms in center of ring.

Mrs. Philip T. Prather.

Pineapple and Orange Ice

Cut fresh pineapple in pieces for serving; sugar and put in ice-box. Make an orange ice. Serve sliced pineapple in fruit cocktail glasses with the orange ice on top. Suggested as a first or last course for summer luncheon.

Grapefruit and Mint Ice

Peel and separate grapefruit into sections free from skin and bitter portions. Sweeten slightly and set away to chill. Make a mint ice. Serve the grapefruit in fruit cocktail glasses with the mint ice on it. Suggested as first or last course for a summer luncheon.

Chili

25c round steak   2½ tsp. chili powder
1 onion   1 can chili beans
2 pods garlic   red pepper to taste
1 can of tomatoes   double spoonful flour

Grind meat, onion and garlic in meat grinder; take double spoonful of lard and fry this meat until brown, then stir in a double spoonful of flour, the tomatoes, chili powder and beans and red pepper. Cook one or two hours and add tea cup of hot water, if necessary.

Mrs. Collett Munger.

Spanish Chili Con Carne

Boil 1 beef tongue until tender; in another vessel boil 2 cups or more of Mexican chili beans, seasoned and salted. Grind the tongue with 2 cups of the cooked beans. In a vessel on the stove, put ¼ cup grease; when hot, add ground tongue and beans. Fry until grease is taken up; then with sauce of beans, add red pepper to taste; let boil; add juice of pound can of tomatoes and salt. Serve at once with cooked rice, remainder of beans and crackers.

Mrs. Rhea Miller.

Cheese Souffle

2 tbsp. butter	4 eggs (beaten
1 cup milk (scant)	separately)
2 tbsp. flour	1 cup cheese (grated)

Make cream sauce of milk, flour, and butter, season with salt and red pepper, add cheese and well beaten yolks, then add stiffly beaten whites. Put in buttered baking dish and bake slowly 15 or 20 minutes. Serve at once.

Mrs. Chas. Dexter, Jr.

Luncheon Sandwich

1 cup grated cheese	2 beaten eggs
2 tbsp. milk	dash red pepper

Add cheese to beaten eggs, then add milk and red pepper. Cook until thick. Spread on toast. Serve hot.

Mrs. Frank C. Cullinan.

Potato Souffle

Peel good mealy potatoes, cut ¼ inch thick. Fry in moderately warm lard 10 minutes. Lift out, let cool few minutes, then plunge into boiling hot fat, fry few seconds. Serve immediately. *Mrs. W. E. Crow.*

Cheese Sandwich

1 small cake of Star
    brand cheese or
    McLaren's cream
    cheese

2 tbsp. melted butter
3 tbsp. chili sauce

Cream butter and cheese together until smooth, then add chili sauce and beat until smooth. This will make a dozen small tea sandwiches.

R. L. B.

Cheese Sandwich

¾ lb. American cheese
1 level tsp. dry mus-
    tard
    paprika to taste
1 egg beaten

butter size of a wal-
    nut
    salt to taste
½ cup milk
1 small garlic button

Cook in double boiler to a smooth paste. Spread between bread and toast.

Mrs. J. L. Driebelbis.

Boston Baked Beans

1 lb. tiny navy beans
½ lb. salt pork
2 tbsp. black molasses

1 onion
1 tsp. dry mustard
    salt and pepper

Soak beans over night. Parboil them in morning before preparing them. Place onion with teaspoon of mustard sprinkled over it in bottom of baking dish. Cover with one-half pound of the beans. Add salt pork and molasses and cover with rest of beans. Cover all with water and bake slowly in oven all day, adding water when needed.

Mrs. Robert Maxwell.

238

Salmon With Green Mayonnaise

1 salmon steak   1 onion
1 carrot   bouquet of herbs

Boil salmon with water, salt, pepper, onion, carrot cut in small slices and bouquet of herbs. Remove the skin when salmon is cooked. This can be served either hot or cold. Serve with green mayonnaise.   *Mrs. S. W. King, Jr.*

Welsh Rarebit

1 lb. American cheese   salt and pepper
2 cups of cream   1 tbsp. Worcestershire
4 eggs   sauce
1 tbsp. butter

Cut cheese into little pieces. Melt until creamy in double boiler. Add butter, then the eggs beaten well. Cream and season. Stir until it begins to thicken. Pour over toast and serve hot.   *Mrs. Robert Maxwell.*

Chili

2 lbs. ground meat   6 tbsp. bacon drippings
1 large can kidney beans   ½ cup chili powder
1 can tomatoes   2 cloves garlic

Put 6 tbsp. of bacon drippings in a skillet and fry onions and garlic until well done. Add meat to mixture and fry. In a deeper pan put the tomatoes, ½ cup chili powder (mixed with warm water) salt and pepper to taste. Add first mixture to this. Add 1 qt. warm water and cook by slow fire several hours. Add more water if necessary. Serves from 10 to 14 people.

Mrs. John O. Wharton.

Chili

2 lbs. tender round steak	1½ cups chili beans
½ lb. salt pork	1 can tomato soup
½ button garlic	2 tbsp. cominos seed
3 or 4 onions	chili powder to taste

red pepper to taste

Soak beans over night. Cut bacon in very small pieces and cook with beans in about 2 qts. water. Add tomato soup. Cut steak (with scissors) into very small pieces, salt and flour well and set aside. Cut onions fine, salt and flour well and set aside. When beans are well done, add cominos seed, which has been pounded and sifted, garlic and chili powder. Put a large cooking spoon of fat in skillet, when quite hot fry steak, stirring occasionally. When done add to beans. Fry onions same way and add to beans. Season with salt and red pepper to taste and let cook about ten minutes.

Mrs. Devereux Dunlap.

Pyramid Chops

lamb steaks	fresh tomatoes
onions	parsley
lemon	butter
salt	pepper

mushrooms

Cut round pieces of bread and toast. Cut the steaks into round pieces and bind with strips of thin bacon (your butcher can make them for you). Broil them and place on toast. Make a sauce of 1 tablespoon butter, juice of half lemon, teaspoon chopped parsley creamed together. (A teaspoon of onion chopped fine or onion juice may be added). Spread on top of each chop and on top of that place a slice of tomato ½ in. thick, which has been broiled. On top of tomato place a slice of onion that has been broiled in butter and on top of that a broiled mushroom and stick a small sprig of parsley in the top of the pyramid. Hot rolls and coffee and peas can be served with this as a meat course for luncheon.

Mrs. John O. McReynolds.

Mushrooms on Toast

½ lb. fresh mushrooms
2 tbsp. butter
1 tbsp. flour
1 cup cream
⅛ tsp. salt
pepper to taste

Chop mushrooms fine and cook in butter for 20 minutes. Stir in flour, and cream, blended together, with salt and pepper. Cook in double boiler for additional 20 minutes. Place on rounds of buttered toast, brown for 1 minute under flame and serve at once. *Mrs. H. R. Aldredge.*

Eggs in Aspic

6 eggs
¼ oz. leaf gelatine
6 slices of tongue
truffles
1 gill aspic jelly
lemon juice
2 gills Bechamel sauce

The eggs are poached in salted water with a little lemon juice. Then trim and set to cool. The Bechamel sauce is heated and added to gelatine and two tablespoons of aspic are stirred in. When the mixture is nearly cold the eggs are mashed with it. This mashing must be done twice, allowing the first to set before adding the second. Then decorate with slices of truffles. As many circles of tongue as there are eggs are cut and the eggs on the circles of tongue are arranged around the side of the platter in a border with a colorful salad of fresh vegetables in the center.

Mrs. Lewis Grinnan.

Bechamel Sauce

1 oz. butter	1 oz. flour
½ carrot	½ small onion
cloves	½ pt. milk
1 gill white stock	½ bay leaf

Melt butter in small pan. Stir in flour and cook a few minutes. To this add sliced carrot, onion, clove and bay leaf. The mixture is then diluted with white stock and milk and allowed to simmer gently for 20 minutes. It is then strained and seasoned to taste.

Mrs. Lewis Grinnan.

Golden Ball Fritters

Put 1 cup of boiling water in a saucepan and add one tablespoon butter. While it is boiling hot add at once a cup of sifted flour and stir briskly until it is smooth dough. Take from the fire and add one by one, four eggs beating each one in well before adding the next. Let stand until cold. Heat a pot of shortening to boiling and drop in by the teaspoon the dough and fry to a golden brown. The puff should be hollow inside and very light. Drain a moment on paper and dust with a little powdered sugar.

Miss Paulula Dunn.

Green Pepper and Bacon Sandwiches

Fry bacon very crisp, cut up very fine. Chop fine or grind equal amount of green pepper and mix the two together. Mix with well seasoned mayonnaise and use as a sandwich filling.

Shrimp Chili

1 pt. shelled shrimp
1 tbsp. butter
1 clove garlic (chopped)
1 tbsp. flour

1 cup milk
1 tbsp. tomato catsup
2 tsp. chili powder
1 tsp. parsley (chopped)

1 tbsp. sherry or lemon juice

Melt butter, add chopped garlic and fry for a few minutes. Then add flour. When blended, add milk and mix thoroughly. Then add catsup, sherry or lemon juice, chili powder and chopped parsley. Mix well, add shrimp, place in casserole and bake ½ hour. Serve hot. 4 servings.

Mrs. T. W. Griffiths, Jr.

Chili

2 lbs. meat chopped, not
     ground
1 piece suet
1 lb. chili beans, soaked
     over night
4 large onions

4 cloves garlic
1 tsp. cominos seed
     (mashed)
2 No. 2 cans tomatoes
½ bottle Gebhart's chili
     powder, 35c size

Fry out suet. Add onions, cook gently, but do not brown. Add chopped meat, let cook until brown. Have beans on boiling in large pot with good amount of water and tomatoes. When meat is nicely browned, add to beans. Season well with salt and add cut up garlic and cominos seed. Cook slowly several hours, adding chili powder (mixed smooth with a little water). About the last 1½ hours, add cayenne if wanted.

Mrs. Ed T. Staten.

Cucumber and Cheese Filling

Mix Philadelphia cheese with a light, highly seasoned mayonnaise and add ground cucumber, which has been drained dry. Season well and spread.

Egg Timbales

6 eggs
1 pt. milk
1 tbsp. flour

½ onion (chopped fine)
½ can tomatoes
olives

1 tbsp. butter

Make a white sauce of milk, butter and flour, pour into the well beaten eggs (reserving 3 tablespoons of white sauce for later) season with salt, onion juice and pepper to taste and put into individual Pyrex dishes. Set in pan of water and cook until set. To remaining 3 tablespoons of white sauce, add tomatoes, chopped olives and onion, cook and serve poured over eggs. An entree or luncheon dish.

Mrs. Lewis Dabney.

German Tamales

1 large head cabbage
1 lb. ground pork

2 cups rice
1 large onion

Boil rice 5 minutes in water to just cover. Fry one large onion very lightly, not brown, mix pork, cooked rice and onion together, season with salt and pepper. Take cabbage and scald in boiling water until leaves are wilted. Remove leaves, fill each leaf with mixture and roll like tamale. Place in covered vessel, add cup water, 1 large spoon dripping and 1 large spoon vinegar. Simmer slowly for about 1 hour. Serve hot. *Mrs. M. H. Thomas.*

Breast of Chicken With Mushrooms

Boil chicken until tender. Cook fresh mushrooms in butter and when cooked, add flour and cream to make white sauce. Slice breast of chicken in large pieces, put into mushroom sauce and serve on toast.

Mrs. Glenway Maxon, Jr.

California Chicken Pie

1 can tuna fish (13 oz.)	1 cup green peas
2 carrots, diced	1 tbsp. butter
2 medium potatoes, diced	2 tbsp. flour
	1 cup milk
1 medium onion, chopped	1 tsp. salt
	¼ tsp. paprika

⅛ tsp. pepper

Pastry—Boil carrots, potatoes, onions and peas together in a small amount of salted water. Make a white sauce as follows: Melt butter, add flour and cook until bubbling. Add milk gradually and cook until smooth and thickened. Add seasonings and mix sauce with the tuna. Line a baking dish with pastry, fill with the vegetables and creamed fish in layers, cover with an upper crust in which holes have been made and bake until crust is brown. *Miss Paulula Dunn.*

Cheese Sandwiches

½ lb. cheese (American)	1 tbsp. Worcestershire sauce
¼ tsp. mustard	pinch salt, dash of cayenne pepper
½ cup mayonnaise or cream	

Grate cheese and cream it well, adding mayonnaise, salt, pepper, etc. Slice bread very thin in round slices. Spread dressing between slices and brown in hot oven.

Mrs. S. I. Munger, Jr.

Rolled Cheese Sandwiches

One-half lb. Kraft's Old English cheese. Grate and cream with mayonnaise and seasonings and spread on slices of bread ¼ inch thick. Roll bread like jelly roll. Slice off ¼ inch rolls and put in ice box until ready to toast in oven just before serving.

Breast of Guinea on Toast

Parboil guinea till tender. Slice off breasts whole. Take dark meat, chop fine, season well, make a rich white sauce with sherry. Use part to mix with ground dark meat. Have crisp toast, put on some of the ground dark meat and top with a large slice of breast and pour sauce over all.

Mrs. Lang Wharton.

Individual Oyster Loaves

Buy oblong rolls. Cut a slice off of top and hollow the roll entirely out. Butter roll inside and toast crisp and light brown. Broil oysters, mix well with chopped celery and picalilli and season to taste with salt and cayenne. Fill shells and dot well with butter and tomato catsup. Put in oven to heat thoroughly. It is necessary to order the rolls.

Miss Ed Dela Wright.

Baked Bananas

8 peeled bananas	juice of 2 lemons
1 scant cup sugar	butter

Squeeze lemon juice over bananas and sprinkle with sugar. Put a good sized lump of butter on each banana and bake in a moderate oven twenty-five minutes, turning so the bananas will be a uniform golden brown.

Eggs a la Benedict

English muffins or toast	tomatoes
ham	eggs
Hollandaise sauce	

Split and toast the muffins and on each half put a piece of broiled ham, then a slice of broiled tomato, next a poached egg. Serve hot with Hollandaise sauce.

Mrs. Frank Austin.

Preserves and Pickles

Watermelon Preserves

Pare in cubes watermelon rinds; soak over night in salt water, drain and weigh. Then boil in clear water until tender. Remove rinds. Thin syrup with equal weight of sugar; let boil five minutes; add rind, well drained, and one lemon sliced; boil until transparent; then add 1 can grated pineapple; cook 20 to 30 minutes. To each quart jar, add 1 dozen Maraschino cherries.

Mrs. Guss W. Thomasson.

Pear Chips

1 bushel pears	2 boxes dried cocoanut
4 pineapples (grated)	sugar and water

Peel and core the pears; slice on a potato slicer; cover with water and cook until tender. Drain well; add sugar, 1 pound to 1 pound of fruit. Cook until done, stirring carefully. Add pineapple, cocoanut (½ can pineapple and ¼ package cocoanut to 4 lbs. fruit. Drain juice from pineapple. Cook 15 minutes—after pineapple and cocoanut are added. One bushel pears makes about 30 pints of chips.

Mrs. Walter Dealey.

Conserve

2 lbs. grapes (seeded)	4 lbs. sugar
2 lbs. plums (seeded)	2 lbs. nuts chopped
4 oranges (seeded and	(pecans or walnuts)
cut fine)	2 lbs. seeded raisins

Put grapes, plums and oranges together and cook about 30 minutes, until oranges are tender. Add raisins, sugar and nuts and cook slowly until thick like jam. Seal.

Mrs. Josephine Tutton.

Apricot-Pineapple Conserve

1 large cup English
   walnuts
3 cups sugar

2 lbs. dried apricots
1 large can pineapple

Wash apricots well; soak over night in 6 cups cold water. Cut apricots and pineapple in small pieces. Add pineapple juice and sugar and the water apricots were soaked in. Cook slowly one and one-half hours. Add chopped nuts just before taking from fire.

Mrs. Chas. Dexter, Jr.

Spiced Grapes

Take pulp from Concord grapes, preserving the skins. Boil pulp and rub through a colander to remove seeds. Then add the skins to the strained pulp and boil with vinegar, sugar and spices. To every seven pounds of grapes, use 4½ lbs. sugar, one pt. vinegar. Spice quite highly with ground cloves, allspice and a little cinnamon.

Miss Marquerite Dale.

Orange Marmalade

3 large juicy oranges   3 lemons
2 grapefruit

Slice very fine; be careful to remove all seeds, as one seed left will make it bitter. The grapefruit should be peeled and all white part removed from rind, then slice rind in small strips, then slice fruit and be sure all white part is removed from it. Measure fruit and juice and to every pint, add 3 pints of water. Let soak in a cool place for 48 hours. Measure again and to every pint of fruit, add 1 pint of sugar, then boil until done.

Kate Hardie Miller.

Citron or Watermelon Rind

Peel off green rind; cut thick rind in small pieces; soak in strong salt water 12 hours. Then soak in alum water 12 hours. Boil in two plain waters thoroughly. Make a syrup with equal parts sugar and water and boil with lemon and ginger-root until sugar is dissolved. Then add melon rind. Cook until rinds are perfectly clear and tender. Boil syrup down very thick. *Mrs. J. H. Shelton.*

Orange Marmalade

Six large oranges, not over ripe, 2 lemons. Shred fruit very fine, peeling it all. Then weigh. To every pound of fruit, add 3 pints of water. Let stand over night, then boil for 1½ hours. Again let stand until next day. Then weigh fruit and water and to every pound add 1¼ pounds of sugar. Boil for one hour or until it jells. *Mrs. A. G. Joyce.*

Plum Conserve

4 qts. plums	1 lb. seedless raisins
4 scant quarts water	½ lb. pecans or English
4 oranges sliced and cut fine	walnut meats (chopped)

Cut plums in one-half and remove seeds; add oranges, sugar and raisins. Cook until thick. Add nuts just before removing from fire. *Mrs. Seth Miller.*

Golden Marmalade

One grapefruit, 1 orange; skin and cut 1 lemon. Slice in tiny pieces; add 3 times as much water as fruit; let stand over night and boil 10 minutes, next morning. Set aside until following day. Then add ¾ cup sugar to 1 pint fruit. Boil 1 hour. *Mrs. J. L. Dreibelbis.*

Quince Preserve

Wash quinces very thoroughly; cover with water; let cook until tender; testing with a straw. Lift out of water (saving water). When cool enough to handle, peel, quarter and core (saving peeling and cores for jelly). Weigh fruit. Make syrup with water quinces were cooked in and sugar, using ¾ to 1 lb. sugar to 1 lb. fruit. Add fruit to syrup after sugar is well dissolved and let cook until thoroughly clear and soft. Put fruit in jars; boil syrup down thick; pour over quince and seal. *Mrs. T. L. Lauve.*

Brandied Peaches

Three-fourths pounds of sugar to 1 pound of fruit. Add ½ gill water to each pound of sugar; let come to a high boil; skim when a thick syrup; add fruit; boil 5 minutes; add 1 gill (or more) of grape brandy to each pound of fruit; mix thoroughly; pour over fruit. Screw tops down at once.
Mrs. Chas. Padgitt.

Grape Conserve

5 lbs. Concord grapes	6 oranges
1 lb. seeded raisins	1 lb. pecan meats

Skin and seed grapes. Put oranges thru food chopper; cover with water and let stand over night. Chop raisins and nuts; add ¾ cup sugar to 1 cup fruit. Cook to a thick marmalade. *Mrs. C. W. Lamberth.*

Chili Sauce

66 ripe tomatoes	11 onions
33 bell peppers	11 cups vinegar
7 tbsp. salt	22 tbsp. sugar

Peel tomatoes; cut tomatoes, peppers and onions fine, boil two hours and bottle while hot.

Mrs. J. B. Shelmire.

Sweet Cucumber Pickle

4 lbs. light brown sugar   ¼ cup whole black
3 pts. vinegar   pepper
                    1/3 cup allspice

Put in kettle and boil 15 minutes. Add 48 sour cucumber pickles of medium size, sliced around ¼ inch thick. Boil 15 or 20 minutes. Set aside until entirely cold; then stir in ½ cup olive oil and put in jars. Let set 10 days. Will then be fine.   *Mrs. J. B. Oldham.*

Beet Relish

1 qt. cooked beets,   2 cups sugar
    chopped fine   2 tbsp. salt
1 small head cabbage   2 tsp. celery seed
1 cup grated horse radish   2 tsp. mustard
                1 pint vinegar

Wait 24 hours before using. Will keep indefinitely.
                    Mrs. P. G. Claiborne.

Chili Sauce

1 peck ripe tomatoes   2 tsp. nutmeg.
3 cups chopped green   3 cups sugar
    peppers   3 pints vinegar
2 cups chopped onions   1 cup salt
3 tsp. cinnamon   3 tsp. cloves

Boil three hours.   *Mrs. Charles Maillot.*

Cucumber Relish

Four quarts sliced cucumbers mixed with 1 cup salt. Soak 3 hours; strain. One pint olive oil, 3 onions, sliced thin, 1 ounce white mustard seed, 1 ounce celery seed, 1 ounce whole black pepper or paprika. Mix all together, cover with vinegar and seal.
                    Mrs. Walter M. Peck.

Heavenly Jam

6 lbs. Concord grapes   4 lbs. sugar
4 oranges   1 lb. seeded raisins

Wash oranges; squeeze out juice; remove white, bitter part and then put skins through meat grinder. Remove skins of grapes, saving them. Heat pulp and put through colander to remove seed. Add grape skins and orange peel and orange juice, raisins and sugar. Let boil in kettle 20 minutes. Pour in jelly glasses and cover with paraffin.

Mrs. Eugene Munger, Birmingham.

Cucumber Pickle Recipe

Into 4 pints of apple vinegar, put 15 pounds of sugar, 1 package of whole black pepper, 1 package of whole spice. Put on to boil. In a 4-gallon jar, cut up 100 school pickles into 1-inch pieces; over them, pour a pint of Tarragon vinegar, 1 pint of olive oil and 12 garlic buttons pierced. When syrup has boiled, pour over pickles and let stand about two weeks before using.   *Mrs. C. W. Hobson.*

Chili Sauce

27 large ripe tomatoes   2 cups vinegar
4 large onions   2 tbsp. Worcestershire
4 gr. peppers   sauce
1 tbsp. cloves   10 tbsp. sugar (more if
2 tbsp. salt   liked sweet)
1 tbsp. ginger   1 tbsp. cinnamon
3 tbsp. horse radish   1 tbsp. allspice
cayenne to taste   1 tbsp. nutmeg
                 1 bunch celery

Chop all vegetables together. Mix with syrup made of all other ingredients and cook slowly until done. Seal while hot. Make as sweet as you like.

Mrs. W. E. Crow.

Green Tomato Pickle

4 qts. green tomatoes	3 tsp. allspice
4 red peppers (hot)	3 tsp. cloves
16 green sweet peppers	3 tsp. cinnamon
4 large onions	3 tsp. mustard
2 tsp. pepper	2 qts. vinegar
¾ cup salt	2 cups sugar
½ cup white mustard seed	

Slice vegetables very thin and place in a stone crock with alternate layers of salt. Let stand 24 hours; drain; rinse with clear water and put in preserving kettle. Add spices, sugar, etc., to vinegar and pour over vegetables. Cook for 30 minutes after the boiling point has been reached. Pour into jars and seal. *Mrs. J. L. Dreibelbis.*

Piccalilli

1 peck green tomatoes	2 heads cabbage
1 dozen green peppers	1 pint salt
1 dozen medium onions	

Chop all together; add salt and let soak over night. Next morning, squeeze out juice. Add 2 quarts vinegar, 2 cups syrup, juice of sweet pickles; 1 or 2 cups sugar, 1 pound whole pepper, allspice, ground cloves, cinnamon, mustard seed, celery seed. Bring to boil. *Fannie T. Horner.*

Piccalilli

1 peck green tomatoes	1 tsp. mustard seed
6 onions	1 cup salt
1 tsp. cloves	4 green peppers
1 tsp. cinnamon	1 pint vinegar

Cut tomatoes and onions in thin slices, and pack in layers with the salt over night. Pour off liquid, add green peppers, vinegar, and spices. Sweeten to taste and cook until soft. *Mrs. Charles Maillot.*

Chili Sauce for Hot or Cold Meats

2 cans tomatoes	2 tbsp. sugar
2 large peppers (cut fine)	1½ tbsp. salt
	1 cup vinegar
2 large onions (cut fine)	1 tsp. cloves
1 tsp. allspice	1 tsp. celery
1 tsp. nutmeg	1 tsp. cinnamon

Tie spices in a thin muslin bag, put all on and boil until thick. This quantity will make about 2 pints. Seal while hot. Will keep indefinitely.   *Mrs. W. L. Neill.*

Cucumber Rings

2 dozen firm dill pickles	10c whole black pepper
25c mustard seed	1 gal vinegar
	5 lbs. sugar
garlic	

Make a syrup of vinegar and sugar; cut pickles in rings about ¼ inch thick, put in crock; sprinkle very lightly with powdered alum. Add mustard seed and pepper to syrup, add garlic to taste (about 6 or 8 buttons cut in pieces). Pour hot syrup over pickles and let stand for a week or more.

Mrs. Collett Munger.

Corn Salad

2 dozen ears corn (cut from cob)	4 cup sugar
1 dozen gr. peppers (chopped and seeded)	4 tbsp. mustard seed
	2 tbsp. salt (or more)
	1½ tsp. tumeric
8 onions chopped	

Put all on to boil and cook hard for 25 minutes. Seal while hot. You can add to the recipe 1 teaspoon cayenne, 1 clove garlic (chopped) and 2 tablespoons celery seed.

Mrs. Josephine Tutton.

Green Tomato Pickle

1 qt. gr. peppers (chop fine)

2 qts. gr. tomatoes sliced thin

2 qts. white onions (sliced thin)

4 qts. cabbage, chop fine

2 tbsp. allspice

1 oz. celery seed

1 oz. tumeric

3 lbs. sugar

4 tbsp. salt

2 tbsp. cloves

1 gal. vinegar

Mix all well, boil slowly ½ hour. Put in jars and seal.

Mrs. Frank Callier.

Mustard Pickle

4 qts. green tomatoes

1 small cabbage

1 bunch celery

1 qt. small onions

1 cauliflower

6 green peppers (have 1 or 2 red)

Cut all in small pieces, cover with salt brine and let stand twenty-four hours. Place pickles in brine on stove and let boil ten minutes. Then drain and dry.

Paste:

6 tbsp. Coleman's mustard

1 tbsp. tumeric powder

2 qts. vinegar

¼ cup mustard seed

2 cups sugar

1 cup flour

1 pt. water

¼ cup celery seed

Mix mustard, tumeric powder, sugar and flour with water to form paste. Bring to boiling point vinegar and 1 pt. water. Stir paste in the vinegar and water and let cool until like custard. Then stir in the pickles. Add mustard seed and celery seed.

Mrs. J. L. Dreibelbis.

Mustard Pickle

2 large size cabbage	8 peppers
5 doz. small onions (pearl onions)	1¾ lbs. Coleman mustard
2 doz. cucumbers (don't peel cucumbers)	1½ lbs. sugar
	2 oz. celery seed

2 oz. tumeric

Chop about the size of a nickel, not too fine and let it stand in salt over night, drain off and put in. Cover with vinegar and cook for 20 minutes.

Mrs. Collett Munger.

Peach Pickles

7 lbs. fruit	3 lbs. sugar
1 qt. vinegar	cloves
1 tbsp. whole spices	1 tbsp. cinnamon

Put vinegar, sugar and spices on, let come to a boil. Drop fruit in slowly. Let boil until can stick fork in fruit. Remove fruit from syrup. Put in jars. Pour syrup in jars while boiling hot. *Mrs. Frank Cullinan.*

Pickled Onions

Pour boiling water over onions and let stand 1 hour. Skim, make a brine, by adding a pint of salt to a gallon of boiling water, and pour over onions. Let stand until morning, drain and reheat brine and pour back over onions. Repeat twice. Third morning drain and wash well in cold water. Fill jars with onions and add a green and a red pepper to each jar. Make a liquid of 1 pt. of water, to each quart of vinegar, add a little celery seed, mustard seed, and a cup of sugar. When it comes to a boil, fill jars and seal. To a small basket of onions, use two quarts and a pint of vinegar.

Mrs. Lewis G. Spence.

Green Tomato Pickles

1 pk. green tomatoes	1 qt. onions
1 medium size white cabbage	12 green peppers
	1 tsp. ground allspice
¼ lb. dry mustard rubbed to smooth paste with vinegar	2 cups brown sugar
	1 oz. celery seed
1 tsp. ground mace	½ lb. white mustard seed
1 tsp. ground cloves	

red and black pepper to taste

Cut up vegetables. Stir in 1 cup of cooking salt. Let stand over night. Squeeze. Put in pot. Pour over enough vinegar to thin. Boil 1 hour. When cold add mustard and celery seed and 1 qt. of vinegar.

Mrs. F. M. Butt.

Spiced Crab Apples

2 doz. large crab apples	whole cloves
2 cups sugar	whole allspice
cider vinegar	stick cinnamon

Thoroughly wash the crab apples, leaving the stems on. Place in a kettle and just cover with cider vinegar. Add sugar and whole spice to taste and boil for 15 minutes. Seal in jars. Ready for use in about 2 weeks.

Mrs. O. T. Poynz.

Index

Menus
PAGE

Dinner Menus.... 16, 17, 18, 19, 20, 21
Luncheon Menus...... 11, 12, 13, 14, 15
Supper Menus............ 21, 22, 23, 24

Hors d'Oeuvres and Cocktails

Almonds, Deviled _____ 27
Alligator Pear Cocktail _____ 29
Artichokes, Jellied _____ 30
Artichokes, Stuffed Hearts _____ 26
Avacado Cocktail _____ 29
Canape, Pastry _____ 25
Canape, Tuna Fish_____ 25, 28
Cheese and Bacon_____ 26
Cheese Crackers _____ 25
Chutney and Bacon _____ 30
Eggs Stuffed with Caviar_____ 26
Eggs Stuffed with
    Pate de Fois Gras_____ 26
Eggs Stuffed with Sardines_____ 27
Ham, Cheese and Chutney_____ 26
Hors d'Oeuvres _____ 28
Oyster Hors d'Oeuvres_____ 30
Oysters, Pickled _____ 28
Philadelphia Scrapple Canape_____ 27
Potato Chips and Cheese_____ 26
Sardines and Bacon_____ 25
Shrimp _____ 27
Shrimp Cocktail _____ 29
Tomato and Egg Hors d'Oeuvre____ 30
Tomato with Sauce_____ 27

Soups

Almond Soup _____ 31
Bortsch _____ 38
Bouillabaisse _____ 35
Bouillon _____ 34
Cream of Corn Soup_____ 37
Cream of Mushroom_____ 32
Creamed Onion Soup au Gratin.... 36
Creme Cressonniere _____ 39
Fresh Mushroom Soup_____ 33
Grape Juice Bouillon_____ 37
Gumbo _____ 32
Gumbo File _____ 36
Italian Stew _____ 33
Pot au Feu _____ 34
Mulled Wine for Twelve_____ 34
Mushroom Soup _____ 31

Soups—(Cont'd)
PAGE

New Orleans Gumbo_____ 38
Okra Gumbo _____ 31
Oyster Soup _____ 33, 39
Shrimp or Crawfish Bisque_____ 37
Tomato Bisque _____ 32

Fish and Oysters

Fish, Cream _____ 50
Fish, Baked _____ 43
Fish, Broiled _____ 41
Fish, In Aspic _____ 44
Fish, Moulded with Mushrooms
    and Lobster Sauce_____ 47
Fish, with Marguery Sauce_____ 43
Halibut, Baked Steak_____ 44
Little Pigs _____ 46
Lobster, Fried _____ 47
Oysters, a la Italienne_____ 52
Oysters, a la St. Anthony_____ 52
Oysters and Noodles_____ 42
Oysters au Gratin_____ 46
Oysters, Broiled _____ 42
Oysters, Deviled _____ 51
Oysters, en Brochette_____ 46
Oysters, Fricasse of_____ 48
Oysters, Keebobbed _____ 40
Oysters, Rockefellow I_____ 40
Oysters, a la Rockefellow II_____ 40
Salmon Loaf _____ 45, 48
Salmon, Moulded _____ 50
Salmon Souffle _____ 48
Sauce, Cocktail _____ 45
Sauce for Fish _____ 50
Sauce, Lemon, for Fish_____ 51
Sauce Victoria _____ 45
Sauce, White _____ 47
Shrimp, Baked _____ 49, 52
Shrimp, Cocktail Sauce for____ 41
Shrimp Creole _____ 49
Shrimp Curry with Rice_____ 51
Shrimp Cutlets _____ 49
Shrimp, Deviled _____ 43
Shrimp, Manhattan _____ 42
Shrimp, Sauted _____ 46

Poultry and Game

Chafing Dish Birds_____ 56
Chicken, a la King_____ 56, 65

Poultry and Game—(Cont'd)

	PAGE
Chicken, Barbecue I	60
Chicken, Barbecue II	63
Chicken, Creamed	61
Chicken, Creole	58
Chicken Croquettes	54
Chicken, Curry	61
Chicken in Creole Sauce	62
Chicken, Jellied	59
Chicken, Paprika en Casserole	62
Chicken, Pressed	55
Chicken Pie	62
Chicken, Scotti	64
Chicken, Spaghetti	64
Cold Chicken Mousse	57
Dressing for Fowls	53
Ducks, a la Carte	55
Fricassee Chicken	54, 59
Hot Chicken Mousse	58
Hot Jellied Chicken	54
Oyster Dressing	53
Pigeon Pie	60
Quail, Broiled on Toast	57
Sauce, Bechamel	63
Sauce, Cumberland	61
Terrapin Chicken	55
Turkey, Roast	53

Meats and Meat Accompaniments

	PAGE
Apples Stuffed with Sausage	71
Baked Ham	69, 75
Barbecue Sauce	75
Brain Entree	69
Brains	73
Breaded Veal Cutlets	72
Braised Brains	74
French Griande	70
Ham and Noodles	67
Ham Sauce	74
Hams, Virginia Style	66
Kentucky Ham	75
Lamb Noisettes	73
Lamb or Venison Sauce	73
Leg of Lamb Roast	74
Meat Loaf	68
Meat Sauce	77
Noodles	67
Roast Beef	72
Sauce for Baked Ham	67, 69
Spaghetti	66, 76

Meats and Meat Accompaniments—(Cont'd)

	PAGE
Spiced Tongue	70
Steak and Spaghetti	71
Steak Creole	68
Tamale Loaf	77
Tomato Gravy	77
Tomato Sauce for Meats	72
Tomato Stuffed with Rice	70
Veal Loaf	68, 77
Yorkshire Pudding	71

Vegetables

	PAGE
Asparagus Loaf	85
Asparagus Pudding	87
Baked Egg Plant	80
Baked Onions	78
Baked Potatoes	84
Baked Stuffed Potatoes	89
Braised Celery	82
Cabbage au Gratin	78
Caramel Sweet Potatoes	86
Carrot Pudding	80
Celery au Gratin	80
Egg Plant	79, 81
Egg Plant Fritters	90
French Fried Onions	90
Fried Celery	83
Fried Parsley	82
Hot Slaw	86
Okra and Tomatoes	83
Okra Patties	81
Pea Roast	89
Potatoes au Gratin	88
Potatoes with Savory Sauce	79
Simple Hollandaise Sauce	85
Spinach Mousse	85
Spinach Ring	86
Spinach Souffle	84
Spinach Timbales	78
Squash Souffle	87
Stuffed Artichokes	82
Stuffed Cabbage	89
Stuffed Egg Plant a la Creole	81
Stuffed Squash	83
Stuffed Tomatoes	88
Sweet Potato Balls	84
Sweet Potato Croquettes	90
Sweet Potato Pone	90
Sweet Potato with Pineapple	88
Sweet Potato with Sherry	87

PAGE

Breads and Muffins

Baking Powder Biscuits 99
Batter Bread 103
Beaten Biscuits 98
Beauregard Biscuit 91
Blueberry Muffin 105
Bran and Fig Muffin 106
Brioche Cake (Crescent Rolls) 99
Brown Bread 95, 96
Cheese Biscuits 107
Cheese Muffins 102
Cheese Puff 105
Cheese Straws 91
Cincinnati Coffee Bread 92
Cinnamon Rolls 94
Corn Bread 92
Cream Fruit Rolls 102
Date Loaf 103
Drop Biscuits 93
English Muffins 101
Flop Crumbles 98
Kentucky Spoon Bread 97
Light Baking Powder and
  Soda Biscuits 98
Light Bread 93, 97
Louisiana Calar 104
Muffins 99, 101
Nut Biscuits 95
Nut Bread 95, 101
Nut Mixture 92
One Egg Muffins 100
Orange Biscuits 98
Orange Bread 94
Orange Nut Bread 103
"Pain Perdu" or Lost Bread ... 104
Pocket Book Rolls 100
Potato Flour Muffins 104, 107
Pop Overs 107
Potato Rolls—Plain 96
Refrigerator Rolls 106
Rice Muffins 106
Salad Rolls 93
Sally Lunn 95, 98
Salt-Rising Bread 94
Scotch Short Bread 91
Spoon Bread 105
Sweet Potato Biscuits 97
Virginia Corn Bread 96
Waffles 100, 102, 107

PAGE

Cakes and Icings

Almond Cake 116
Almond Sticks 141
Angel Food Cake ... 112, 122, 128, 136
Apple Cake 119
Blackberry Cake I 134
Blackberry Jam Cake 143
Black Fruit Cake 129
Brownies 131
Burnt Sugar Cake 117
Carmel Cookies 137
Caramel Icing 123
Cream Almond Filling 127
Cocoanut Drops 132
Cocoanut Filling (Very Moist) .. 125
Cookies 120, 134, 142
Chocolate Angel Food Cake ... 122
Chocolate Cake ... 109, 126, 138, 140
Chocolate Cookies 130
Chocolate Filling 138
Chocolate Fudge Cake ... 124, 132
Chocolate Nut Cake 118
Chocolate Roll 111
Chocolate Sponge Cake 130
Citron Cake 139
Coffee Cake 114, 128
Dainty Yellow Cake 111
Date Cookies 118
Date Loaf 112
Date Sticks 124
Devil's Food Cake ... 123, 136, 142
Doughnuts 119
Drop Cake 129
Eggless Ginger-Bread 120
Elephant Ears 143
Favorite Layer Cake 137
Finland Cookies 142
Frosting 139
Fruit Cake 108, 127
Fruit Cookies 109
Fruit Snaps 134
Fudge Frosting 133
Fudge Icing 121, 140
Ginger-Bread 118
Golden Angel Food 133
Hermits 113
Icing 130
Icing for Mahogany Cake ... 135
Irish Potato Cake 112
Jam Cake 137, 140

Cakes and Icings—(Cont'd)

PAGE

Jelly Roll _____ 115
Kisses _____ 122
Kisses Shells _____ 138
Lace Cookies _____ 141
Lady Baltimore Filling _____ 121
Lemon Jelly Filling _____ 125
Mahogany Cake _____ 135
Marshmallow Meringue Cake _____ 110
Meringue Cake _____ 129
Meringue Strawberry Shortcake _____ 109
Mock Angel Cake _____ 117
Nut Loaf _____ 135
Oatmeal Cookies _____ 116, 125
Orange Cake _____ 131
Orange Filling _____ 131
Orange Icing _____ 132
Pecan Macaroons _____ 125
Pineapple Up-Side-Down Cake _____ 139
Preserve Cake _____ 114
Prune Cake _____ 113
Rocks _____ 116
Rolled Wafers _____ 141
Short Cake _____ 111, 126
Small White Cake _____ 121
Sour Cream Cake _____ 114, 133
Sponge or Muffin Cake _____ 113
Strawberry Short Cake _____ 126
Sugar Icing _____ 134
Superior Soft Ginger Bread _____ 115
Swedish Wafers with Nuts _____ 128
Thanksgiving Cake _____ 136
Westinghouse Cookies _____ 120
White Cake _____ 123
White Cake with Chocolate Filling _____ 110
White Fruit Cake _____ 108
White Icing _____ 124

Salads

Almond Salad _____ 156
Argyle Salad _____ 148
Asparagus Salad _____ 166
Avocada Dressing _____ 155
Avocada Salad _____ 145
Bean Salad _____ 163
Cheese Apples _____ 146
Cheese Fruit Salad Baskets _____ 164
Cheese Mould Salad Ring _____ 161
Cheese Ring Salad _____ 166
Cheese Salad _____ 147

Salads—(Cont'd)

PAGE

Cherry Salad _____ 147, 159
Cole Slaw _____ 145
Congealed Asparagus Salad _____ 163
Cooked Salad Dressing _____ 158
Cream French Dressing _____ 154
Cucumber and Shrimp Salad _____ 156
Cucumber Cheese _____ 150
Delicious Salad _____ 155
Frozen Cheese Salad _____ 144, 153
Frozen Cream Mayonnaise _____ 160
Frozen Fruit Salad _____ 154, 158, 165
Frozen Salad _____ 144
Frozen Salad Dressing _____ 159
Frozen Tomato _____ 160, 164
Frozen Tomato Salad _____ 146
Frozen Vegetable Salad _____ 162
Fruit Salad _____ 159
Fruit Salad Dressing _____ 149
Grapefruit Salad _____ 147, 161
Green Mayonnaise _____ 161
Ginger Ale Salad _____ 148
Heart of Palm Salad _____ 153
Italian Salad _____ 163
Kentucky Cheese Salad _____ 152
Marshmallow Salad _____ 151
Mixed Salad _____ 165
Moquin Salad _____ 166
Old Fashioned Lettuce Salad _____ 152
Orange Salad _____ 151
Parsley Ring _____ 160
Pineapple and Cucumber Salad _____ 146
Potato Salad _____ 153
Roquefort Cheese Salad Dressing _____ 151
Rouquefort Slaw _____ 165
Russian Dressing _____ 147, 158
Salad Dressing _____ 149
Shrimp Ring _____ 157
Spaghetti Salad _____ 162
Summer Dressing _____ 166
Thousand Island Dressing _____ 149
Tomato Aspic _____ 154
Tomato Gelatine Cheese Salad _____ 157
Tomato Stuffed with Anchovies _____ 150
Tomato with Caviar _____ 152
Whipped Cream Salad _____ 155

Pastry

Amber Pie _____ 172
Apple Merinque Pie _____ 174
Brama Cream Pie _____ 173

INDEX

PAGE

Pastry—(Cont'd)

Butterscotch Pie 171, 172, 173
Caramel Custard 167
Cherry Pie 168
Chocolate Pie 170, 174
Cocoanut Cream Pie 172
Cream Pie 169
Date Pie 175
French Lemon Pie 175
Hot Water Pastry 170
Lemon Pie 174
Mince Meat 169
Molasses Pie 175
Oh! So Good Pie 168
Orange Pie 168
Pecan Pie 171
Pineapple Pie 171
Pumpkin Ice Cream Pie 169
Spice Pie 170
Transparent Pies 173
Washington Pie 167

Puddings and Desserts

Almond and Mocha Pudding 191
Almond Tartlets 189
Apple Batter Pudding 180
Apple Dumpling 195
Bancroft Pudding 182
Batter Pudding 199
Boston Cream Pie 178
Brittle Pudding 193
Burnt Almond Charlotte 177
Cabinet Pudding 184
Candy Pudding 182
Caramel Pudding 185
Carrot Pudding 196
Charlotte Russe 187, 199
Chocolate Pudding 177
Chocolate Sauce 194
Chocolate Souffle 186
Cocoanut Pudding 181
Coffee Chocolate Pudding 189
Coffee Mousse 194
Cream Puffs 189
Date Meringue 196
Date Pudding 181, 187
Date Tarts 176
Delmonico Pudding 180
Fig Pudding 185
Frozen Orange Pudding 192
Frozen Plum Pudding 183
Frozen Pudding 184

PAGE

Puddings and Desserts —(Cont'd)

Gelatine Bessie 200
Graham Pudding 188
Hansel Pudding 193
Hot Chocolate Pudding 196
Ice Box Cake 191
Ice Box Chocolate Freeze 179
Lady Fingers and Fruit Dessert ... 187
Laurabelle Cake 190
Lemon Pudding 183
Macaroon Pudding 183
Marshmallow Pudding 179
Nesselrode Pudding 198
Nut Souffle 186
Old English Plum Pudding 181
Orange Charlotte 198
Orange Marmalade Pudding 194
Orange Pudding 179
Orange Trifle 188
Pineapple Bavarian Cream 197
Pineapple Cake 192
Prune Charlotte 185
Pudding Sauce 197
Raisin and Nut Pie 198
Raspberry Pudding 193
Refrigerator Cake 186
Rice Pudding 176
Sharky Custard 197
Simple Dessert 180
Spanish Cream 188
Steam Apple Pudding 184
Strawberry Souffle 200
Three In One Ice Cream 195
Velvet Pudding 192
Woodford Pudding 176

Eggs and Omelets

Bread Crumb Omelet 203
Cheese Souffle 202
Chicken Omelet 202
Eggs and Green Peppers 201
Eggs Poached in Milk 202
Plain Omelet 201
Poached Eggs—A La Boeldien 201
Scrambled Eggs au Parmesian 203
Scrambled Eggs, with Peppers 202

Ices and Ice Cream

Almond Ice 211
Almond Orange Ice Cream 211
Angel Parfait 210

Ices and Ice Cream—(Cont'd)

	PAGE
Cafe Parfait	206
Canton Sherbet	205
Cranberry Ice	204
Cream Sherbet	208
Frozen Buttermilk	212
Frozen Chocolate Bisque	205
Frozen Egg-Nogg	204
Frozen Fruit	208
Frozen Pumpkin Pie	209
Frozen Strawberries	210
Frozen Strawberries with Cream	212
Good Ice Cream	206
Grape Ice	207
Green Gage Ice Cream	210
Hot Chocolate Sauce I	205
Hot Chocolate Sauce II	207
Loganberry Ice	208
Macaroon and Walnut Ice Cream	209
Maple Mousse	207, 209
Maple Parfait	207
Marron Mousse	212
Melon Mould Ice Cream	212
Orange Souffle	208
Peanut Brittle Ice Cream	204
Pear Melba	212
Peppermint Ice Cream	206
Pineapple Sponge	206
Raspberry or Strawberry Bombe	211
Victoria Pudding	210

Beverages

Blackberry Cordial	214
Chocolate	215
Drip Coffee	215
Egg-Nogg	213
Formula for Mixing Tea	214
Fruit Punch	213
Old-Fashioned Boiled Coffee	215
Pink Milk	215
Punch for 75 People	214
Russian Tea	214
Twelfth Night Bowl	213

Candies

Black Walnut Candy	219
Butterscotch	218
Candy from Wythville, Va.	219
Chocolate Caramels	221
Chocolate Creams	216
Chocolate Fudge	217
Cocoanut Candy	217
Dandy Candy	218

Candies—(Cont'd)

	PAGE
Date Loaf	220
Fluffy Ruffle Kisses	217
Fudge	216, 221
Mints	220
Molasses Candy	220
Panocha	222
Patience	218
Patience II	219
Peanut Candy	222
Pecan Pralines	221
Sugared Nuts	216
Turkish Delight	222

Luncheon Dishes and Sandwiches

Apples and Conserve	226
Baked Bananas	246
Baked Brains	232
Baked Grits	231
Baked Oranges	226
Bechamel Sauce	242
Bird-Nest Toast	231
Broiled Pineapple	225
Boston Baked Beans	238
Breast of Chicken with Mushrooms	244
Breast of Guinea on Toast	246
Brown Bread Sandwiches	230
California Chicken Pie	245
Cheese Ball	235
Cheese London	231
Cheese Sandwich	238, 245
Cheese Souffle	237
Chicken and Brains in Ramekins	227
Chicken Cheese Sandwiches	232
Chicken Loaf	227
Chicken Sandwiches	229
Chili	234, 236, 239, 240, 243
Chili Loaf	230
Cornmeal Souffle	233
Cucumber and Cheese Filling	243
Egg and Mushrooms	224
Egg Croquettes	235
Egg Timbales	244
Eggs a la Benedict	246
Eggs in Aspic	241
English Cream Entree	223
German Tamales	244
Golden Ball Fritters	242
Grapefruit and Mint Ice	236

Luncheon Dishes and Sand-wiches—(Cont'd)

PAGE

Green Pepper and Bacon Sandwiches ... 242
Green Pepper Sandwich ... 228
Ham and Cheese Souffle ... 232
Ham Mousse ... 233
Hominy Souffle ... 225
Hot Cheese Sandwiches ... 224
Individual Oyster Loaves ... 246
Luncheon Dish ... 235
Luncheon Sandwich ... 237
Moulded Sweetbreads ... 234
Mushrooms on Toast ... 241
Neufchatel Cheese Sandwiches ... 228
Onion Souffle ... 226
Oranges ... 225
Orange Toast ... 223
Philadelphia Scrapple ... 229
Pigs in Blanket ... 234
Pineapple and Orange Ice ... 236
Potato Souffle ... 237
Prune and Cheese Balls ... 230
Pyramid Chops ... 240
Relish ... 224
Rice Croquettes—Cheese Sauce ... 229
Ring Noodles ... 236
Rolled Cheese Sandwiches ... 245
Salmon with Green Mayonnaise ... 239
Salted Almonds ... 228
Sandwiches ... 228
Santa Claus Sandwiches ... 225
Sauted Sweetbreads ... 235
Shrimp Chili ... 243
Simple Lunch Dish ... 233

Luncheon Dishes and Sand-wiches—(Cont'd)

PAGE

Spanish Chili Con Carne ... 237
Spanish Stew ... 230
Tuna Fish in Ramekins ... 226
Welsh Rarebit ... 239

Preserves and Pickles

Apricot-Pineapple Conserve ... 248
Beet Relish ... 251
Brandied Peaches ... 250
Chili Sauce ... 250, 251, 252
Chili Sauce for Hot or Cold Meats ... 254
Citron or Watermelon Rind ... 249
Conserve ... 247
Corn Salad ... 254
Cucumber Pickle ... 252
Cucumber Relish ... 251
Cucumber Rings ... 254
Golden Marmalade ... 249
Grape Conserve ... 250
Green Tomato Pickles ... 253, 255, 257
Heavenly Jam ... 252
Mustard Pickle ... 255, 256
Orange Marmalade ... 248, 249
Peach Pickles ... 256
Pear Chips ... 247
Piccalilli ... 253
Pickled Onions ... 256
Plum Conserve ... 249
Quince Preserve ... 250
Spiced Crab Apples ... 257
Spiced Grapes ... 248
Sweet Cucumber Pickle ... 251
Watermelon Preserves ... 247

MEMORANDA